The Creative Class Goes Global

D1104382

The whole landscape of research in urban studies was revolutionized by the publication of Richard Florida's *The Rise of the Creative Class* in 2002, and his subsequent book entitled *The Flight of the Creative Class* has helped to maintain a decade-long explosion of interest in the field. While these two books examine the creative class in the context of the United States, research has emerged which investigates the creative class worldwide.

The Creative Class Goes Global brings together detailed studies of the creative class in cities across the globe, examining the impact of the creative class on growth and development. The countries covered include the United Kingdom, the Netherlands, Germany, Australia, China, Japan and Canada, in addition to the United States. Taken together, the contributions deepen our understanding of the creative class and the various factors that affect regional development, highlighting the similarities and differences between the creative class and economic development across countries.

This book will be of great interest to scholars of economic geography, regional economics, urban sociology and cultural policy, as well as policy-makers involved in urban development.

Charlotta Mellander is Professor of Economics at Jönköping International Business School, Sweden. She also holds a visiting faculty position at the Martin Prosperity Institute, Rotman School of Management, University of Toronto, Canada.

Richard Florida is Director of the Martin Prosperity Institute in the Rotman School of Management at the University of Toronto, Canada, and is also Global Research Professor at New York University, USA. He is the author of the best-selling book, *The Rise of the Creative Class*.

Bjørn T. Asheim is Professor and Chair in Economic Geography at the Department of Human Geography, Lund University, Sweden. He is Co-founder, previously Director and now Research Director of CIRCLE, one of the largest research organisations on innovation in Europe.

Meric Gertler is President and Professor of Geography and Planning at the University of Toronto, Canada.

Regions and Cities

Managing Editor:
Gillian Bristow, *University of Cardiff, UK*

Editors:
Maryann Feldman, *University of Georgia, USA*
Gernot Grabher, *HafenCity University Hamburg, Germany*
Ron Martin, *University of Cambridge, UK*
Martin Perry, *Massey University, New Zealand*

In today's globalised, knowledge-driven and networked world, regions and cities have assumed heightened significance as the interconnected nodes of economic, social and cultural production, and as sites of new modes of economic and territorial governance and policy experimentation. This book series brings together incisive and critically engaged international and interdisciplinary research on this resurgence of regions and cities, and should be of interest to geographers, economists, sociologists, political scientists and cultural scholars, as well as to policy-makers involved in regional and urban development.

For more information on the Regional Studies Association visit www.regionalstudies.org

There is a **30% discount** available to RSA members on books in the ***Regions and Cities*** series, and other subject related Taylor and Francis books and e-books including Routledge titles. To order just e-mail alex.robinson@tandf.co.uk, or phone on +44 (0) 20 7017 6924 and declare your RSA membership. You can also visit www.routledge.com and use the discount code: **RSA0901**

The Creative Class Goes Global

Edited by
Charlotta Mellander,
Richard Florida, Bjørn T. Asheim
and Meric Gertler

Routledge
Taylor & Francis Group

LONDON AND NEW YORK

First published 2014
by Routledge
2 Park Square, Milton Park, Abingdon, Oxon OX14 4RN

and by Routledge
711 Third Avenue, New York, NY 10017

Routledge is an imprint of the Taylor & Francis Group, an informa business

© 2014 Selection and editorial material, Charlotta Mellander, Richard Florida, Bjørn T. Asheim and Meric Gertler; individual chapters, the contributors

British Library Cataloguing in Publication Data
A catalogue record for this book is available from the British Library

Library of Congress Cataloging in Publication Data
The creative class goes global/edited by Charlotta Mellander, Richard Florida, Bjørn T. Asheim and Meric Gertler.
pages cm
Includes bibliographical references and index.
1. Creative ability—Economic aspects. 2. Creative ability—Social aspects. 3. Work ethic—United States. 4. Leisure. 5. Social classes. 6. Creative ability in technology. 7. Technology and civilization. 8. Human capital. I. Mellander, Charlotta.
HD53.C743 2013
306.4'7—dc23
2013013909

ISBN: 978-0-415-63360-4 (hbk)
ISBN: 978-0-415-63361-1 (pbk)
ISBN: 978-0-203-09494-5 (ebk)

Typeset in Times New Roman
by Book Now Ltd, London

Printed and bound in the United States of America by Publishers Graphics, LLC on sustainably sourced paper.

Contents

x *Contents*

Figures

Tables

Contributors

Bjørn T. Asheim, Professor in Economic Geography, CIRCLE/Department of Human Geography, Lund University, Sweden.

Oedzge Atzema, Professor of Economic Geography, Department of Human Geography and Urban & Regional Planning, Faculty of Geosciences, Utrecht University, Netherlands.

Ron Boschma, Professor and Director, CIRCLE, Lund University, Sweden.

Markus M. Bugge, Senior Researcher, Nordic Institute for Studies in Innovation, Research and Education, Oslo, Norway.

Federica Calidoni, PhD, Swedish Agency for Growth Policy Analysis, Östersund, Sweden.

Nick Clifton, Reader in Economic Geography and Regional Development, Cardiff School of Management, Cardiff Metropolitan University, UK.

Richard Florida, Professor of Business and Creativity, The Martin Prosperity Institute, Rotman School of Management, University of Toronto, Toronto, Ontario, Canada, and Global Research Professor at New York University, USA.

Michael Fritsch, Professor, Friedrich-Schiller-University Jena, School of Economics and Business Administration, Jena, Germany; German Institute for Economic Research (DIW) Berlin, and Halle Institute for Economic Research (IWH), Germany.

Meric Gertler, Dean, Faculty of Arts & Science, Professor of Geography, University of Toronto, Canada.

Høgni Kalsø Hansen, Associate Professor, Department of Geosciences and Natural Resource Management, University of Copenhagen, Denmark.

Arne Isaksen, Professor, University of Agder, Grimstad, Norway.

Mark Lorenzen, Professor of Innovation, Entrepreneurship and Industrial Dynamics, Department of Innovation and Organizational Economics, Copenhagen Business School, Denmark.

Gerard Marlet, Groningen University, Utrecht School of Economics and Atlas voor gemeenten, Netherlands.

Charlotta Mellander, Professor of Economics, Department of Economics, Jönköping International Business School, Jönköping, Sweden; The Martin Prosperity Institute, Rotman School of Management, University of Toronto, Toronto, Ontario, Canada.

Haifeng Qian, Assistant Professor of Economic Development, Levin College of Urban Affairs, Cleveland State University, USA.

Mika Raunio, Senior Researcher, Research center for Knowledge, Science, Technology and Innovation Studies/TaSTI, University of Tampere, Tampere, Finland.

Kevin Stolarick, Research Director, The Martin Prosperity Institute, Rotman School of Management, University of Toronto, Toronto, Ontario, Canada.

Michael Stuetzer, Technical University Ilmenau, Chair of Economic Policy, Ilmenau, Germany.

Kristina Vaarst Andersen, Assistant Professor, Department of Innovation and Organizational Economics, Copenhagen Business School, Copenhagen, Denmark.

Irina van Aalst, Assistant Professor of Urban Geography, Department of Human Geography and Urban and Regional Planning, Urban and Regional Research Center Utrecht, Utrecht University, Netherlands.

Frank van Oort, Professor of Urban Economics, Department of Economic Geography, Faculty of Geosciences, Utrecht University, Netherlands.

Clemens van Woerkens, Utrecht School of Economics and Atlas voor gemeenten, Netherlands.

Hans Westlund, Professor, KTH Royal Institute of Technology, Stockholm, Sweden; Jönköping International Business School, Jönköping, Sweden; Institute for Developmental and Strategic Analyses, Ljubljana, Slovenia.

Acknowledgements

It goes without saying that a volume like this draws off the research of a wide variety of people. We want to thank all the contributors and their research teams and staff. We also thank those, including many of the contributors to this volume as well as others, who acted as reviewers and referees for the studies and chapters contained herein.

We are also grateful to members of Martin Prosperity Institute team who provided invaluable assistance putting this volume together. Karen King did the initial work of bringing the original studies together. Taylor Brydges helped to organize, edit and proof the chapters and overall volume in detail. Kimberly Silk effectively supported us in the reprint rights process and helped us prepare the book for the publisher. Zara Matheson helped with the production of numerous figures and maps. Garrett Morgan provided additional research and editorial assistance.

We thank the supportive publishing team at Routledge, especially Natalie Tomlinson.

1 The creative class goes global

Richard Florida and Charlotta Mellander

This book examines the global reach of the creative class. Richard Florida's seminal book, *The Rise of the Creative Class*, published in 2002, garnered the attention of academics, city-leaders, urbanists and economic developers around the world. The book outlined a theory in which the creative class—scientists, technologists, innovators and entrepreneurs; artists, designers, musicians, entertainers, media workers and cultural creatives, and knowledge-based professionals in business, education and healthcare—had become the central force propelling economic growth. Comprising roughly a third of the workforce in the United States, its rise had led to sweeping changes in norms, values, geography, and everyday life. It further argued that since creative people prefer places that are diverse, tolerant, and open to new ideas, the 3Ts of economic development—technology, talent and tolerance—are the keys to attracting the creative class to a city or region.

A follow-up volume, *The Flight of the Creative Class*, extended the theory globally, documenting the rise of the creative class across the nations of the world, while a 2012 update, *Rise of the Creative Class Revisited* charted the creative class across 78 countries. Of the countries studied, Singapore leads, with 47.3 percent of its workforce in the creative class, followed by the Netherlands with 46.2 percent and Switzerland with 44.8 percent. Australia is fourth, with 44.5 percent of its workforce in the creative class. Scandinavian and Northern European countries take many of the top spots: Sweden (43.9 percent), Belgium (43.8 percent), Denmark (43.7 percent), Finland (43.4 percent), Norway (42.1 percent), and Germany (41.6 percent). Canada ranks 12th with 40.8 percent, and the United States is 27th, with 35 percent of its workforce in the creative class.

The past decade has seen a tremendous amount of research on the creative class across the world's nations and cities. This book brings together the very best of that research. It is organized around 13 chapters that examine the creative class in the United States and Canada; Europe, Scandinavia and the Nordic countries, and Japan, China and Australia in Asia.

There has been considerable debate about the significance of the creative class and even its definitions. Some argue that as a predictor of urban success, the creative class approach is not dissimilar to the more traditional measure of human capital, which uses educational attainment or the percentage of adults with college degrees. Edward Glaeser (2004) argued that human capital in fact provided a better measure of a region's economic potential. But a growing body of research, much of it conducted by scholars featured in this volume, has found that the two approaches differ significantly, and that while each has its strengths, the creative class approach provides a superior measure of some key aspects of regional economic performance.

As Florida (2002) noted in his original book, the creative class is an alternative measure of skill that is based not on education but on the actual work that people do. It is not a proxy for but a direct measure of jobs. He also noted that while the educational attainment measure typically allows one overall value for a city or region, for example, the percentage of adults who hold bachelors degrees, the creative class measure can isolate specific occupations and occupational clusters which affect regional economic performance.

And while there is considerable overlap between human capital and the creative class, they are not the same thing. A careful study of the United States (2012) by Kevin Stolarick of the University of Toronto and Elizabeth Currid-Halkett of the University of Southern California, found that nearly three-fourths (72.2 percent, to be exact) of adults with college degrees are members of the creative class. But less than 60 percent (59.3 percent) of the members of the creative class have college degrees, according to a detailed analysis. In other words, four in ten members of the creative class—16.6 million workers—do not have college degrees. As Stolarick and Currid-Halkett write:

> Thus, while some correlation would be expected, our results indicate that human capital and the creative class do not necessarily capture the same people nor is a measure of each's respective presence in a regional economy indicative of similar trends.

A study by Todd Gabe of the University of Maine (2011) found that the creative class has a substantial effect on regional economic growth, even when controlling for the effects of education and other factors. Moreover, his research found that having a creative class job adds another 16 percent to wages, over and above the effects of a college degree, roughly equivalent to 1.5 years of additional education. A (2007) study by David McGranahan and Timothy Wojan used sophisticated statistical techniques to gauge the effects of the creative class versus human capital on regional growth. These techniques, they note, allowed them to undertake a "critical examination of the most cutting critique of Florida's analysis: that he is merely substituting employment in highly skilled occupations as a proxy for the endowment of human capital." Their key findings confirm the "strong independent influence on employment growth from both the initial share employed in the recast creative class occupations and its growth over the decade. By contrast, the statistical association with human capital variables is quite weak." Based on this, they conclude: "The econometric test of the creative class thesis provides strong support for the notion that creativity has an effect on growth independent of the endowment of human capital."

Another detailed study by Marlet and van Woerkens (2004), investigating regional development in the Netherlands, found that the creative class considerably outperformed the standard human capital measure in accounting for employment growth. The study concludes that the creative class approach sets a "new standard" for measuring skill and talent, especially when considering regional labor productivity. "With our Dutch data set we do find evidence that Florida's creative class is a better predictor of city growth than traditional education standards," they wrote. They continued:

> Therefore we conclude that Florida's major contribution is his successful attempt to create a population category that is a better indicator for levels of human capital than average education levels or amounts of highly educated people. The point is, as Florida stated, not which or how much education people can boast of, but what they really do in working life.

Others have criticized the construct of the creative class as a "hodge-podge," saying it includes too broad a spectrum of types of work to be really meaningful. McGranahan and Wojan's detailed research (2007) found this not to be the case, documenting the underlying knowledge and creative skills that underpin and unify the occupations included in the creative class. Using detailed data from the Bureau of Labor Statistics' Occupational Information Network (O*NET) to specify the skills for each of the occupations in the creative class, they found that, with small exceptions, the original definition was valid and the correlation between the original and their updated definition was substantial.

Another line of criticism argues that as a theory of urban development, the creative class approach falls victim to the proverbial chicken-and-egg problem. What typically comes first, these critics argue, are jobs. Once a region has those, the people—as well as the amenities, lifestyle, and tolerance—will follow. Creative class theory argues that this is a false dichotomy. Regional development is a long-run cumulative process that occurs in places that bring people and jobs together. More to the point, the creative class measure is by design and definition not a measure of amenity or even of indirect skill, as with the educational attainment measure of the human capital approach, but a direct measure of employment and the actual jobs people do.

A study by Jesse Shapiro (2006) found that though "roughly 60 percent of the employment growth effect of college graduates is due to enhanced productivity growth," with the "rest" being "caused by growth in quality of life." Shapiro added that "this finding contrasts with the common argument that human capital generates employment growth in urban areas solely through changes in productivity." A (2011) study by Falck, Fritsch and Heblich conducted a unique and powerful natural experiment by examining the long-term effects on talent attraction and economic growth of seventeenth- and eighteenth-century Baroque opera houses in Germany. These opera houses, as they explain, are "exogenous to the distribution of high human capital employees that originates from the period of and after the Industrial Revolution." Even so, they found the location of these opera houses had a strong relationship to a region's later ability to attract highly skilled talent and to grow. "Proximity to a baroque opera house is a strong predictor of a region's equilibrium share of high-human-capital-employees," they write—and this despite the fact that the opera houses and the cultural amenity they provide came well before the jobs, in this case, by centuries.

Over the past decade, a large body of research has emerged that is aimed at testing the creative class approach and applying it in different national and urban contexts across the world. A particularly notable effort to collect and organize data for Western Europe and the Nordic countries was organized by Bjørn T. Asheim from Lund University in Sweden, with Ron Boschma of Utrecht University; Phillip Cooke of Cardiff University; Michael Fritsch of Friedrich-Schiller University, Jena; Meric Gertler from the University of Toronto; Arne Isaksen of Norway's University of Agder; Mark Lorenzen of the Copenhagen Business School; and Markku Sotarauta, University of Tampere, Finland.

This book gathers together the best studies of the creative class in a global context, including both published and unpublished research by authors from the USA, the UK, Germany, the Netherlands, Sweden, Denmark, Finland, Norway, and China. Its chapters examine the geography of the creative class, the factors that influence its location, and its effects on economic growth and development in various nations. Taken together, they deepen our understanding of the creative class and the various factors that act on regional development, highlighting the similarities and differences between the creative class and economic development across countries.

Outline of the book

Part I considers the creative class in the United States and Canada. Chapter 2, "Inside the Black Box of Regional Development Human Capital, the Creative Class and Tolerance" by Richard Florida, Charlotta Mellander and Kevin Stolarick, considers the United States. Chapter 3, also by Florida, Mellander and Stolarick, uses a similar framework to examine the creative class in Canada.

Part II of the book turns to Scandinavia, the Nordic countries and Europe. Chapter 4, a new contribution by Høgni Kalsø Hansen, examines to what extent creative class theory and the 3T approach fit Sweden, a relatively small nation with 9 million people, but which tops the list on the global creativity index (Florida, 2005; Florida *et al.*, 2011). When it comes to Sweden, Hansen concludes, the creative class theory applies more to larger city-regions than smaller ones.

Chapter 5, by Kristina Vaarst Andersen and Mark Lorenzen, examines how well the creative class theory fits the case of Denmark, a nation even smaller than Sweden. It fits it quite well. The Danish creative class is concentrated in Copenhagen and Denmark's larger cities, which are able to provide a diverse range of service and cultural offerings and tolerance of alternative lifestyles, and in smaller Danish cities as well. The interviews carried out for the study indicate that many creatives are attracted to smaller cities because of the cost advantages, specialized employment offerings, attractive work–life balance, authenticity, and sense of community.

Chapter 6 explores the creative class theory across the Nordic nations of Sweden, Denmark, Norway, and Finland. Its authors, Kristina Vaarst Andersen, Markus M. Bugge, Høgni Karlø Hansen, Arne Isaksen, and Mika Raunio, find the creative class to be unevenly distributed across these nations and to be more highly concentrated in "capital regions" which possess thicker labor markets. Exploring the relative effects of the "people climate" and the "business climate" in the location of the creative class, they find that both play a role. While the people climate is important, an attractive job market or business climate is even more important to creative class location decisions in the Nordic countries. The chapter makes the important point that people climates are heterogeneous, that they vary considerably from place to place. The authors conclude with an examination of the impact of welfare state policies in the Nordic countries.

Chapter 7, a new analysis by Gerard Marlet and Clemens van Woerkens, looks at the Netherlands. Their previous research had found that the creative class outperformed educational measures of human capital in accounting for the economic performance of Dutch regions. In this chapter, they look at the role of job opportunities, aesthetic factors, and tolerance in the location of the creative class in the Netherlands. They found that job opportunities, urban amenities, and aesthetics play key roles in the growth of the creative class in Dutch cities, while tolerance plays a smaller role.

Chapter 8, newly written by Irina van Aalst, Oedzge Aztema, Ron Boschma and Frank van Oort, also looks at the Netherlands and finds a substantial relationship between the creative class and employment growth, and a smaller but still significant connection between the creative class and the growth of new businesses across Dutch regions. They find only a weak association between regional openness and the presence of the creative class and, in contrast to Chapter 7, they find no association between recreational and socio-cultural amenities and the creative class. However, they do find that the presence of the creative class may be an important regional condition in the case of labor mobility.

Chapter 9, by Nick Clifton, highlights the uneven and concentrated geography of the creative class in the UK. Its findings are in sync with Chapters 2 and 3 on the United States and Canada. The creative class is strongly associated with economic performance across the UK, but its concentration increases with regional size, with traditional manufacturing regions lagging behind.

Chapter 10, an updated version of a (2009) study by Michael Fritsch and Michael Stuetzer, considers the creative class in Germany. Although it is especially concentrated in larger cities, there are considerable creative class concentrations in smaller cities and rural places as well. In contrast to the findings for the Dutch studies in Chapters 7 and 8, Fritsch and Stuetzer found that employment opportunities play only a minor role in the location of the creative class, compared to ethnic and cultural diversity. They also found that education and public healthcare are strongly associated with the creative class.

Chapter 11, a newly written contribution by Ron Boschma and Michael Fritsch, applies the key results of a large-scale EU project aimed at testing creative class theory in a European context to its examination of the creative class across seven

European countries: Denmark, Finland, Germany, the Netherlands, Norway, Sweden, and the United Kingdom. The chapter looks at two things: the geography of the creative class across European cites and the factors that shape that geography. It finds the creative class to be over-represented in larger cities across Europe, with London as the winner in terms of creative class shares. It also finds that tolerance and openness have a positive effect on the regional share of the creative class, while the provision of public facilities in healthcare and education have only minor, if any, impact, which is in line with the findings of Chapter 2.

Part III turns to the creative class in Australia and Asia. Chapter 12, by Kevin Stolarick, examines the creative class and the 3Ts across Australia's Local Government Areas. It finds that the creative class is strongly associated with tolerance and diversity. Two of the 3Ts, talent and tolerance, are more strongly associated with greater income growth across Australian regions than the third T, technology.

Chapter 13, by Hans Westlund and Federica Calidoni, turns to the creative class in Japan. An updated version of their (2011) study, it compares and contrasts Richard Florida's theory about openness and tolerance to Robert Putnam's theories on social capital, highlighting their differences and similarities. The study does not find any support for either the role of tolerance or social capital theories in relation to growth in Japan, but it does find that there are significant relations between human capital and accessibility, on one hand, and population growth and high tech, on the other. The overall weak results are in part a reflection of data limitations, according to the authors.

Chapter 14 by Richard Florida, Charlotta Mellander, and Haifeng Qian examines the creative class and the 3Ts in China, a country that is currently seeking to transform its economic structure from a traditional industrial to a more innovative, human capital-driven and knowledge-based economy. An updated and revised version of a study that originally appeared in *Environment and Planning A* (2012), it finds that the distribution of the creative class and talent is considerably more concentrated in China than in the USA or any other advanced economies. Universities were found to be the key factor in shaping the distribution, both of talent and of technological innovation, while tolerance also plays an important role. Perhaps most striking is the finding that neither talent nor technology is associated with the economic performance of Chinese regions: a finding that stands in sharp contrast to the pattern in advanced economies.

The final chapter by Florida and Mellander pulls together the broad cross-national themes and learning from these studies. We will have more to say in this last chapter, but generally speaking, three things stand out. First, taken as a whole, the studies reinforce the validity of the creative class approach and of occupational-based analysis across a wide range of countries. Second, they substantiate the uneven geography of the creative class and its tendency to concentrate in large cities or those with knowledge-based institutions such as universities. Third and most interesting are the findings emerging from these studies involving the role of openness and tolerance. Studies of small countries, for example, Sweden in Chapter 4 or the Netherlands in Chapters 7 and 8, find little or no effect of tolerance and openness.

But studies of large countries, like the United States in Chapter 2, or which consider a relatively large number of European countries, as in Chapter 11, find that tolerance and openness do play a significant role in both the geography of the creative class and of regional economic development. The issue here is likely to reflect scale. The effects of openness are likely to be muted in small countries with relatively homogeneous populations and more pronounced in large countries and in cities and regions across countries with greater diversity of cities and populations.

We hope this volume will help to inform and stimulate future research and more efficacious public policy-making on this vital subject.

Bibliography

Falck, O., Fritsch, M. and Heblich, S. (2011) "The phantom of the opera: Cultural amenities, human capital, and regional economic growth," *Labour Economics*, 18(6): 755–766.

Florida, R. (2002) *The Rise of the Creative Class*, New York: Basic Books.

Florida, R. (2005) *The Flight of the Creative Class: The New Global Competition for Talent*, New York: HarperCollins.

Florida, R. (2012) *The Rise of the Creative Class: Revisited*, New York: Basic Books.

Florida, R., Mellander, C. and Stolarick, K. (2011) "Creativity and prosperity: The global creativity index," Martin Prosperity Institute Report. Available at: http://martinprosperity.org/media/GCI%20Report%20Sep%202011.pdf (accessed August 29, 2013).

Florida, R., Mellander, C. and Qian, H. (2012) "China's development disconnect," *Environment and Planning A*, 44: 628–648.

Fritsch, M. and Stuetzer, M. (2009) "The geography of creative people in Germany," *International Journal of Foresight and Innovation Policy*, 5: 7–23.

Gabe, T. (2011) "The value of creativity," in D. Andersson, A. Andersson and C. Mellander (eds), *Handbook of Creative Cities*, Cheltenham: Edward Elgar, pp. 128–145.

Glaeser, E. L. (2004) "Book review of Richard Florida's 'The Rise of the Creative Class'," available at: http://www.creativeclass.com/rfcgdb/articles/GlaeserReview.pdf (accessed August 29, 2013).

McGranahan, D. and Wojan, T. (2007) "Recasting the creative class to examine growth processes in rural and urban counties," *Regional Studies*, 41(2): 197–216.

Marlet, G. and Van Woerkens, C. (2004) *Skills and Creativity in a Cross-Section of Dutch Cities*, Utrecht: Utrecht School of Economics. Available at: http://igitur-archive.library.uu.nl/USE/2005-1129-200137/04-29.pdf (accessed August 29, 2013).

Shapiro, J. M. (2006) "Smart cities: Quality of life, productivity, and the growth effects of human capital," *The Review of Economics and Statistics*, 88(2): 324–335.

Stolarick, K. and Currid-Halkett, E. (2012) "Creativity and the crisis: The impact of creative workers on regional unemployment," *Cities*. doi:10.1016/j.cities.2012.05.017.

Westlund, H. and Calidoni, F. (2011) "The creative class, social capital and regional development in Japan," *Review of Urban and Regional Development Studies*, 22(2–3): 89–108.

Part I
The United States and Canada

2 Inside the black box of regional development*

Human capital, the creative class, and tolerance

Richard Florida, Charlotta Mellander and Kevin Stolarick

Introduction

What *really* drives economic development? It is a complex question, so it is not surprising that lots of opinions and answers have been offered. If you ask the typical person on the street, they will tell you the key is jobs. This seems to jive with common sense: When a place attracts new jobs, more wealth and other good things follow. This conventional wisdom is the backbone of a good deal of economic development policy, as economic developers scramble to lure companies to their towns. Others say technology is key. Pointing out places like Silicon Valley, they say success lies in a high-tech cluster of great research universities, abundant venture capital and entrepreneurial startup companies. But according to current thinking and research in economics, geography and social science broadly, the underlying driver of economic development is highly skilled and educated people—what some call talent and what economists and social scientists frequently refer to as human capital. Places that have more of it thrive, while those with less stagnate or decline.

The central role played by human capital in economic development has been documented both in large-scale studies of national economic performance (Barro, 1991) and across regions in the US and other advanced countries (Rauch, 1993; Simon and Nardinelli, 1996; Simon, 1998). It is also clear from recent studies that human capital levels are diverging, and the differences are growing larger and more pronounced across regions (Berry and Glaeser, 2005).

Understanding the role of the cultural economy in regional development is also an interesting question. Prior work suggests that people working in culturally creative occupations are likely to have an impact on both the production and consumption of a variety goods and services. The cultural economy could have significant and direct relationships with regional wages, income and labor productivity. As prior work by Stolarick and Florida (2006) found direction connections between the artistic/cultural and technology/innovation communities of a specific city (Montréal), these relationships could be more meaningfully investigated in a broader context. The strong presence of culturally creative individuals can act as a signal of openness and

* This chapter was previously published as: Florida, R., Mellander, C., and Stolarick, K. (2008) 'Inside the Black Box of regional development–Human capital, the creative class, and tolerance', *Journal of Economic Geography*, 8: 615–649.

inclusiveness across a region which enhances regional attractiveness to other talented individuals. Additionally, a significant cultural economy can also be related to the *consumption* of cultural goods which act as a regional amenity that could help attract others to the region.

Our research focuses on two key questions over which there remains considerable debate. The first concerns how best to understand and measure human capital. The standard measure for human capital is educational attainment, usually the share of a population with a bachelor's degree and above. But, recent studies show that this measure captures only a part of a person's capability which reflects accumulated experience, creativity, intelligence, innovativeness, and entrepreneurial capabilities as well as level of schooling. One line of research (Florida, 2002a, 2002b, 2002c, 2004b) suggests an alternative measure for human capital, based on the occupation, specifically a set of occupations that make up the 'creative class', including science, engineering, arts, culture, entertainment, and the knowledge-based professions of management, finance, law, healthcare and education. Comparative studies show that the creative class measure outperforms conventional human capital measures in accounting for regional development in Sweden (Mellander and Florida, 2006) and the Netherlands (Marlet and Van Woerken, 2004).

If we understand that human capital drives economic growth and we also know that human capital levels are becoming more divergent or uneven, this raises a second question: Exactly what are the factors that shape the distribution of human capital in the first place? On this score, three different competing theories have been offered. The first argues that universities play a key role in creating initial advantages in human capital, which becomes cumulative and self-reinforcing over time (Glaeser *et al.*, 2001). The second argues that amenities play a role in attracting and retaining highly-educated, high-skilled households (Glaeser, 1994; Glaeser *et al.*, 2001; Shapiro, 2006; Clark, 2003). The third theory argues that tolerance and openness to diversity are important (Florida, 2002a, 2002b, 2002c). We suggest that these three approaches need not be seen as mutually exclusive. It is more likely that these factors play complementary roles in the distribution of talent and in regional development.

To shed light on these issues, we present a stage-based general model of regional development. In the first stage, we examine how factors such as tolerance, universities and consumer service amenities affect the location of talent (measured as human capital and the creative class). In the second stage, we look at how the concentration of talent in turn affects technology. And in the third stage, we examine the effects of technology, talent, and tolerance on both regional wages and income. This stage-based model structure enables us to isolate the direct and indirect effects of these factors in the overall system of regional development. We use structural equations and path analysis models to examine the independent effects of human capital, the creative class, technology, tolerance and other factors identified in the literature on both regional wages and incomes. We examine these issues via a cross-sectional analysis of 331 geographic metropolitan regions in the United States, and test explicitly for the effects of regional size.

Our modeling approach is designed to address a significant weakness of previous studies of the effects of human capital and the creative class on regional development. Most of these studies use a single equation regression framework to identify the direct effects of human capital and other factors on regional development. The findings of these studies, not surprisingly, indicate that human capital outperforms other variables. But that does not establish that these other variables do not matter. First, something has to affect the initial distribution of human capital. Variables that have not performed well in other studies may exert influence by operating through human capital and thus indirectly affect regional development or certain variables may operate through different channels. By using a system of equations our model structure allows us to parse the direct and indirect effects of key variables on each other as well as on regional development. Furthermore, our model is based on a strong *a priori* theory of the relationships between and among key variables as they shape regional development.

Our results inform three main findings. First, we find that human capital and the creative class play different but complementary roles in regional development. The creative class—or occupational skill—operates through the channel of wages and exerts its effect on regional labor productivity. Human capital—or education—operates by increasing regional income and wealth.

Second, we find that certain occupations affect regional development to a greater degree than others. Education and healthcare have a relatively small association with regional development, while occupations like computer science, engineering, management and business and financial operations evidence much higher levels of association. A particularly interesting finding is the relatively high levels of association between artistic and entertainment occupations and regional labor productivity. These occupations, which are typically seen as consumers of local resources, appear to affect regional productivity to a significant degree when controls for other key factors are included.

Third, we find that tolerance is significantly associated with both human capital and the creative class and also with regional wages and income. Universities and consumer services also affect the regional distribution of human capital and the creative class, but substantially less so than tolerance. These three factors do not operate in competition with one another, but tend to play complementary roles in the geographic distribution of human capital and the creative class and in regional development broadly.

Theory and concepts

The literature on economic development is vast. Solow (1956) noted the effect of technology on economic growth. Solow's model treated technology as exogenous and not affected by the marginal rate of substitution between capital and labor. Ullman (1958) noted the role of human capital in his work on regional development. Jacobs (1961, 1969) emphasized the role of cities and regions in the transfer and diffusion of knowledge; as the scale and diversity of cities increase, so do the connections between economic actors that result in the generation of new ideas and innovations. Andersson (1985a, 1985b) explored the role of creativity historically in regional economic development, stressing the importance of knowledge, culture, communications, and creativity, while arguing that tolerance also plays a role in stimulating creativity in cities and regions. Romer's (1986, 1987, 1990) endogenous growth model connected technology to human capital, knowledge, and economic growth. Invention in the neoclassical framework is no longer exogenous, but a purposeful activity demanding real resources.

Lucas (1988) further developed and explicitly identified the role of human capital externalities in economic development. Building on Jacobs' and Romer's work, Lucas highlighted the clustering effect of human capital, which embodies the knowledge factor. He recognized the role of great cities, which localize human capital and information, create knowledge spillovers, and become engines of economic growth. Cities reduce the cost of knowledge transfer, so ideas move more quickly, in turn giving rise to new knowledge more quickly.

A wide range of empirical studies have documented the role of human capital in regional growth. Barro (1991), Rauch (1993), Simon and Nardinelli (1996) and Simon (1998) all confirm the relation between human capital and growth on a national level. Glaeser (2000) provides empirical evidence on the correlation between human capital and regional economic growth. Firms locate in areas of high human capital concentration to gain competitive advantages, rather than letting suppliers' and customers' geography alone dictate their location. Other studies find that human capital is becoming more concentrated (Florida, 2002b; Berry and Glaeser, 2005), and there are reasons to believe that this division will continue, affecting not only regional growth levels, but also housing values (Gyourko *et al.*, 2006; Shapiro, 2006).

The current debate revolves around two key issues. The first is how best to measure and account for human capital. Traditionally, human capital has been measured as education and training, simply because those are seen as the most important investments in human capital. The conventional measure of human capital is educational attainment—generally, the share of the population with a bachelor's degree and above. The educational attainment measure, it has been pointed out, leaves out a small but incredibly influential group of entrepreneurs, like Bill Gates or Michael Dell, who for various reasons did not go to or finish college. These two entrepreneurs and many others like them have added immense value to the US and global economies through their skill even though they would not make the cut of the standard education attainment measure of human capital. Furthermore, the educational attainment measure is broad, and therefore does not allow for nations or regions to identify specific types of human capital or talent. Education measures potential talent or skill, but occupation provides a potentially more robust measure of utilized skill—that is how human talent or capability is absorbed by and used by the economy. While studies have shown that education is one way of improving the productivity of labor, other factors such as creativity, intelligence, and on-the-job knowledge and accumulated experience function interchangeably with education in affecting labor productivity (Smith *et al.*, 1984). Education provides an underlying level of capability, but such capability has to be converted into productive work. Thus occupation is the mechanism through which education is converted into skill and labor productivity.

For these reasons, others have argued that occupation is a better and more direct measure of skill. Recent studies (Marlet and Van Woerken, 2004; Mellander and Florida, 2006) find that occupational measures significantly outperform conventional educational attainment in accounting for regional development in Sweden and in the Netherlands. Using occupations as a measure for skill has the additional advantage of allowing one to isolate the effects of specific occupations on income and regional labor productivity in terms of wages. Our models enable us to isolate the effects of human capital, the creative class and also of individual creative occupations on regional development.

Furthermore, there are good theoretical reasons to expect that human capital and creative occupations—education and skill—affect regional development through different channels. Human capital theory postulates that wages rise with the level of knowledge or skill (Becker, 1964, 1993; Mincer, 1974). Optimally, wage levels should be in proportion to the stock of human capital, since this affects the value of workers' marginal product. Wages are thus set by the regional *supply and demand* for labor. More to the point, as pay for work, wages are directly related to regional labor productivity. In this macro context, wages and knowledge are considered in aggregate. On a micro level they may be distributed unevenly. Two regions can reach the same wage levels based on (1) a homogeneous labor force or (2) a labor force consisting of high and low knowledge labor that together reach the same result. But at the mean, the regional wage level will reflect the regional labor productivity.

Income is a composite measure which includes wages plus gains, rents, interest, transfers and the like. On average, wages make up about 70 percent of US income. If wages measure regional labor productivity, income reflects regional wealth. In this sense, income is less place-dependent. For example, there are a lot of rich people in regions like Southern Florida, but they made their money elsewhere. Income is much more easily moved between regions. Furthermore, non-wage sources of income such as capital gains, interest, subsidies and the like have little to do with regional skill or the ability of a region to utilize skill in production. Our models test for the effects of human capital, the creative class, and individual occupations on both regional wages and incomes.

The second key issue in the current debate is over the factors that affect the geographic distribution of human capital or the creative class in the first place. Since we know that these sorts of talent are associated with economic development, and we also know that they are spread unevenly, it is important to understand the factors that account for their varied geography. Most economists conceptualize human capital as a stock or endowment, which belongs to a place in the same way that a natural resource might. But the reality is that human capital is a *flow*, a highly mobile factor that can and does relocate. The key question then becomes: What factors shape this flow and determine the divergent levels of human capital and the creative class—education and skill—across regions?

Three different answers to that question have been offered. The first approach offered by Glaeser and his collaborators (2001) is that human capital builds off itself. Places with an initial advantage tend to build on and gain from that advantage. The presence of major research universities has been found to be a key factor in this set of initial advantages as well in both the production and distribution of human capital. Yet, the distribution of education and skill need not be coincident with the distribution of universities. While some regions with great universities have large concentrations of talent, others operate mainly in the production of human capital, serving as exporters of highly educated people to other regions (Florida *et al.*, 2006). Florida (2005) argues that the geographic connection from education to innovation and economic outcomes *in that same locale* may no longer hold. This is a result of the increased mobility of highly-skilled and educated people within countries and even across borders. However good a region's educational system might be, it is no guarantee it can hold on to its educated and skilled people. One way to think of the university is as a necessary but insufficient condition for attracting educated and skilled populations to a region or even holding on to the ones it produces.

The second approach argues that the distribution of education and skill is affected by the distribution of amenities. Roback (1982) expanded the traditional neoclassical model, where migration occurs in response to wage levels and land rent to include quality-of-life amenities. Glaeser, Kolko and Saiz (2001) find that consumer and personal service industries such as restaurants, theatres, and museums tend to be localized and thus demand geographical closeness between producer and consumer. Lloyd and Clark (2001) as well as Florida (2002a, 2002b, 2002c) stress the role of lifestyle—in the form of entertainment, nightlife, culture, and so on—in attracting educated populations. Florida (2002c) introduces a measure of observed locational preferences of the producers of artistic and cultural amenities, the 'Bohemian Index', and found it to be associated with concentrations of human capital and innovation. Shapiro's (2006) detailed study of regional productivity growth finds that 'roughly 60 percent of the employment growth effect of college graduates is due to enhanced productivity growth, the rest being caused by growth in quality of life'.

The third approach to the factors that influence the flow of talent among regions argues that tolerance and openness to diversity affect the level and geographic distribution of education and skill. Jacobs (1961) and Quigley (1998) have argued that firm-based diversity is associated with economic growth, but Jacobs also argued that diversity of individuals is important as well. Recent research has focused on the role of demographic diversity in economic growth. Ottaviano and Peri (2005) show how diversity among individuals, in the form of immigrants, increases regional productivity. Immigrants have complementary skills to native-born, not because they perform different tasks, but also because they bring different skills to the same task. A Chinese cook and an Italian cook will not provide the same service nor good; neither will a German-trained physicist substitute perfectly for a US-trained one. Noland (2005) finds that tolerant attitudes toward gay and lesbians are associated with both positive attitudes toward global economic activity and international financial outcomes. Florida and Gates (2001) find a positive association between concentrations of gay households and regional development. Florida (2002a) further argues that tolerance—specifically 'low barriers to entry' for individuals—is associated with geographic concentrations of talent, higher rates of innovation, and regional development. The more open a place is to new ideas and new people—in other words, the lower its entry barriers for human capital—the more education and skill it will likely capture.

There is considerable debate over the salience of these measures, approaches and findings. Clark (2003) finds that the relationship between the Gay Index and regional development holds only for high population regions. Glaeser (2004) ran linear regressions with human capital, the Gay Index and the Bohemian Index and found that the effects of human capital overpower the effects of these other tolerance measures when looking at change in population between 1990 and 2000, an admittedly crude measure of economic development. Florida (2004a, 2004b) counters that these frameworks and models are crude and do not capture the interactions among the system of factors that act on regional development. He suggests a general model of regional development according to the 3Ts of economic development: technology, talent and tolerance. He argues that each alone is necessary but insufficient in generating regional development: All three must act together with substantial and balanced performance to result in higher levels of development.

It is important to state at the outset that our model does not argue for a mechanistic relationship between regional tolerance (measured as concentrations of artists and or gays) and regional development. Rather, we argue that tolerance or openness to diversity makes local resources more productive and efficient acting through four key mechanisms. First, locations of bohemian and gay populations reflect low barriers to entry for human capital. Such locations will have advantages in attracting a broad range of talent across racial, ethnic and other lines, increasing the efficiency of human capital accumulation. Page (2008) provides the basis for a general economic theory of tolerance and improved economic outcomes. He finds that not only does cognitive diversity lead to better decision-making but that it is associated with identity diversity, the diversity of people and groups, which enable new perspectives. Diversity broadly construed, he finds, is associated with higher rates of innovation and growth.

Second, larger bohemian and gay populations signal underlying mechanisms that increase the efficiency of knowledge spillovers and human capital externalities that Lucas (1988) identifies as the primary engine of economic growth. Recent studies (Markusen and Schrock, 2006; Currid, 2007) note the role of artistic networks as conduits for the spread of new ideas and knowledge transfer across firms and industries. Stolarick and Florida (2006) demonstrate the 'spill-acrosses', which can be more wide-ranging than spillovers, that can be generated by the interaction between bohemians and the traditional technology community. Greater concentrations of artists and gays thus reflect regional mechanisms that accelerate human capital externalities and knowledge spillovers.

The third mechanism for making local resources more productive is that artistic and gay populations reflect regional values that are open-minded, meritocratic, tolerant of risk, and oriented to self-expression. Inglehart *et al.* (Inglehart and Norris, 2003; Inglehart and Welzel, 2005) have noted the correlation between self-expression values and GDP growth at the national level. In detailed research tracking more than 60 countries over four decades, Inglehart (Inglehart and Norris, 2003; Inglehart and Welzel, 2005) identifies tolerance or what he calls 'self-expression' to be a core element of a new value systems associated with higher levels of GDP and economic growth. He notes that openness toward gay and lesbian populations is the best indicator of overall tolerance. Psychological studies (Amabile, 1996; Sternberg, 1999; Fredrickson, 2001) indicate that self-expression is associated with higher levels of creativity, innovation and entrepreneurial behavior. Lucas (1988) explicitly notes the similarities in values and orientation as 'creative' actors between technological and entrepreneurial labor and artistic and cultural populations.

Fourth, locations with larger artistic and gay populations signal underlying mechanisms which increase the productivity of entrepreneurial activity. Because of their status as historically marginalized groups, traditional economic institutions have been less open and receptive to bohemian and gay populations, thus requiring them to mobilize resources independently and to form new organizations and firms. We thus suggest that regions where these groups have migrated and taken root reflect underlying mechanisms which are more attuned to mobilization of such resources, entrepreneurship and new firm formation. These four factors, when taken together, improve the efficiency and productivity of regional human capital, innovation and entrepreneurship.

We also note that according to our theory, tolerance, universities and consumer service amenities need not operate exclusively or in competition with each other. Rather, we suggest that they are likely to have complementary effects on the geographic distribution of education and skill. Universities, consumer amenities, and tolerance act on regional economic development directly, as well as indirectly, via their effects on the levels of educated and skilled people. Also, there may be reasons to believe that these factors are affected by the size of regions (McGranahan and Wojan, 2007). Larger regions, by virtue of their size and market reach, may be able to support more of these options. We test explicitly for the effects of region size across various permutations of the model.

Model

A schematic picture of our general model for the system of regional development is outlined in Figure 2.1. The model allows us to overcome several limitations of previous studies. First, it considers regional development as a system of relationships. It allows us to test the independent relations between human capital, the creative class, technology, tolerance and regional development. Second, it allows us to test for and more precisely identify the role of educational human capital versus the creative class on regional wages and incomes. Third, it allows us to

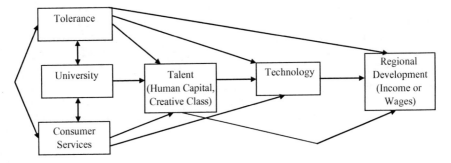

Figure 2.1 Path model of the regional development system

parse the effects of wages and income, and to identify the factors that act on regional labor productivity and regional wealth. And fourth, it enables us to parse the relations between tolerance, consumer services, and universities and the distribution of human capital and the creative class which in turn act on regional wages and income. The arrows identify the hypothesized structure of relationships among the key variables.

Variables

We now describe the variables in the empirical model. The variables cover all 331 metropolitan statistical areas in the USA, and are for the year 2000. Descriptive statistics for all measures and variables are provided in Table 2.1.

Outcome variables

It is common in studies of regional development to use factors like population change or job growth as measures of development. But those measures are quite crude in that they cannot specify the quality of development. Not all jobs are created equal; some pay a good deal more than others. Regions increasingly specialize in different kinds

Table 2.1 Descriptive statistics

	Mean	Standard deviation	Minimum	Maximum
BA or above	23.72	7.43	11.05	52.38
Creative class	20.30	5.88	8.55	42.73
Super-creative	7.86	3.14	1.77	25.20
University	2.11	2.00	0.00	11.93
Tolerance	0.876	0.281	0.44	2.87
Consumer services	221.43	23.49	41	253
Technology	0.701	2.253	0.00	29.96
Wages (000)	13.428	3.700	5.153	30.311
Income (000)	20.607	3.972	9.899	51.462

of economic activity, and therefore different kinds of jobs (Markusen, 2004). When we say regional development, what we really want to know is the overall level of development and living standards of a region. We thus need to know how much people in a region earn and what the total income of the region is. We use two measures of regional development as outcome variables: wages and incomes. It is important to remind readers of the differences between the two. Wages are remuneration for work. Most economists suggest that wages are thus a good proxy for regional labor productivity. Income includes wages but also earnings from interest, capital gains, self-employment income, transfers, and so on. Wages exclude non-earned income.

Wages

This measure is based on the sum of the wages and salaries and based on total money earnings received for work performed as an employee in the region. This measure includes wages, salary, armed forces pay, commissions, tips, piece-rate payments, and cash bonuses earned before deductions were made for taxes, bonds, pensions, union dues, etc. It is measured on a per worker basis and is from the 2000 US BLS.

Income

Income is the sum of the amounts reported separately for wage or salary income including net self-employment income; interest, dividends, or net rental or royalty income or income from estates and trusts; social security or railroad retirement income; Supplemental Security Income (SSI); public assistance or welfare payments; retirement, survivor, or disability pensions; and all other income. It is measured on a per capita basis and is from the 2000 US Census.

Wages and incomes are related (see Table 2.2 and see Figure 2.2).The correlation coefficient between them is 0.723. Still there are considerable differences among regions. As we noted earlier, wages are a good proxy for regional productivity, while income is a good proxy for regional wealth. To get a better handle on this, we looked at the wage-to-income ratio across regions. The higher the score, the relatively larger the share of their total regional income or wealth comes from wages, in other words a relatively large share of their total regional income or wealth comes from labor productivity. Regions with a lower score are more dependent on capital gains accrued elsewhere or on non-wage income streams. The differences are considerable, ranging from more than 90 percent wages to around 20 percent wages in resort destinations. Our models enable us to look into the effects of both wages and income on regional development, and also at the factors that affect each of them.

Human capital

This variable is the conventional measure based on educational attainment, measured as the percentage of the regional labor force with a bachelor's degree and above. It is from the 2000 US Census.

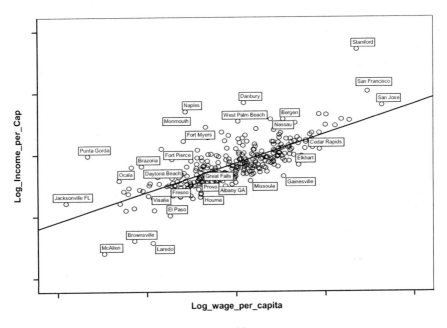

Figure 2.2 Scatter graph of regional wages and income

Creative class

We use several definitions of the creative class based on occupation. Each of them is measured as share of the regional labor force. All data are from the US Bureau of Labor Statistics for the year 2000. Following Florida (2002a), we examine the effects of the creative occupations or the 'creative class', defined as those in which individuals 'engage in complex problem solving that involves a great deal of independent judgment and requires high levels of education or human capital'. Specifically, it includes the following major occupational groups: computer and math occupations; architecture and engineering; life, physical, and social science; education, training, and library positions; arts and design work; and entertainment, sports, and media occupations—as well as other professional and knowledge work occupations including management occupations, business and financial operations, legal positions,

Table 2.2 Correlation matrix for key variables

	Human capital	Creative class	Super-creative	Wages	Income
Human capital	1				
Creative class	0.727**	1			
Super-creative	0.665**	0.868**	1		
Wages	0.653**	0.840**	0.695**	1	
Income	0.701**	0.474**	0.399**	0.723**	1

Note: ** Indicates significance at the 0.01 level.

healthcare practitioners, technical occupations, and high-end sales and sales management. McGranahan and Wojan (2007) utilized BLS data on the actual skill content of tasks to recalculate creative class occupations on a slightly narrower basis. We also include this revised definition of the creative class in our analysis (see Appendix Table A1 which shows results consistent with those presented below).

Super-creative core

We include a variable to test for the effects of the super-creative core, a narrower group of creative occupations which Florida (2002a) defines as those which involve more intense use of creativity on the job: computer and math occupations; architecture and engineering; life, physical, and social science; education, training, and library positions; arts and design work; and selected entertainment, sports, and media occupations. We also include McGranahan and Wojan's (2007) revised definition.

Individual creative occupations

We also completed analysis for each of the major clusters of creative occupations: computer and math; architecture and engineering; life and physical science; management; business and financial specialists; arts, design, media and entertainment; education; law; and healthcare.

The relation between our two primary measures of talent— human capital and the creative class— is illustrated in the scatter graph provided in Figure 2.3. The two are

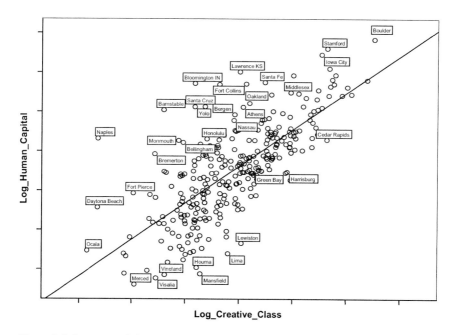

Figure 2.3 Scatter graph between human capital and creative occupations

related but clearly not the same. The correlation coefficient between the two of them is .727, while the correlation coefficient for super-creative occupations and education is slightly less, .665 (Table 2.2).

Technology variables

Tech Pole Index

We include a technology variable to account for the effects of technology on regional development. This technology variable is based on the Tech Pole Index from 2000, published by the Milken Institute. This index ranks metropolitan areas based on: (1) high-technology industrial output as a percentage of total US high-technology industrial output; and (2) the percentage of the region's own total economic output that comes from high-tech industries compared to the nation-wide percentage. We also test for a more narrow definition of the high-tech sector based on industries that use a more skilled labor force (Hecker, 1999).

Tolerance and related variables

To examine the question of what accounts for the geographic distribution of educated and skilled populations, we include three key variables reflecting the current literature.

Tolerance

This variable is measured as a combination of the concentration of gay and lesbian households and the concentration of individuals employed in the arts, design and related occupations. Here we follow Florida *et al.* (Florida and Gates, 2001; 2002a, 2002b, 2002c, 2005) and combine the Gay and Bohemian Indexes. The data are from the US Census for the year 2000. It is important to note that the bohemian measure here which is based on the household survey of the US Census thus differs considerably from the occupational measures used in the talent and creative class measures described above which are from the employer surveys of the Bureau of Labor Statistics.

Universities

This variable measures number of university faculty per capita. It is based on 2000 data from IPEDS (Integrated Post-Secondary Data Set) from the US Department of Education.

Consumer service amenities

We use the diversity of consumer service firms as our proxy for regional amenities, following Glaeser (1994) and Shapiro (2006). This variable reflects the number of service industries represented within the metropolitan region that could be regarded as attractive to consumers. It is based on 2000 industry data from the Census.

Methods

We use path analysis and structural equations to examine the relationships between variables in the model. In order to analyze the dynamics between this set of variables adequately, structural equation modeling is used. Structural equation models (SEM) may be thought of as an extension of regression analysis and factor analysis, expressing the interrelationship between variables through a set of linear relationships, based upon their variances and covariances. In other words, a structural equation replaces a (usually large) set of observable variables with a small set of unobservable factor constructs, thus minimizing the problem of multicollinearity (for further technical description, see Jöreskog, 1973). The parameters of the equations are estimated by the maximum likelihood method.[1]

It is important to stress that the graphic picture of the structural model (Figure 2.1) expresses direct and indirect correlations, not actual causalities. Rather, the estimated parameters (path coefficients) provide information on the relation between the set of variables. Moreover, the relative importance of the parameters is expressed by the standardized path coefficients, which allow for interpretation of the direct as well as the indirect effects. We do not assume any causality among university, tolerance and consumer services but rather treat them as correlations.

From the relationships depicted in the model (Figure 2.1, above), we estimate three equations:

$$\ln Talent = \beta_{11} \ln Tolerance + \beta_{12} \ln University + \beta_{13} \ln ConsumerServices + e_3 \quad (2.1)$$
$$\ln Technology = \beta_{21} \ln Tolerance + \beta_{23} \ln ConsumerServices + \beta_{24} \ln Talent + e_2 \quad (2.2)$$
$$\ln Wages = \beta_{31} \ln Tolerance + \beta_{34} \ln Talent + \beta_{35} \ln Technology + e_1 \qquad (2.3a)$$
$$\ln Incomes = \beta_{31} \ln Tolerance + \beta_{34} \ln Talent + \beta_{35} \ln Technology + e_1 \qquad (2.3b)$$

Findings

We begin with the results of the bivariate analysis. We then turn to the results of the path analysis and structural equations models, looking at the roles played by human capital and the creative class on regional wages and incomes. The next section examines the roles played by specific occupations in regional development. After that we discuss the role of tolerance as well as consumer service amenities and universities in affecting the distribution of human capital and the creative class.

Table 2.2 provides a correlation matrix for the key variables. The correlation coefficient for human capital and income (.701) is higher than that for the creative class or (.474) or super-creative occupations (.399). But the opposite pattern appears for wages. The correlation between the creative class and wages (.840) is higher than that for human capital and wages (.653). This provides a first glimpse of the different channels through which human capital and the creative class affect regional development.

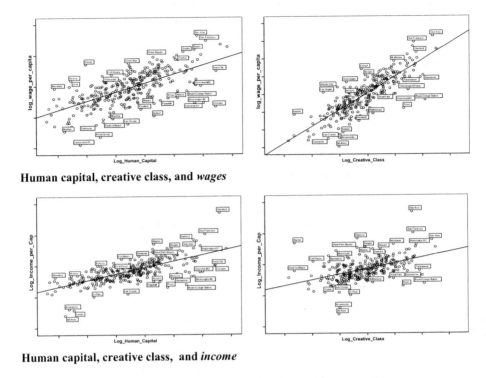

Human capital, creative class, and *wages*

Human capital, creative class, and *income*

Figure 2.4 Scatter graphs for human capital, creative class and income and wages

Figure 2.4 is a series of scatter graphs which further illustrate the relation-ships between human capital and the creative class on wages and income. The slope for human capital and income is steeper than for the creative class and income. But the slope for the creative class and wages is much steeper than for human capital and wages. There are fewer outliers and the observations cluster tightly around the line. This reinforces the notion that human capital and the creative class act on different channels of regional development.

Inside the black box of regional development

To further gauge the differential effects of human capital and the creative class in relation to regional development, we turn to the key to the findings from the structural equations models and path analysis. We ran separate models for human capital and the creative class using both wages and income as measures of regional development. We analyzed models based on creative and super-creative occupations using Florida's (2002a) definition as well as the revised, narrower definition introduced by McGranahan and Wojan (2007), as well as for the major groupings of creative occupations. We also investigated exclud-ing the arts, design, entertainment, media and sports occupations from the creative class occupations and super-creative core occupations to check for the possible collinearity between the tolerance measure and this group. We completed analysis for four regional size classes: regions over a million population; 500,000 to 1 million; 250,000 to 500,000; and less than 250,000. The results proved to be extremely robust to these different formulations of the basic model.

The models examine the relation between the different measures of human capital and the creative class and income and wages and also isolate the effects of three key factors—tolerance, consumer services and universities—on the level and geographic distribution of human capital and the creative class as well as their consistency with income and wages. A path analysis is provided for each model based on the standardized β-coefficients. This standardized coefficient is based upon the regression where all the variables in the regression have been standardized first by subtracting each variable's mean and dividing it by the standard deviation associated by each variable. These coefficients can be used to analyze the relative importance of the explanatory variables in relation to the dependent variable. Also, the other structural equation results are reported for.

Figure 2.5 summarizes the findings for the path analysis where income is the outcome variable, while Figure 2.6 shows the findings for wages. Tables 2.3 and 2.4 report the SEM results.

Looking at the findings for the income models in Table 2.3, the R^2 for education on income (.559) is considerably higher than for creative (.486) or super-creative occupations (.476). Turning to the wage models in Table 2.4, the R^2 for creative occupations (.769) and super-creative occupations (.602) are both higher than for educational human capital (.518). The same models were run for the occupational definitions used by McGranahan and Wojan (2007) with only minor differences in the results (see Appendix Table A2). Nor did excluding arts, design, entertainment, sports and media occupations from the creative class and the group of super-creatives significantly change the results. (Results available from the authors on request.) Furthermore, the path coefficients between human capital (.44) and income are much stronger than those for the creative class (.13) and super-creative occupations which is insignificant. Conversely, the path coefficients between wages and the creative class (.70) and super-creative occupations (.49) are stronger than for human capital (.45).

Our models include a technology variable so we can parse its effects alongside the two major talent variables as well as tolerance on regional development. The findings indicate that while technology plays a role in regional development, the relation to talent—whether measured as human capital or the creative class—is stronger. When included alongside human capital, the coefficient between technology and wages is .36. This is smaller than the coefficient of .45 between human capital and wages. The coefficient for technology and income is .22, about half the size of the coefficient of .44 between human capital and income. When the creative class is used, the coefficient for technology and wages (.18) is significantly smaller than the coefficient of .70 between the creative class and wages. Technology performs better in the models

Human capital

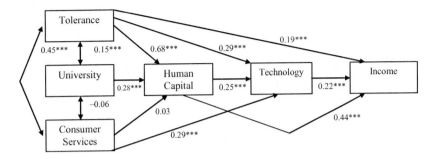

Creative class

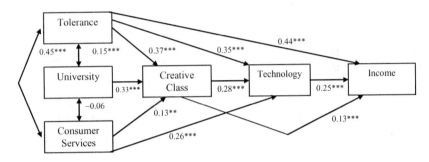

Super-creative occupations

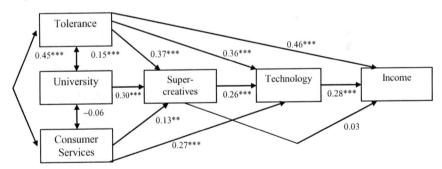

Figure 2.5 Path analysis for human capital, the creative class and income

with creative class and income. The coefficient between technology and income is .25, about twice as much as that for the creative class and income (.13). When super-creative occupations are used, the coefficient between technology and income is .28 while the coefficient for super-creative occupations and income is insignificant. Since some industries within the high-technology sector will have progressed further along the life cycle and become more

Human capital

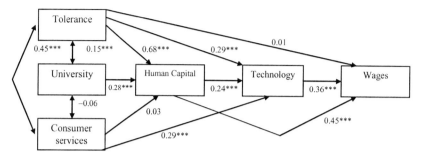

Creative class

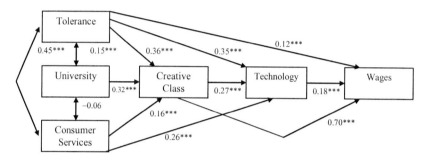

Super-creative occupations

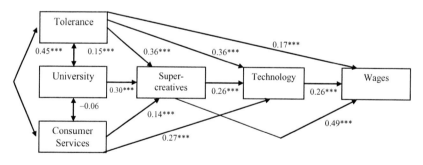

Figure 2.6 Path analysis for human capital, creative class, and wages

standardized in their production (and thereby less dependent on skill and knowledge), we ran the model with another, narrower definition of high-technology industry based on highly skilled labor intensity (Hecker, 1999). In these versions of the model, technology is slightly stronger in explaining wages and incomes, but there are no major changes in the significance, direction or path of the results.

Table 2.3 SEM results for income

Income	Human capital			Creative class			Super-creative core		
	Talent	Technology	Income	Talent	Technology	Income	Talent	Technology	Income
Variables	Eq 1	Eq 2	Eq 3	Eq 1	Eq 2	Eq 3	Eq 1	Eq 2	Eq 3
Tolerance	0.713***	2.576***	0.120***	0.362***	3.110***	0.270***	0.501***	3.230***	0.286***
Consumer services	0.063	5.500***		0.258**	5.026***		0.357**	5.051***	
University	0.112***			0.121***			0.155***		
Talent		2.128***	0.257***		2.607***	0.082***		1.700***	0.012
Technology			0.015***			0.017***			0.019***
Observations	331	331	331	331	331	331	331	331	331
R^2	0.619	0.453	0.559	0.332	0.486	0.486	0.315	0.475	0.476

Note: ** Indicates significance at the 0.05 and ***at the 0.01 level.

Table 2.4 SEM results for wages

Wages	Human capital			Creative class			Super-creative core		
Variables	Talent	Technology	Wages	Talent	Technology	Wages	Talent	Technology	Wages
	Eq 1	Eq 2	Eq 3	Eq 1	Eq 2	Eq 3	Eq 1	Eq 2	Eq 3
Tolerance	0.713***	2.595***	0.013	0.355***	3.140***	0.111***	0.494***	3.192***	0.158***
Consumer services	0.063	5.601***		0.326***	4.995***		0.414***	5.058***	
University	0.112***			0.121***			0.157***		
Talent		2.061***	0.400***		2.476***	0.659***		1.719***	0.338***
Technology			0.037***			0.018***			0.027***
Observations	331	331	331	331	331	331	331	331	331
R^2	0.619	0.451	0.518	0.332	0.482	0.769	0.316	0.477	0.602

Note: *** Indicates significance at the 0.01 level.

It is important to note that both human capital and creative class act on technology directly and as such also act indirectly through technology to have an additional effect on regional development. The path coefficient between human capital and technology is .24 in the wage model and .25 in the wage model. The coefficient between the creative class is .27 in the wage model and .28 in the income model. The coefficient between super-creative occupation and technology is .26 in the wage mode and .26 in the income model.

Region size effects

We also completed this analysis based on four groupings based on regional population. The key findings hold regardless of region size. (Results available.) Human capital remains more closely associated with income, while the creative class is more closely associated with regional wages or productivity. The path coefficients for human capital and income range from .86 in the largest regions to .31 in the smallest. When wages are used, the path coefficients for human capital and wages range from .81 in the largest regions to .44 in the smallest. For the creative class, the path coefficients between it and wages range from .81 in the largest regions to .79 in the smallest; and for income the path coefficients range from .27 in the largest regions to .16 in the smallest. The difference between the creative class and human capital is most pronounced among the 144 regions with less than 250,000 people. Here the creative class has a much stronger positive relationship with wages.

The overall findings from both the SEMs and the path analyses are clear. Human capital and the creative class are not substitutes. Rather, they act on regional development through different channels. Human capital or education operates through the channel of income, raising overall regional wealth. The creative class acts through wages and is much more closely associated with regional labor productivity. This is a non-trivial difference. Wages indicate a region's ability to generate labor productivity and wealth, while income can be, and frequently is, based on the ability of a region to attract wealth generated elsewhere. Wages reflect a Silicon Valley style of regional development where the wage-to-income ratio in Silicon Valley is .924, while income can and frequently does reflect a South Florida style of regional development—the wage-to-income ratio in Naples, Florida, is .333. The creative class is much more likely to be associated with regional labor productivity, while the human capital level reflects some regional labor productivity but also wealth accumulated over time and (potentially) in other locations. In our view, high human capital regions may be wealthier, but this can be, and frequently is, due their attractiveness to individuals and households who have accumulated wealth elsewhere. The creative class is much more closely associated with current regional labor productivity—the basic mechanism through which wealth is generated in the first place.

How and why occupations matter to regional development

Most studies treat human capital as monolithic, but clearly it is not. There is good reason to believe that some occupations and specific types of skill play a relatively larger role in regional development. There is a long tradition in industrial organization economics of identifying particular industries which contribute to overall growth. For example, Gordon (2003) found that computers and related industries accounted for a large share of US productivity growth in the 1990s. We introduce the concept of *occupational organization economics* by probing the effects of occupations on economic development.

Table 2.5 provides the correlations for the major occupational groupings, between both wages and income with the share of the regional workforce in that occupation. Several things are evident. First, the correlation coefficients are consistently higher for wages than for income, reinforcing the finding that occupations act on regional development through the channel of regional labor productivity. Second, while the correlations are all positive and significant, there is a wide range in the value and strength of the coefficients. Certain occupations appear to contribute relatively more to regional labor productivity.

Business and financial operations (.830) and computer and mathematical (.822) top the list. High-end sales (.774) and arts, design and media (.736) form a second cluster. A third cluster is composed of management (.668) and architecture and engineering (.649). Legal (.593) and scientific occupations (.540) form a fourth cluster. The effects of healthcare (.364) and education occupations (.232) are much weaker, and insignificant in terms of regional income.

Figure 2.7 supplements this with scatter graphs for the major occupations and wages. The scatter graphs show the steepness of the slopes for computer and mathematics occupations; business and financial operations; and architecture and engineering. Art and entertainment occupations and high-end sales occupations also have steep slope and cluster neatly around the line. Education and healthcare evidence a much weaker relation to wages which stays at approximately at the same level no matter what the regional wage levels are, with only a few exceptions.

Table 2.5 Correlation matrix for occupations, wages and income

Occupation	Wages	Income
Business and financial operations	0.830**	0.549**
Computer and mathematical occupations	0.822**	0.659**
High-end sales and sales management	0.774**	0.480**
Arts, design, entertainment, sports and media	0.736**	0.511**
Management	0.668**	0.358**
Architecture and engineering	0.649**	0.472**
Legal	0.593**	0.390**
Life, physical and social sciences	0.540**	0.393**
Healthcare	0.364**	0.052
Education and training	0.232**	0.055

Note: ** Significant at the 0.01 level.

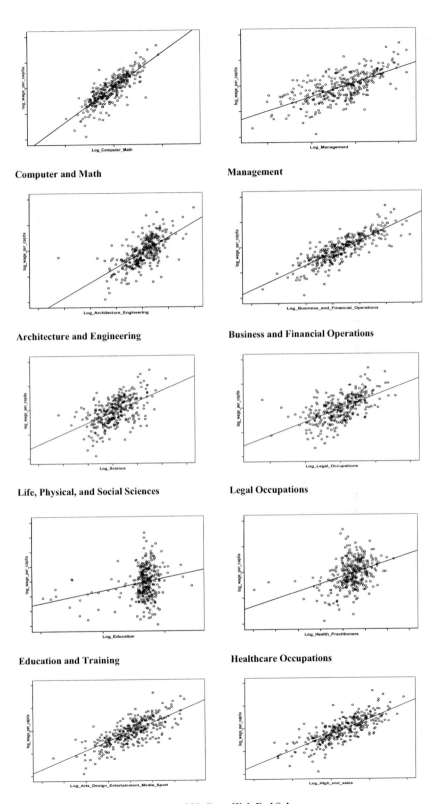

Computer and Math

Management

Architecture and Engineering

Business and Financial Operations

Life, Physical, and Social Sciences

Legal Occupations

Education and Training

Healthcare Occupations

Arts, Design, Entertainment, Sports and Media   **High-End Sales**

Figure 2.7 Scatter graphs for occupations and regional wages

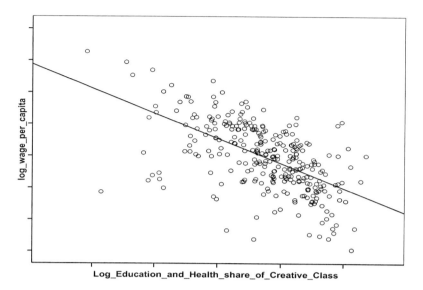

Figure 2.8 Education and healthcare occupations and wages

Figure 2.8 plots education and healthcare occupations as a share of the creative class against regional wages. The slope is distinctly negative. As the share of these two increases, the lower average regional wages. There are several possible explanations for this. It is likely that the demand for these occupations does not increase with incomes or wages but rather with population. It may also reflect demographic characteristics. Regions, for example, with a larger share of students will have a greater demand for education and a smaller share of population to engage in other productive activities. Regions with larger populations of elderly households will have a greater demand for healthcare, more healthcare occupations, and smaller share of the workforce employed in other productive activities. Needless to say, education and healthcare do not appear to add significantly to regional labor productivity and wealth. These occupations might be understood as a regional floor or constant. All regions will need some floor or threshold of these occupations, but the ones that experience productivity improvement and growth are those which have relatively higher concentrations of other occupations such as computer and math, science and engineering, business and management, or arts and entertainment.

SEM and path analysis findings for major occupations

We completed structural equation modeling and path analyses for each of the major occupational groups, technology and wages. The key results of the SEM models are summarized in Table 2.6, while Figure 2.9 presents the findings for the path analysis.

Table 2.6 SEM results for major occupations

Variables	Talent	Technology	Wages per capita
Business and financial operations			
	Eq 1	*Eq 2*	*Eq 3*
Gay Index	0.613***	3.168***	0.107***
Consumer services	0.683***	4.586***	
University	0.088***		
Talent		1.553***	0.399***
Technology			0.018***
Observations	331	331	331
R²	0.293	0.479	0.735
High-end sales and sales management			
Tolerance	0.279***	3.644***	0.177***
Consumer services	0.558***	4.589***	
University	0. 050**		
Talent		1.811***	0.528***
Technology			0.023***
Observations	331	331	331
R²	0.212	0.461	0.703
Computer and math occupations			
Tolerance	1.488***	2.282***	0.025
Consumer services	1.054***	4.336***	
University	0.142***		
Talent		1.232***	0.239***
Technology			0.014***
Observations	331	331	331
R²	0.427	0.513	0.689
Arts, design, media and entertainment			
Gay Index	0.250***	2.060***	−0.005
Consumer services	0.965***	6.240***	
University	0.235***		
Talent		1.368***	0.323***
Technology			0.038***
Observations	331	331	331
R²	0.269	0.394	0.646
Management			
Tolerance	0.302***	3.620***	0.215***
Consumer services	0.136	5.440***	
University	0.083***		
Talent		1.637***	0.400***
Technology			0.030***
Observations	331	331	331
R²	0.138	0.463	0.628

(Continued)

Table 2.6 (Continued)

Variables	Talent	Technology	Wages per capita
Architecture and engineering			
Tolerance	0.635***	3.333***	0.227***
Consumer services	0.661***	4.773***	
University	0.082**		
Talent		1.268***	0.193***
Technology			0.026***
Observations	331	331	331
R^2	0.177	0.496	0.564
Legal occupations			
Tolerance	0.692***	3.558***	0.188***
Consumer services	0.626***	5.075***	
University	0.094**		
Talent		0.852***	0.173***
Technology			0.034***
Observations	331	331	331
R^2	0.217	0.453	0.533
Healthcare			
Tolerance	−0.039	4.160***	0.284***
Consumer services	0.196	5.517***	
University	0.160***		
Talent		0.539*	0.239***
Technology			0.041***
Observations	331	331	331
R^2	0.124	0.429	0.522
Life, physical and social sciences			
Tolerance	0.814***	3.601***	0.196***
Consumer services	0.484*	5.318***	
University	0.184***		
Talent		0.651***	0.123***
Technology			0.038***
Observations	331	331	331
R^2	0.236	0.447	0.500
Education			
Tolerance	0.098	4.103***	0.273***
Consumer services	0.250	5.527***	
University	0.256***		
Talent		0.375*	0.070***
Technology			0.043***
Observations	331	331	331
R^2	0.129	0.431	0.451

Note: ** Indicates significance at the 0.05 and *** at the 0.01 level.

Computer and math

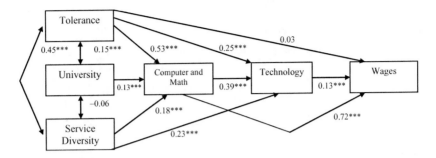

Business and financial operations

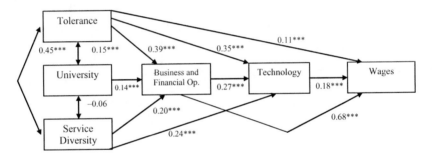

High-end sales

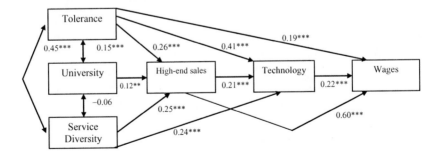

(Continued)

(Continued)

Arts, design, entertainment, and media

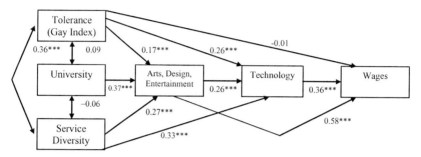

Management

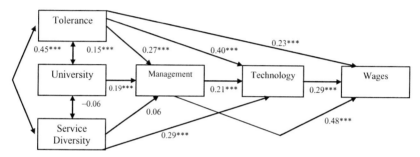

Architecture and Engineering

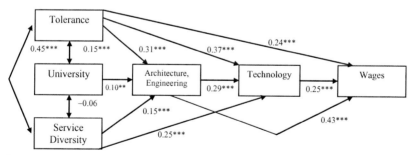

Legal

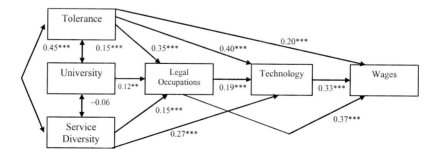

Scientific occupations

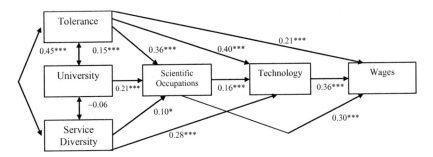

Healthcare

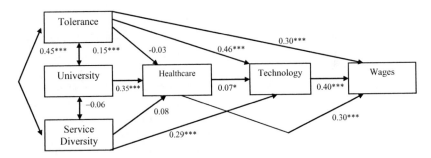

Education occupations

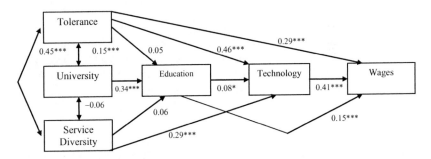

Figure 2.9 Path analysis for key occupational groups

Computer and math occupations have the strongest relation to wages with a path coefficient of .72. It is followed by two occupations with path coefficients greater than .6: business and financial operations (.68) and high-end sales (.60). Arts, design, entertainment and media occupations are close behind with a path coefficient of .58. This may be considered surprising since both the conventional wisdom and academic research view these groups as consumers as opposed to producers of resources. We should point out, however, that the models for the arts and entertainment occupations are slightly different than the others, including just the gay measure of tolerance in this model due to potential collinearity between some of these occupations and the bohemian measure. Overall, the gay measure is slightly weaker than the combined tolerance measure, which may work to strengthen the relative importance of these arts-related occupations. However, the model proved robust when the overall tolerance index returned results approximately the same (.56). Next in line are a cluster of occupations with path coefficients greater than 0.4: management (.48), architecture and engineering (.43).

Computer and math occupations also have the highest path coefficient for technology (.39). It is followed by: architecture and engineering (.29); business and financial operations (.27); and arts, design, entertainment and media (.26). Of these three occupations, the SEM which includes arts and entertainment generates the highest overall R^2 in explaining wages together with tolerance and technology. The path coefficients for management (0.21); high-end sales (0.21); legal (0.19) and scientific occupations (0.16) are smaller. The coefficients for education (0.08) and healthcare (0.07) are weakest and significant only at the 0.1 level.

We have examined the role of particular occupational groups in regional labor productivity. We find that the effects of these occupational groups on wages vary widely. Occupations such as computer and mathematics, business and financial operations, engineering and architecture, and, somewhat surprisingly, arts and entertainment are very closely associated with regional labor productivity and wages. However, occupations like education and healthcare are much less so. From a public policy standpoint, it seems that regions would want to foster a healthy mix of the former and they would be wise to avoid becoming too heavily specialized in education and healthcare if they want to improve their labor productivity and develop their economies.

Explaining the uneven distribution of human capital

Our research is concerned with a second key question: How to explain the uneven distribution of human capital or the creative class in the first place. Our models examine the roles played by three factors: tolerance, consumer amenities measured by the diversity of service firms, and universities. We now present the key findings for this aspect of our research.

University

The findings indicate that universities are consistently associated with both human capital and the creative class. The coefficient between the university and human capital is (.28) in both the wage and income models (see Figure 2.2). The coefficient between it and the creative class is (.32) in the wage model and (.33) in the income model. The coefficient between the university variable and super-creative occupations is (.30) in both models. In terms of individual occupations, the university variable is strongly related to science occupations as might be expected, since these occupations are closely related to university science and universities are major employers of scientists. It is strongly associated with education and healthcare, where again universities and university-affiliated hospitals are major employers.

The university is closely associated with arts, design and entertainment occupations, but again recall that the tolerance measure includes only the gay index in this version of the model, potentially damping down its effect. The university is less closely related to other, more business-oriented occupations, including engineering and architecture.

Consumer service amenities

The variable for consumer service amenities has mixed effects. It is associated with the creative class but not with human capital. The path coefficient between it and the creative class is .16 in the wage model and .13 in the income model. The results are similar for super-creative occupations. The path coefficient between consumer services and super-creative occupations is .14 in the wage model and .13 in the income model. Furthermore, the variable for consumer services plays a role in all of the major occupational categories, with the path coefficients ranging from .10 to .29 for arts and entertainment, although the coefficient for arts and entertainment may be affected by the fact that it includes only the gay index as noted earlier. The path coefficients between consumer services and human capital are insignificant in both models. Consumer services appear to play an additional role on technology, being closely associated with it in both the wage and income models with path coefficients ranging from .26 to .29. The variable for consumer services is more highly correlated to business-oriented occupations like management, sales and business and financial operations, than with scientific or artistic and cultural occupations.

Tolerance

Our findings indicate that tolerance plays an important set of roles in regional development. The coefficients between tolerance and human capital and it and the creative class are consistently high and significant. The coefficient between tolerance and human capital is .68 in both the wage and income models. It ranges from .37 to .38 for the creative class and super-creative occupations in both models. The path coefficients also show sizeable relations between tolerance and all the major occupational categories, especially computer and math where the coefficient is .53. The variables for tolerance also have a sizeable and consistent effect on technology. The path coefficients range from .29 in the models with human capital to .35 in the models with the creative class, and 0.36 in the models with super-creative occupations.

Furthermore, the variable for tolerance is directly consistent with wages and income in many permutations of the model. The path coefficient is .44 in the model for the creative class and income, and .46 in the model for super-creative occupations and income. In these two models, tolerance is the factor most strongly related to income. Interestingly, in models with the creative class, tolerance is actually the factor with the strongest relationship to income, which may be a reflection of the role of tolerance in attracting higher income individuals and retirees. The coefficient between tolerance and income is .19 in the model with human capital. Overall, tolerance adds considerable additional explanatory power to the model of human capital and income.

These findings suggest that tolerance plays a key role in regional development. It is strongly associated with both human capital and the creative class. And it is closely associated with technology, wages and incomes as well. In other words, tolerance is significantly related to the other two Ts—talent and technology—as well as regional development outcomes. In a very fundamental sense, this third T, tolerance, plays a key role in the overall system of regional development.

It is important to note that while our theory and model posit a strong set of underlying mechanisms for the effects of tolerance on regional development, our empirical models and evidence do not specify the precise nature and direction of causality. One concern may be that empirical results for tolerance reflect the fact that gay and artistic populations are themselves a function of higher wage, higher income locations. But the nature of our models which isolate the independent effects of human capital, the creative class, and technology as well as the university and consumer amenities on each other as well as regional wages and income gives us confidence in the role played by tolerance in the system of regional development. We initially expected the tolerance variable would exert its influence on regional development only by directly acting on the human capital and creative class variables. In addition, we have found that tolerance has a positive and direct relationship with wages and income.

It is also important to recall that our theory of the effects of tolerance on regional development does not posit a mechanistic relationship between regional tolerance (measured as concentrations of artists and/or gays) and regional development. Rather, we argue that tolerance or openness to diversity makes local resources more productive and efficient by acting through four key mechanisms. First, locations of bohemian and gay populations reflect low barriers to entry for human capital. Such locations will have advantages in attracting a broad range of talent across racial, ethnic and other lines, increasing the efficiency of human capital accumulation. Second, larger bohemian and gay populations signal underlying mechanisms that increase the efficiency of knowledge spillovers and human capital, as artistic networks act as conduits for the spread of new ideas and knowledge transfer across firms and industries. Third, artistic and gay populations reflect regional values that are open-minded, meritocratic, tolerant of risk, and oriented to self-expression which are in turn associated with higher levels of creativity, innovation and entrepreneurial behavior. Fourth, locations with larger artistic and gay populations signal underlying mechanisms which increase the productivity of entrepreneurial activity. These four factors, when taken together, improve the efficiency and productivity of regional human capital, innovation and entrepreneurship.

Region size effects

We also looked at the effects of tolerance, universities and consumer services by region size. In particular, we wanted to test whether the results are being driven by large regions with bigger markets, more options and more cosmopolitan attitudes. The findings indicate that the overall pattern of results holds across region sizes for tolerance and the university, but not for consumer services. Tolerance remains significant on both human capital and the creative class, except for the creative class in the smallest regions. It is also significantly related to wages and income in most permutations of the model across region sizes. The role of the university increases in medium and small regions. The variable for consumer services plays its most important role in smaller regions.

The cultural economy

The cultural economy has both direct and indirect relationships to regional development and impacts both production and consumption. First, the cultural economy is an important part of the regional economy. The *arts, design, media, and entertainment* occupational cluster has strong significant correlations with both regional wages and income. And, although potential collinearity with the tolerance measures necessitates caution, the occupation group is still found to have a strong and significant relationship to wages and regional labor productivity when the other factors are taken into consideration in the structural equation modeling. Second, the direct, significant and positive relationship, that is consistently found, between tolerance and technology is at least, in part, the complementarity between cultural occupations and the development of high-technology. These occupations also create significant value in other more traditional technologies by leveraging design and other creative skills into the final product and production process. The 'creative milieu' as identified by Stolarick and Florida (2006) results in finding high levels of technology and innovation with high levels of 'bohemians' even when the level of regional talent is taken into consideration. Third, the strong presence of culturally creative individuals is a reflection of regional tolerance which we have found to be significantly and positively associated with various measures of regional talent and regional income levels. While a gay and lesbian presence is not always visible, a bohemian presence is clearly and intentionally identifiable in a region. This enhances the ability of bohemians to act as a signal of inclusiveness within a region which enhances regional attractiveness. While these first three relationships have been related to regional *production* (and not just of cultural goods), a large regional cultural economy is also related to the *consumption* of cultural goods which act as a regional amenity that could serve to help attract others to the region. The positive relationship between the tolerance and talent measures can also be a reflection of the positive correlation between the availability of cultural goods and services in a region and the number and size of the (more broadly defined) creative class and/or skilled, talented, educated individuals.

Conclusion

Our research has examined the role of human capital, the creative class, and tolerance in regional development. We distinguished between two channels of regional development, regional labor productivity and regional wealth and included measures of both of wages and income in as outcome variables in our models. We tested for the direct and indirect relations between human capital, the creative class, and individual occupations, and regional wages and income, using path analysis and structural equations models. We advanced a stage-based model for regional development to separately and jointly examine the effects of talent, technology, and tolerance on regional development. In the first stage, factors such as tolerance, universities and consumer service amenities act on the location of talent (measured as human capital and the creative class). In the second stage, the concentration of talent in turn affects technology. And in the third stage technology, talent, and tolerance combine to affect regional wages and income. This stage-based model structure enabled us to isolate the direct and indirect relations of these factors in the overall system of regional development. We used structural equations and path analysis models to examine the independent effects of human capital, the creative class, technology, tolerance and other factors identified in the literature on both regional wages and incomes. We believe this modeling approach is an improvement over previous studies, because it enables us to examine the roles of technology, talent, tolerance and other factors on each other as well as on regional development in a system context.

Our results inform three overall findings. First, we find that human capital and the creative class play different but complementary roles in regional development. The creative class—or occupational skill—operates through the channel of wages and exerts its effect on regional labor productivity. Human capital—or education— operates by increasing regional income and wealth. Our findings here reinforce Marlet and Van Woerken's (2004) claim that the creative class sets a 'new standard' for measuring human capital especially when considering regional labor productivity.

Second, we find that certain occupations affect regional development to a much greater degree than others. Education and healthcare have little effect on regional development, while occupations like computer science, engineering, management and business and financial operations have a relatively large effect. A particularly interesting finding is that artistic and entertainment occupations exert considerable direct influence on regional development. Our findings indicate that these occupations are not just consumers of regional resources; they are producers of them as well. Based on this, we suggest that future studies of regional and cross-national development make use of occupational measures which provide important information not captured by standard educational or industry variables.

Third, we find that tolerance is significantly associated with human capital and the creative class. Universities and consumer services also affect the regional distribution of educated and skilled populations, but less so than tolerance. Tolerance thus plays a key role in the regional development system being associated with regional income and wages as well as the other two Ts—talent and technology. These findings substantiate and deepen Florida's (2002a, 2002b, 2005) theory of the 3Ts of economic development. More research is needed on how these and other factors shape the increasingly uneven distribution of human capital, especially in light of the increasing divergence of human capital levels across regions. It is important to future research to zero in more precisely on the factors that affect not just the current stock but the flow of human capital or the creative class at the margins.

We have also found that the cultural economy has both direct and indirect relationships to regional development. The cultural economy is an important part of the region's wages, income, and labor productivity. There is a complementarity between cultural occupations and the development of high-technology and other products and services. The strong presence of culturally creative individuals is a reflection of regional tolerance and inclusiveness. A large regional cultural economy also generates goods and services which act as a regional amenity that could help attract others to the region.

Generally speaking, our findings suggest that the structure of relationships between technology, talent and tolerance in regional development is complex and that regional development cannot be understood as a series of either-or phenomena. Human capital is important but so is the creative class. Education captures one element of regional capability, but occupational skill is critical. The creative class acts to improve regional labor productivity directly, while human capital is more closely associated with increased regional wealth.

Our findings also indicate that the relations between tolerance and regional development must be taken seriously. Our models, which are much more appropriate methodologically for understanding the broad system of regional development, show the consistently significant role of tolerance on technology, on talent, and on regional wages and income directly. We do not argue here that gays and artists are the direct producers of regional economic growth. Rather, our combined measure of artists and gays is a proxy for the much broader impacts of tolerance and openness generally on regional development. As we have argued and shown, tolerance acts on regional development by making other inputs, such as education and occupational skill, more efficient. In our view, tolerance increases the efficiency of key regional resources by lowering barriers to entry for highly skilled and educated people across ethnic, racial, sexual orientation lines; by creating a regional culture that is more oriented to new ideas and tolerates higher levels of risk; by helping to foster a broad environment which facilitates networking, accelerates spillovers, and generates new combinations of talent and resources; and by encouraging the entrepreneurial mobilization of resource in new and more productive firms and organizations.

We hope our research helps clarify some key issues in the ongoing debate over the role of technology, talent and tolerance in regional development. And we also hope it draws more attention and interest in this debate and motivates others to engage in research on how these factors affect regional productivity, income, and living standards across the globe.

Note

1 We are aware of the fact that there could be feedback loops in this model's framework, but building them into the model itself would restrict the actual tests that could be performed. Also, the very same model has been used in other national contexts, and several alternate model specifications have been tested. The use of structural equation modeling/path analysis and the implications of this were raised by the reviewers. While we are aware of the implications, it is by far the best alternative in relation to the task at hand. The conceptualization of the model was developed first and SEM was determined to be the best approach given the model and available data. Our goal is to test these relationships in sequence; factors related to the distribution of talent, in relation to technology and then their relation to overall regional economical performance. In our earlier work on this chapter, we did try various simultaneous equation specifications with a far less satisfying or tractable results. We also tried seemingly unrelated

regression (SUR) and many variations of OLS. SUR did not work since there were way too many interdependencies. OLS would not allow for the indirect relationships which are an important expectation of our model. In the current version of the chapter we use maximum likelihood estimation, which is the most common when using structural equation modeling. We did, however, also run the same regressions using GLS estimation with no significant differences.

Bibliography

Amabile, T. (1996) *Creativity in Context*, Boulder, CO: Westview Press.

Andersson, Å. E. (1985a) 'Creativity and regional development', *Papers of the Regional Science Association*, 56: 5–20.

Andersson, Å. E. (1985b) *Creativity: The Future of Metropolitan Regions*, Stockholm: Prisma.

Barro, R. J. (1991) 'Economic growth in a cross-section of countries', *Quarterly Journal of Economics*, 106: 407–443.

Becker, G. (1964) *Human Capital*, New York: Columbia University Press for the National Bureau of Economic Research.

Becker, G. (1993) *Human Capital: A Theoretical and Empirical Analysis, with Special Reference to Education*, Chicago: University of Chicago Press.

Berry, C. R. and Glaeser, E. L. (2005) 'The divergence of human capital levels across cities', NBER Working Paper No. 11617.

Clark, T. N. (2003) 'Urban amenities: Lakes, opera and juice bars. Do they drive development?', *Research in Urban Policy*, 9: 103–140.

Currid, E. (2007) *The Warhol Economy*, Princeton, NJ: Princeton University Press.

Florida, R. (2002a) *The Rise of the Creative Class*, New York: Basic Books.

Florida, R. (2002b) 'The economic geography of talent', *Annals of the Association of American Geographers*, 92: 743–755.

Florida, R. (2002c) 'Bohemia and economic geography', *Journal of Economic Geography*, 2: 55–71.

Florida, R. (2004a) 'Revenge of the squelchers', *The Next American City*, Issue 5.

Florida, R. (2004b) 'Response to Edward Glaeser's review of "The Rise of the Creative Class",' available at: http://creativeclass.com/rfcgdb/articles/ResponsetoGlaeser.pdf (accessed 19 August 2009).

Florida, R. (2005) *Cities and the Creative Class*, New York: Routledge.

Florida, R. and Gates, G. (2001) 'Technology and tolerance: The importance of diversity to high-technology growth', in T. N. Clark (ed.), *The City as an Entertainment Machine*: *Research in Urban Policy*, vol. 9, Oxford: Elsevier, pp. 199–220.

Florida, R., Gates, G., Knudsen, B. and Stolarick, K. (2006) 'The university and the creative economy', available at: http://www.creativeclass.org/rfcgdb/articles/University%20For%20City%20and%20Community%204.pdf (accessed 2 August 2009).

Fredrickson, B. L. (2001) 'The role of positive emotions in positive psychology: The broaden-and-build theory of positive emotions', *American Psychologist*, 56: 218–226.

Glaeser, E. L. (1994) 'Cities, information, and economic growth', *Cityscape*, 1(1): 9–47.

Glaeser, E. L. (2000) 'The new economics of urban and regional growth', in G. Clark, M. Feldman and M. Gertler (eds), *The Oxford Handbook of Economic Geography*, Oxford: Oxford University Press.

Glaeser, E. L. (2004) 'Book review of Richard Florida's "The Rise of the Creative Class"', available at: http://post.economics.harvard.edu/faculty/glaeser/papers/Review_Florida.pdf (accessed 29 August 2013).

Glaeser, E. L., Kolko, J. and Saiz, A. (2001) 'Consumer city', *Journal of Economic Geography*, 1: 27–50.

Gordon, R. (2003) 'Hi-tech innovation and productivity growth', NBER Working Paper No. 9437.

Gyourko, J., Mayer, C. and Sinai, T. (2006) 'Superstar cities', NBER Working Paper No. 12355, July.

Hecker, D. (1999) 'High-technology employment: A broader view', *Monthly Labor Review*, June.

Inglehart, R. and Norris, P. (2003) *Rising Tide*, New York: Cambridge University Press.

Inglehart, R. and Welzel, C. (2005) *Modernization, Cultural Change and Democracy*, New York: Cambridge University Press.

Jacobs, J. (1961) *The Death and Life of Great American Cities*, New York: Random House.

Jacobs, J. (1969) *The Economies of Cities*, New York: Random House.

Jöreskog, K. G. (1973) 'Analysis of covariance structures', in P. R. Krishnaiah (ed.), *Multivariate Analysis*, vol. III. New York: Academic Press.

Lloyd, R. and Clark, T. N. (2001) 'The city as an entertainment machine', *Research in Urban Sociology*, 6: 357–378.

Lucas, R. E. (1988) 'On the mechanics of economic development', *Journal of Monetary Economics*, 22: 3–42.

McGranahan, D. and Wojan, T. (2007) 'Recasting the creative class to examine growth processes in rural and urban counties', *Regional Studies*, 41: 197–216.

Markusen, A. (2004) 'Targeting occupations in regional and community economic development', *Journal of the American Planning Association*, 70: 253–268.

Markusen, A. and Schrock, G. (2006) 'The artistic dividend: Urban artistic specialisation and economic development implication', *Urban Studies*, 43(10): 1661–1686.

Marlet, G. and Van Woerkens, C. (2004) *Skills and Creativity in a Cross-section of Dutch Cities*. Available at: http://www.uu.nl/uupublish/content/04-29.pdf (accessed 11 December, 2008).

Mellander, C. and Florida, R. (2006) 'The creative class or human capital? Explaining regional development in Sweden', Working Paper Series in Economics and Institutions of Innovation No. 79, Royal Institute of Technology, CESIS – Centre of Excellence for Science and Innovation Studies.

Mincer, J. (1974) *Schooling, Experience and Earnings*, New York: Columbia University Press for the National Bureau of Economic Research.

Noland, M. (2005) 'Popular attitudes, globalization and risk', *International Finance*, 8: 199–229.

Ottaviano, G. I. P. and Peri, G. (2005) 'Cities and cultures', *Journal of Urban Economics*, 58: 304–337.

Page, S. E. (2008) *The Difference: How the Power of Diversity Creates Better Groups, Firms, Schools, and Societies*, new edn, Princeton, NJ: Princeton University Press.

Quigley, J. M. (1998) 'Urban diversity and economic growth', *Journal of Economic Perspective*, 12: 127–138.

Rauch, J. E. (1993) 'Productivity gains from geographic concentration of human capital: Evidence from the cities', *Journal of Urban Economics*, 34: 380–400.

Roback, J. (1982) 'Wages, rents, and the quality of life', *Journal of Political Economy*, 90: 1257–1278.

Romer, P. M. (1986) 'Increasing returns and long-run growth', *Journal of Political Economy*, 94: 1002–1037.

Romer, P. M. (1987) 'Crazy explanations for the productivity slowdown', in *Macroeconomics Annual*, New York: National Bureau of Economic Research, Inc.

Romer, P. M. (1990) 'Endogenous technological change', *Journal of Political Economy*, 98: S71–S102.

Shapiro, J. M. (2006) 'Smart cities: Quality of life, productivity, and the growth effects of human capital', *Review of Economics and Statistics*, 88: 324–335.

Simon, C. J. (1998) 'Human capital and metropolitan employment growth', *Journal of Urban Economics*, 43: 223–243.

Simon, C. J. and Nardinelli, C. (1996) 'The talk of the town: Human capital, information, and the growth of English cities, 1861 to 1961', *Explorations in Economic History*, 33: 384–413.

Smith, G., Carlsson, I. and Danielsson, A. (1984) *Experimental Examinations of Creativity*, Lund: Lund University.

Solow, R. M. (1956) 'A contribution to the theory of economic growth', *The Quarterly Journal of Economics*, 70: 65–94.

Sternberg, R. J. (1999) *Handbook of Creativity*, Cambridge: Cambridge University Press.

Stolarick, K. and Florida, R. (2006) 'Creativity, connections and innovation: A study of linkages in the Montréal Region', *Environment and Planning*, 38(10): 1799–1817.

Ullman, E. L. (1958) 'Regional development and the geography of concentration', *Papers and Proceedings of the Regional Science Association*, 4: 179–198.

Appendix

Table A1   SEM results for McGranahan and Wojan revised creative class

Wages	Florida creative class			McGranahan and Wojan creative class		
	Talent	Technology	Wages	Talent	Technology	Wages
Variables	Eq 1	Eq 2	Eq 3	Eq 1	Eq 2	Eq 3
Tolerance	0.355***	3.140***	0.111***	0.471***	3.149***	0.085***
Consumer services	0.326***	4.995***		0.227	5.329***	
University	0.121***			0.127***		
Talent		2.476***	0.659***		1.908***	0.541***
Technology			0.018***			0.024***
Observations	331	331	331	331	331	331
R^2	0.332	0.482	0.769	0.325	0.472	0.742

Income	Florida creative class			McGranahan and Wojan creative class		
	Talent	Technology	Income	Talent	Technology	Income
Variables	Eq 1	Eq 2	Eq 3	Eq 1	Eq 2	Eq 3
Tolerance	0.362***	3.110***	0.270***	0.479***	3.125***	0.255***
Consumer services	0.258**	5.026***		0.149	5.351***	
University	0.121***			0.125***		
Talent		2.607***	0.082***		2.007***	0.099***
Technology			0.017***			0.016***
Observations	331	331	331	331	331	331
R^2	0.332	0.486	0.486	0.324	0.473	0.498

Note: ** Indicates significance at the 0.05 and *** at the 0.01 level.

Table A2 SEM results for redefined creative class (without education and healthcare)

Narrow creative occupations (without healthcare and education)

	Talent	Technology	Wages
Variables	Eq 1	Eq 2	Eq 3
Tolerance	0.551***	2.750***	0.071**
Consumer services	0.456***	4.626***	
University	0.090***		
Talent		2.400***	0.579***
Technology			0.010***
Observations	331	331	331
R^2	0.333	0.506	0.807

Narrow super-creative occupations (without education)

Tolerance	0.424***	3.034***	0.099***
Consumer services	0.372***	4.860***	
University	0.103***		
Talent		2.396***	0.635***
Technology			0.014***
Observations	331	331	331
R^2	0.306	0.491	0.811

Note: ** Indicates significance at the 0.05 and *** at the 0.01 level.

3 Talent, technology and tolerance in Canadian regional development*

Richard Florida, Charlotta Mellander and Kevin Stolarick

Introduction

What are the drivers of regional economic development in Canada? Traditionally, the answer has been jobs. The availability of high-quality, high-paying employment opportunities has long been seen as central to the ability of regions to attract people and raise incomes. With the globalization of manufacturing and the movement of many manufacturing jobs to lower-cost locations, technology and entrepreneurship have come to be seen as increasingly important sources of regional development. Others point to the role of human capital in regional economic growth, arguing that a key element is the ability of regions to attract and retain highly-educated, highly skilled people. More recent approaches emphasize the roles played by urban amenities, quality of life, energetic artistic and cultural scenes, and openness to diversity in regional development.

This chapter examines the role of technology, talent or human capital, and tolerance in Canadian regional development. It seeks to shed light on four related issues. First, what are the relative contributions of technology and human capital – two factors identified in the broad literature – on the development of Canadian city regions? Second, what is the relative contribution of two alternative measures of human capital – one based on education and the other based on occupations, namely, creative occupations – on regional development in Canada? Third, what is the relative contribution of regional institutions – in terms of universities, service diversity, and levels of tolerance – on levels of technology and human capital? And fourth, how does the system of relationships among these factors and variables ultimately work to shape income level across Canadian regions?

Our research methodology builds upon and extends earlier research by Florida *et al*. (2008b) and Mellander and Florida (2009) on the United States and Sweden. However, the Canadian context is different in many aspects (Lipset, 1990). Canada is a large country with a relatively small, highly urban population. With a recent influx of immigrants it is both culturally and geographically diverse. As a consociational

* This chapter was previously published as: Florida, R., Mellander, C., and Stolarick, K. (2010) 'Talent, technology and tolerance in Canadian regional development', *The Canadian Geographer*, 54(3): 277–304.

nation, Canada is populated by several distinct cultural groups: Anglophone, Francophone, and Aboriginal, as well as new immigrants. Stretching from the Atlantic to the Pacific to the Arctic Ocean, Canadian regions differ greatly in natural resources and climate. Canada's regions are physically and socially heterogeneous. Wellstead's (2007) examination of the contemporary staples thesis finds that the Canadian economic geography is a mix of Schumpetarian and Ricardian competitive states. Thus, understanding economic development in Canada requires understanding the factors that shape growth across heterogeneous Canadian regions. The fact is, most of the regional development literature has a strong focus on the US regions, which may in the end have very different structures and processes compared to what we can identify in Canadian regions.

Our research seeks to add to the understanding of regional development in Canadian regions. To shed light on these issues, we present a stage-based general model of regional development. This stage-based model structure enables us to isolate the direct and indirect effects of these factors in the overall system of regional development. We use structural equations and path analysis models to examine the independent effects of human capital, the creative class, technology, tolerance and other factors identified in the literature on both regional wages and incomes. We examine these issues via a cross-sectional analysis of 46 geographic regions in Canada. Our modeling approach is designed to address relations between our explanatory and dependent variables in a Canadian regional context. It will also enable us to make comparisons with earlier similar studies for US regions.

Theory and concepts

This section introduces our theoretical and conceptual framework. It begins with a discussion of the factors that have been found to shape Canadian regional development and then moves onto broader, but more abstract, conceptualizations of the underlying factors that shape regional development in general.

Theories of Canadian regional development

Innis (1956) was a strong proponent of development theories designed uniquely for a place. His argument was that any comprehensive theory would need a strong foundation supported by the unique characteristics of a situation. He claimed that a theory developed in Europe would not be applicable or relevant for Canada. It is hardly coincidence then that his 'staples' thesis was the first significant development theory that specifically addressed Canada's unique conditions. The theory was a modified version of export base theory and claimed that Canada's development was a response to certain 'staple' resources, and the demand for these resources decided the success of a region (ibid.). The theory was used to explain regional disparities within the country, a problem that contradicted neoclassical theories.

The staples thesis was prominent until the 1960s, at which point academics began to challenge certain aspects of it that failed to explain regional disparities (Savoie, 1997). Regional development in Canada was approached for a long time through the lens of regional disparities. Examining and understanding these disparities were thought to be the path through which regional development would occur (ibid.) . For a brief period Perroux's growth pole theory became popular and was applied within the Canadian context (ibid.). Innis' staples thesis was still relevant in the early 1990s as Barnes reexamined the theory in light of post-Fordism and flexible specialization (Barnes, 1996). Bradfield in the late 1980s wrote a book detailing the most prominent theories that have affected Canadian policy. Again staples theory played a prominent role, as did the issue of regional disparities (Bradfield, 1988) .

The overwhelming focus on regional disparities is no doubt in response to the unique physical and cultural situations within Canada. Like Innis, Bradfield argued for the creation of distinct country-specific development theories. Bradfield also stressed the importance of developing theories that not only looked at economic gain, but cultural, social and political costs as well. He felt that 'cultural differences can impose economic costs, either to overcome the difference or as a penalty for ignoring them' (ibid.). Geographers have increasingly included culture as a key element in development theories.

Geographical literature on regional development in Canada has progressed significantly over the last two decades as the Canadian economy and its regions have evolved. Theories have focused far less on regional disparities, and much more attention has been paid to local and regional characteristics that can foster growth. Barnes *et al.* (2000) reiterate earlier sentiments expressed by Barnes that economies need to be understood as local and contingent. It is clear that Canadian geographers have become aware of the historical settings and narrative of place. This has encouraged Canadian geographers to comprehensively adapt popular theories of economic development for Canada. As Barnes *et al.* (2000) acknowledge, globalization has made place more important, not less, and this has led to the creation of regional development theories that focus on innovation and creativity as the drivers of growth.

Creativity and Canadian regional development

The idea of the creative city in the Canadian context was examined by Gertler (2001) who looked at the change in the flow of people, capital and ideas over time. Gertler linked the urbanization of Canada's spatial form (1945–1975) to rising wages, the post-war housing boom, car ownership and significant infrastructure investment post-war. Limited research and case studies have been conducted on regional innovation systems and clusters within Canada (Holbrook and Wolfe, 2000). Recent work has led to the development of a Canadian-specific cluster methodology, that more appropriately acknowledges Canada's unique characteristics (Spencer *et al.* 2010) .

Florida's creative class theory (2002a) was first analytically applied to the Ontario context by Gertler *et al.* (2002), with unique results reflecting the differences in Canada's occupational composition. Slack *et al.* (2003) conducted a detailed report discussing the importance of the city-region to economic and regional development in Ontario, highlighting many of the social and economic challenges faced by the province. The idea has been further expanded upon with the creative city concept and its application to cities nationwide. Duxbury (2004) provides examples of how policy-makers from Toronto to Halifax are adopting many of the indicator statistics developed for American metropolitan areas by Florida. Stolarick and Florida's (2006) analysis of the Montreal region documented the links between technology, talent, tolerance and creativity in the region. Smith and Warfield's (2008) case study of creative values associated with the Vancouver region did not find the city to be a paradigm example of creative theory. They did, however, stress the importance of creativity and its connectivity to economic results. Hall and Kahn (2008) examined the relation between immigrants and high-tech regions, and found that immigrants in larger Canadian regions with high levels of high-tech concentrations have significantly lower income earnings than immigrants in mid-sized and smaller regions. Peripheral regions are struggling to maintain their position within the Canadian geographic hierarchy (Polèse and Shearmur, 2006).

Human capital and economic development

There is an enormous body of literature which has sought to explain the factors that drive economic growth (Solow, 1956; Romer, 1986, 1987; Barro, 1991; Barro and Sala-i-Martin, 1997; Barro and Lee, 2000). Solow (1956) identified the role of technology as an exogenous factor. Romer's 'new growth theory' (1986, 1987, 1990) identified the endogenous accumulation of knowledge as the primary engine of economic growth (see also Grossman and Helpman, 1991; Aghion and Howitt, 1992).

Empirical studies by Barro (1991), Rauch (1993), Simon and Nardinelli (1996) and Simon (1998), all confirm the relationship between human capital and growth at the national level. Several studies (Rauch, 1993; Audretsch and Feldman, 1994; Feldman, 1999; Duranton and Puga, 2003) have also shown the link between national economic growth and the distribution of knowledge in large urban regions. Large, dense areas create an environment in which knowledge can move quickly and at a low cost between firms and individuals. This results in an increase in knowledge flows and knowledge exchange, which in turn gives rise to new knowledge and new goods and productions (Jacobs, 1969; Kremer, 1993; Carlino *et al.*, 2001).

Glaeser (2000) provides empirical evidence on the correlation between human capital and regional economic growth. Firms locate to gain competitive advantages, rather than letting suppliers and customers determine location choice. Firms seek out areas of high human capital concentration. Studies by Florida (2002b) and Berry and Glaeser (2005) find that human capital is becoming more concentrated and there are strong reasons to believe that this division will continue, affecting not only regional growth levels, but also housing values (Shapiro, 2006; Gyourko *et al.*, 2006). Capturing the effects from human capital is tricky for many reasons. There is now an emerging debate over alternative levels of human capital. Most economists argue for a traditional measure based on educational attainment. Others (Florida, 2002a; Markusen, 2004; Gabe, 2006; McGranahan and Wojan, 2006) suggest an alternative measure based on occupation. Several studies (Marlet and Van Woerkens, 2004; Gabe, 2006; Florida *et al.*, 2008a; Mellander and Florida, 2009) have found that occupational measures can and do outperform educational attainment measures in accounting for some aspects of regional development.

Alternative measures of human capital: education vs. occupation

Our research keys into this reasonably open question in the current debate: How to best measure and account for human capital? Laroche and Mérette (2000) note that no satisfactory measure of human capital exists for Canada, that education as the measure of human capital fails to capture all the activities related to knowledge acquisition that occur in the country. The breadth of the measure also prevents nations or regions from identifying specific types of human capital or talent. Education measures potential talent or skill but does not measure actual skill as it is utilized and consumed by the economy.

We look explicitly at an alternative measure of human capital based on occupation, which, we suggest, provides a potentially more robust measure of human capital capable of capturing what people do as opposed to what people know. The models we develop below enable us to isolate the effects of human capital, the creative class and also of individual creative occupations on regional development. Previous research (Florida *et al.*, 2008b) has found that these two types of human capital and creative occupations affect regional development by operating through different channels. Human capital, that research found, had a bigger effect on regional income, a broad measure which includes wages plus gains, rents, interest, transfers and the like, while creative occupations affect wages. We include both measures initially in this analysis.

Factors affecting the distribution of human capital

The second key issue in the current debate involves identifying the factors that shape the geographic distribution of human capital measured either way – by educational attainment or as creative occupations. Most economists conceptualize human capital as a stock or endowment, which belongs to a place in the same way that a natural resource might. But the reality is that human capital is a *flow*, a highly mobile factor that can and does relocate. Gertler (2001) notes the importance that the flow of people has had on shaping the Canadian urban landscape. The flow of people from one region to the next has major policy implications that can only be properly understood from a well-rooted theory of individual migration. In Canada, the current flow of people – both native and foreign-born – tends to be from the Atlantic and Prairie provinces to Ontario, Alberta and British Columbia (Edmonston, 2002). Our research examines the factors that shape this flow and determine the divergent levels of human capital and the creative class – education and skill – across Canadian regions.

Four possible answers to the question of human capital mobility or flow have been offered. The first argues that the distribution of education and skill is affected by the distribution of amenities. Roback (1982) expanded the traditional neoclassical model of migration to include not only the response to wages and land rent but to quality-of-life amenities as well. Glaeser *et al.* (2001) find that consumer and personal service industries such as restaurants, theatres, and museums tend to be localized and thus demand geographical closeness between producer and consumer. Beyond service and consumer goods, Glaeser highlights the importance of other amenities such as public goods, aesthetics and transportation. Lloyd and Clark (2001) impart a strong emphasis on the role of lifestyle – in the form of entertainment, nightlife, culture, and so on – in attracting talent. Shapiro's (2006) detailed study of regional productivity growth finds that 'roughly 40% of the employment growth effect of college graduates is due to quality of life', the rest being caused by enhanced productivity growth.

The second approach offered by Berry and Glaeser (2005) is that the concentration of human capital builds off itself. Places with an initial advantage tend to build upon that strength, seeing increases over time. The presence of major research universities has been found to be a key factor in this set of initial advantages as well in both the production and distribution of human capital. The distribution of education and skill need not be coincident with the distribution of universities (Florida, 2002a; Berry and Glaeser, 2005). While some regions with great universities have large concentrations of talent, others operate as producers of human capital, serving as unrewarded exporters of highly educated people to other regions (Florida *et al.*, 2006). Florida (2005) argues that the geographic assembly line connection from education to innovation and economic outcomes *in that same locale* may no longer hold. This is a result of the increased mobility of highly skilled and talented people within countries and even across national borders. The quality of a region's post-secondary institutions is no guarantee it can hold onto its educated and skilled people. The university is neither a *necessary* nor *sufficient* condition for attracting educated and skilled populations to a region or even holding on to the ones it produces.

The third approach is that the mobility of human capital is a response to the availability of jobs (Bartel, 1979; Carlino and Mills, 1987; Blanchard and Katz, 1992). The economic reasoning is straightforward. Individuals who are perfectly rational will relocate to regions with the greatest economic opportunity – highest wages and largest labor markets. Ferguson *et al.* (2007) find that in the Canadian context this is more or less true for rural regions. Urban centers in Canada are similar to those in the US, where it is a combination of amenities and economic factors that determine the location decision of individuals (ibid.). This is in agreement with Wellstead's heterogeneous depiction of the Canadian economic geography.

Diversity, openness and tolerance

The final approach to the factors that influence the flow of talent among regions argues that tolerance and openness to diversity affect the level and geographic distribution of education and skill. Jacobs (1961) and Beckstead and Brown (2003) have argued that firm-based diversity is associated with economic growth, but Jacobs also argued that diversity of individuals is important as well. Recent research has focused on the role of demographic diversity in economic growth. Ottaviano and Peri (2005) show how diversity among individuals, in the form of immigrants, increases regional productivity. Noland (2005) finds that tolerant attitudes toward gays and lesbians are associated with both positive attitudes toward global economic activity and international financial outcomes. Florida and Gates (2003) find a positive association between concentrations of gay households and regional development. Florida (2002a, 2002b, 2002c) further argues that tolerance – specifically 'low barriers to entry' for individuals – is associated with geographic concentrations of talent, higher rates of innovation, and regional development. The more open a place is to new ideas and new people, the larger the net it casts in the global competition for talent, in other words, the lower its entry barriers for human capital – the more talent it will likely capture.

There is considerable debate over the salience of these measures, approaches and findings. Clark (2003) finds that the relationship between the Gay Index and regional development holds only for regions with large populations. Glaeser (2004) ran linear regressions with human capital, the Gay Index and the Bohemian Index and found that the effects of human capital overpower the effects of these other tolerance measures when looking at change in population between 1990 and 2000. Florida (2004a, 2004b) counters that these frameworks and models are insufficient and do not capture the interactions among the system of factors that act on regional development. He suggests a general model of regional development according to the 3Ts of economic development: technology, talent and tolerance. He argues that each alone is necessary but insufficient in generating regional development. All three must act together with substantial and balanced performance to result in higher levels of development.

It is important to state at the outset that our model does not argue for a mechanistic relationship between regional tolerance (measured as concentrations of artists and gays or immigrants) and regional development. Rather, we argue that tolerance or openness to diversity makes local resources more productive and efficient by acting through four key mechanisms.

1   *Low barriers to entry*: High concentrations of bohemian, gay/lesbian and immigrant populations reflect low barriers to entry for human capital. Such locations will have advantages in attracting a broad range of talent across racial, ethnic and other lines, increasing the efficiency of human capital accumulation. Page (2008) provides the basis for a general economic theory of tolerance and improved economic outcomes. He finds that not only does cognitive diversity lead to better decision-making but that it is associated with identity diversity, the diversity of people and groups, which enable new perspectives. He finds that diversity broadly understood is linked with higher growth and rates of innovation. Work by Florida *et al.* (2008a, 2008b) and Mellander and Florida (2009) on nations such as the United States, Sweden

and China, illustrates that the tolerance factor might influence the distribution of talent and technology in different ways. In addition, there is a national subjectivity to what is regarded as tolerance.

2 *Knowledge spillovers and human capital externalities*: Larger bohemian and gay populations signal underlying mechanisms that increase the efficiency of knowledge spillovers and human capital externalities that Lucas (1988) identifies as the primary engine of economic growth. Recent studies (Markusen and Schrock, 2006; Currid, 2007) note the role of artistic networks as conduits for the spread of new ideas and knowledge transfer across firms and industries. Stolarick and Florida (2006) demonstrate the importance of 'spillacrosses' – interaction between bohemians and the traditional technology community. Concentration of artists and gays/lesbians thus reflects the regional mechanisms that tend to accelerate human capital externalities and knowledge spillovers.

3 *Signals of openness and meritocracy*: Significant artistic, gay/lesbian and immigration populations reflect regional values that are open-minded, meritocratic, tolerant of risk, and oriented to self-expression. Inglehart and Norris (2003) and Inglehart and Welzel (2005) have noted the correlation between values and GDP growth at the national level. In research over four decades and across more than 60 countries, Inglehart and Norris (2003) and Inglehart and Welzel (2005) identify tolerance or what they call 'self-expression' to be a core element of a new value system associated with higher levels of GDP and economic growth. They note that openness of people towards gay and lesbian populations is the best indicator of overall tolerance. People in tolerant places are not happier because they themselves are tolerant but due to the general level of tolerance experienced in society. Psychological studies (Amabile, 1996; Sternberg, 1999; Fredrickson, 2001) indicate that this is associated with higher levels of creativity, innovation and entrepreneurial behavior. Lucas (1988) explicitly notes the similarities in values and orientation as 'creative' actors between technological and entrepreneurial labour and artistic and cultural populations.

4 *Resource mobilization*: Locations with larger artistic, gay and immigrant populations signal underlying mechanisms which increase the productivity of entrepreneurial activity. Traditional economic institutions have tended to marginalize these groups, thus requiring them to mobilize resources independently and to form new organizations and firms. We suggest that regions where these groups have migrated and taken root reflect underlying mechanisms which are more attuned to mobilization of such resources for entrepreneurship and new firm formation. These four factors, when taken together, improve the efficiency and productivity of regional human capital, innovation and entrepreneurship.

We also note that, according to our theory, tolerance, universities and consumer service amenities need not operate exclusively or in competition with each other. Rather, we suggest that they are likely to have complementary effects on the

geographic distribution of education and skill. Tolerance, universities and consumer amenities act on regional economies through direct and indirect channels,
as they effect the concentration of talented and skilled people in regions.

Model, variables, and methods

A schematic picture of our general model for the system of regional development
is outlined in Figure 3.1. The model allows us to overcome several limitations
of previous studies. First, it considers regional development as a system of
relationships. It allows us to test the independent effects of human capital, the
creative class, technology, and tolerance on regional development. Second, it
allows us to test for, and identify more precisely, the role of educational human
capital versus the creative class on regional wages and incomes. Third, it
allows us to parse the effects on wages and income, and to identify the factors
that act on regional labour productivity and regional wealth. And, fourth, it
enables us to parse the effects of tolerance, consumer services, and universities
in the distribution of human capital and the creative class which in turn act on
regional wages and income. The arrows identify the hypothesized structure of
relationships among the key variables. The model is based on earlier work by
Florida *et al.* (2008b). The model has been modified to include two relationships that were insignificant in the US. For Canada, it was found that there
were strong relationships between tolerance and technology and tolerance and
our overall development indicators. This model will enable us to make comparisons between the earlier results shown for the United States. It is important
to note that our path models do not imply empirical causality or uni-directional
relationships. As Simon (1954) notes, the unidirectional arrows in our paths
are not meant to imply uni-directional causality, but associative relationships
that might work in both directions. Our theory, however, leads us to believe
that the causal ordering of the relationships flows more or less in the direction
of the arrows, and we will analyze these relationships using data that is temporally
consistent with our theoretical assertions.

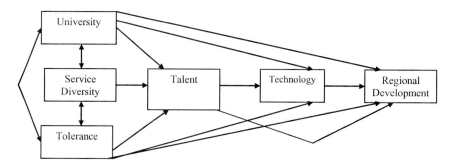

Figure 3.1 Model of key regional development paths

Variables

We now describe the variables in the empirical model. The variables cover 46 CMAs (Census Metropolitan Areas) and CAs (Census Agglomerations) in Canada. The small number of observations is not optimal, but the study includes *all* Canadian CMAs and some of the more populous CAs. The number of observations is, in other words, a reflection of the Canadian economic geography. This analysis is based on a *population* and not a sample. Although the technique being applied (structural equation modeling) is more robust with a greater number of observations, Canada has a limited number of cities. While a finer geography would create more observations, it would not be compatible with our underlying theory which is regional. The lower number of observations limits the value of the χ^2-based goodness of fit tests for the overall model, but does not otherwise impact the analysis or results.

All variables in equations 3.1 and 3.2 are for the year 2001, while the dependents in equation 3.3 (Regional Development) are from 2006 (see p. 000). The reason for those differences in time is that we do not expect the full effect to come in the same year, but rather some years later. We will also test and report for changes in income levels between the years 2001 and 2006. Descriptive statistics for all measures and variables are provided in Table 3.1. These numbers are

Table 3.1 Descriptive statistics: all regions

	Obs	*Mean*	*Standard deviation*	*Minimum*	*Maximum*
Talent:					
BA or above	46	0.170	0.054	0.097	0.310
Creative class	46	0.302	0.045	0.227	0.449
Super-creative	46	0.162	0.029	0.112	0.270
Creative professionals	46	0.140	0.019	0.108	0.180
Decomposed creative occupations:					
Managers	46	0.064	0.013	0.043	0.100
Business and finance	46	0.032	0.007	0.022	0.050
Science	46	0.059	0.017	0.034	0.127
Health	46	0.043	0.008	0.027	0.064
Education/social science	46	0.079	0.013	0.056	0.111
Arts and culture	46	0.024	0.007	0.015	0.040
Regional characteristics:					
University (faculty)/1000	46	2.299	1.973	0	8.445
Self-expression	27	0.982	0.394	0.494	1.906
Mosaic Index	46	0.126	0.089	0.009	0.437
Visible minorities	46	0.072	0.979	0.006	0.369
Service diversity	46	210.93	13.92	186	233
Effects:					
Technology	46	0.831	0.353	0.349	1.788
Avg. income	46	35,007	3,816	28,823	48,878
Avg. employment income	46	35,146	4,060	29,075	48,931

based on the 46 regions included in our analysis, and not the Canadian totals (which we, however, would expect to be very similar).

Outcome variables

It is common in studies of regional development to use factors like population change or job growth as measures of development. But those measures are quite crude in that they cannot specify the quality of development. Not all jobs are created equal; some pay a good deal more than others. Regions increasingly specialize in different kinds of economic activity, and therefore different kinds of jobs (Barbour and Markusen, 2007). When we say 'regional development', what we really want to know is the overall level of development and living standards of a region. We thus need to know how much people in a region earn and the total income of the region. Based on earlier research (Florida *et al.*, 2008b), we use two measures of regional development as outcome variables: average income and average employment income, but will also include changes in income levels.

- *Average income*: This includes employment income, income from government programs, pension income, investment income and any other money income received by persons age 15 or older in 2005 as collected by Statistics Canada in 2006.
- *Average employment income*: This variable refers to total income received by persons 15 years of age and older. It includes wages and salaries, net income from a non-farm unincorporated business and/or professional practice, and net farm self-employment income in 2005 as collected by Statistics Canada in 2006.

Employment incomes and total incomes are related. For Canada, the correlation coefficient between them is 0.974. Still, earlier studies for the United States (Florida *et al.*, 2008b) have shown a considerable difference between the two across regions. As we noted earlier, wages are a good proxy for regional productivity (Becker, 1962, 1993), while income is a good proxy for regional wealth.

- *Average income change 2001 to 2006:* We include an additional variable based on changes in income between the years 2001 and 2006. The data is from Statistics Canada for years 2001 and 2006, but reflects the period 2000–2005.

Human capital or talent variables

The next class of variables concerns talent. As noted above, our research uses several different measures for talent.

- *Human capital*: This variable is the measure based on educational attainment, measured as the share of the regional labour force with a bachelor's (four-year university) degree and above. It is from the 2001 Canadian Census.
- *Creative class*: We use several definitions of the creative class, based on occupation. Each of them is measured as the share of the regional labor force. All data is from the Census of Canada for the year 2001. Following Florida (2002a), we examine the effects of the creative occupations or the 'creative class', defined as those in which individuals 'engage in complex problem solving that involves a great deal of independent judgment and requires high levels of education or human capital'. The original creative class measure includes the following major occupational groups: computer and math occupations; architecture and engineering; life, physical, and social science; education, training, and library positions; arts and design work; and entertainment, sports, and media occupations, as well as other professional and knowledge work occupations including management occupations, business and financial operations, legal positions, healthcare practitioners, technical occupations, and high-end sales and sales management.

Statistics Canada defines occupation according to National Occupational Classification (NOC) which is different from the classification system used by the Bureau of Labor Statistics in the United States. This creative class measure will be adjusted according to the Canadian definitions. However, they are still defined based on the complex problem solving and independent judgment conditions.

- *Super-creative core*: Florida (2002a) defines the super-creative core as: computer and math occupations; architecture and engineering; life, physical, and social science; education, training, and library positions; arts and design work; and entertainment, sports, and media occupations. We define the super-creative core as follows: Professional occupations in natural and applied sciences, technical occupations related to natural and applied sciences (referred to as 'Science'), judges, lawyers, psychologists, social workers, ministers of religion, and policy and program officers, paralegals, social services, workers and occupations in education and religion, n.e.c. ('Education and Social Science'), Professional occupations in art and culture, technical occupations in art, culture, recreation and sports ('Arts and Culture').
- *Creative professionals*: Florida (2002a) includes the following professional occupations in the creative class: management occupations, business and financial operations, legal positions, healthcare practitioners, technical occupations, and sales management. We include the following occupations: Senior management occupations, specialist managers, other managers (referred to as 'Managers', Professional occupations in business and finance,

finance and insurance administration occupations ('Business and Finance'), Professional occupations in health, nurse supervisors and registered nurses, technical and related occupations in health ('Health'). We also analyze key creative occupations separately: managers, business and finance, science, health, education and social science, and arts and culture.

Technology variable

Techpole: We include a technology variable to account for the effects of technology on regional development. This technology variable is the product of the location quotient and regional share for Canadian High Tech industry employment. The techpole ranks CMA and CA by multiplying regional: (1) regional high-tech industrial employment as a percentage of regional employment; by (2) the national high-tech employment as a percentage of national employment. This is based on Canadian Business Patterns data from Statistics Canada for the year 2001.

Variables that affect the distribution of human capital or talent

To examine the question of what accounts for the geographic distribution of educated and skilled populations, we include three key variables reflecting the current literature: tolerance, universities and service diversity.

We use three measures for tolerance – the self-expression index, visible minorities and the mosaic index:

- *Self-expression index:* This variable combines the concentration of self-identified partnered or married gay and lesbian households and the concentration of individuals employed in the arts, design and related occupations. Both are location quotients. The self-expression index is the average of the two. The data is from the Canadian Census for 2001. The data from 2001 is only available from Statistics Canada for the 27 CMAs.
- *Visible minorities*: We will also employ a measure based on the visible minority share of the population. Visible minorities are defined as 'persons, other than Aboriginal peoples, who are non-Caucasian in race or non-white in color' according to The Employment Equity Act. This data is from Canadian Census for the year 2001.
- *Mosaic index:* This variable is the share of population that is foreign-born immigrants to Canada. The data is from Canadian Census for the year 2001.

Other variables

- *Universities*: This variable measures number of university professors per capita. University professors teach courses to undergraduate and graduate students and conduct research at universities and degree-granting colleges. It is based on NOC data from the 2001 census. There are many ways to measure the university effect, and at earlier stages of this work we did try other variables (e.g. fixed effects for larger universities, students, researchers only, etc.). This research led us to find that faculty per capita is the best measure we can come up with given the context. This is a proxy for the ability to produce talent in the form of human capital, and at the same time a proxy for the connection to the industry. If, for example, we had used grants oriented towards spin-offs, that would only work as a proxy for the university–industry link, and the primary interest is the relationship between the strength of local university presence and regional talent levels.

- *Service diversity*: We use the diversity of consumer service firms as our proxy for regional amenities. This variable reflects the number of service industries represented within the metropolitan region that could be regarded as attractive to consumers. It is based on 2001 industry data from Statistics Canada.

Methods

We use path analysis and structural equations to examine the relationships between variables in the model. In order to analyze the dynamics between this set of variables adequately, structural equation modeling (SEM) is used. Structural equation models may be thought of as an extension of regression analysis and factor analysis, expressing the relationship between variables through a set of linear relationships, based upon their variances and covariances. In other words, structural equations replace a (usually large) set of observable variables with a small set of unobservable factor constructs, thus minimizing the problem of multi-collinearity (Jöreskog, 1973). The parameters of the equations are estimated by the maximum likelihood method.

It is important to stress that the graphic picture of the structural model (Figure 3.1) expresses direct and indirect correlations, not actual causalities. Rather, the estimated parameters (path coefficients) provide information of the relation between the set of variables. Moreover, the relative importance of the parameters is expressed by the standardized path coefficients, which allow for interpretation of the direct as well as the indirect effects. We do not assume any causality among university, tolerance and service diversity but rather treat them as correlations.

From the relationships depicted in the model (Figure 3.1) we estimate three equations:

$$\text{lnTalent} = \beta_{11}\,\text{lnUniversity} + \beta_{12}\,\text{lnServiceDiversity} + \beta_{13}\,\text{lnTolerance} + e_3 \quad (3.1)$$
$$\text{lnTechnology} = \beta_{21}\,\text{lnUniversity} + \beta_{22}\,\text{lnTolerance} + \beta_{24}\,\text{lnTalent} + e_2 \quad (3.2)$$
$$\text{lnRegional Development} = \beta_{31}\,\text{lnUniversity} + \beta_{33}\,\text{lnTolerance} +$$
$$\beta_{34}\,\text{lnTalent} + \beta_{35}\,\text{lnTechnology} + e_1 \quad (3.3)$$

Findings

We now turn to our findings. We begin by examining the effects of the two primary talent measures: human capital and the creative class. We then provide the findings for specific occupations.

Table 3.2 Talent and occupations, correlation coefficients

	Human capital	*Creative class*
Managers	0.679**	0.748**
Business and finance	0.609**	0.630**
Science-*	0.732**	0.827**
Health	0.281	0.320*
Education and social science	0.601**	0.654**
Arts and culture	0.830**	0.855**
Technology	0.774**	0.757**
Income	0.512**	0.507**
Employment income	0.516**	0.502**

Note: Significance levels *** $p < 0.001$, ** $p < 0.05$, * $p < 0$.

Table 3.2 summarizes the results of the correlation analysis of occupation and outcome variables with the traditional human capital and our creative class. The correlation coefficient between conventional human capital (educational attainment) and the creative class (what people do) is 0.914. While there is a high correlation between these two groups in Canada's 46 largest urban areas, Mellander (2009) finds that only 1 out of 4 people within the creative class in Sweden hold a university degree of 3 years or more. This illustrates that a university degree by no means is a prerequisite for a creative occupation but that the probability of having a creative occupation increases with the education level.

Human capital and the creative class are closely related to most key occupational groups. In many cases both human capital and the creative class are highly correlated with both the same occupational variables and outcome variables, For example, human capital and creative class have a strong relationship to arts and culture occupations (0.830 and 0.855), while both have a weak correlation with health occupations. These results imply that both measures, human capital and creative class, are associated with regional outcomes in Canada. However, the work by Florida *et al.* (2008b) shows that even if the two groups collocate and are similarly related to different occupational sub-groups, they tend to work differently in the structural equation context that will be used in the empirical part of this chapter.

If we turn to the relationship between various talent measures and regional income, we see that little difference between the relationships between human capital and the creative class with income and employment income can be found. In earlier studies of the United States (Florida *et al.* 2008b), human capital was found to be more closely related to regional income levels, while the creative class is more closely related to wages. However, as Table 3.2 shows, this is not the case in Canada. Both human capital and creative class have similar relationships to both income and employment incomes. The correlation coefficient for human capital and income is 0.512 and employment income is 0.516. The correlation for the creative class and income is 0.507 and employment income, 0.502. We will therefore, from here on, only focus on average income levels and changes in those, and exclude employment income (wages) from the analysis.

Findings from path analysis and structural equations

To further gauge the differential effects of human capital and the creative class on regional development measured using regional income levels, we now turn to the key findings from the structural equations models and path analysis. We ran separate models for human capital, the creative class, and the super-creative core.

The models examine the effects of the different measures of human capital and the creative class on income, and also isolate the effects of three key factors – tolerance, service diversity and universities – on the level and geographic distribution of human capital and the creative class as well on income. A path analysis is provided for each model based on the standardized β-coefficients, while the unstandardized β-coefficients will be presented in the related tables. This standardized coefficient is based upon the regression where all the variables in the regression have been standardized first by subtracting each variable's mean and dividing it by the standard deviation associated by each variable. These coefficients can be used to analyze the relative importance of the explanatory variables in relation to the dependent variable. We ran the models for both average income levels and for income change between 2001 and 2006, and report the results for each below.

Figure 3.2 is the path analysis for human capital. Human capital has a sizeable and significant direct effect on income. It also has a significant direct effect on technology, while technology also has a significant direct effect on income. Looking at the factors which affect the distribution of human capital, tolerance (i.e., the self-expression index) has the largest effect. The university variable is also positive and significant on talent, while service diversity has no significant effect on the distribution of talent. The self-expression variable also has a strong relationship to technology. It is also interesting to notice the negative and significant relationships for both the university and self-expression variables and regional income. The relationship between the university variable and technology is also negative and significant in relation to technology. This could be caused by a multicollinearity effect, but in

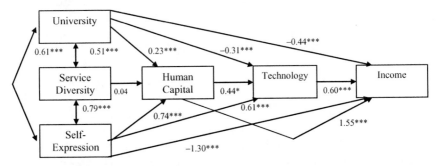

Figure 3.2 Path analysis for human capital and self-expression

Note: Significance levels *** $p < 0.001$, ** $p < 0.05$, * $p < 0.1$.

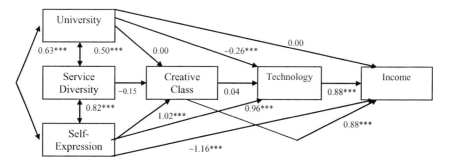

Figure 3.3 Path analysis for the creative class and self-expression

Note: Significance levels *** $p < 0.001$, ** $p < 0.05$, * $p < 0.1$.

a bivariate correlation with technology it is still only weakly related (0.344 at the 0.05 level). The university variable lacks a significant bivariate relation with income as well. Generally speaking, regional income is positively and significantly explained by human capital and technology.

When we run the models with change in regional income levels between 2001–2006, none of the explanatory variables are significant. In other words, the distribution of talent, technology and the university factor did not have an impact on the average income growth during the subsequent five years.

Figure 3.3 summarizes the path analysis for the creative class. Generally speaking, the relationships are similar to those for human capital. The creative class has a significant direct effect on regional income, but the relationship between it and technology is insignificant. The relationship between the creative class and self-expression is somewhat stronger than in the human capital model. The university variable is insignificant on the creative class, technology and income.

Table 3.3 provides the results for SEM models for human capital and the creative class. The R^2 values for equations 3.1 and 3.2 are between 0.72–0.87. However, those factors together explain less in equation 3.3 where the R^2 value is approximately 0.53–0.67 (Table 3.4). The overall results suggest a strong direct relationship between both human capital and the creative class and income. They also suggest a strong relationship between tolerance (measured by the self-expression index) and both talent measures, technology, and regional income.

When we run the models for income change, the creative class and the self-expression variables both become significant at the 0.05 level. This is an interesting result. While the conventional human capital measure had no effect on income change, the distribution of creative class occupations in combination with higher levels of self-expression levels is associated with increases in income levels across Canadian regions. This suggests that creative class occupations have a larger effect on changes in regional incomes than does the human capital level measured as educational attainment.

Table 3.3 SEM results for human capital, creative class and self-expression

Income	Human capital			Creative class		
	Talent	Technology	Income	Talent	Technology	Income
Variables	Eq 1	Eq 2	Eq 3	Eq 1	Eq 2	Eq 3
Self-expression	0.508***	2.549***	−0.323***	0.323***	3.937***	−0.282***
Service Diversity	0.199			−0.335		
University	0.060***	−0.495***	−0.041***	0.000	−0.422**	0.000
Talent		2.672*	0.560***		0.560	0.677***
Technology			0.036***			0.052***
Observations	46	46	46	46	46	46
R^2	0.872	0.722	0.665	0.812	0.740	0.528

Note: Significance levels *** $p < 0.001$, ** $p < 0.05$, * $p < 0.1$.

Table 3.4 SEM results including visible minorities

Income	Human capital			Creative class		
	Talent	Technology	Income	Talent	Technology	Income
Variables	Eq 1	Eq 2	Eq 3	Eq 1	Eq 2	Eq 3
Visible minorities	0.094***	0.007	0.043***	0.014	0.072	0.056***
Service diversity	1.395***			1.022***		
University	0.132***	−0.091	−0.035**	0.039***	−0.027	−0.023**
Talent		1.033***	0.199***		1.674***	0.350***
Technology			−0.009			−0.021
Observations	46	46	46	46	46	46
R^2	0.758	0.439	0.539	0.545	0.463	0.560

Note: Significance levels *** $p < 0.001$, ** $p < 0.05$, * $p < 0.1$.

Immigrants and visible minorities

We now substitute the self-expression index with variables for visible minorities and the Mosaic index.

Figure 3.4 is the path analysis for visible minorities. Human capital continues to have a strong relationship with income, as well as technology. The visible minorities variable performs somewhat differently than self-expression. It is both positive and significant in relation to income. Its effect on human capital is weaker than that for self-expression and it is not significantly related to technology. Both the university and service diversity variables are positively related to human capital in this model. When we run the model with change in income levels, we again find no effect from either human capital or visible minorities.

Figure 3.5 is the path analysis for visible minorities and the creative class. The creative class remains positively and significantly related to income. Visible

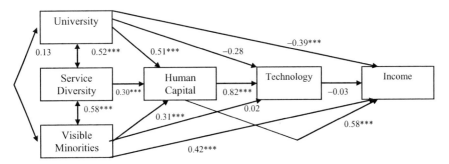

Figure 3.4 Path analysis for human capital and visible minorities

Note: Significance levels *** $p < 0.001$, ** $p < 0.05$, * $p < 0.1$.

minorities are significantly related to regional income levels, but not to the creative class. Thus, visible minorities appears to work directly on income rather
than on or through the creative class. Recall that the visible minority measure
is positive and significant in relation to human capital. A possible explanation is
that while visible minorities possess higher education, they are relatively concentrated in non-creative class jobs.

Figure 3.6 summarizes the results for the mosaic index. The creative class
continues to have a direct effect on income and technology. The mosaic index is
positively and significantly related to human capital, technology and income but
not the creative class (Table 3.5). This suggests that immigrants tend to have
direct effects on technology and income but not on or through the creative class.
When we run the model for income change, neither the mosaic index nor the
creative class variable is significantly related to income growth. This indicates
that the creative class only has a positive impact on income growth in regions
with higher levels of self-expression.

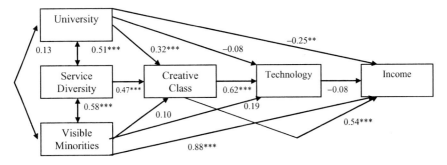

Figure 3.5 Path analysis for the creative class and visible minorities

Note: Significance levels *** $p < 0.001$, ** $p < 0.05$, * $p < 0.1$.

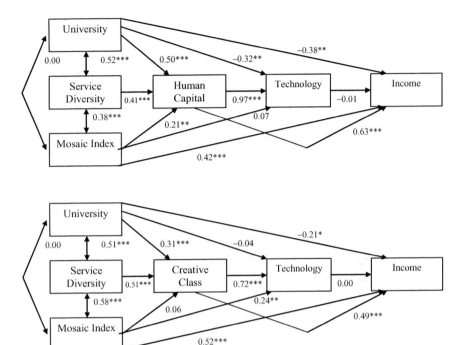

Figure 3.6 Path analysis for human capital, the creative class and the mosaic index
Note: Significance levels *** $p < 0.001$, ** $p < 0.05$, * $p < 0.1$.

Table 3.5 SEM results including the Mosaic Index

Income	Human capital			Creative class		
	Talent	Technology	Income	Talent	Technology	Income
Variables	Eq 1	Eq 2	Eq 3	Eq 1	Eq 2	Eq 3
Mosaic Index	0.074**	0.151	0.051***	0.038	0.072**	0.063***
Service Diversity	1.892***			1.103***		
University	0.129***	−0.502*	−0.051**	0.038**	−0.065	−0.019*
Talent		5.934***	0.216***		9.307***	0.360***
Technology			0.000			0.000
Observations	46	46	46	46	46	46
R^2	0.734	0.666	0.569	0.545	0.633	0.577

Note: Significance levels *** $p <0.001$, ** $p <0.05$, * $p <0.1$

The super-creative core

We now use our general model to examine the role of the two main groups that make up the creative class – the super-creative core and creative professionals.

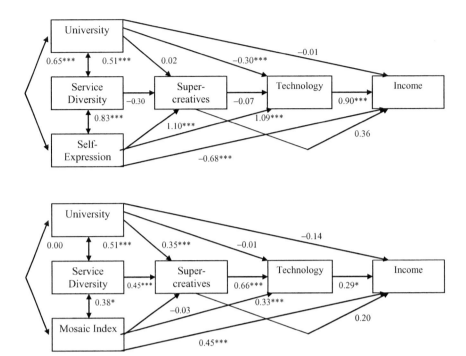

Figure 3.7 Path analysis for the super-creative core

Note: Significance levels *** p < 0.001, ** p < 0.05, * p < 0.1.

We then turn to specific occupational groups: managers, business and finance, science, health, education and social science, and arts and culture.

We start with the results for the super-creative core. Figure 3.7 shows the key findings from the path analysis.

The super-creative core has no direct effect on income. It has a positive and significant effect on technology in just one of the two models. In turn, it is shaped by the self-expression index but not the mosaic index. The university variable is positively and significantly related to super-creatives in one of the two models. When we run the model with income change, we find that the super-creative core is insignificantly related to regional income change.

Figure 3.8 provides the path analysis for creative professionals. There is a positive and significant relationship between creative professionals and income and a slightly stronger one between them and technology. In the model with the self-expression index, the relationship between creative professionals and the university is weak. But when we substitute the mosaic index, the university factor becomes slightly significant, and the relationship between creative professionals and technology becomes stronger. The mosaic index has a positive and significant effect on income, while the self-expression index is negative and significant.

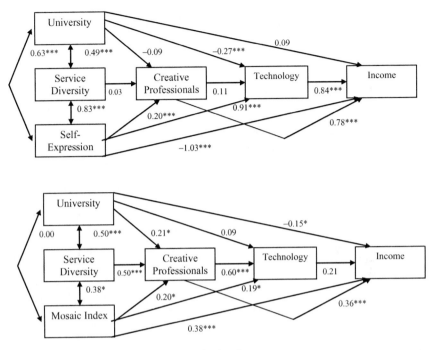

Figure 3.8 Path analysis for creative professionals

Note: Significance levels *** $p < 0.001$, ** $p < 0.05$, * $p < 0.1$.

Interestingly, when we run the model for income change, we find a significant relationship for creative professionals (Table 3.6). This stands in contrast to the result for super-creatives. The result holds both in combination with the self-expression index and the mosaic index. This indicates that the group of creative professionals appears to have a significant impact on both absolute income levels as well as changes in income levels over time where super-creatives do not.

Occupations and regional development

We now turn to our findings for more specific occupational groupings, 'decomposing' the creative class into its constituent occupations to probe for their separate effects on regional incomes. Below we summarize the results of SEM and path analyses for each of the major occupational groups, technology and wages. Table 3.7 provides the key results of the SEM models, while Figures 3.9A–F present the findings for the path analysis.

Basically, we find positive and significant direct relationships between three of the six occupational groups and income – management occupations, business and finance occupations, and scientific occupations. We find no significant relationship for health, education or arts and culture occupations on income. However,

Table 3.6 SEM results for the super-creative core and creative professionals

Income	Self-expression			Mosaic Index		
	Super-creative core			Super-creative core		
	Talent	Talent	Talent	Talent	Technology	Income
Variables	Eq 1	Eq 1	Eq 1	Eq 1	Eq 2	Eq 3
Tolerance	0.398***	−0.006	−0.006	−0.006	3.676***	−0.242***
Service diversity	−0.781**	1.179***	1.179***	1.179***		
University	0.003	0.051***	0.051***	0.051***	−0.433**	−0.008
Talent					1.496	0.649***
Technology						0.050***
Observations	46	46	46	46	46	46
R^2	0.774	0.477	0.477	0.477	0.730	0.594

Income	Creative professionals			Creative professionals		
	Talent	Talent	Talent	Talent	Technology	Income
Variables	Eq 1	Eq 1	Eq 1	Eq 1	Eq 2	Eq 3
Tolerance	0.236***	0.236***	0.236***	0.031*	0.413*	0.048***
Service diversity	0.056	0.056	0.056	0.995***		
University	−0.010	−0.010	−0.010	0.024*	0.138	−0.015
Talent					8.430***	0.299**
Technology						0.013
Observations	46	46	46	46	46	46
R^2	0.653	0.653	0.653	0.513	0.543	0.549

Note: Significance levels *** $p < 0.001$, ** $p < 0.05$, * $p < 0.1$.

Table 3.7 SEMs for key occupational groups

Tolerance	Self-expression			Mosaic Index		
	Managers			Managers		
Income	Talent	Technology	Income	Talent	Technology	Income
Variables	Eq 1	Eq 2	Eq 3	Eq 1	Eq 2	Eq 3
Tolerance	0.319***	2.956***	−0.172***	0.068**	0.204	0.043***
Service diversity	0.388			1.477***		
University	−0.063**	−0.368**	0.021	−0.004	0.337**	−0.006
Talent		2.795**	0.407***		6.434***	0.258***
Technology			0.035***			0.007
Observations	46	46	46	46	46	46
R^2	0.544	0.776	0.582	0.461	0.621	0.572

Income	Business and finance			Business and finance		
	Talent	Technology	Income	Talent	Technology	Income
Variables	Eq 1	Eq 2	Eq 3	Eq 1	Eq 2	Eq 3
Tolerance	1.218*	3.280***	−0.127*	0.070***	0.318	0.048***
Service diversity	0.178*			1.655***		
University	−0.084*	−0.481**	0.012	−0.007	0.373**	−0.007
Talent		1.803*	0.227**		5.083***	0.097
Technology			0.044***			0.019**
Observations	46	46	46	46	46	46
R^2	0.484	0.757	0.462	0.513	0.510	0.509

Income	Science			Science		
	Talent	Technology	Income	Talent	Technology	Income
Variables	Eq 1	Eq 2	Eq 3	Eq 1	Eq 2	Eq 3
Tolerance	0.570***	3.086***	−0.120	−0.015	0.716***	0.071***
Service diversity	−0.997			1.950***		
University	−0.073**	−0.445**	−0.008	0.009	−0.268**	−0.005
Talent		1.905**	0.177**		4.823**	0.248***
Technology			0.041**			−0.005
Observations	46	46	46	46	46	46
R^2	0.827	0.671	0.499	0.262	0.703	0.621

Income	Health			Health		
	Talent	Technology	Income	Talent	Technology	Income
Variables	Eq 1	Eq 2	Eq 3	Eq 1	Eq 2	Eq 3
Tolerance	0.122	3.679***	−0.082	−0.063**	0.744***	0.055***
Service diversity	−1.313*			−0.270		
University	0.083***	−0.104	0.001	0.083***	0.769***	−0.066
Talent		−3.313***	−0.022		−2.447	−0.004
Technology			0.052***			0.025***
Observations	46	46	46	46	46	46
R^2	0.294	0.826	0.377	0.340	0.357	0.495

Income	Education and social science			Education and social science		
	Talent	Technology	Income	Talent	Technology	Income
Variables	Eq 1	Eq 2	Eq 3	Eq 1	Eq 2	Eq 3
Tolerance	0.212***	4.197***	−0.062	−0.013	0.914***	0.054***
Service diversity	−1.024**			0.136		
University	0.061***	−4.269***	−0.002	0.087***	0.606**	−0.001
Talent		2.716	−0.019		−0.253	−0.061
Technology			0.049***			0.025***
Observations	46	46	46	46	46	46
R^2	0.530	0.803	0.368	0.441	0.321	0.501

(Continued)

Table 3.7 (Continued)

Income	Arts and culture*			Arts and culture		
	Talent	Technology	Income	Talent	Technology	Income
Variables	Eq 1	Eq 2	Eq 3	Eq 1	Eq 2	Eq 3
Tolerance	0.286***	2.123***	−0.043	0.027	0.427**	0.057***
Service diversity	1.301**			2.622***		
University	0.000	−0.251	−0.003	0.036	−0.054	0.001
Talent		2.577**	−0.070		4.758***	−0.118*
Technology			0.052***			0.036***
Observations	46	46	46	46	46	46
R^2	0.683	0.694	0.375	0.591	0.623	0.524

Notes: Significance levels *** $p < 0.001$, ** $p < 0.05$, * $p < 0.1$.

(a) The tolerance factor is only proxied by the Gay Index and not the Boho Index in this case to rule out collinearity problems with the talent group of arts and culture.

these three occupations can be said to have an indirect effect on regional incomes working through technology.

The findings suggest that management occupations are most strongly associated with income. The coefficients for management occupations are significant in models with both the self-expression and the mosaic index. The correlation coefficient between management occupations and income is also high (0.673). Scientific occupations also have a strong association with income. In the model which includes the mosaic index, it becomes slightly stronger than that for management occupations with an R^2 value of 0.621, compared to 0.572 for management occupations. Business and finance occupations are also positively associated income in the path structure, but only in models with the self-expression index. Arts and culture occupations are weakly related to income in a bivariate context (0.335, significant at the 0.05 level). Health and education occupations have no significant direct relation with regional average income, and are not even correlated to income in a bivariate context (-0.192 and -0.004).

When we substitute regional income levels with income change, we find a positive and significant relation for business and finance (0.386) and health (0.392) when combined with the self-expression index. When the mosaic index is employed, only business and finance are significant (0.404). The result for health occupations is also worth noting. While health-related occupations show no significant relation to current regional income levels, they are associated with regional income growth.

The findings also indicate the consistent role played by tolerance in regional talent formation. The self-expression index is closely related to each and every one of the occupational groups, and has its strongest effect on management occupations. The mosaic index is weaker, and is negative or not significantly related to science, health, education, and social science, and arts and culture occupations.

The tolerance variables are also positively and significantly related to technology. Both the self-expression index and the mosaic index are strongly related to the

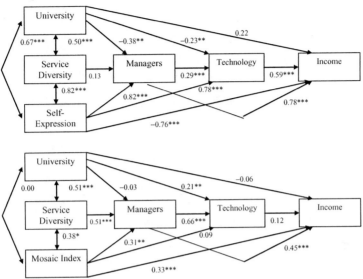

Managers

Figure 3.9A Path analysis for managers

Note: Significance levels *** $p < 0.001$, ** $p < 0.05$, * $p < 0.1$.

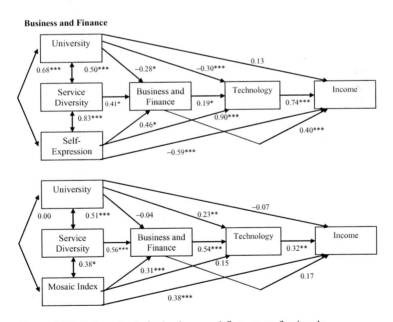

Business and Finance

Figure 3.9B Path analysis for business and finance professionals

Note: Significance levels *** $p < 0.001$, ** $p < 0.05$, * $p < 0.1$.

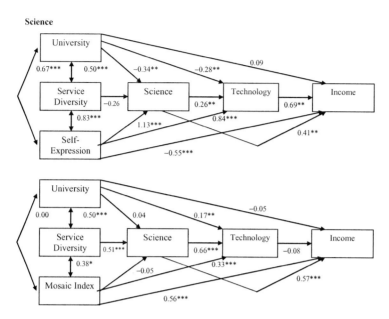

Figure 3.9C Path analysis for science professionals

Note: Significance levels *** $p < 0.001$, ** $p < 0.05$, * $p < 0.1$.

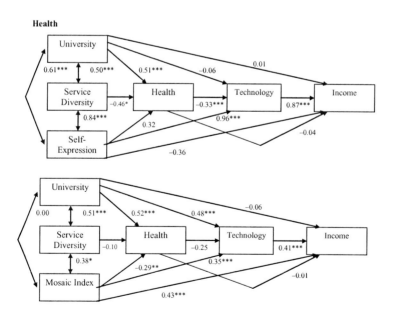

Figure 3.9D Path analysis for health professionals

Note: Significance levels *** $p < 0.001$, ** $p < 0.05$, * $p < 0.1$.

Education and Social Science

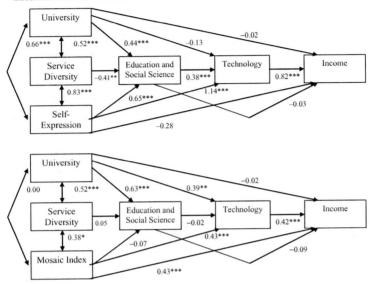

Figure 3.9E Path analysis for education and social science professionals

Note: Significance levels *** $p < 0.001$, ** $p < 0.05$, * $p < 0.1$.

Arts and Culture

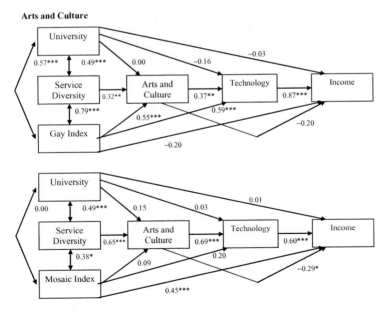

Figure 3.9F Path analysis for arts and culture professionals

Note: Significance levels *** $p < 0.001$, ** $p < 0.05$, * $p < 0.1$.

technology variables, often being stronger than the relationships between the individual occupation groups and technology. We find that the tolerance measures play different roles in relation to regional income. The mosaic index is frequently positive and significant, while the self-expression index is either negative or insignificant. It is also interesting to note the role of the service diversity measure. When used together with the self-expression index, it is negative or insignificant, but when used with the mosaic index, it is frequently positive and significant.

The effect of the university variable is relatively weak across almost all occupational groups with the exception of health and education and social science – two groups which are quite closely related to the university as employer. Surprisingly, the university variable is also in general weakly associated with technology. It becomes significant in the cases where talent plays no role. This may be an artifact of a relative overestimation because of the missing talent–technology link.

Conclusion

Our research has provided an empirical examination of the factors that shape regional development in Canada. Specifically, we explored the role of human capital and the creative class, as well as technology, on regional incomes. We also examined a series of factors – universities, tolerance, and service diversity – on talent and on regional income and on income change. We provided an analysis of the role of specific occupational groupings on income as well.

Our research generated several key findings. First, our findings shed light on the effects of two different measures of talent or human capital on regional development – educational attainment and creative occupations. Generally speaking, our findings show that both measures are strongly associated with regional development (measured as regional income level) in Canada, when we looked at the factors that affect change in regional incomes between 2001 and 2006, the creative class variable was significant while the human capital variable was not.

The findings suggest that the educational human capital measure has a significant effect on technology, while the creative class does not. Of the two main groups that make up the creative class, creative professionals are more strongly related to regional income. If we compare these results with the outcome for the United States analysis (Florida *et al.*, 2008b), we can conclude that human capital is weaker than the self-expression index in order to explain technology in Canada. For the United States· these two factors were equally strong in relation to technology.

Second, our findings show that technology plays an important role in Canadian regional development. The technology variable has a positive and significant effect on income in models with the self-expression index. In these models, this technology effect holds alongside both human capital and the creative class, though it is relatively stronger in models with the latter. However, the effect of technology on income becomes insignificant in models with visible minorities and the mosaic index – variables which have a strong direct effect on income. We are led to conclude that technology affects regional development in conjunction with the self-expression variables (that is openness to gays and bohemians). Recent work by Hall and Kahn (2008) has shown how immigrants in tech-intensive larger Canadian regions have significantly lower income earnings than immigrants in mid-sized and smaller regions. These results suggest a weaker relation between technology and incomes in regions with a higher share of immigrants. The results for Canada are similar to the ones for the United States (Florida *et al.*, 2008b). However, in the United States, the relation between technology and income levels tends to stay significant, also in a multivariate analysis including immigration-related variables.

Third, our findings shed light on the role of specific occupations in Canadian regional development – management; business and finance; science; health; education and social science; and arts and culture occupations. Management and scientific occupations have the strongest association with regional income, while business and finance occupations also are associated with regional income. Arts and culture occupations have a strong association with technology, roughly the same strength as for scientific occupations.

However, we find the effects of these occupational groups on incomes to be weaker compared to the results from comparable studies of the United States (Florida *et al.*, 2008b) using a similar methodology. This can partly be explained by differences between the Canadian and the United States' occupational definitions. But it may also be a pattern of lower productivity levels, since wage levels tend to be a reflection of those, and in the Canadian case the wage and income levels are closely related. Human capital theory postulates that wages rise with the level of knowledge or skill (Becker, 1964, 1993; Mincer, 1974). Optimally, wage levels should be in proportion to the stock of human capital, since this affects the value of workers' marginal product. However, wages are set by the regional *supply and demand* for labour and in order to increase wage levels based on talent, industry must have a need for this in order to be willing to pay for it. Health and education occupations have no significant relationship to regional income. This is in line with the findings of previous studies of the United States (Florida *et al.*, 2008b) and Sweden (Mellander and Florida, 2009).

Fourth, our findings shed light on the differential role played by tolerance, universities, and service diversity on regional development. Of the three, our findings indicate that tolerance plays by far the most significant role, acting directly on both talent production and regional income. We also find that different measures – and kinds – of tolerance affect regional development in different ways. The self-expression index is positively associated with both talent variables and with technology. The two other measures of tolerance – visible minorities and the mosaic index – have a direct significant and positive link to income levels.

We thus find that openness to or tolerance of gays and bohemians and visible minorities and immigrants operate on regional development through distinctive channels. The former appears to operate indirectly on income through the channel of regional talent, signaling for regional openness to or attractiveness for talent, as well as through regional technology, while the latter operates more directly on income.

The results for tolerance differs from the United States results (Florida *et al.*, 2008b), where only the self-expression index was found positive and significant in relation to talent and technology, but immigration-based measures showed a negative and significant relation with those variables. At the same time, the self-expression index in Canada shows a negative and significant relation to income, while this is significant and positive for most of the cases in the United States. The results make us believe that immigration groups in Canada are better absorbed into more productive economic activities, but it is not necessarily through higher education, creative occupations or high tech jobs.

Fifth, our findings indicate that university's role in Canadian regional development is relatively weak. It has a positive and significant relation to human capital but is insignificant in relation to the creative class. The university has little association to technology or regional income. There are several reasons why this may be so. It may reflect the flow of talent between regions. Certain regions may provide research and education which is then exported to other regions which perform more commercial functions. It is a signal that the universities that produce talent may not keep the talent in the region. It might also reflect a university focus on education and talent as opposed to commercially relevant research or startup firms. The results for the university factor are in line with the results from earlier studies for the United States (Florida *et al.*, 2008b), where the university variable in general was strong in relation to talent, but only weakly associated with technology and income levels. While we know that many universities, especially in the United States, have quite extensive relations to industry, this does not seem to be a general pattern across regions, neither in the United States nor in Canada, but that the university mainly plays the role as the talent producer.

In short, our findings shed new light on the ways that Canadian regional development is shaped by the 3Ts of technology, talent and tolerance. Talent in the form of human capital and the creative class is strongly associated with regional income. Technology affects regional income alongside human capital, the creative class and openness to gays and bohemians. The university's role in technology development and regional income is relatively weak. This suggests an ongoing policy challenge to find new and better ways for connecting Canadian universities more directly to regional talent, technology and income. Tolerance is a strong suit in Canadian regional development providing considerable direct and indirect effects on talent and regional income. Tolerance towards gays and bohemians is strongly associated with both human capital and the creative class, while tolerance in the form of openness to immigrants and visible minorities is strongly related to regional income. The effects of these forms of tolerance on income are greater than that played by technology. This suggests that Canada's experiment in opening up to immigration is paying significant economic development dividends.

Acknowledgments

Ronnie Sanders and Michael Wolfe provided research assistance. We are grateful for research support from the Martin Prosperity Institute and the Ontario Provincial Government.

Bibliography

Aghion, P. and Howitt, P. (1992) 'A model of growth through creative destruction', *Econometrica*, 60: 323–351.

Amabile, T. M. (1996) *Creativity in Context: Update to the Social Psychology of Creativity*, Boulder, CO: Westview Press.

Audretsch, D. B. and Feldman, M. P. (1994) 'R&D spillovers and innovative activity', *Managerial and Decision Economics*, 15: 131–138.

Barbour, E. and Markusen, A. (2007) 'Regional occupational and industrial structure: Does one imply the other?', *International Regional Science Review*, 30: 72–90.

Barnes, T. J. (1996) *External Shocks: Regional Implications of an Open Staple Economy, in Canada and the Global Economy: The Geography of Structural and Technological Change*, Montreal: McGill-Queen's Press.

Barnes, T. J., Britton, J. N., Coffey, W. J., Edgington, D. W., Certler, M. S. and Norcliffe, G. (2000) 'Canadian economic geography at the millennium', *Canadian Geographer / Le Géographe canadien*, 44: 4–24.

Barro, R. J. (1991) 'Economic growth in a cross-section of countries', *The Quarterly Journal of Economics*, 106: 407–443.

Barro, R. J. and Sala-i-Martin, X. (1997) 'Technological diffusion, convergence, and growth', *Journal of Economic Growth*, 2: 1–26.

Barro, R. J. and Lee, J. W. (2000) 'International data on educational attainment: Updates and implications', *Oxford Economics Paper*, 53: 541–563.

Bartel, A.P. (1979) 'The migration decision: What role does job mobility play?', *The American Economic Review*, 69: 775–786.

Becker, G. (1962) 'Investment in human capital: Effects on earnings', *Journal of Political Economy*, 7: 9–49.

Becker, G. (1964) *Human Capital*, New York: Columbia University Press for the National Bureau of Economic Research.

Becker, G. S. (1993) *Human Capital: A Theoretical and Empirical Analysis, with Special Reference to Education*, Chicago: University of Chicago Press.

Beckstead, D. and Brown, M. (2003) *From Labrador City to Toronto: The Industrial Diversity of Canadian Cities 1992–2002*, available at: http://dsp-psd.pwgsc.gc.ca/Collection/Statcan/11-624-M/11-624-MIE2003003.pdf (accessed 10 November 2008).

Berry, C. R. and Glaeser, E. L. (2005) 'The divergence of human capital levels across cities', *Papers in Regional Science*, 84: 407–444.

Blanchard, O. J. and Katz, L. (1992) 'Regional evolutions', *Brookings Papers on Economic Activity*, 1–75.

Bradfield, M. (1988) 'Introduction', in *Regional Economics: Analysis and Policies in Canada*, Toronto: McGraw-Hill Ryerson, pp. 1–19.

Carlino, G. A. and Mills, E. S. (1987) 'The determinants of county growth', *Journal of Regional Science*, 27: 39–54.

Carlino, G. A., Chatterjee, S. and Hunt, R. (2001) 'Knowledge spillovers and the new economy of cities', Working Paper No. 01-14, Federal Reserve Bank of Philadelphia.

Clark, T. N. (2003). 'Urban amenities: Lakes, opera and juice bars. Do they drive development?', *Research in Urban Policy*, 9: 103–140.

Currid, E. (2007) *The Warhol Economy: How Fashion, Art, and Music Drive New York City*, Princeton, NJ: University Press.

Duranton, G. and Puga, D. (2003) 'Micro-foundations of urban agglomeration economies', in J. V. Henderson and J-F. Thisse (eds), *The Handbook of Regional and Urban Economics*, Amsterdam: North Holland.

Duxbury, N. (2004) *Creative Cities: Principles and Practices*. Available at: http://www.cpm.com/documents/31347_en.pdf (accessed 10 November 2008).

Edmonston, B. (2002) *Research on Immigration and Integration in the Metropolis*, Vancouver, BC: Vancover Centre of Excellence.

Feldman, M. P. (1999) 'The new economics of innovation, spillovers and agglomeration: A review of empirical studies', *Economics of Innovation and New Technology*, 8: 5–25.

Ferguson, M., Ali, K., Olfert, M. R. and Partridge, M. (2007) 'Voting with their feet: Jobs versus amenities', *Growth and Change*, 38: 77–110.

Florida, R. (2002a) *The Rise of the Creative Class: And How It's Transforming Work, Leisure, Community, and Everyday Life*, New York: Basic Books.

Florida, R. (2002b) 'Bohemia and economic geography', *Journal of Economic Geography*, 2: 55–71.

Florida, R. (2002c) 'The economic geography of talent', *Annals of the Association of American Geographers*, 92: 743–755.

Florida, R. (2004a) 'Revenge of the squelchers', *The Next American City*.

Florida, R. (2004b) Response to Edward Glaeser's Review of "The Rise of the Creative Class", available at: http://creativeclass.com/rfcgdb/articles/ResponsetoGlaeser.pdf (accessed 19 August 2009).

Florida, R. (2005) *Cities and the Creative Class*, New York: Routledge.

Florida, R. and Gates, G. (2003) 'Technology and tolerance: The importance of diversity to high-technology growth', in T. N. Clark (ed.), *The City as an Entertainment Machine*: *Research in Urban Policy*, vol. 9, Oxford: Elsevier, pp. 199–220.

Florida, R., Gates, G., Knudsen, B. and Stolarick, K. (2006) *The University and the Creative Economy*, available at: http://www.creativeclass.org/rfcgdb/articles/University%20%For%20City%20and%20Community%20204.pdf (accessed 10 November 2008).

Florida, R., Mellander, C. and Qian, H. (2008a) 'Creative China? The university, tolerance and talent in Chinese regional development', Working Paper Series in Economics and Institutions of Innovation No. 145, Royal Institute of Technology, CESIS – Centre of Excellence for Science and Innovation Studies.

Florida, R., Mellander, C. and Stolarick, K. (2008b) 'Inside the Black Box of regional development—human capital, the creative class and tolerance', *Journal of Economic Geography*, 8: 615–649.

Fredrickson, B. L. (2001) 'The role of positive emotions in positive psychology: The broaden-and-build theory of positive emotions', *American Psychologist*, 56: 218–226.

Gabe, T. M. (2006) 'Growth of creative occupations in US Metropolitan Areas: A shift-share analysis', *Growth and Change*, 37: 396–415.

Gertler, M. S. (2001) 'Urban economy and society in Canada: Flows of people, capital and ideas', *The Canadian Journal of Policy Research*, 2: 119–130.

Gertler, M. S., Florida, R., Gates, G. and Vinodrai, T. (2002) 'Competing on creativity: Placing Ontario's cities in North American context', available at: http://www.investinginchildren.on.ca/Communications/articles/Competing%20on%20Creativity.pdf (accessed 7 August 2009).

Glaeser, E. L. (2000) 'The new economics of urban and regional growth', in G. Clark, M. Feldman and M. Gertler (eds), *The Oxford Handbook of Economic Geography*, Oxford: Oxford University Press.

Glaeser, E. L. (2004) 'Book review of Richard Florida's "The Rise of the Creative Class"', available at: http://post.economics.harvard.edu/faculty/glaeser/papers/Review_Florida.pdf (accessed 29 August 2013).

Glaeser, E. L., Kolko, J. and Saiz, A. (2001) 'Consumer city', *Journal of Economic Geography*, 1: 27–50.

Grossman, G. M. and Helpman, E. (1991) *Innovation and Growth in the Global Economy*, Cambridge, MA: MIT Press.

Gyourko, J., Mayer, C. and Sinai, T. (2006) 'Superstar cities', Working Paper No. 12355, Washington, DC: National Bureau of Economic Research.

Hall, P. V. and Kahn, A. J. (2008) 'Differences in hi-tech immigrant earnings and wages across Canadian cities', *Canadian Geographer / Le Géographe canadien*, 52: 271–290.

Holbrook, A. J. and Wolfe, D. A. (2000) *Innovations, Institutions and Territory: Regional Innovation Systems in Canada*, Montreal: McGill-Queen's University Press.

Inglehart, R. and Norris, P. (2003) *Rising Tide: Gender Equality and Cultural Change around the World*, Cambridge: Cambridge University Press.

Inglehart, R. and Welzel, C. (2005) *Modernization, Cultural Change, and Democracy: The Human Development Sequence*, Cambridge: Cambridge University Press.

Innis, H. A. (1956) *The Fur Trade in Canada: An Introduction to Canadian Economic History*, Toronto: University of Toronto Press.

Jacobs, J. (1961) *The Death and Life of Great American Cities*, New York: Random House.

Jacobs, J. (1969) *The Economy of Cities*, New York: Random House.

Jöreskog, K. G. (1973) 'Analysis of covariance structures', in P. R. Krishnaiah (ed.), *Multivariate Analysis*, vol. III, New York: Academic Press.

Kremer, M. (1993) 'Population growth and technological change: One million BC to 1990', *The Quarterly Journal of Economics*, 108: 681–716.

Laroche, M. and Mérette, M. (2000) 'Measuring human capital in Canada', available at: http://dsp-psd.pwgsc.gc.ca/Collection/F21-8-2000-5E.pdf (accessed 11 December, 2008).

Lipset, S. (1990) *Continental Divide: The Values and Institutions of the United States and Canada*, New York: Routledge.

Lloyd, R. and Clark, T. N. (2001) 'The city as an entertainment machine', *Research in Urban Sociology*, 6: 357–378.

Lucas, R. E. (1988) 'On the mechanics of economic development', *Journal of Monetary Economics*, 22: 3–42.

McGranahan, D. and Wojan, T. (2007) 'Recasting the creative class to examine growth processes in rural and urban counties', *Regional Studies*, 41: 197–216.

Markusen, A. (2004) 'Targeting occupations in regional and community economic development', *Journal of the American Planning Association*, 70: 253–268.

Markusen, A. and Schrock, G. (2006) 'The artistic dividend: Urban artistic specialisation and economic development implications', *Urban Studies*, 43: 1661–1686.

Marlet, G. and Van Woerkens, C. (2004) *Skills and Creativity in a Cross-section of Dutch Cities*, available at: http://www.uu.nl/uupublish/content/04-29.pdf (accessed 11 December 2008).

Mellander, C. (2009) 'Creative and knowledge industries: An occupational distribution approach', *Economic Development Quarterly*, 23: 294–305.

Mellander, C. and Florida, R. (2006) 'The creative class or human capital? Explaining regional development in Sweden', Working Paper Series in Economics and Institutions of Innovation No. 79, Royal Institute of Technology, CESIS – Centre of Excellence for Science and Innovation Studies.

Mellander, C. and Florida, R. (2009) 'Human capital or the creative class – explaining regional development in Sweden', *The Annals of Regional Science*.

Mincer, J. (1974) *Schooling, Experience and Earnings*, New York: Columbia University Press for the National Bureau of Economic Research.

Noland, M. (2005) 'Popular attitudes, globalization and risk', *International Finance*, 8: 199–229.

Ottaviano, G. I. P. and Peri, G. (2005) 'Cities and cultures', *Journal of Urban Economics*, 58: 304–337.

Page, S. E. (2008) *The Difference: How the Power of Diversity Creates Better Groups, Firms, Schools, and Societies*, Princeton, NJ: Princeton University Press.

Polèse, M. and Shearmur, R. (2006) 'Why some regions will decline: A Canadian case study with thoughts on local development strategies', *Papers in Regional Science*, 85: 23–46.

Rauch, J. E. (1993) 'Productivity gains from geographic concentration of human capital: Evidence from the cities', *Journal of Urban Economics*, 34: 380–400.

Roback, J. (1982) 'Wages, rents, and the quality of life', *Journal of Political Economy*, 90: 1257–1278.

Romer, P. M. (1986), 'Increasing returns and long-run growth', *Journal of Political Economy*, 94: 1002–1037.

Romer, P. M. (1987) 'Crazy explanations for the productivity slowdown', in *Macroeconomics Annual*, National Bureau of Economic Research, Inc.

Romer, P. M. (1990) 'Endogenous technological change', *Journal of Political Economy*, 98: S71–S102.

Savoie, D. J. (1997) *Canada: Regional Development Theories and Their Application*, ed. B. Higgins and D. J. Savoie, Edison, NJ: Transaction Publishers.

Shapiro, J. M. (2006) 'Smart cities: Quality of life, productivity, and the growth effects of human capital', *Review of Economics and Statistics*, 88: 324–335.

Simon, C. J. (1998) 'Human capital and metropolitan employment growth', *Journal of Urban Economics*, 43: 223–243.

Simon, C. J. and Nardinelli, C. (1996) 'The talk of the town: Human capital, information, and the growth of English cities, 1861 to 1961', *Explorations in Economic History*, 33: 384–413.

Simon, H. A. (1954) 'Spurious correlation: A causal interpretation', *Journal of the American Statistical Association*, 49: 467–479.

Slack, E., Bourne, L. and Gertler, M. S. (2003) *Vibrant Cities and City-Regions: Responding to Emerging Challenges. The Panel on the Role of Government*, available at: https://ospace. scholarsportal.info/bitstream/1873/3486/1/244174.pdf (accessed 21 October 2008).

Smith, R. and Warfield, K. (2008) 'The creative city: A matter of values', in C. P. Lazzeretti (ed.), *Creative Cities, Cultural Clusters and Local Economic Development*, Cheltenham, UK: Edward Elgar Publishing.

Solow, R. M. (1956) 'A contribution to the theory of economic growth', *The Quarterly Journal of Economics*, 70: 65–94.

Spencer, G. M., Vinodrai, T., Gertler, M. S. and Wolfe, D. A. (2010) 'Do clusters make a difference? Defining and assessing their economic performance', *Regional Studies*, 44: 697–715.

Sternberg, R. J. (1999) *Handbook of Creativity*, Cambridge: Cambridge University Press.

Stolarick, K. and Florida, R. (2006) 'Creativity, connections and innovation: A study of linkages in the Montréal Region', *Environment and Planning*, 38(10): 1799–1817.

Wellstead, A. (2007) 'The (post) staples economy and the (post) staples state in historical perspective', *Canadian Political Science Review*, 1: 8–25.

Part II

Scandinavia, the Nordic countries and Europe

4 Florida's creative class in a Swedish context

The problem of measuring tolerance and amenity-driven growth

Høgni Kalsø Hansen

The theory of the creative class, location dynamics and the welfare state

The central idea of the creative class theory is that people move for places rather than jobs. In that sense, one of the most important outcomes of the creative class debate is that the focus of the regional development debate has moved away from focusing on attracting companies towards attracting creative and highly educated people – henceforth called talents – by creating stimulating and authentic cities with a wide range of amenities (Wojan *et al.*, 2007; Asheim and Hansen, 2009). Attracting the right people will attract the right investments, it is argued. Companies wish to invest where the most creative and innovative workforce are located, because this gives them a better chance to be competitive in tomorrow's market.

A fundamental mechanism in Florida's reasoning is that talented people are footloose and will migrate from one region to another if their needs are not fulfilled. Jobs are of course important in this respect, but according to Florida and his followers, talented people find a thick labour market and a wide scope of leisure activities more important and thus are attracted to places that can offer a wide range of amenities. Consequently, regions can become more attractive to talented people, and organisations seeking talented people, by upgrading urban space and offering better welfare services (Florida, 2002).

However, such a fundamental mechanism requires at least two fundamental parameters: a potentially mobile labour force and a variety of regions to migrate between. A central question, however, is whether these mechanisms are present in a welfare state like Sweden where labour mobility and the number of large regions are less distinct compared to its North American counterpart where the theory was developed.

A central point is whether amenities can be used to boost urban space and thereby attract the creative class. According to Florida (2002), Glaeser (2005) and Rappaport (2009), this holds true for North America. In North America, however, the number of cities of a size that allows for thick labour markets is higher than in most European countries, and the labour market structures are different from those of European countries such as Sweden. Following this argument, Clifton *et al.* (forthcoming) look into the geography of talent in Sweden, as a representative of a coordinated market economy, and the UK, as a representative of a liberal market economy as defined by Hall and Soskice (2001). Clifton *et al.* find that the creative class is more equally distributed in a coordinated market economy and argue that this is due to more equal distribution of welfare services and welfare jobs including social unemployment benefits, which do not force people to move between regions. Moreover, Clifton *et al.* find that to some extent indicators of quality of place have less effect on the concentration of the creative class and talent in coordinated market economies compared to liberal market economies if the nature of regional hierarchies are left out. The different effects that varieties of capitalism potentially have on the location and dynamics of the creative class call for a more context-regulated understanding of how, where and why the talented people locate.

In the following section, studies on the role of amenities for regional development in Sweden will be discussed with the aim of highlighting the importance of regional and national contextual differences, e.g. the varieties of capitalism, when testing whether the basic dynamics of the creative class theory will work in this context. Empirical findings within the amenity growth paradigm come from at least three different directions, according to Hansen and Winther (2012). First, regional economists have touched upon the subject by including amenities as one of several parameters in their econometric models (Sjaastad, 1962; Glaeser, 2005; Rappaport, 2009). Second, the perspective of amenities as a factor of attraction has a long tradition within migration studies, though pull-push factors rather than economic development have been the main research focus in these studies (Roback, 1982; Adamson *et al.*, 2004; Chen and Rosenthal 2008). Third, a growing literature is emerging within the field of economic geography with a research focus on uneven regional growth as the primary concern (Hansen and Winther, 2010; Storper and Scott, 2009; Boschma and Fritsch, 2009). This section emphasises the latter; the relations between talent and creativity and regional uneven development is the focus here.

Findings and research agendas tend to be considerably different between North America and Europe. There are different urban and regional hierarchies, national welfare state regimes, modes of growth and economic structures between the USA and Europe. These differences support and react to economic changes in very different ways. Two important issues come into play in the amenity growth framework. First, differences in how to organise capitalism have resulted in a system with more double income families in especially the Nordic countries compared to the USA, which results in lower mobility rates, as two new jobs rather than one need to be found (Asheim, 2009; Asheim and Hansen, 2009). The share of female participation on the labour market is one central contextual difference between the USA and Sweden. Both in Sweden and in the USA approximately 94 per cent of the women who are part of the labour market are employed. However, the share of women who take part in the labour market differs significantly. The participation rate among women in the labour force in USA is only 57.5 per cent, while the figure for Sweden is 76 per cent (Statistics Sweden, [2005] 2007; US Census Bureau, [2000] 2007). Thus, while the employment rates among women who take part in the labour market is the same in the USA and Sweden, the share of women having or seeking jobs is markedly different. Lower participation of women in the labour force therefore cannot be assigned to the difficulty for women to get a job, but rather to a structural difference between the two societies. All things being equal, two rather than one earned income in a family can be expected to lower mobility both in regard to moving from one place to another and in regard to commuting. And everything else being equal, we can therefore expect mobility to be constrained with less friction in the USA compared to Sweden. Consequently, it can be argued that context is an important factor when discussing the importance of the creative class for theories on regional development.

In a broader perspective, the contextual differences between countries can also be seen in the varieties of capitalism (Hall and Soskice, 2001). Whether labour market are organised within a liberal market economy such as the USA or the coordinated market economy such as Sweden has to be taken into consideration as this will influence labour market functions as well as the role of the public sector with respect to social security and unemployment benefits, which clearly have effects on people's choice of place to live and their willingness to move. Deeply rooted (i.e. civil society-based) cultural differences, such as the presence of social capital (Putnam, 1993; 2000), which Florida has contrasted to creative capital when it comes to contributing to economic growth, will influence people's and even firms' behaviour, and, thus, have to be taken into consideration when analysing the relative importance to the people climate and the business climate for promoting regional economic development in various regions and countries.

Second, in most parts of Europe and especially in the Nordic countries, the regional hierarchy differs considerably from that in North America. The number of large city regions that compete on almost equal terms is low. In all the Nordic countries for example, the capital regions are the only city regions with more than 1,000,000 inhabitants, and their position in the very top of each national regional hierarchy is indisputable, both in terms of economic power, employment opportunities and the largest share as well as variety of amenities (Andersen *et al.*, 2010a ; 2010b).

A number of studies have been produced which bring us closer to an understanding of the links between amenities and urban as well as regional growth. The key to understanding the role of amenities in promoting urban and regional growth is to identify what the most important location factors are for firms and labour. Hansen and Niedomysl (2009) and Niedomysl and Hansen (2010) approached this question by asking approximately 5000 people in Sweden who recently moved from one region to another about their motives and decisions to move. The findings do not support the amenity growth paradigm. The main conclusion is that jobs and carrier opportunities are the single most important reason why people migrate, no matter what the migrants' level of education and income. Further, personal social relations come before factors that can be categorised as amenities. But this does not necessary mean that amenities are unimportant for migrants. It can be expected that amenities do play a vital role if migrants have to choose between two locations offering equal opportunities in regard to jobs and personal social relations. But this would not give amenities a leading role in regard to regional development, rather the findings presented above suggest that evolutionary, path-dependent industrial dynamics are the leading drivers when discussing urban growth, and imply that the direct influence of amenities on regional growth is questionable.

This does not mean that amenities do not play a role in migration and knowledge-based growth all together. Asheim and Hansen (2009) apply the knowledge base approach[1] to a study of location factors of highly skilled labour. Asheim and Hansen divide knowledge into three ideal types of knowledge bases: analytical (science-based), synthetic (engineering-based), and symbolic (arts-based). By identifying occupations that draw primarily on one of the three knowledge bases, Asheim and Hansen produce an analytical framework that can diversify the amenity growth debate further. Accordingly, they rank 70 Swedish labour market regions according to how well they perform on people climate and business climate (patents, technology intensity of production). This is correlated with the regions grouped according to their concentrations of knowledge bases. This exercise shows that regions that rely more on synthetic knowledge bases tend to perform better on the business climate variables than on the people climate variables, and those regions that depend more on analytical and especially symbolical knowledge bases tend to perform better on people climate variables and less well on business climate variables. These finding suggest that the role of amenities differs depending on the type of highly educated labour. Amenities might be important for regions that have high concentrations of industries and labour that draw on symbolic knowledge (artists) bases, while it might be less important for regions that are more dependent on synthetic (engineers) knowledge. Therefore, the impact that amenities are likely to have on regional development depends on the mix of knowledge bases or the types of highly skilled labour that are dominating in a particular setting.

Sweden and the geography of talent – and the problem of measuring tolerance

Above, a critical discussion and reflection on potential problems that can follow if a model is uncritically implemented in another setting than the one it is developed in were presented. Contextual difference has to be taken into consideration. Now follows a related attempt to unfold and develop the idea of measuring tolerance so that it would fit better in a Swedish context and maybe also an American context. However, before doing this, a few figures on the demography and geography of talent in a Swedish context will be helpful in order to understand the figures presented later. Sweden only consists of three cities that it is fair to count as large cities – namely Stockholm, Gothenburg and Malmö.[2] Hence, all the Swedish labour market regions are included in the analysis. Table 4.1 shows the population ranking of the 25 largest regions in 2002, the share of creative class and the location quotient.

Table 4.1 The creative class's share of the workforce in the Swedish regions (2002)[1]

A-region	Population rank	Creative class (%)	Creative core (%)	Creative professionals (%)	Location quotient of the creative class (LQ)
Sweden		35.68	11.43	24.25	1.00
Stockholm/ Södertälje	1	45.98	14.95	31.03	1.29
Uppsala	5	44.69	19.16	25.52	1.25
Linköping	11	42.29	17.58	24.71	1.19
Malmö/Lund/ Trelleborg	3	41.40	14.67	26.73	1.16
Gothenburg	2	40.19	13.02	27.17	1.13
Västerås	13	37.38	12.06	25.32	1.05
Umeå	16	36.28	14.56	21.72	1.02
Luleå/Boden	24	36.04	12.60	23.44	1.01
Sundsvall	19	34.88	10.69	24.19	0.98
Karlstad	9	33.09	10.60	22.49	0.93
Örebro	7	33.01	11.10	21.90	0.92
Eskilstuna	21	32.87	10.14	22.73	0.92
Jönköping	14	32.69	9.51	23.18	0.92
Helsingborg/ Landskrona	4	31.69	8.60	23.09	0.89
Östersund	18	31.62	9.57	22.05	0.89
Växjö	15	31.59	9.07	22.52	0.89
Norrköping	10	31.37	9.61	21.76	0.88
Borlänge/Falun	12	31.12	10.38	20.74	0.87
Trollhättan/ Vänersborg	23	30.71	8.37	22.34	0.86
Halmstad	22	29.92	8.33	21.59	0.84
Kalmar/Nybro	20	29.88	9.25	20.62	0.84
Kristianstad	25	29.81	9.13	20.68	0.84
Borås	6	29.48	7.65	21.82	0.83
Gävle/ Sandviken	8	28.92	9.17	19.75	0.81
Uddevalla	17	28.80	8.41	20.39	0.81

Note: [1] The categorisation of the creative class and the sub-categorisation follow Florida (2002) and can be seen in detail in Hansen (2007).

To some extent the geographical distribution of the creative class in Sweden follows the population size of the Swedish regions. Some differences are present, but most of these can be explained by large plant sites and the presence of a university or other types of institutions offering higher education. What can be read from Table 4.1 is that the regions with the highest creative class LQ are primarily found in the southern parts of Sweden. In northern Sweden, only Umeå and Luleå/Boden have LQs above 1, which is equal to the Swedish national average.

In many ways, the geography of human capital is similar to the geography of the creative class. The regions with major universities top this list (Hansen, 2007). This is due to the university activities and the related industries. The regions with the major universities also top the list if only the level of education within high-tech industries is considered. This suggests that the most knowledge-intensive productions are located within the regions that also have the major universities.

One thing that the Swedish data permit is a closer look into the educational background of the creative class. Table 4.2 illustrates the level of education in creative and non-creative groups.

The data show that the largest share of highly educated people is found in the creative core. It is, however, noteworthy that a relatively high share of the creative core, going from 20 per cent to 40 per cent, does not have a university degree equal to or above the bachelor's level. This has to be interpreted as a combination of small errors in two different variables (education and occupation), combined with the fact that architects, engineers, etc., can achieve their title through practice-orientated programmes and not only through theoretical programmes. This brings us one of the most dominating critiques of Florida put forward by Glaeser (2004).

Table 4.2 The share of people (aged 18–64) with a bachelor's degree or above in the creative class, the creative core, the creative professionals and the non-creative occupations in Sweden, 2002

City region	Creative class (all)	Creative core	Creative professionals	Non-creative occupations
Sweden	41.0	68.5	28.0	5.9
Uppsala	53.9	79.3	34.8	10.4
Umeå	52.4	80.8	33.4	8.5
Linköping	50.2	76.7	31.5	6.5
Malmö/Lund/ Trelleborg	47.9	76.3	32.3	9.4
Luleå/Boden	46.2	72.3	32.1	5.3
Gothenburg	44.1	72.3	30.6	8.4
Stockholm/ Södertälje	43.8	65.8	33.3	10.5
Västerås	40.0	67.9	26.7	5.1
Kristianstad	39.8	71.7	25.8	4.3
Karlstad	39.5	70.8	24.8	4.6
Örebro	39.3	65.7	25.9	5.5
Kalmar/Nybro	39.3	72.5	24.4	4.7
Halmstad	39.2	71.0	26.9	4.3
Borlänge/Falun	39.2	67.6	24.9	3.6
Jönköping	39.1	71.6	25.8	4.9
Östersund	38.6	64.1	27.5	4.4
Växjö	37.2	71.4	23.4	4.7
Helsingborg/ Landskrona	36.4	66.4	25.2	4.6
Gävle/Sandviken	35.4	63.3	22.5	3.9
Uddevalla	35.2	67.9	21.7	3.6
Norrköping	35.0	63.2	22.6	4.2
Trollhättan/ Vänersborg	34.6	60.6	24.8	3.6
Eskilstuna	34.5	58.3	23.9	4.1

He argues that talent and the creative class are the same to a large extent. This, however, shows that a large share of the assumed most creative people do not have the formal education that Glaeser uses as his key variable.

In general, according to Hansen (2007), the relationship between the presence of a creative class and human capital fits well with employment growth in Sweden. These statistical correlations underpin Florida's argument in Sweden. This does not, however, mean that the causality that the 3T model argues for is what drives growth in Sweden. And it does not mean that the proxies that Florida (2002) develops fit into a Swedish context or can be developed into better proxies. In the following pages how to measure tolerance will be discussed.

One of the more novel ideas that Florida launched in 2002 was that tolerance and openness have an important role in regard to attracting and retaining talented people. Several indicators are introduced such as the now famous Gay Index, indicating the concentration of homosexuals as a proxy for how tolerant a region is. Other proxies for tolerance are the Bohemian Index, measuring the concentration of artists, and the Melting Pot Index, measuring the concentration and composition of the foreign-born population. All indicators show positive correlations with regional growth.

However, it can be questioned whether the concentration of the foreign-born population can be understood as a proxy for openness. It can also be seen as a proxy for segmentation and ghettoisation. Below, this relation will be looked into with the aim of introducing a complementary measurement for openness using Sweden as a case study.

Openness towards different people living by different norms, etc., is difficult to measure quantitatively. As mentioned above, one way to do this has been by looking at the foreign-born population as a proxy of tolerance toward differentness. At least two different indexes can be used: in Sweden, Hansen (2007) has used Openness 1, indicating only non-Western foreign-born persons as a share of the total population, and Openness 2 indicating all foreign-born people as a share of the total population.[3] In the Openness 1 and Openness 2 Indexes, a high score, equal to a high rate of foreign-born people, is seen as a positive indication of a tolerant environment. This is of course problematic. It does not say anything clear about tolerance in terms of integration, acceptance, etc. High concentrations of foreign ethnic groups can lead to conflicts and to the collapse of city districts. Therefore, based on findings from Hansen (2007), the following section will discuss and unfold the concept of openness using Swedish data.

Figure 4.1 is the Openness 1 Index measured as the share of the population that originates from a non-Western country. The Swedish average is close to 4.5 per cent, and the figure reveals that Stockholm has almost double the average. Uppsala, Gothenburg and Malmö/Lund/Trelleborg follow, but with shares that are almost 2 percentage points lower. Västerås, number five on the list, has a non-Western population share closer to Malmö/Lund/Trelleborg than Örebro which comes in six. The high rankings of Stockholm, Uppsala, Gothenburg and Malmö are most likely related to the attractive effect urban areas have on foreign people. The high ranking of Västerås can most likely be explained by the immigration of foreigners assigned to jobs at ABB – a large

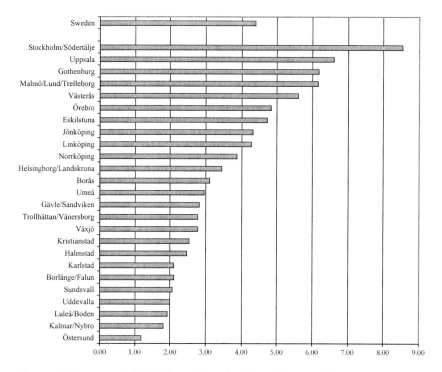

Figure 4.1 Openness 1 (2002) share of people of non-Western origin

Swedish industrial corporation. The figure also shows that with some exceptions, the ranking comes close to the ranking of the population. The most significant exceptions are Helsingborg/Landskrona, Borås and Karlstad with a lower share than expected from the ranking according to population, and Västerås and Eskilstuna which have a higher share than expected.

An argument for looking at non-Western-born population is that it can expected that the non-Western-born population differ more explicitly from the Swedish-born population than the Western-born population in regard to, for example, culture. A high share of non-Westerns should therefore indicate a high level of tolerance. To avoid only looking at non-Westerns, Hansen (2007) also used an Openness 2 Index measuring the share of all foreign-born people, including people of a Western as well as a non-Western origin. One particular reason for looking at all foreign-born populations is that refugees given asylum and residence permits are to some extent located due to political actions rather than their own choices. Thereby, the Openness 1 Index may be influenced by the placement of the foreign-born persons at the time of entering the country rather than their own original choice. The potential impact of such, however, can be considered to be low, since the refugees given asylum will first register in the statistics when they are given citizen rights and thereby can move and locate freely and independently from where refugee camps are located.

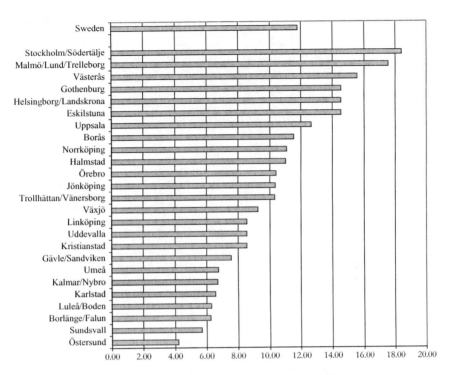

Figure 4.2 Openness 2 (2002) share of people of non-Swedish origin

Figure 4.2 is close to the pattern of Figure 4.1. The large city regions are at the top together with a few of the smaller regions that have a relatively large foreign-born population, due to the fact that factories experienced a shortage of labour and therefore engaged guest workers in the 1960s and 1970s.

There is, however, more to tolerance than a high share of a foreign-born population. Measuring tolerance as the share of foreign-born population is fairly problematic. High concentrations of a foreign-born population can lead to segregation. Therefore, the next step is to introduce a third index, the Integration Index, based on the relation between the share of foreign-born people in the population and the share of employed foreign-born people of all employed people. By putting the two variables in relation to each other, we obtain an indication of the degree to which the foreign-born population is integrated into the labour market. This helps to present a nuanced picture of the interaction between the foreign- and the domestic-born populations, and, hence, an indication of integration.

The following two figures investigate tolerance understood as integration in the labour market. We believe that tolerant regions are successful in integrating foreign-born people into the labour market, while a less tolerant environment will have a lower employment rate among foreign-born people.

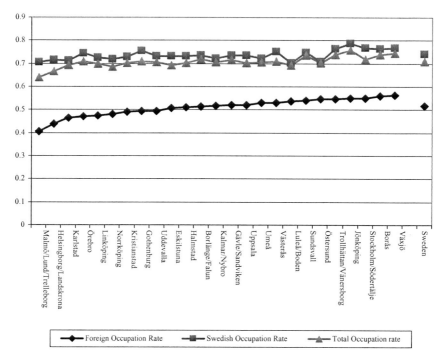

Figure 4.3 Occupation rate for Swedish-born and all foreign-born populations (aged 18–64), 2002

Three curves are plotted in Figure 4.3. The upper curve illustrates the occupation rate among the Swedish-born population. The curve in the middle indicates the occupation rate in total, and, finally, the lower curve represents the occupation rate among the foreign-born population. An equal divide would mean that the upper and the lower curves should lie on the same values – the middle curve. Figure 4.3 reflects differences between the occupation rates for the ethnic Swedes and 'non-ethnic' Swedes. The ethnic Swedes have a higher rate of participation in the labour market in all the regions, and the gap between the foreign occupation curve and the Swedish population curve is significant in all regions.

In general, Figure 4.3 indicates a weak trend between the total occupation rate and the foreign occupation trend. The higher the occupation rate, the higher the foreign occupation rate.

It is noteworthy that both the Malmö/Lund/Trelleborg and Helsingborg/Landskrona regions have significantly low occupational rates for the foreign-born population. These two regions are located in Scandia and both serve as entry points to Denmark and Europe. Hence, trans-border commuting has been controlled for. Adding Swedish-born and non-Swedish-born people living in the two regions but working in Denmark only incurs very limited changes. Malmö/Lund/Trelleborg still come out last with a notably low occupational rate for the foreign-born population. Only Helsingborg/Landskrona marginally climb one position up, switching position with Karlstad. Accordingly, while adding the cross-border commuters helps Helsingborg/Landskrona one position up, it does not hide the fact that the two largest Scandia urban areas have low labour market participation rates for the foreign-born population.[4]

At the other end of Figure 4.3, Sundsvall, Östersund, Trollhättan/Vänersborg, Jönköping, Stockholm/Södertälje, Borås and Växjö all have occupational rates for foreign-born of a similar level. With the exception of Östersund, all the seven regions have high occupation rates in general, and this may of course be an important factor in explaining the higher foreign occupational rates in these regions. A high occupational rate in general typically results in a higher participation rate on the labour market for weaker social groups. Hence, regions that experience strong economic development will be more tolerant, or to put it simply: demand for all types of labour increases with the economic performance of a region.

Östersund, however, has a low employment rate in general and still a high participation rate for foreign-born people on the labour market. This is one reason why employment rates have to be seen in relation to each other. This is done in the Integration Index (Figure 4.4). If a total match between the Swedish-born and

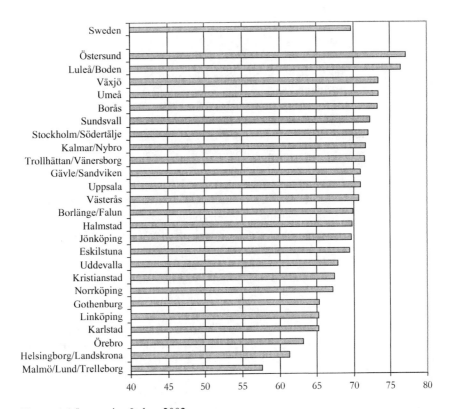

Figure 4.4 Integration Index, 2002

the foreign-born occupation rate were present, the Integration Index would have a value of 100. Consequently, the smaller the gap is between the two occupation rates, the higher the score becomes in the index.

The index shows that Malmö/Lund/Trelleborg and Helsingborg/Landskrona still obtain the least favourable scores and that Karlstad and Örebro have switched places compared to Figure 4.3. Again Malmö/Lund/Trelleborg and Helsingborg/ Landskrona have been controlled for cross-border commuting. Malmö/Lund/ Trelleborg still come out last while Helsingborg/Landskrona again climb up one position, switching with Örebro, but with a value closer to Karlstad, Linköping and Gothenburg than to Örebro. The top of the list shows the regions that are, relatively, best at integrating the foreign-born labour force into the labour market. Östersund and Luleå/Boden come out with good scores. Relating these findings to the findings in Figure 4.3, it is evident that both Östersund and Luleå/Boden have considerably lower occupation rates than many of the other regions. Figure 4.3 showed a tendency towards a higher integration of foreign-born people into the labour market as the employment rate rose. Östersund and Luleå/Boden reflect a different image. Östersund and Luleå/Boden only have the 18th and the 22nd positions respectively, the best employment rates among the 25 regions presented here. Four of the ten best performing regions on the Integration Index are ranking below the ten best performing regions on employment rates. This might imply that different parameters from employment rates play an important role in the integration of foreign-born population into the labour market.

However, there is one striking feature; 7 of the 10 regions with best integration scores perform poorly on the Openness 2 Index, which indicates that higher shares of foreign-born population in most cases lead to a tendency to have lower scores on the Integration Index. Stockholm is an outstanding exception. The combination of a high level of foreign-born population and a high level of integration on the labour market seen in Stockholm proves that successful integration on the labour market cannot only be narrowed down to a discussion on the share of foreign-born people.

When analysing some of the regions that have high and low scores, it turns out that Östersund has a high level of education among Western-born foreigners and that Luleå/Boden has a good educational level among the foreign-born in general. Naturally, this can be one of the explanations why the two regions experience such a high score on the Integration Index; but the educational level may also be the result of better integration of foreigners into the labour market. Linköping, however, also has a relatively high educational level among the foreign Western-born population in jobs, but Linköping has a low score on the Integration Index. Therefore the educational level among the foreign-born population does not result in a high integration score alone. Stockholm/Södertälje, Gothenburg, Malmö/Lund/ Trelleborg and Helsingborg/Landskrona all reflect relatively small differences between the educational level among the Swedish and the foreign-born population in jpbs. Additionally, looking at the relative difference between the educational level of the Swedish-born and the foreign-born population shows that no systematic patterns of better integration are evident where the educational level is higher.

In general, the non-Western foreign-born population has a lower level of education, whereas the Western foreign-born population, in general, has a slightly higher level of education. This does not, however, really influence the employment rate in general. Actually, Stockholm comes out well on the Integration Index, but has the largest gap in percentage points between the non-Western foreign-born population and the Swedish population. Again this produces a very muddy picture of possible patterns between origin, employment rate and educational level. Hence, explanations of the participation level of the foreign-born population in the labour market can be linked to some kind of tolerance indication – stating that the higher score a region obtains on the Integration Index, the more tolerant the region is.

The Integration Index seems sensitive to the share of foreigners in the population. This can be an argument for using the Openness Indexes as well as the Integration Index – and the Bohemian Index – to indicate tolerance. Östersund and Luleå/Boden and Malmö/Lund/Trelleborg are extremes by being at the top of one and last in another index. However, additionally when combining Openness and Integration, it is notable that Stockholm is first on the Openness 1 and 2 Indexes but comes out 7th in the Integration Index with a significantly better score than Malmö/Lund/Trelleborg or Gothenburg. The same holds for e.g. Växjö, Borås and Västerås which all obtain good scores in all three indexes. To us, this indicates a higher tolerance level in these regions compared to Malmö/Lund/Trelleborg, Gothenburg and Helsingborg/Landskrona.

To sum up, when the Openness parameter is examined, primarily the large regions achieve good scores. However, if the openness measure is problematised by introducing the Integration Index, a more differentiated picture occurs, where the connection between population and rank on the index is less evident; the large regions are no longer at the top, and the small regions are no longer at the bottom.

Location context and theory

The theory of the creative class has been very influential since it was presented in the early 2000s. Advocates of this approach to regional development have been extremely successful in selling their thoughts and ideas to policy-makers and planners across the globe. Sweden is no exception in this respect. Here the ideas have been implemented in regional development plans both in large and smaller communities. One reason for this is that Sweden has been highlighted as one of the best examples of how powerful the theory can be (e.g. Florida and Tinagli, 2004; Mellander and Florida, 2007).

However, in this chapter, central assumptions in the theory have been challenged. Based on previously published material, some of the basic dynamics of the theory have been discussed with the aim of highlighting the role of context for a model like the creative class. The studies presented in this chapter show that mobility on the labour market is less pronounced in Sweden compared to the studies done in North America. This is crucial in regard to how effective the implementation of the model is. Also stressed in this chapter is that the welfare system, women's participation in the labour market and the nature of the regional hierarchy all play important roles with regard to the effect that regional strategies based on Florida's theory will have.

Moreover, this chapter has presented a modified measurement of the proxies normally used in Florida-inspired studies. By looking at the differences in the employment rates among ethnic Swedes compared to the foreign-born population, an index has been developed in order to present the complete measurement differences in the tolerance level of regions. In the presented form, the Integration Index is a supplement to openness and is thought of as a way to balance out the risk of running ghettoisation effects rather than tolerance, openness and inclusiveness.

Finally, the empirical material used in this chapter was produced before the economic crisis that started in 2007. Data comes from a period where Sweden was heading towards high growth. Although Sweden has been one Europe's most successful countries in dealing with the economic crisis, the crisis has had an impact on the supply of jobs. Some regions, especially the less urban and the ones that are characterised by traditional manufacturing, have been suffering job loss, lack of investments and finding the creative and highly skilled labour are moving out. In light of the rising unemployment that occurred especially during the first years of the crisis, it can be expected that migration for jobs has been even more important compared to amenity-based migration. This just emphasises that jobs are a highly important factor in migration in Sweden. If the data were more recent, it is expected that the data would show the same patterns. One distinction would be that the differences between the regions that have high shares of human capital and creative people and the regions that have lower shares have increased. That is at least a pattern that can be seen in Denmark where knowledge production is centralising in the main urban areas (Hansen and Winther, 2012) and this is a process that is most likely to happen in Sweden as well. Moreover, it can be expected that the regions that were heavily dominated by traditional manufacturing in the early 2000s would have had a harder time during the crisis. This is due to the fact that the crisis has increased the speed of industrial transformation of the Swedish economy towards a more knowledge- and service-based economy.

Summing up, this chapter has pointed out problems with the current theory of regional development based on the creative class. It has been argued that context has to be taken into consideration: something that is also evident from studies based on data from Sweden. Moreover, this chapter has indicated areas where the established theory can be developed and has pinpointed some of the pitfalls that should be avoided. Based on the findings by Andersen *et al.* (2010b), Hansen (2007) and others, Florida's theories of a creative class propelling regional growth fit well in the case of Sweden. This work suggests that the theory is more applicable to the larger regions, as the smaller regions are less sensitive to change based on the concentration of the creative class or a tolerant environment. Thus, the lesson from this chapter has to be that before praising the theory of the creative class – or most other theories, for that sake – one needs to do some basic studies on the context and thereby enable adjustment for causal relations that might be true in some contextual settings while not in others.

Notes

1 The knowledge base approach suggests that knowledge can be divided into three groups: synthetic, analytic and symbolic. Synthetic knowledge is engineer-based and more tacit than codified and based on know-how. Analytical knowledge is science-based and characterised by codified knowledge and know-why, and finally the symbolic knowledge base is art-based and characterised by tacit knowledge and know-who.
2 The unit used is labour market regions (A-regioner). Sweden consists of 70 A-regioner which are defined based on dominant travel to work patterns.
3 *Non-Western*: Africa, Asia, South America. *Western*: Sweden, Nordic Countries without Sweden, EU25 without Denmark and Finland, North America (including Mexico), Oceania (unknown and stateless are left out).
4 Only trans-border commuter data from Scandia to Sealand in Denmark was available. Trans-border commuting can also be relevant for some of the regions located along the Norwegian and the Finnish borders as well as for the Stockholm/Södertälje region. Therefore, we have decided not to add the commuting data from Malmö/Lund/Trelleborg and Helsingborg/Landskrona to the graphic figures.

Bibliography

Adamson, D. W., Clark, D. E. and Partridge, M. D. (2004) 'Do urban agglomeration effects and household amenities have a skill bias?', *Journal of Regional Science*, 44: 201–223.

Andersen, K. V., Bugge, M. M., Hansen, H. K., Isaksen, A. and Raunio, M. (2010a) 'One size fits all? Applying the creative class thesis onto a Nordic context', *European Planning Studies*, 18: 1591–1609.

Andersen, K. V., Hansen, H. K., Isaksen, A. and Raunio, M. (2010b) 'Nordic city regions in the creative class debate: Putting the creative class thesis to a test', *Industry & Innovation*, 17: 215–240.

Asheim, B. T. (2009) 'Guest editorial: Introduction to the creative class in European city region', *Economic Geography*, 85: 355–362.

Asheim, B. T. and Hansen, H. K. (2009) 'Knowledge bases, talents and contexts: On the usefulness of the creative class approach in Sweden', *Economic Geography*, 85: 425–442.

Boschma, R. and Fritsch, M., (2009) 'Creative class and regional growth: Empirical evidence from seven European countries', *Economic Geography*, 85: 391–423.

Chen, Y. and Rosenthal, S. S. (2008) 'Local amenities and life-cycle migration: Do people move for jobs or fun?', *Journal of Urban Economics*, 64: 519–537.

Clifton, N., Cooke, P. and Hansen, H. K. (forthcoming) 'Towards a reconciliation of the "context-less" with the "space-less"? The creative class across varieties of capitalism: New evidence from Sweden and the UK', *Regional Studies*.

Florida, R. (2002) *The Rise of the Creative Class: and How It's Transforming Work, Leisure, Community, and Everyday Life*, New York: Basic Books.

Florida, R. and Tinagli, I. (2004) *Europe in the Creative Age*, London: Demos.

Glaeser, E. L. (2004) 'Book review of Richard Florida's "The Rise of the Creative Class"', available at: http://post.economics.harvard.edu/faculty/glaeser/papers/Review_Florida. pdf (accessed 9 November 2012).

Glaeser, E. L. (2005) 'Smart growth: Education, skilled workers, and the future of cold-weather cities', *Policy Briefs*, PB-2005-1, Rappaport Institute for Greater Boston and Taubman Center for State and Local Government, Harvard University.

Hall, P. and Soskice, D. (eds) (2001) *Varieties of Capitalism: The Institutional Foundations of Comparative Advantage*, Oxford: Oxford University Press.

Hansen, H. K. (2007) 'Technology, talent and tolerance: The geography of the creative class in Sweden', *Rapporter och Notiser* 169, Department of Social and Economic Geography, Lund University.

Hansen, H. K. and Niedomysl, T. (2009) 'Migration of the creative class: Evidence from Sweden', *Journal of Economic Geography*, 9: 191–206.

Hansen, H. K. and Winther, L. (2010) 'The spatial division of talent in city regions: Location dynamics of business services in Copenhagen', *Tijdschrift voor Economische en Sociale Geografie*, 101: 55–72.

Hansen, H. K. and Winther, L. (2012) 'On a road to nowhere: A comment on amenities and urban and regional development', in B. van Heur and A. Lorentzen (eds), *Cultural Political Economy of Small Cities*, London: Routledge.

Mellander, C. and Florida, R. (2007) 'The creative class or human capital? Explaining regional development in Sweden', *CESIS Electronic Working Paper Series*, Paper No. 79, available at: www.infra.kth.se/cesis/documents/WP79.pdf (accessed 29 August 2013).

Niedomysl, T. and Hansen, H. K. (2010) 'What matters more for the decision to migrate: Jobs versus amenities', *Environment and Planning A*, 42: 1636–1649.

Putnam, R. (1993) *Making Democracy Work: Civic Traditions in Modern Italy*, Princeton, NJ: Princeton University Press.

Putnam, R. (2000) *Bowling Alone: The Collapse and Revival of American Community*, New York: Simon & Schuster.

Rappaport, J. (2009) 'The increasing importance of quality of life', *Journal of Economic Geography*, 9: 779–804.

Roback, J. (1982) 'Wages, rents, and the quality of life', *Journal of Political Economy*, 90: 1257–1278.

Sjaastad, L.A. (1962) 'The costs and returns of human migration', *The Journal of Political Economy*, 70: 80–93.

Statistics Sweden ([2005] 2007) 'Extract from the public accessible database of Statistics Sweden', available at: http://www.ssd.scb.se/databaser/makro/Visavar.asp?yp=tansss&xu=C9233001&huvudtabell=YREG1&deltabell=K1&deltabellnamn=The+population+16%2B+years+by+municipality%2C+employment+status+%28gainfully+employed+population%29%2C+age+and+sex%2E+Year&omradekod=AM&omradetext=Labour+market&preskat=O&innehall=Befolkningen&starttid=2001&stopptid=2007&Prodid=AM0208&fromSok=&Fromwhere=S&lang=2&langdb=2 (accessed 29 August 2013).

Storper, M. and Scott, A. J. (2009) 'Rethinking human capital, creativity and urban growth', *Journal of Economic Geography*, 9: 147–167.

US Census Bureau ([2000] 2007) *Profile of General Demographic Characteristics: 2000*, Washington, DC: US Census Bureau, available at: http://censtats.census.gov/data/US/01000.pdf (accessed 29 August 2013).

Wojan, T. R., Lambert, D. M. and McGranahan, D. A. (2007) 'Emoting with their feet: Bohemian attraction to creative milieu', *Journal of Economic Geography*, 7: 711–736.

5   Different creative cities*

Exploring Danish data to adapt the creative class argument to small welfare economies

Kristina Vaarst Andersen and Mark Lorenzen

Introduction

During the last two decades, research on how individual creativity, skill and talent relates to innovation-based competitiveness and economic growth has boomed. The theory on the *creative class* by Richard Florida and associates (Florida, 2002a; 2002b; 2002c; 2005a; 2005b) is one of the most influential discourses in this field (e.g. Montgomery, 2005; Boyle, 2006; Raush and Negry, 2006; Weick and Martin, 2006; Andersen and Lorenzen, 2009; Lorenzen and Andersen, 2009; Andersen *et al.*, 2010). The reason is, arguably, that the creative class theory manages to combine relatively uncontroversial insights from sociology, psychology and labour market studies with economic geography and urban planning, amounting into claims that are able to attract attention – and controversy (e.g. Malanga, 2004; Glaeser, 2005; Peck, 2005; Scott, 2006).

Simplified, Florida argues that in a globalized economy where innovation constitutes competitive advantage, it is possible to identify a segment in the labour force that is particularly important because it is engaged with innovating through applying technical, social and/or artistic creativity. This 'creative class' has particular preferences for amenities such as high-quality housing, work empowerment and specialized consumption. While the creative class shares these preferences with highly educated labour, Florida is able to demonstrate empirically that the creative class has a more unique trait: it prefers to locate in cities with particular high levels of cultural services, ethnic diversity and tolerance towards non-mainstream lifestyles. Florida further claims that as a result of this preference-driven pattern of location of the creative class, diverse and ethnically and culturally rich cities prosper economically, as innovation-intensive firms pursue the creative workers to these cities.

The creative class theory attracts notable policy attention, and policy-makers across Europe and Asia have a tendency to apply remarkably similar policies in order to stimulate creativity and attract the creative class. However, the theory is based on

* This chapter was previously published as: Lorenzen, M. and Vaarst Andersen, K. (2012) 'Different creative cities: exploring Danish data to adopt the creative class argument to small welfare economies', *Creative Industries Journal*, 4(2): 123–136.

empirical studies of United States and subsequently Canada. This North American context is characterized by big, highly mobile, populations, large-scale cities, vast geographical spaces and liberal market economies (Hall and Soskice, 2001). Hence, while we might accept as generally valid the theory's general foundation (the role of individual creativity for economic growth), its more particular claims about the location preferences of creatives and geographical distribution of growth may not apply to small countries with small populations, low mobility and coordinated, welfare-based market economies. For example, in welfare states, creatives may have other location preferences than cultural services and tolerance, or such factors may be more evenly distributed across cities. Small distances and/or well-functioning public transport systems may also distribute creatives more evenly across geographical space than was the case for North America. If small welfare economies are indeed different, policies carbon-copied from the North American experience are likely to be insignificant, or even harmful, to economic development elsewhere.

In this chapter, we investigate whether and how the creative class theory should be adapted to small welfare economies, by way of a study of a small European country with a population of only 5.5 million, short geographical distances, a well-developed infrastructure and a universal welfare state: Denmark. First, we test Florida's central theses in the Danish context, and find that policy-makers need to recognize that in small welfare economies, cities that attract creatives may be very different. Second, we use qualitative interviews to build theory elements that go beyond those of Florida's. We suggest that different creative cities are faced with fundamentally different policy challenges.

The creative class theory is in an intermediate state of development, and as is suitable for testing and adding to such theory, we applied a mixed-method approach (Creswell, 2002). In econometric analyses of large-scale register data, we analysed the composition and location of the creative class in Denmark, and correlated the growth and place qualities of Danish cities with their presence of the creative class. Subsequently, we used qualitative interviews to explore causalities. In the econometric exercise, the chosen geographical analytical unit was municipalities. We then followed all Florida's technical definitions (2002b; 2002c) and approximated the creative class using Statistics Denmark's labour market database. Florida defines the creative class as three types of job functions: *Bohemian*, entailing artistic forms of creativity (e.g. artists, designers and writers); *creative core* functions, entailing mostly technical creativity (e.g. researchers, engineers and doctors); and *creative professional* functions, entailing creativity in a generic and managerial sense (e.g. managers, finance people and lawyers). In the theory, the creative core has the highest skill levels and accounts for most of the innovation created by the creative class. However, even if the bohemians are relatively few and account for only a modest part of the creative class's contribution to economic growth, according to Florida, this has the most specialized preferences and is pioneering the preferences of the creative class in general. Aspects of the preferences of the bohemians disseminate to the rest of the creative class, stimulating its 'bourgeoisie-bohemian' ethos (Brooks, 2001). In the qualitative part of our study, we carried out a total of 92 interviews in nine cities: the national and regional centres (Copenhagen, Aarhus, Odense and Aalborg), cities with a large share of the creative class compared to the size of their populations (Svendborg, Sønderborg, Ærø and Fanø), and one city with a small share of the creative class compared to the size of its population (Esbjerg). The interviews were done on-site, used a semi-structured interview protocol and were subsequently transcribed/summarized. We asked politicians, public servants and local business managers of knowledge-intensive companies about the economic and political impact of the creative class. Furthermore, group interviews with members of the creative class explored their location preferences and lifestyle choices.

The remainder of the chapter is structured as follows. The next section briefly describes the characteristics and geographical distribution of the Danish creative class. The following sections test the applicability to Denmark of Florida's theses that the creative class propels technology-based economic growth (third section) and that the creative class is attracted to cities with particular service offer and tolerance to particular lifestyles (fourth section). In the sections, we also present qualitative evidence that is used for subsequent theory building: The fifth section identifies and discusses policy challenges for four stylized Danish creative city types.

The Danish creative class

The creative class constituted 25 per cent of the Danish labour force in 2004, but as this figure did not include freelancers or self-employed, the creative class may realistically comprise a third of the Danish workforce. The creative professionals is the largest group, constituting approximately two-thirds, with the creative core making up one-third (bohemians is a very small subgroup of a few per cent). Being knowledge workers, the creative class has a high average education: 44 per cent have completed a higher education of three or more years, as compared to 22 per cent for the population in general.

It is worth noting the cultural consumption patterns of the Danish creative class. While Florida suggested that the creative class in North America is attracted to cities with high cultural opportunities, his work did not engage in much detail. This issue has been addressed in the Danish context (Andersen and Lorenzen, 2009; Bille, 2010). The Danish creative class consumes culture differently than the rest of the labour force: It is more culturally active, attends more pop and rock concerts and visit art exhibitions and art museums, city landscapes and cultural sites more often. In short, the creative class is a major consumer of urban cultural activities that tend to be consumed in an individual and flexible manner.

In Florida's North American findings, the larger the population of a city, the larger its attraction of the creative class (Florida, 2002a; 2002c). A survey of European cities has confirmed this size dynamics: Cities below a certain population size have too small labour markets and markets for services to attract the creative class (Lorenzen and Andersen, 2009). This size effect could, with some variation, be traced in Denmark. Copenhagen is the only Danish city with a population of more than a million, and Aarhus, the second largest city, has a population

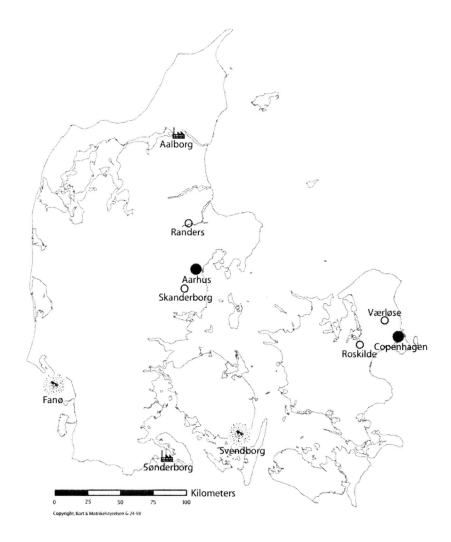

Notes: □□□= Hub; O = Satellite; 🏭 = Cluster; ☀ = Quaint

Figure 5.1 Examples of Danish cities with high creative class presence

For elaboration of the different city types, see the later section 'Different creative cities'.

of a mere 300,000. Nevertheless, we found that the Danish creative class did agglomerate in these two national centres, measured both by absolute figures and share of the labour market. After Aarhus, the size effect seemed to taper off – the third largest Danish city, Odense, did not attract the third largest share of the creative class, and many larger provincial cities had low shares of the creative class, even if several of these cities had good infrastructures and universities. Surprisingly,

Table 5.1 Correlation of presence of creative class and economic growth

Indicator of economic growth	Correlation with presence of creative class
Prosperity: Share of inhabitants with incomes above the Danish mean	$p = 0.537$***
Technology intensity: Share of employees working in high-tech industries	$p = 0.315$***
Industrial activity: Number of employers (private as public) per 1,000 inhabitants	$p = 0.043$***

Note: *** Denotes significance level = 0.01.

a range of smaller cities attracted higher shares of the creative class than their population size would suggest. Some of these (e.g. Roskilde, Randers, Værløse and Skanderborg) were cities in relative proximity to Copenhagen or Aarhus, but others (e.g. Sønderborg, Aalborg, Svendborg and Fanø) were located far away from the national centres. The above examples of cities with a high presence of the creative class are shown in Figure 5.1.

The Danish creative class and economic growth

Florida proposes that the creative class boosts city prosperity because creative knowledge workers start and attract high-technology and high-growth companies (2002c). In order to test this proposition, we measured the economic impact of the creative class on Danish cities by correlating the cities' presence of the creative class (measured by its share of the local labour force) with different statistical indicators – one of prosperity, one of the technology intensity of local industry and one of the activity level of local industry (see Table 5.1). We found that in 2004, the presence of the creative class in these cities correlated significantly and strongly with prosperity, and moderately with technological intensity. However, the correlation between the presence of the creative class in the cities and industrial activity was very weak.

This result with only partial support for Florida's proposition reflects a measurement problem for which earlier empirical work on the North American creative class has also been criticized. While we may reasonably assume that the creative class, being mobile and career-seeking, is attracted to prosperous, high-tech cities with highly active industries and ample employment opportunities, Florida suggests that the creative class also reinforces, or may even kick off, growth. But a statistical correlation between the presence of the creative class and various indicators of prosperity, technology and industrial activity cannot elucidate the causalities at play (Malanga, 2004). Having rich statistical data at our disposal, we therefore addressed this problem by using time series: we correlated the cities' presence of the creative class in the year 1996 with how the other statistical indicators developed in the subsequent eight-year period (see Table 5.2). This statistical exercise provided strong support for Florida's proposition. We found that the Danish cities' creative class in 1996 correlated significantly and

Table 5.2 Correlation of the presence of the creative class and economic growth in subsequent eight years

Indicator of economic growth, 1996–2004	Correlation with presence of creative class, 1996
Prosperity: Share of inhabitants with incomes above the Danish mean	$p = 0.624***$
Technology intensity: Share of employees working in high-tech industries	$p = 0.293***$
Industrial activity: Number of employers (private as opposed to public) per 1,000 inhabitants	$p = 0.243***$

Note: *** Denotes significance level = 0.01.

strongly with subsequent prosperity growth, moderately with technological intensity growth and moderately with industrial activity growth. Hence, the cities that have managed to attract a strong presence of the creative class are more likely to experience subsequent start-ups of new companies, many of which are in high-tech industries, and a general rise in income levels.

Our qualitative interviews lent insights into the causalities at play. The interviewed managers of Danish knowledge-intensive companies pointed out that, given that they increasingly outsource routine work, the ability of these companies to attract knowledge workers is central to competitiveness, and at the time of the interviews, all managers reported that their companies regularly had to decline orders because they were unable to hire the necessary workers. Such problems were particularly prominent for technically creative workers and for workers with a cross-disciplinary skill set, such as engineers with project management experience, artistic creatives with a financial expertise or creative professionals with specialized technical skills. By far, shortages of creatives were most severe in cities with small shares of the creative class. One interviewed manager mentioned that in order to avoid losing creatives, his company had shifted its R&D department away from such a city.

Services, tolerance and the Danish creative class

A second important element in Florida's theory is the proposition that the creative class is attracted by soft city qualities, such as (primarily cultural) service offer and tolerance to diverse (foreign, as well as bourgeoisie-bohemian) lifestyles (2002c). In order to test this proposition, we correlated two indicators of Danish cities' service offer and three indicators of their tolerance with the development of their creative class (see Table 5.3). These correlations were all significant, but none of them were strong. Concerning service offer, we found that cities' cultural opportunities, and public generic service levels, both in 1996, correlated weakly with their growth in the creative class in the subsequent eight-year period. Concerning tolerance, cities' presence of foreign nationals, as well as social inclusion of non-Western immigrants, both

Table 5.3 Correlation of growth of creative class, service, and tolerance

Indicator of service and tolerance, 1996	Correlation with growth of creative class, 1996–2004
Cultural opportunities: Number of employees in restaurants, bars, nightclubs and other entertainment, sport, libraries, museums and other recreational and cultural activities	$p = 0.037***$
Public generic service level: Number of public teachers, health workers and social workers per 1,000 inhabitants	$p = 0.099***$
Presence of foreign nationals: Share of inhabitants born outside Denmark	$p = 0.129***$
Social inclusion of non-Western immigrants: Employment rate of inhabitants born outside Scandinavia, the European Union, United States, Canada, Australia and New Zealand.	$p = 0.102***$
Share of bohemians in the labour force	$p = 0.316***$

Note: *** Denotes significance level = 0.01. In the last correlation, we excluded bohemians from the creative class.

correlated weakly with their subsequent growth in the creative class, while the correlation between cities' share of bohemians in the labour force and subsequent growth in the creative class was moderate.

Although these correlations were moderate or weak, their high significance lent moderate support for Florida's proposition for Denmark, although it is noteworthy that cultural opportunities seemed to matter so little for Danish cities' ability to attract creatives. Our qualitative interviews with members of the Danish creative class allowed us to explain these statistical findings. The considerations of the interviewees suggested that soft attractors were always balanced with hard ones. One example was housing prices: since particularly younger creatives were unwilling to compromise on the quality of housing, but at the same time were unable to afford the expensive and desirable properties in the major cities, they increasingly needed to locate elsewhere. Living in the countryside meant longer commuting to work, but this was often offset by locating close to family, facilitating babysitting for young career-oriented couples. A second example was job opportunities: Career options remained a key variable for the choice of location. While the major cities generally offered better opportunities, a handful of smaller cities that had developed world-class, specialized high-tech firms, offered competitive, even better, career options for particular creative job functions, typically engineers.

Concerning soft factors, interviews suggested that cultural opportunities did matter to the location decisions of the creative class, but not always those opportunities that can be measured statistically. Interviewees highlighted the ambience of a city as vital, particularly beautiful cityscapes, authentic architecture, intimate squares, greenery and proximity to the sea. A sense of social inclusion was also often stressed as very attractive, and several other interviewees said that their preferred cultural activities, in addition to larger events such as concerts and plays, encompassed local community activities. One interviewee mentioned Singapore as an example of a city that, if he should move abroad, would be too 'hardcore' to live in, due to what he felt would be lack of civic participation and inclusion and sense of community, but also a too highly paced lifestyle. The pace of life, and having free time for family and leisure, were stressed by several of the interviewed creatives. Many pointed to Copenhagen as a work environment with an unattractive work/life balance, particularly for those employed in the larger companies. The greater distance between amenities and services in the major cities were mentioned as unattractive. For example, parents among our interviewees emphasized that not just the abundance but also the quality of public generic services such as education and child care were important, and short transport times were a key factor in this respect.

Different creative cities: hubs, satellites, clusters and quaint

Denmark is a small country with rich national statistics, and this allowed us to analyse the geographical distribution of the creative class in more depth than was possible for earlier research on North America. Most notably, we were able to look closely at differences in the ways different Danish cities attract the creative class. In the sections above, we confirmed the Danish version of a general trend: the creative class is attracted to the opportunities offered in larger cities – in Denmark, particularly Copenhagen and Aarhus. However, we were also able to identify factors that attract the creative class to other and smaller cities, such as cheaper housing, higher-quality and more accessible generic public services, specialized job offers and more attractive work/life balance, as well as cultural opportunities that are hard to measure statistically, such as authenticity, greenery and a sense of community. Consequently, Aarhus and Copenhagen, while remaining firmly in place as the first and second most popular choice for the creative class, do not have monopoly on attracting creatives.

In this section, we seek to synthesize these insights into four stylized creative city types that, in fundamentally different ways, are able to attract the creative class. They are listed in Table 5.4. The Danish examples in Table 5.3 were mapped onto Figure 5.1 above.

In the following, we discuss these creative city types in greater detail, and touch upon some of their policy challenges.

Hubs

Cities with populations with more than 500,000 are well connected to global infrastructures and transportation systems, and as they often sport a whole gamut of different industrial clusters and knowledge institutions (e.g. universities), they are simultaneously specialized and diverse (Lorenzen and Frederiksen, 2008).

Table 5.4 Different creative cities

Type	Danish example
Hubs	
Large national centres, competing (globally) on attracting the creative class on account of their size and diversity	Copenhagen Aarhus
Satellites	
Medium-sized satellite cities and small commuter towns around the major cities, offering lower living costs in combination with access to the major cities' specialized service offers and occasionally their labour markets	Roskilde, Randers, Værløse, Skanderborg
Clusters	
Medium-sized cities with industrial cluster(s) offering specialized career options outside the major cities' catchment area	Sønderborg, Aalborg
Quaint	
Small towns with peculiar qualities of place, such as natural beauty, authentic architecture or a thriving local community	Svendborg, Fanø

This means that they are in a 'size game' when attracting the creative class: in major cities, the number of jobs, specialized services and cultural opportunities does not merely grow proportionally with population numbers, they grow exponentially, in a self-reinforcing manner (Lorenzen and Andersen, 2009). Because the Hubs hence possess more of the city qualities the creative class looks for, they also have a disproportionate share of the creative class.

This attractiveness, however, is constantly in danger of eroding through congestion. Hubs may struggle with issues of overpopulation, traffic jams, pollution and pressure on public generic services such as daycare, elder care and healthcare. Furthermore, the global competition for creatives between similar metropolises is growing. This combination of issues constitutes a policy challenge: Hubs need to play the 'size game' without becoming too congested. Across North America and Western Europe, large-scale public investments in infrastructure and environmental improvements are now routinely part of policies to attract the global creative class. However, epic in scope, these policies often fail to also address equally important yet less conspicuous issues in retaining the creative class: public generic services such as healthcare, childcare and elder care, issues where Hubs often fall behind.

In Denmark, the only two cities that play the 'size game' (ibid.) are Copenhagen and Aarhus, and with their unique size and offer of specialized services and jobs, these two cities assert a particular pull on the Danish creative class. Copenhagen and Aarhus are also the only Danish cities big enough to compete globally for international investments as well as the global creative class – the majority of which lives in Copenhagen. When compared to its European neighbours such as London, Paris and Hamburg, Copenhagen is surprisingly competitive, despite its comparatively modest size and cultural homogeneity. The lack of ethnic diversity is offset by the city's other qualities, such as efficient transport infrastructure, good housing and attractive design and architecture. However, without continuous investments in avoiding congestion, architectural uniformity and excessive gentrification, Copenhagen's attractiveness to the creative class may be eroded. Our study of the Danish creative class suggested that already today, the risk of congestion and the erosion of generic public services compared to provincial towns adversely affect the attractiveness of Copenhagen and Aarhus to some members of the Danish creative class.

Satellites

Our study of the Danish creative class indicated that small cities, even those with few jobs or evident city qualities, may attract high shares of the creative class if they are geographically near Hubs. Such small Satellites' limited diversity and specialized services are offset by them being within the Hub's catchment area. Some Satellites may offer some jobs and a (limited) range of generic public services, relying on the proximate Hub for more specialized services (Christäller, 1933). This is the case for some provincial towns that lie near national hubs, such as Newark near New York or Luton near London. Other Satellites are pure commuter towns relying on Hubs for both specialized services and jobs. While depending on Hubs, Satellites compete directly with these for creative class residents. Their attractiveness stems from a combination of easy accessibility to the Hub and lower house prices and cheaper or better public generic services targeting commuters, such as schools and day care institutions.

As the attractiveness of Satellites hinges upon competitive prices and the quality of housing and generic services, the greatest political challenges of such cities are, naturally, price hikes and erosion of service provisions. The inflow of high-income creatives to such cities may boost property prices, and it may tempt policy-makers to increase tax levels and prices of generic public services. However, as Satellites possess no unique city qualities of their own, erosion of their price and generic services advantage would make them very vulnerable to losing creatives to newer commuter towns elsewhere.

In the Danish Copenhagen and Aarhus regions, only the part of the creative class with high purchase power (the creative core, such as doctors and scientists), or those with low expectations of living standards (the bohemians, such as artists) live in Copenhagen or Aarhus cities proper, while the rest of the creative class tends to cluster in small provincial towns (such as Roskilde or Randers) or commuter towns (such as Værløse and Skanderborg) around the central Hubs. In the Copenhagen region, the affluent creatives congregate in the exclusive northern suburbs, while the lower-paid creatives are more likely to live in southern suburbs. But even if the quality of housing in these areas is not comparable, they both sport green spaces, forests and the seaside, as well as good day care and schools.

Clusters

In Denmark as well as elsewhere, specialized economic activity in the guise of industrial clusters plays an increasing role for economic growth (Martin and Sunley, 2003). Many such industrial clusters, particularly those dependent upon international investments, leading universities, or urban project ecologies (Grabher, 2002), are located in Hubs, but others continue to grow in provincial towns or 'new industrial spaces' (Scott, 1988). As industrial clusters offer employment opportunities in highly specialized fields, they exert a pull on some types of creatives. Consequently, a number of relatively small cities that are not near any Hub, but sport an industrial cluster, are able to develop relatively high shares of the creative class.

The policy challenge for such Clusters is twofold. First, an industrial cluster's job offer is highly specialized, and that means that it attracts only certain types of creatives, for example, particular specialties of engineers who are single and in early stages of their career and hence willing to compromise on lifestyle preferences for a period of time. With the progression of their career, and when establishing a family, many such creatives leave Clusters in order to move to Hubs. The policy challenge for Clusters is hence to be able to retain the creative class longer, for example, by offering jobs for spouses. Second, while industrial clusters experience periods of intensive growth, specialization is also risky. Many industrial clusters enter economic lock-in and decline (Martin and Sunley, 2006). Consequently, a policy challenge for Clusters is also to avoid over-specialization of industrial activity, and promote flexibility and transformation, for example, through investing in new fields of technology and education.

In Denmark, examples of Clusters are Sønderborg, specialized in mechatronics, and Aalborg, with a dominant ICT cluster. After decades of specialized growth, both these Danish cities face notable policy challenges: Sønderborg has problems retaining its mechanical engineers due to the lack of local cultural opportunities and employment opportunities for spouses, and Aalborg is in a difficult process of de-locking its local industry from its narrow specialization as the world markets for ICT shift.

Quaint

A fourth city type has managed, without being Hubs, Satellites or Clusters, to attract high shares of the Danish creative class. Cities such as Svendborg and Fanø are members of an exclusive club of small Danish cities enjoying natural beauty in combination with a particular history mirrored authentically in their contemporary urban landscapes. Artists and bohemians have flocked to such Quaint cities for many decades, infusing them with active local communities and arts scenes. Today, with the growing bourgeoisie-bohemian lifestyle of the creative class, many creatives are willing to sacrifice the specialized services and career opportunities in Hubs, Satellites or Clusters for a lifestyle oriented towards authenticity, beauty and community in a Quaint city. As their purchasing power grows and their jobs get increasingly digitized, many creatives are able to import the specialized services they seek, and work wholly or partly from home. This makes a life in a Quaint, but remote, city less inconvenient.

The main policy challenge for the Quaint cities is to strike the right balance between quaintness and convenience. These cities' authenticity, beauty and strong local sense of community are often due to their remote location, their small size and their slow pace of change. Living in such a city means limited opportunities for shopping and, for many who are not self-employed or have digitized jobs, arduous long work commutes to a Hub, Satellite or Cluster. Consequently, policy-makers in Quaint cities often see it as necessary to infuse them with Hub-type shopping and entertainment offers and to improve their accessibility. However, if implemented without respect for beauty and authenticity, such policies tend to destroy small cities' attractiveness, without making them able to compete with Hubs or Satellites on service offer and accessibility. The landscape in Denmark, as in so many other countries, is increasingly dotted with shopping malls, amuse-ment parks, highways and bridges to the benefit of one-day tourists and transit traffic, but to the detriment of those local communities these infrastructures were meant to boost.

Conclusion

In this chapter, we set out to investigate whether Richard Florida's theory of the creative class needs to be adapted to the context of small, culturally and geo-graphically homogenous, coordinated welfare economies. Using a mixed-method empirical approach, we tested the relevance of the theory's central propositions for Denmark. We found that some adaptation of this highly influential theory was indeed in place. On the one hand, regression analyses of labour market data showed that even if Denmark is hugely different from North America where the creative class was first studied, the general trends proposed by Florida can also be recognized here. The creative class is important in creating, or at least reinforcing, economic growth in Danish cities. In turn, the Danish creative class is attracted to soft city qualities, such as diverse service and cultural offers and tolerance of for-eign and bourgeoisie-bohemian lifestyles. Therefore, this crucial segment in the Danish labour force agglomerates, like its North American equivalent, in the major cities. However, on the other hand, the small size of Denmark means that there are only two major cities, and our statistical exercise pointed to a gamut of other and smaller cities that are either in symbiotic relationships to major cities or have their own independent models of attracting creatives.

Our qualitative interviews showed that this relatively diverse pattern of creative cities is shaped by the efficient Danish transportation system and the welfare state. In Denmark, families typically have two wage earners, and a relaxed work/life bal-ance is appreciated. For many creatives, it is feasible to live in proximity to, rather than in, major cities, and for some, it is feasible to opt out of the congestion and high-paced work life in major cities altogether. The four creative city types we have pointed to in this chapter demonstrate that creatives balance hard factors such as job opportunities and living costs with soft factors such as authenticity, beauty and sense of community. However, our study demonstrated that investing in cultural opportunities is not the magic bullet that many policy-makers believe it to be. For some cities, such investments may be a good policy, increasing the city's attractiveness to creatives. However, for other cities, different investments, such as alleviating congestion or improving the housing offer, should take higher priority.

Throughout the last decade, policy-makers across the world have begun to compete to boost local economic growth by applying policies inspired almost exclusively by the research on the North American creative class. However, the study of the Danish creative class presented in this chapter suggests that in order to be able to stimulate creativity and attract creatives, policies need to take differences between national contexts, and between cities, into account. In Denmark alone, we have demonstrated four distinct, and all successful, city models of attracting the creative class. In other national contexts, there may be more, and policy-makers would do well to investigate before intervening. Different creative cities call for different policies.

Bibliography

Andersen, K. V., Hansen, H. K, Isaksen, A. and Raunio, M. (2010) 'Nordic city regions in the creative class debate: Putting the creative class thesis to a test', *Industry and Innovation*, 17: 215–240.

Andersen, K. V. and Lorenzen, M. (2009) *Den Danske Kreative Klasse: Hvem er den, hvordan ser den ud, hvor bor den – og hvad betyder det?* [The Danish creative class: who, how, and where – and so what?], Aarhus: Klim.

Bille, T. (2010) 'Cool, funky and creative? The creative class and preferences for leisure and culture', *International Journal of Cultural Policy*, 16: 466–496.

Boyle, M. (2006) 'Culture in the rise of tiger economies: Scottish expatriates in Dublin and the "Creative Class" thesis', *International Journal of Urban and Regional Research*, 30: 403–426.

Brooks, D. (2001) *Bobos in Paradise: The New Upper Class and How They Got There*, New York: Simon & Schuster.

Christäller, W. (1933) *Die zentralen Orte in Süddeutschland/Central Places in Southern Germany*, Jena: Gustav Fischer.

Creswell, J. W. (2002) *Research Design: Qualitative, Quantitative, and Mixed Methods Approaches*, Thousand Oaks, CA: Sage.

Florida, R. (2002a) 'The economic geography of talent', *Annals of the Association of American Geographers*, 92: 743–755.

Florida, R. (2002b) 'Bohemia and economic geography', *Journal of Economic Geography*, 2: 55–71.

Florida, R. (2002c) *The Rise of the Creative Class: And How It's Transforming Work, Leisure, Community and Everyday Life*, New York: Basic Books.

Florida, R. (2005a) *Cities and the Creative Class*, London: Routledge.

Florida, R. (2005b) *The Flight of the Creative Class: The New Global Competition for Talent*, New York: HarperCollins.

Glaeser, E. L. (2005) 'Review of Richard Florida's "The Rise of the Creative Class"', *Regional Science and Urban Economics*, 35(5): 593–596.

Grabher, G. (2002) 'The project ecology of advertising: Tasks, talents and teams', *Regional Studies*, 36: 245–262.

Hall, P. A. and Soskice, D. (eds) (2001) *Varieties of Capitalism: The Institutional Foundations of Comparative Advantage*, Oxford: Oxford University Press.

Lorenzen, M. and Frederiksen, L. (2008) 'Why do cultural industries cluster? Localization, urbanization, products and projects', in P. Cooke and Rossella Lazzeretti (eds), *Creative Cities, Cultural Clusters, and Local Economic Development*, Cheltenham: Edward Elgar, pp. 155–179.

Lorenzen, M. and Andersen, K. V. (2009) 'Centrality and creativity: Does Richard Florida's creative class offer new insights into urban hierarchy?' *Economic Geography*, 85: 363–390.

Malanga, S. (2004) 'The curse of the creative class', *City Journal*, 4: 36–45.

Martin, R. and Sunley, P. (2003) 'Deconstructing clusters: Chaotic concept or policy panacea?', *Journal of Economic Geography*, 3: 5–35.

Martin, R. and Sunley, P. (2006) 'Path dependence and regional economic evolution', *Journal of Economic Geography*, 6: 395–437.

Montgomery, J. (2005) 'Beware "the creative class": Creativity and wealth creation revisited', *Local Economy*, 20: 337–343.

Peck, J. (2005) 'Struggling with the creative class', *International Journal of Urban and Rural Research*, 29: 740–770.

Raush, S. and Negrey, C. (2006) 'Does the creative engine run? A consideration of the effect of creative class on economic strength and growth', *Journal of Urban Affairs*, 28: 473–489.

Scott, A. J. (1988) *New Industrial Spaces: Flexible Production Organization and Regional Development in North America and Western Europe*, London: Pion.

Scott, A. J. (2006) 'Creative cities: Conceptual issues and policy questions', *Journal of Urban Affairs*, 28: 1–17.

Weick, C. W. and Martin, J. D. (2006) 'Full-time and part-time independent inventors: Rising with the creative class', *International Journal of Entrepreneurship and Innovation*, 7: 5–12.

6   One size fits all?*

Applying the creative class thesis to a Nordic context

Kristina Vaarst Andersen, Markus M. Bugge, Høgni Kalsø Hansen, Arne Isaksen and Mika Raunio

Introduction

In the past few years the creative class thesis put forward by Florida (2002a) has aroused much interest as well as debate. As the primary reactions have calmed, it is time to systematically examine if and how Florida's causal relations actually work in various empirical settings. This chapter seeks to apply the creative class thesis to a Nordic context, aiming to see whether and how Florida's thesis proves fruitful in a different geographical context than it was developed.

Theories on regional development have traditionally been based on the assumption that people follow jobs, and policy has focused on nurturing the business climate to attract investments and stimulate the competitiveness of industries. Florida represents an alternative approach to theorising on regional development by arguing that specific qualities of place have become a crucial factor for explaining the location pattern of knowledge-intensive firms. Central to his approach is the claim that 'jobs follow people' rather than 'people follow jobs'. An important analytical pair of concepts in this thesis is 'people climate' and 'business climate'. Business climate refers to the traditional production and location dynamics for industries, such as labour, knowledge resources, capital, infrastructure and physical resources (e.g. Porter, 1990). People climate refers to specific qualities of place that attract and retain knowledgeable people to particular places.

Former studies by the authors of this chapter demonstrate statistical correlations between indicators of people climate and the creative class, and between the creative class and economic growth in the Nordic countries (Andersen and Lorenzen, 2005; Isaksen, 2005; Raunio and Sotarauta, 2005; Hansen, 2007). The creative class in these papers and this chapter is defined as the working population within specific occupations that include a high degree of problem-solving and decision-making responsibility, more exactly, many academic occupations, administrative managers and artists (e.g. Florida, 2002a: 328; Andersen and Lorenzen, 2005: 17). However, the statistical analyses referred to above are only significant for the largest Nordic

* This chapter was previously published as: Vaarst Andersen, K., Bugge, M. M., Hansen, H. K., Isaksen, A., and Raunio, M. (2010) 'One size fits all? Applying the creative class thesis onto a Nordic context', *European Planning Studies*, 18(10): 1591–1609. Reprinted by permission of the publisher, Taylor & Francis Ltd, http://www.tandfonline.com.

city regions (Hansen, 2008). This suggests that Florida's 3Ts of technology, talent and tolerance may be a relevant analytical concept only in some Nordic regions. Our objective in this chapter is therefore to test the relevance of the concepts of people climate and business climate in three types of city regions: Capital regions, Regional centres and Semi-peripheral regions, in each of the four Nordic countries. The chapter is based on semi-structured interviews with 110 informants from 14 regions in Denmark, Finland, Norway and Sweden, and it analyses how people climate and business climate affect the location dynamics of firms and the creative class in the three types of city regions. Furthermore, the study aims to examine the causality of the creative class approach. Florida's work (2002b) has proven statistical correlations between aspects of people climate and the creative class, and between the creative class and high-technology industry and economic growth. Other statistical exercises also demonstrate strong independent influence on regional employment growth from the share of creative class occupations and its growth in regions (e.g. Marlet and van Woerkens, 2007; McGranahan and Wojan, 2007). This chapter supplements such studies by drawing on interviews and focus groups, and by asking whether the creative class thesis and related policy formulations apply in three quite different types of Nordic city regions.

The chapter is structured as follows: Section two presents the main arguments behind the creative class thesis and provides a theoretical framework for the current empirical exercise. Section three describes the method, information sources and the regions that are included in the study. Section four presents the empirical analysis and compares the importance of people climate and business climate for the location of firms and the creative class. Finally, section five concludes on the relevance of people climate and business climate in different spatial settings, and discusses how the empirical evidence relates to policy initiatives in various types of city regions.

Theoretical framework

Florida's theorizing needs to be seen in a wider theoretical context that seeks to improve our understanding of the driving forces and mechanisms of regional development and economic growth.

Traditionally theorizing on regional development has often been based on the assumption that people follow jobs, and policy has focused on nurturing the business climate to attract investments and increase the competitiveness of firm, industries and clusters. Many studies in economic geography and beyond have thus tended to focus on the capabilities and the organization of the firms, networks and organizations that constitute these industries, and on the institutional set-up surrounding industries. Studies have conceptualized the industrial landscape in terms of clusters and innovation systems. Parts of this literature have focused on how different countries or groups of countries hold different features and characteristics and how they may be described in terms of national innovation systems (NIS) (Freeman, 1987; Lundvall, 1992; Nelson, 1993) or varieties of capitalism (Hall and Soskice, 2001). Related and supplementing approaches include technological innovation systems (TIS) (Carlsson, 1995), sectoral innovation systems (SIS) (Breschi and Malerba, 1997) and regional innovation systems (RIS) (Cooke, 1992; Asheim and Isaksen, 1997). Common to these approaches is that they apply a systemic understanding of economic development and industrial dynamics. The focus is often on how organizations like firms, research institutes and public agencies interact with each other in knowledge production and distribution. Individual actors and individual location choices have been far less emphasized. To the degree that these studies have dealt with policy formulation, they have often focused on how policy may support (infrastructure for) given industries, networks of firms or industry organizations, and also interlinkages between industry, public sector and universities (Etzkowitz and Leydesdorff, 2000).

One of the recent trends in the innovation systems literature questions generic policies (Miller and Floricel, 2004) and the one size fits all approach (Tödtling and Trippl, 2005; Cooke *et al.*, 2007). This literature emphasizes that the validity of best practice is limited and relative to various regional and innovation contexts. This questioning of a one size fits all approach likewise underpins the present study, as this seeks to examine how Florida's thesis works in a different spatial context than that in which it was initially developed. The findings by McGranahan and Wojan (2007) that the urban creative class in the US is different from the rural creative class make such a focus no less relevant.

According to Florida, most theorizing within economic geography and beyond has until now been preoccupied with the notion of business climate. Without rejecting the impact of business climate altogether, Florida stresses the notion of people climate as a complementary viewpoint to the business climate perspective. It is maintained that creative workers are attracted to exciting firms and to jobs with autonomy, responsibility and challenges (Florida 2002a), but the argument that specific qualities of place have become a crucial factor for explaining the location patterns of knowledge-intensive firms represents a new approach to theorizing on regional development.

Creative people are assumed to have similar preferences and are thus expected to be attracted to places holding specific qualities (ibid.). The qualities in question are openness, tolerance and heterogeneity. The cultural diversity of these places is seen as an indication of low entry barriers which enable many kinds of people to settle down and become part of the local community (ibid.: 294). Besides cultural diversity, a variety of sporting, leisure and entertainment opportunities, authentic places and vibrant street life are also seen as central elements of an attractive people climate for the creative class (Florida, 2002a: 228, 259). These arguments are supported by results from a survey of the consumption of cultural offers by the Danish creative class (Bille, 2009). The creative class is comparatively eager consumers of very specialized cultural offers, such as concerts, exhibitions, museums, performing art and city architecture, and, thus, supposed to prefer large cities having such offers rather than smaller cities.

Florida (2002b) demonstrates correlations between indicators of people climate and high-tech jobs in US city regions. Similar correlations are found in empirical data from Canada (Gertler *et al.*, 2002), European countries (Boschma and Fritsch, 2007) and the Nordic countries (Andersen and Lorenzen, 2005; Isaksen, 2005; Raunio and Sotarauta, 2005; Hansen, 2007). Larger Nordic cities with a high share of artists (bohemians) and cultural jobs have a relatively large creative class and a high share of high-tech jobs. These correlations are positive and significant as regards large Nordic city regions (with more than 100,000 inhabitants), but not in small and medium-sized regions (with 10,000 to 49,999; 50,000 to 99,999 inhabitants).[1] This observation forms some of the background for the current study and the wish to test Florida's thesis in various spatial contexts.

By putting emphasis on people climate and quality of place, the *individual*, its *location choice*, and its *occupation* supplement the industry and the firm as the prime objects of study. In this sense Florida intends to expand the prevailing understanding of economic growth as being promoted by regional clusters of firms. The growth of clusters is traditionally explained by the upgrading mechanisms and competitive advantages accruing to collocated similar and related firms, for example, the possibility for firms to benefit from a pool of experienced labour and specialized suppliers, and to pick up ideas and knowledge simply by being located in an information-intense industrial milieu (Marshall, 1890; Asheim, 1996; Malmberg and Maskell, 1997; Maskell and Malmberg, 1999; Bathelt *et al.*, 2004). But, according to Florida, these are 'only partial answers … the real force behind this clustering is people. Companies cluster in order to draw from concentrations of talented people who power innovation and economic growth' (Florida, 2002a: 220). Florida's contribution is to highlight the importance of creative persons and how their choice of place to live triggers regional industrial growth. Then, 'the bottom line is that cities need a *people climate* even more than they need a business climate' (ibid.: 283, original italics).

Since the publication of *The Rise of the Creative Class* (Florida, 2002a), the creative class thesis has gained significant impact both within economic geography and beyond. But parallel to the public acclaim and policy implementation of the creative class thesis, the theory has also been widely criticized.

First, it has been criticized for its method and inability to address the causal relations between the presence of the creative class in a city region and the city's economic performance. Storper and Scott (2009) thus argue that Florida fails to explain how local concentrations of talented people emerge in the first place, and preserves the importance of production as locational determinant. Peck (2005) criticizes Florida for implicitly suggesting that there is a causal relationship between the presence of the creative class and economic growth, whereas his quantitative method only suggests a statistical correlation between the two. Markusen (2006) criticizes Florida's method of using occupational groups as an indicator for measuring creativity. However, occupational groups or educational level are the most suitable and international comparable indicators of job creativity when using census and registered data.

Second, the theory has been criticized for its notion of the creative class. Markusen (2006) discusses the fact that the creative class constitutes one-third of the American population and problematizes the grouping of all their values and preferences under one heading. Asheim and Hansen (2009) have elaborated on this by introducing the knowledge base approach to point to the diversity of priorities of the creative class according to the knowledge bases that different segments of the creative class draw upon. Kotkin (2003), Malanga (2004) and Glaeser (2005) do not share the belief that the creative class gravitates towards urban areas and state that instead the middle class wants affordable and safe suburban lives. Glaeser (2005) questions the relevance of the creative class concept by arguing that human capital has almost the exact same effect on regional growth as the creative class. Glaeser thus stresses that the creative class category only reproduces the well-established concept of human capital which consists of highly skilled people. This may be debated, as data from Sweden indicates that less than half of the creative class holds a higher education (Hansen, 2007). Marlet and van Woerkens (2007) also found that the creative class is a better predictor of employment growth in Dutch cities and towns, and these authors maintain that 'Richard Florida has found better standards for measuring human capital than the often used education level' (p. 2617).

Third, the theory has been criticized for its policy implications. Lehmann (2003) criticizes Florida for not evaluating the inequality generated by the economic importance of the creative class, and Markusen (2006) criticizes the creative class for not playing any political role. Peck (2005) condemns Florida's theory for ignoring the class polarization that exists between those who are included in the creative class and those who are not, for glorifying the creative class and for lacking a critical attitude towards the class perspective he presents. Peck (2005) also points to the problems associated with the 'one size fits all' policy recipe for all cities which Florida prescribes. Most of these leftist critics point to the lack of a class perspective, a lack of solutions for the ordinary region and a tendency to blame the victim when the approach does not pay off. On the other hand, conservatives and market liberals such as Kotkin (2003) and Malanga (2004) criticize Florida for using the people climate perspective as an excuse to legitimize an active state and public policy interventions.

Much of the critique directed at Florida's theorizing is legitimate and opportune, and many of the points raised do highlight important weaknesses. There are many aspects of the creative class thesis that surely need further debate and refinement. Yet, Florida's conceptualization of the creative class and people climate is highly interesting and deserves to be treated as a serious contribution to our understanding of the dynamics of the knowledge economy. When trying to pin down the present overall socio-economic picture in a highly accessible jargon and format, which may be Florida's principal achievement, there will always be elements that can be further nuanced and developed. As in any broad assertion and overarching theory, there is an imminent risk of oversimplification and unfortunate generalization. We see Florida's contribution to the analysis of regional growth as an approach in the making. The following sections examine and discuss the validity of the approach in different contextual settings. In this effort we discuss the relevance of Florida's theory on the relatively small job markets in different types of Nordic city regions. The main research question is:

- To what extent and how does the impact of people climate and business climate vary across different types of city regions?

This research question is underpinned and specified by the following sub-questions:

- What factors are important for attraction and retention of the creative class and businesses in the Nordic countries, and how do these vary in different types of city regions?
- What is the (potential) causal relationship between people climate and the creative class?
- How are people climate and business climate implemented in regional strategies and policies in different types of city regions?

Design and method

Florida focuses on metropolitan areas, particularly the largest ones. Due to a quite different Nordic regional hierarchy, this chapter examines the impact of people climate and business climate from a wider sample of city regions (see also McGranahan and Wojan, 2007). While North America and especially the US are characterized by numerous metropolitan areas, each of the four Nordic countries has only one region with more than one million inhabitants. Consequently, the urban hierarchy is fundamentally different from the one constituting the empirical basis for Florida's development of the creative class approach. The capital regions of the Nordic countries, Copenhagen, Helsinki, Oslo and Stockholm, dominate within the national economy and urban hierarchy. Further, each of the Nordic countries has only three to four city regions that can be termed regional centres, but which are considerably smaller than the capital regions. Except for Gothenburg, which has half the population of Stockholm, these secondary cities typically have from one-third to one-fifth of the population of the capital regions.

This chapter divides the studied regions into three groups, based on a combination of geography, scale and power: (1) capital cities; (2) regional centres; and (3) semi-peripheral regions (Table 6.1). All capital regions are centres of economic and political power in their countries. The regional centres have a secondary position in the urban hierarchy. The four regional centres studied in this chapter all have universities and knowledge-based industries, and they also have a vibrant cultural supply. The semi-peripheral regions are located on the fringe of more dominating regions. These regions often hold a combination of traditional industrial production mixed with more knowledge-intensive industries.

The difference in population size between the various types of regions may affect the significance of people climate and business climate in different ways. We understand people climate as factors related to quality of place, e.g. cultural amenities, attractive public spaces and public provision such as schools, health care or public transport. People climate is a common denominator of elements that affect the attractiveness of a certain location. Though people climate differs between a dynamic capital region and a quiet, semi-peripheral region, both

Table 6.1 Overview of the studied regions and number of interviews conducted

	Capital city regions (>1 000 000 inhabitants)	*Regional centres (250 000–1 000 000 inhabitants)*	*Semi-peripheral regions (<250 000 inhabitants)*
Denmark	Copenhagen (10 informants + 2 group interviews)	Aarhus (9 informants + 2 group interviews)	Svendborg (11 informants + 2 group interviews) Sønderborg[1] (8 informants) Esbjerg (12 informants + 2 group interviews)
Finland[2]	Helsinki (5 informants)	Tampere (13 informants)	Oulu (5 informants)
Norway	Oslo (6 informants + 2 group interviews)	Trondheim (8 informants + 1 group interview)[3]	Grenland (8 informants + 2 group interviews)
Sweden	Stockholm (6 informants + 2 group interviews)	Malmö/Lund (6 informants + 2 group interviews)	Karlskrona (7 informants + 2 group interviews)

Notes:

1   No group interviews were conducted in Sønderborg.
2   Finnish data is based on three preceding studies concerning the same questions and the same target group as this chapter. These studies, conducted between 2001 and 2004, include hundreds of personal interviews and thousands of responses to questionnaires in the same city regions as are subjects to this analysis. To control for the usability of those previously conducted interviews, five new interviews were made in both Helsinki and Oulu. When no systematic deviations between these new and the previously conducted interviews were found, 10 interviews from the previous study were used for detailed analyses.
3   One planned group interview in Trondheim was cancelled.

deviations might still attract the creative class, but probably different parts and age groups (McGranahan and Wojan, 2007).

Business climate involves factors that more directly influence the competitiveness of businesses, such as infrastructure, government support, educational institutions, and network building between organizations. A vital business climate will stimulate existing industries and attract new businesses to a region and hopefully pay off by an increasing number of jobs. Consequently, a job market with many and varied high skilled jobs become an indicator of an attractive and well-functioning business climate. The business climate and its resulting job opportunities are most often affected by the population size. There are more career opportunities in big cities, which is important for the dual career families of the Nordic countries.[2]

Interviews and informants

The empirical material consists of individual and group interviews with 110 informants in 14 city regions in the Nordic countries of Denmark, Finland, Norway, and Sweden as seen in Table 6.1. The informants in each region include government officials, business leaders, civic leaders, representatives of marginalized and minority groups, and were supplemented by focus group interviews with representatives of the creative class. The selection of informants should illustrate different aspects of the people and business climate in the regions. Thus, lifestyle preferences of the creative class have been gathered through 19 group interviews with 4–6 representatives of the creative class. The creative class respondents represented a broad variety of professions stretching from artists to university researchers and from librarians to ICT professionals.

The perspective on the local tolerance level has been covered through interviews with at least one representative of marginalized or minority groups. Perspectives on if and how the creative class influences upon the local business climate and location decisions have been achieved through interviews with at least two local business leaders in each region, including at least one knowledge-intensive company, and, where possible, one company with a recent history of relocation. Views on strategies to attract the creative class have been gathered through interviews with at least one key person in the local government in each city region, and through interviews with at least two civic leaders, e.g. local politicians.

The data collection was carried out by the authors. Very few informants refused to take part in the interviews. We tried to provide for a high reliability of the data in different ways (Berg, 2007). We carried out semi-structured interviews by use of the same interview guides in each region. We prepared a specific interview guide adapted to each target group of informants, i.e., to representatives of minority groups, private firms, politicians, local authorities, and the creative class. In the interviews we deliberately avoided using the 'creative class language' in order to get the informants' 'real' opinion, and not what they thought would be 'the right answer' according to the creative class thesis. Instead of using, for example, the concept of the creative class, we used labels such as 'knowledge workers', 'artists', 'engineers', and 'professionals'. The primary data material consists of texts from the informant interviews. The texts have been condensed and restructured and made into case descriptions of each region (Yin, 2008). The case descriptions were sent to the informants for evaluation, which sometimes led to correction of factual faults and new information. Finally, we provided for reliability by gathering information about the same subject from several informants in each region and by cross-checking information through focus group discussions.

The study has been part of a larger comparative European study[3] on applying the creative class thesis to a European context which has included discussing and defining central concepts and indicators, such as tolerance, talent, creative class, knowledge-intensive industries, etc. Thus, the validity of the concepts used has been closely emphasized and examined. The external validity or transferability of the results includes first of all the Nordic countries. The study included the same type of regions in the four Nordic countries, and the authors find similarities and differences in the results within similar types of regions across the four countries. This indicates that the results are transferable across the Nordic countries.

People climate, business climate and the many faces of attractiveness

Capital regions: skewed spatial structure of job and educational markets

The spatial urban structure of the Nordic countries constitutes a rather different starting point in competition for talent than in the US. The US has a thick job market for the creative class with more than 50 metropolitan areas of more than one million inhabitants. These agglomerations differ remarkably from each other in terms of their people climate, i.e.,, by their natural climate, social atmosphere, cultural offerings, physical appearance, diversity and social cohesion. In contrast, each Nordic country has only one region with more than one million people (the capital regions) and three or four regional centres with notably smaller populations and thinner job markets. In terms of the physical environment, even the Nordic capitals are more 'small town-like', 'close to nature' and less urban than many of their European counterparts.

The key feature that differentiates the Nordic capital city regions from the remaining Nordic regions is the relative size of their labour markets and educational opportunities. In addition, they serve as political and administrative centres. The attractive factors that pull people to the capital regions are most often related to work or studies. In the case of Finland, 50 per cent of all jobs in the information sector are found in Helsinki and less than 9 per cent in the second biggest city region of Tampere. The same applies in terms of university students, of which 36 per cent are located in Helsinki and less than 15 per cent in Tampere (Finnish Ministry of the Interior, 2006). The biographies of the respondents reveal that especially for newcomers starting their job careers, the best opportunities are generally found in the thick job markets of the Nordic capital city regions. This particularly applies to dual career couples.

The importance of the large job market in capital city regions is related to general changes in the labour market, in particular regarding 'creative jobs'. In the Fordist economy until the 1970s, job security was rather high, or was at least an aim in economic policy (Piore and Sabel, 1984). Employers often offered long-term vertical career paths, which are less usual in the 'new knowledge economy'. Now job circulation is higher, careers are more horizontal than vertical, and advancement requires increased expertise rather than promotions based on seniority (Miles and Snow, 1996). Due to these altered dynamics in the labour market, people with high-expertise careers tend to seek thick local job markets in large cities in which they may accumulate knowledge and experience from specialized niches or across various firms, industries and sectors. A former deputy mayor of Copenhagen puts it this way: 'I think Copenhagen is the only international brand this country has. It's the only place where you can place knowledge institutions and attract big international companies.'

The high living standards, public services and cultural amenities are highlighted as strengths of the capital city regions. However, not all of these qualities provide strong competitive advantages for the capital city regions at a national level due to a rather uniform quality of services across all types of city regions. An intentional national policy aiming to lower regional differences in welfare and economic growth is important in the Nordic countries, and has succeeded in producing comparatively small regional differences compared to e.g. the USA. Nordic respondents assume that basic services like schools and health care work rather well also in more peripheral regions. In short, the Nordic capital city regions are clearly different from other Nordic city regions as regards their job markets, but less so in terms of public services. A comment from a representative of the creative class in Sweden seems to capture the general view: 'Maybe you would think about the public service level if you have children, but it is not a big issue.'

Respondents frequently report that the capital city regions are regarded as modern cities with a vibrant cultural supply and a rich selection of restaurants and cafés. According to creative class respondents in the Nordic capital cities, one does not necessarily make much use of the cultural offer, but there is an option value of easy access to a variety of cultural activities. The capital city regions are clearly the most diverse locations in the Nordic countries. Diversity and tolerance are often mentioned and discussed by the respondents, but these factors do not seem to have a strong impact on actual moving decisions, if the persons in question do not belong to minority groups themselves. A creative class member in Stockholm puts it this way: 'My child does not meet other cultures which I find very unfortunate but the alternative is to move my child to another school and that I'm not prepared to do.'

In terms of ethnicity, the Nordic countries are rather homogeneous (with the exception of Sweden[4]), and diversity is not an important pull factor in moving decisions. Florida states that tolerance and diversity are crucial factors of attractiveness, but in the Nordic case these values seem to be appreciated when they are present but they are not factors of attractiveness as such. Diversity in cultural offer seems to be more important to the creative class than tolerance.

The attraction of the capital city regions as places to study and to find a first job seems to be especially related to early life phases when people tend to be most mobile, not just because they rarely have established their own families but also due to more 'mobile mind-sets'. However, it seems that the attractiveness of the capital city regions is also related to a lack of job opportunities in less urban areas. Thus, moves are not always voluntary but rather forced solutions when people want to start or proceed with their careers (see also Raunio and Linnamaa, 2000; Raunio, 2001).

The factors that push members of the creative class away from capital city regions or prevent them from moving there are mostly housing prices, congestion, or lack of integration or a sense of community. These factors are thus channelling people to regional centres or other regions. A common problem is that adequate housing at reasonable prices and in reasonable distance from the workplace is not available. Within the last decade, all four Nordic countries have experienced an explosive increase in real estate prices in the capital regions. In Finland, the average price of an apartment was €2634/sqm^2 in the capital region a few years ago, whereas it was €1599/sqm^2 in the second largest and fastest growing city region of Tampere (Finnish

Ministry of Interior, 2006). One result of this is that commuting distances and the number of commuters have grown substantially in the capital city regions from the 1960s and onwards. More than 150,000 employees commute to central Helsinki every day; more than 36,000 of them come from outside the Helsinki region, and the commuting area is continuously expanding. In Denmark, the number of commuters into the greater metropolitan area of Copenhagen has increased by 33 per cent from 1995 to 2005 from approximately 100,000 to 133,000 (Statistics Denmark, 2007). This pattern is concurrent throughout the Nordic countries. This applies even if the current crises has led to somewhat lower housing prices, since it has also become more difficult to get loans for newcomers on the housing market. Throughout recent years this has led not only to an increasing number of commuters but also a growing commuting distance. On the one hand, this has opened up a more diverse set of alternatives of living environments within the same labour market region, especially with well-functioning public transport. On the other hand, increasing housing prices lead to problems of obtaining a labour force holding the right composition of skills. The head of strategic planning in Stockholm addresses the problem of expensive housing this way: 'It is important that the city does not become too expensive to live in to secure the fundamental services.'

The Nordic capital city regions lead the transition towards more knowledge-based economies in their countries. All capital city regions have an international focus, and to some extent Stockholm, Copenhagen, Helsinki and Oslo see each other as competitors. This concerns both recruitment of highly skilled workers and attraction of firms in knowledge-intensive industries. In terms of international competition for knowledge, a factor that may affect the attractiveness of the Nordic capitals is that wage disparities in the Nordic countries are the lowest in the world (OECD, 2002). The income level for highly educated people is thus not notably higher compared to blue-collar workers or craftsmen.

In general, the capital city regions have changed the focus in industrial policy from attracting and retaining businesses towards developing appealing public spaces and other attractions for human capital. All capital cities refer to a growing competition for talent and try to approach this by planning for attractive housing areas and a rich and multifaceted cultural supply, which seems to be the new strategy of industrial policy in the Nordic capital cities. One example is the Danish focus on creative industries and on the significance of creativity for the attractiveness and economic future of cities. The municipality of Copenhagen has thus initiated an analysis of how to improve the conditions for the creative industries (Mathiasen *et al.*, 2006). Another example of educational innovation is the new 'Aalto University' in Finland, which is a merger of three existing universities in Helsinki: the University of Technology, the Helsinki Business School and the University of Industrial Design and Art.

Knowledge-intensive companies interviewed argue that capital cities are the place to be due to their knowledge-generating institutions, a constant talent flow and not least because the capital cities are centres of power. A recently established Stockholm office of a Danish consultancy argued that it is important to be where political decisions are taken in order to win projects. A saying in some local government offices in

Southern Sweden is: 'What doesn't happen in Stockholm doesn't happen at all.' The same is the case of Copenhagen, Helsinki and Oslo. The respondents in the companies state that if they do not look for highly specialized, local competencies, the capital region often provides the best mix of talent, infrastructure and power. However, start-up firms, in particular outside the central city areas, often base their locations on social relations rather than on economic rationality; a finding which is in line with entrepreneurship research (Stam, 2007) and which has also been identified in a study on Copenhagen (Winther and Hansen, 2006).

Regional centres: affordable alternatives to capital city regions

The attractiveness of the regional centres is partly based on the qualities that push people away from capital city regions or prevent them from moving there, i.e., more affordable housing, a stronger sense of community and a local identity and authenticity.

Although thinner job markets may prevent these regions from being attractive alternatives to capital regions, the four regional centres studied have both large universities and a considerable pool of jobs for highly educated people. Nevertheless, regional centres have more specialized job markets compared to the capital city regions, for example Trondheim houses the national technical university and Tampere has specialized in jobs for engineers.

The term 'right size', often used by respondents, refers to the regional centres. In particular, it refers to their social atmosphere which is still rather small town-like where people 'are not too alienated from each other', but still 'everybody does not know what everybody is doing'. Certain groups of people tend to avoid the 'hectic and alienated' capital city regions and instead prefer the smaller regional centres, especially if these are close to their region of origin. Regional centres do not actually have to offer more high-quality living environments than the capital city regions since their key attractive factors are their smaller size: namely, low congestion, local social cohesion and affordable housing prices. If reasonable job opportunities are available, regional centres offer attractive alternatives for the creative class. A member of the creative class in Malmö-Lund puts it this way: 'You have all the convenience of a capital city within commuting range but you avoid the inconveniences like high housing prices, pollution, etc.'

An attractive people climate is, however, also of importance. Interviews indicate that the creative class often look for qualities of place that may provide other inputs and inspirations than those related to their jobs. These may be found in a diverse cultural life (concerts, exhibitions, theatre, sport), urbanity (street life, public spaces, meeting places) and professional communities outside the place of work. A creative environment, in terms of a place where one can meet many people in different professions is regarded as important. Regional centres with their educational opportunities and relatively large job markets often include such creative milieus.

The regional centres are preferred by people in certain life phases, in particular, families who may find that apartments or houses are too expensive in the capital city regions. Such a life phase pattern corresponds with recent results from studies in the US where 'the rural creative class is older and more likely to be married than the urban creative class' (McGranahan and Wojan, 2007: 205). It should be noticed that generally people with children of school age are quite immobile, whereas students and young single people (in their twenties and early thirties) are the most mobile. Thus, as regards the number of 'stable inhabitants', the typical life phase of the members of the creative class settling in certain regions is of importance.

Firms that have relocated from other regions to regional centres often want proximity to universities or other knowledge-creating institutions. However, personal networks also play a central role in location decisions – small-scale entrepreneurs tend to start up businesses where they live and thus pay more attention to social relations than to more business-oriented location factors (Winther and Hansen, 2006). While personal networks play a role for small enterprises, the university plays a major role for many medium and large enterprises located in the regional centres. A director of innovation in a larger company in Aarhus puts it this way: 'It is an advantage to us that there is an academic environment in Aarhus – the university and the other companies. It provides opportunities for cooperation and recruiting.'

In contrast to the capital cities, regional centres often have a more national focus in their industrial policies, although international competition is also recognized. Regional centres focus to some extent more on poorly defined, national competitors than on capital regions. However, Tampere created, for example, development programmes already at the beginning of the 2000 with the aim of becoming the world leader in some areas of business, technology and information society's services (e-Tampere program). Similarly other regional centres like Aarhus and Malmö address the issue of a well-equipped infrastructure that will enable the cities to tap into international pipelines of knowledge flows. Improvement of infrastructure and active participation in international networks tend to be an explicit strategy in regions below the capital level whereas it is more implicit in the capital city regions.

Semi-peripheral regions: entrepreneurship and place identity

Many smaller Nordic towns make attempts to strengthen their people climate; the town centres are being revitalized and they arrange a broad range of festivals. At the same time the number of cafés has increased and many cities are experiencing growing cultural supply. Still, many smaller towns lack the urban qualities to attract people who are looking for urbanity and a vibrant city life. Thus, they experience problems in retaining or attracting the young members of the creative class looking for a greater variety of leisure opportunities and a larger professional community. This is strengthened by the fact that smaller towns in more peripheral areas also have a comparatively thin job market.

People climate factors have, however, played an important role for the economic growth of some semi-peripheral regions. The Danish region of Svendborg exemplifies how an exceptionally high quality of living environment may support job growth. Svendborg has lost many jobs in traditional industries, but local entrepreneurship and commitment have prevented an economic recession. Svendborg is known for its natural beauty, cultural amenities and tolerance due to its history as a port city. Comments like 'you can't discharge the beauty of the nature – this region is so beautiful' or 'that might be the trademark of our town – broad and rich music life' are not rare in Svendborg and reflect a strong local pride. People are commuting to surrounding city regions or are self-employed in order to stay. However, Svendborg experiences difficulties in attracting people with highly specialized skills. Thus, it is the *retaining* effect rather than the attracting effect that has ensured Svendborg the position as the Danish town with the third largest share of the creative class. The head of Svendborg business council enhances the regions' qualities in this way: 'Svendborg is an attractive place to be for creative people because of both the cultural life of the city and the nature surrounding it.'

A parallel example is found in the case of Oulu in Finland. Parts of Oulu's success as a high-tech town seem to derive from its people climate, or more precisely from its social environment and local place identity. Oulu has gained a substantial net migration compared to the rest of Northern Finland due to its relatively thick job market and a social environment which is more 'Northern' than other alternative job markets in southern Finland. This quality cannot be replicated since it is based on the authenticity of the city. Consequently, Oulu is also known for its entrepreneurial spirit building on historical roots.[5]

The two examples illustrate that the 'right' people climate combined with an entrepreneurial milieu may benefit the economic growth of semi-peripheral regions. Local identity helps retain people in these regions. In addition also, long-term commitment to a particular region ensures social capital. Contrary to 'transient people' who come to a place merely due to careers and jobs and move further if other interesting possibilities arise, people committed to a community will be more motivated to seek or create jobs in order to be able to stay in a place they appreciate (see Martin and Sunley, 2006).

Semi-peripheral regions generally have a thinner industrial milieu than more central parts of the countries. However, being small brings advantages different from the larger city regions. An ICT entrepreneur in a semi-peripheral town in Sweden stressed that: 'Karlskrona is small, so there are not many jobs here. On the other hand, it is easier for firms to help each other. This is not possible to the same degree in larger cities.' This view resembles the role attributed to social capital in stimulating the competitiveness of Italian industrial districts as described by, for example, Brusco (1982), Piore and Sabel (1984), Asheim (1996) and Markusen (1996). In line with this, Putnam (1993) also emphasizes how social capital stimulates collaboration and economic development. Contrary to this view, Florida asserts that social capital restrains innovation and progress as entry barriers rise. The role of social capital may in fact be an important division between small, semi-peripheral regions and larger regions. Large regions have a large number of companies, knowledge organizations and 'meeting places'. Here weak ties between large numbers of economic actors may

Table 6.2 Main characteristics of the three types of regions

	Capital city regions	*Regional centres*	*Semi-peripheral regions*
Business climate	Thick job markets and promising career opportunities	Somewhat thick job markets but limited career opportunities	Narrow job markets
People climate	Abundance and variety of cultural opportunities	Variety of cultural opportunities	Community activities and local identity
Attractive factor	People are 'forced' to the city regions because of jobs and careers	People are attracted to both jobs and people climate	People are attracted to people climate and local focus/clusters

stimulate the generation and diffusion of new ideas and increase innovation activities. In contrast, economic development in semi-peripheral regions may rely more on joint action among a smaller number of relevant actors stimulated by socially embedded networks. This illustrates the need to unpack and diversify the creative class approach, as the approach is rarely directly applicable to all types of regions (Asheim and Hansen, 2009).

In each of the four Nordic countries, the capital city region stands out due to the combination of an appealing business climate and an attractive people climate. While some people are attracted to the vibrant life of the Nordic capital regions, the creative class primarily locates in these regions because of the thick job market with promising career opportunities. In contrast, the main appeal of the regional centres is the *combination* of a somewhat thick job market, rich cultural opportunities and a small-town feeling which the capital regions lack. People are drawn to the peripheral regions especially because of this small town feeling of community and local identity in spite of thin or narrow job markets and limited cultural opportunities (Table 6.2).

The semi-peripheral regions tend to struggle more than the larger regions in the quest for highly skilled labour and knowledge-intensive firms. Thus, a more hands-on policy is needed to attract highly skilled labour and knowledge-intensive firms to semi-peripheral regions compared to more urbanized regions. Consequently, the business policy perspective of attracting and retaining businesses is more explicit in the semi-peripheral regions, including actively establishing networks between businesses and strengthening education, research and government on a local level.

Conclusion and implications for theory and policy formulation

This chapter has analysed aspects of people climate and business climate of 14 regions in four Nordic countries. A main objective has been to critically examine what roles people climate and business climate play in the location of the creative class, in the location of businesses and in policy formulation in the different types of regions. So to what extent and how can the creative class thesis be applied to a Nordic context, and how can the findings from this study help develop the creative class approach?

Two main findings can be derived from the present study. The first finding is that people climate is generally considered to be important for the creative class, but it is still secondary to attractive job markets when making actual decisions about moving. The second finding is that what attracts or repels the creative class varies between types of regions, and the notion of people climate is perceived differently in different places.

The secondary role of people climate to business climate may be explained by the urban structure and hierarchy in the Nordic countries and by the role of the Nordic welfare states. First, the opportunities of getting an attractive job and a subsequent career are vital for the location of the creative class. The uneven spatial distribution of relevant jobs for creative class members in the Nordic countries, especially for highly skilled people, implies that the capital city regions possess a much thicker labour market than the regional centres. The capital regions are the only cities that offer a really thick labour market and a great variety in career opportunities for many members of the creative class. Then, people cannot actually choose between several cities to live in, and consequently people climate is valued but is not decisive for location decisions. However, to the degree that the capital regions compete on an international level with other large cities, a prime focus on people climate may be justified.

Second, the welfare state policies in all Nordic countries ensures a fairly equal distribution of goods and services, which in Florida's study of the USA is considered a competitive aspect of people climate. Public schools, eldercare, kindergartens, higher education, infrastructure and public transportation are all regulated by national laws. The Nordic welfare states highly subsidize the cultural industries which enables a relatively equal distribution of cultural amenities such as libraries, theatres and museums between regions. Service levels are also rather equal across different regions, and therefore local governments face difficulties in marketing their city regions by focusing on the level of their welfare goods. These aspects of the Nordic welfare states greatly diminish the effect of people climate as an attractive force. The welfare system also supports and encourages dual-career families which further strengthens the need for thick labour markets. An implication of this is that individual Nordic regions will experience difficulties in creating competitive advantages by merely focusing on people climate. Consequently, regions will face difficulties in marketing themselves on people climate parameters only. The finding that people climate is secondary to business climate is in line with results from a large-scale survey carried out by Hansen and Niedomysl (2009), who conclude that employment opportunities and social relations are the main reasons why creative people migrate.

The second major finding of the study is that what attracts or repels the creative class varies between types of regions, by different parts of the creative class, and by people in different phases of life. The notion of people climate is perceived differently in different places. The capital city regions score highest on Florida's original indicators of people climate, such as diversity, tolerance, cultural opportunities and vibrant street life (Hansen, 2007). However, the capital city regions often struggle with expensive housing, congestion and a lack of social cohesion which have a push-effect on some people, especially families with children, towards the outer parts of the capital region or to other parts of the countries. Therefore, the people climate of capital city regions primarily appeals to young creative workers, often without children. At the same time, educational opportunities and thick job markets are highly important for these groups. Semi-peripheral regions, on the other hand, cannot compete on qualities like diversity and cultural offers. But social relations and local identity may attract the creative class to semi-peripheral regions. The same applies for regional centres which furthermore offer thicker job markets and educational opportunities along with larger cultural supply than the average semi-peripheral region. An additional advantage of the regional centres is that they offer both 'large cities and small towns' environments at the same time – a characteristic by which they may distinguish themselves from the capital city regions. However, it seems that both semi-peripheral regions and regional centres first of all attract creative class members because of job opportunities, but that these regions retain people because of specific aspects of quality of life.

Both people climate and business climate are implemented in regional strategies in the studied regions, but to a varying degree. Attracting and retaining creative and talented people is emphasized in all types of regions, but the traditional strategies of strengthening the business climate are increasingly employed the less densely populated the regions are. Whereas capital cities, and to some extent also regional centres, mainly focus on attracting the creative class, semi-peripheral regions try to attract qualified labour *as well as* to provide a beneficial business climate. According to our findings, there seems to be a mismatch between economic development strategies and the actual key drivers of economic development in the different types of regions. Capital city regions may overstate the focus on people climate compared to the actual significance of this factor for the location of the creative class and businesses in these regions. As regards semi-peripheral regions, a more feasible strategy may be to strengthen their originality and authenticity rather than trying to 'become more global' in their people climate, as they cannot compete in that playground with larger city regions anyway.

Regions should consider various combinations of and approaches to people climate and business climate in regional planning and strategy development. A viable strategy for capital city regions which would help attract creative workers globally is focusing on the housing market in order to make it more affordable for the creative class to live in the city region throughout different phases of life. Due to an often well-developed people climate, regional centres will gain from focusing on their job markets in order to offer alternatives to the capital city regions. Trying to appear as equally international and hectic as the capital cities will, however, probably hinder creative class families from moving to the regional centres. The same applies to semi-peripheral regions; however, here entrepreneurial spirits should be supported and combined with a socially integrated small town environment and hands-on policy to increase networks between firms and to nurture firms with quick and efficient bureaucracy.

These considerations testify an analytical approach that does not suit all types of regions. Our findings point to the fact that an attractive people climate in a Nordic context to some extent differs from the one that Florida emphasizes – particularly for city regions other than the capitals. Consequently, when comparing the Nordic findings to Florida's creative class thesis, we will argue that Florida has an exaggerated focus on people climate parameters such as vibrant street life, music scenes and cultural diversity. These factors are less important to job and career opportunities for 'creative class families' in a Nordic context. In this respect the priorities linked to young and single members of the creative class seem to be overrepresented in Florida's (2002a) research. In this sense the study raises concerns about the potential for applying the creative class approach beyond large city regions which strongly limits the usability of the approach in regional planning. Consequently, more studies of perceptions of the people climate for people in different places and life phases and at more detailed regional levels would further help improve our understanding of the location patterns of highly skilled people.

Acknowledgements

This study is an outcome of the European Science Foundation project, *Technology, Talent and Tolerance in European Cities: A Comparative Analysis*, coordinated by Professor Bjørn T. Asheim, Lund University. We wish to thank the partners in the project for valuable discussions throughout the project. Moreover we wish to thank the granting organizations: European Science Foundation, the Swedish Research Council, the Academy of Finland, the Research Council of Norway and Danish Enterprise and Construction Authority (Erhvervs- og Byggestyrelsen) and the Danish Municipality VAT foundation (Den Kommunale Momsfond). Lastly, we thank the three anonymous referees for valuable constructive comments.

Notes

1 In the Nordic countries, correlations between the share of creative workers and high-tech growth are negative for city regions with 10,000 to 49,999 and insignificant for regions with 50,000 to 99,999 inhabitants (Hansen, 2008: 179).
2 The income levels, social systems and national cultures of the Nordic countries are often based on both a husband's and wife's involvement in the labour market, as opposed to e.g. Germany, where the income taxation system supports a situation where one parent stays home with children.
3 'Technology, Talent and Tolerance in European Cities: A Comparative Analysis'. The project was carried out between 2004 and 2007 by partners from Denmark, Finland, Germany, the Netherlands, Norway, Sweden, Switzerland and the UK. The study was financed by the European Science Foundation and National Research Councils.
4 Sweden has traditionally had the most liberal policy among the Nordic countries towards immigration, people seeking asylum and refugees. Especially in the last decade refugee policy and asylum policy in Sweden have been significantly less strict than in Denmark, Finland and Norway.
5 It should be noted that Oulu is the regional centre of Northern Finland, but due to its rather small size, it may be seen here as a semi-peripheral region.

Bibliography

Andersen, K. V. and Lorenzen, M. (2005) *The Geography of the Danish Creative Class*, Report, Department of Industrial Economics and Strategy, Copenhagen Business School, available at: http://www.kreativeklasse.dk (accessed 29 August 2013).

Asheim, B. T. (1996) 'Industrial districts as "learning regions": A condition for prosperity', *European Planning Studies*, 4: 379–400.

Asheim, B. T. and Hansen, H. K. (2009) 'Knowledge bases, talents and contexts: On the usefulness of the creative class approach in Sweden', *Economic Geography*, 85: 425–442.

Asheim, B. T. and Isaksen, A. (1997) 'Location, agglomeration and innovation: Towards regional innovation systems in Norway?', *European Planning Studies*, 5: 299–330.

Bathelt, H., Malmberg, A. and Maskell, P. (2004) 'Clusters and knowledge: Local buzz, global pipelines and the process of knowledge creation', *Progress in Human Geography*, 28: 31–56.

Berg, B. L. (2007) *Qualitative Research Methods for the Social Sciences*, 6th edn, Boston: Pearson.

Bille, T. (2009) 'Den danske kreative klasses kulturelle profil', in K. V. Andersen and M. Lorenzen (eds), *Den Kreative Klasse*, Århus: Forlaget Klim, pp. 47–66.

Boschma, R. and Fritsch, M. (2007) 'Creative class and regional growth: Empirical evidence from eight European countries', *Economic Geography*, 85(4): 391–423.

Breschi, S. and Malerba, F. (1997) 'Sectoral innovation systems: Technological regimes, Schumpeterian dynamics, and spatial boundaries', in C. Edquist (ed.), *Systems of Innovation*, London: Pinter, pp. 130–156.

Brusco, S. (1982) 'The Emilian model: Productive decentralisation and social integration', *Cambridge Journal of Economics*, 6: 167–184.

Carlsson, B. (ed.) (1995) *Technological Systems and Economic Performance*, Dordrecht: Kluwer.

Cooke, P. (1992) 'Regional innovation systems: Competitive regulation in the new Europe', *Geoforum*, 23: 365–382.

Cooke, P., De Laurentis, C., Tödtling, F. and Trippl, M. (2007) *Regional Knowledge Economies: Markets, Clusters and Innovation*, Cheltenham, UK: Edward Elgar.

Etzkowitz, H. and Leydesdorff, L. (2000) 'The dynamics of innovation: From national systems and "mode 2" to a triple Helix of university-industry-government relations', *Research Policy*, 29: 109–123.

Finnish Ministry of the Interior (2006) 'Suurten kaupunkiseutujen politiikkakokonaisuus. Alueiden kehittäminen', *Sisäasianministeriön julkaisuja*, 45/2006.

Florida, R. (2002a) *The Rise of the Creative Class: And How It's Transforming Work, Leisure, Community, and Everyday Life*, New York: Basic Books.

Florida, R. (2002b) 'The economic geography of talent', *Annals of the Association of American Geographers*, 94: 743–755.

Freeman, C. (1987) *Technology Policy and Economic Performance: Lessons from Japan*, London: Pinter.

Gertler, M., Florida, R., Gates, G. and Vinodrai, T. (2002) *Competing on Creativity: Placing Ontario's Cities in North American Context*, report prepared for the Ontario Ministry of Enterprise, Opportunity and Innovation and the Institute for Competitiveness and Prosperity.

Glaeser, E. L. (2005) 'Review of Richard Florida's "The Rise of the Creative Class"', *Regional Science and Urban Economics*, 35: 593–596.

Hall, P. and Soskice, D. (eds) (2001) *Varieties of Capitalism: The Institutional Foundations of Comparative Advantage*, Oxford: Oxford University Press.

Hansen, H. K. (2007) 'Technology, talent and tolerance: The geography of the creative class in Sweden', *Rapporter och Notitser* 169, Department of Social and Economic Geography, Lund: Lund University.

Hansen, H. K. (2008) 'The urban turn – and the location of economic activities', *Meddelanden från Lunds Universitets Geografiska Institution*, Avhandlingar CLXXVI, Lund: Lund University.

Hansen, H. K. and Niedomysl, T. (2009) 'Migration of the creative class: Evidence from Sweden', *Journal of Economic Geography*, 9: 191–206.

Isaksen, A. (2005) *Den kreative klassen og regional næringsutvikling i Norge*, Arbeidsnotat 22/2005, Oslo: NIFU STEP.

Kotkin, J. (2003) 'Paths to prosperity', *American Enterprise*, July/August: 32–5.

Lehmann, C. (2003) 'Class acts', *Raritan*, 22: 147–167.

Lundvall, B-Å. (ed.) (1992) *National Systems of Innovation: Towards a Theory of Innovation and Interactive Learning*, London: Pinter.

McGranahan, D. and Wojan, T. (2007) 'Recasting the creative class to examine growth processes in rural and urban counties', *Regional Studies*, 41: 197–216.

Malanga, S. (2004) 'The curse of the creative class', *City Journal*, Winter, available at: http://www.city-journal.org/html/14_1_the_curse.html (accessed 29 August 2013).

Malmberg, A. and Maskell, P. (1997) 'Towards an explanation of regional specialization and industry agglomeration', *European Planning Studies*, 5: 25–42.

Markusen, A. (1996) 'Sticky places in slippery space: A typology of industrial districts', *Economic Geography*, 72: 293–314.

Markusen A. (2006) 'Urban development and the politics of a creative class: Evidence from a study of artists', *Environment and Planning A*, 38(10): 1921–1940.

Marlet, G. and van Woerkens, C. (2007) 'The Dutch creative class and how it fosters urban employment growth', *Urban Studies*, 44: 2605–2626.

Marshall, A. (1890) *Principles of Economics*, London: Macmillan.

Martin, R. and Sunley, P. (2006) 'Path dependence and regional economic evolution', *Journal of Economic Geography*, 6: 395–437.

Maskell, P. and Malmberg, A. (1999) 'The competitiveness of firms and regions: "Ubiquitification" and the importance of localized learning', *European Urban and Regional Studies*, 6: 9–25.

Mathiasen, S. B., Poulsen, C. F. and Lorenzen, M. (2006) *Rammebetingelser for Københavns kreative brancher*, Copenhagen: Imagine, Copenhagen Business School.

Miles, R. E. and Snow, C. C. (1996) 'Twenty-first-century careers', in M. B. Arthur and D. M. Rousseau (eds), *The Boundaryless Career: A New Employment Principle for a New Organizational Era*, Oxford: Oxford University Press, pp. 97–116.

Miller, R. and Floricel, S. (2004) 'Value creation and games of innovation', *Research-Technology Management*, 47: 25–37.

Nelson, R. (ed.) (1993) *National Innovation Systems: A Comparative Analysis*, Oxford: Oxford University Press.

OECD (2002) 'Income distribution and poverty in the OECD area: Trends and driving forces', *OECD Economic Studies*, 34, 2002/1.

Peck, J. (2005) 'Struggling with the creative class', *International Journal of Urban and Regional Research*, 29: 740–770.

Piore, M. J. and Sabel, C. F. (1984) *The Second Industrial Divide: Possibilities for Prosperity*, New York: Basic Books.

Porter, M. E. (1990) *The Competitive Advantage of Nations*, Basingstoke: Macmillan.

Putnam, R. D. (1993) *Making Democracy Work: Civic Traditions in Modern Italy*, Princeton, NJ: Princeton University Press.

Raunio, M. (2001) 'Osaajat valintojen kentällä Helsingin, Tampereen, Turun, Jyväskylän, Porin ja Seinäjoen seutujen vetovoimaisuus virtaavassa maailmassa', University of Tampere, Research Unit for Urban and Regional Development Studies, *Sente Publications* 11/2001, Tampere.

Raunio, M. and Linnamaa, R. (2000) 'Asuin- ja elinympäristön laatu ja kaupunkiseudun kilpailukyky. Osaajien preferenssit ja tyytyväisyys Helsingin, Tampereen, Turun, Jyväskylän, Porin ja Seinäjoen seuduilla', University of Tampere, Research Unit for Urban and Regional Development Studies, *Sente Publications* 9/2000, Tampere.

Raunio, M. and Sotarauta, M. (2005) 'Highly skilled labor force in the global field of choices: Case Finland', paper presented at Oxford Round Table, 'Adapting to Globalization in the 21st Century', St. Antony's College, University of Oxford, July 31–August 5.

Stam, E. (2007) 'Why butterflies don't leave: Locational behaviour of entrepreneurial firms', *Economic Geography*, 83: 27–50.

Statistics Denmark (2007) Available at http://www.statistikbanken.dk (accessed 29 August 2013).

Storper, M. and Scott, A. J. (2009) 'Rethinking human capital, creativity and urban growth', *Journal of Economic Geography*, 9: 147–167.

Tödtling, F. and Trippl, M. (2005) 'One size fits all? Towards a differentiated regional innovation policy approach', *Research Policy*, 34:1203–1219.

Winther, L. and Hansen, H. K. (2006) 'The economic geographies of the outer city: Industrial dynamics and imaginary spaces of location in Copenhagen', *European Planning Studies*, 14: 1389–1406.

Yin, R. (2008) *Case Study Research: Design and Methods*, 4th edn, Thousand Oaks, CA: Sage.

7 Tolerance, aesthetics, amenities or jobs?

The attraction of the Dutch city to the creative class

Gerard Marlet and Clemens van Woerkens

Introduction

Ever since the publication of Richard Florida's *The Rise of the Creative Class* (Florida, 2002), Dutch local policy-makers have been trying to stimulate their local economies by attracting the so-called creative class. In his book Florida states that those cities where creative people (the creative class) tend to live are able to attract more (high-tech) industries and perform better economically.

Most Dutch cities and towns try to attract this creative class by handing over old factory buildings to artists, charging no rent or very little. They hope that this *broedplaatsenbeleid* (a policy to create "cauldrons of creativity") will in the near future attract the creative class and thus stimulate the local economy. Hope is the correct word here since very little is known about what exactly attracts creative, highly educated people to certain cities.

Florida's key contribution to the economic development literature is—as he claimed—an answer to the question why some places are better able than others to generate, attract, and retain creative people: "In my view, it is not amenities that account for the why. What accounts for the why is, simply put, openness ... I have come to refer to it as 'Tolerance'" (Florida, 2004). According to Florida, it is not (or not only) job opportunities or urban amenities that attract the creative class to a city, but openness and tolerance towards a diverse urban climate.

Creative and talented people are often individualists with alternative preferences, diverse lifestyles and non-conformist behavior. That is why cities that are open to and tolerant of a wide range of people and their socially and ethnically diverse backgrounds are successful in attracting the creative class. Creative people feel drawn to urban tolerant atmospheres and they like urban cosmopolitan experiences (Florida, 2002). Successful cities are, according to Florida, not consumer cities (Glaeser *et al.*, 2001), nor social capital cities (Putnam, 2000), but places with "low barriers to entry" which are "known for diversity of thought and open-mindedness" (Florida, 2005).

In his later work Florida added aesthetics as another important factor for a city's appeal to creative, highly educated people (Florida, 2007). By aesthetics, Florida means a city's aesthetic qualities, both physical (fine buildings in the urban environment) and natural (the scenery outside the city). In his earlier work Florida had already referred to the importance of authentic inner cities, both in the sense of buildings and cultural venues (Florida, 2002). In a recent survey by Florida in cooperation with the Gallup Organization, young recent university graduates stated that the aesthetic qualities of cities are the most important factor determining their choice for a place to live (Florida *et al.*, 2006).

Aesthetic cities which are tolerant and open to cultural and ethnic diversity attract creative people, who are in turn responsible for economic prosperity in these cities. This view of Richard Florida is opposed to traditional views in urban economics, where living patterns of households are mainly explained either by job opportunities or by choice of amenities. In traditional urban theory, people were not supposed to be attracted by things like tolerance or aesthetics, but by jobs. The location decisions of households were seen as a trade-off between (cheap) residence outside the city center and travel costs to work within the city center (Alonso, 1970).

Other urban scholars have emphasized the role of amenities as a major attraction for people in their location decision. At first, the amenity literature was mainly concerned with natural amenities like climate and environmental beauty (Ullman, 1954). Later, urban amenities like culture and cafés were also seen as a decisive reason for people to live in a particular place (Glaeser *et al.*, 2001; Clark, 2003). In this view, people's decisions where to live no longer depend on the availability of jobs, but on specific living preferences like natural and urban amenities—while jobs follow people, business is attracted to places where people like to live (Boarnet, 1994). But although the role of amenities is generally accepted, and more and more evidence is appearing of a connection between amenities and growth, this does not mean that job opportunities are no longer important in the location decisions of households (Compton and Pollak, 2004).

How does Florida's view fit into this tradition of urban economics? Florida agrees that people do not just follow jobs. But natural and urban amenities are not, for him, enough as an alternative explanation for a city's appeal. Creative and highly educated people prefer cities which have aesthetic assets and which are open and tolerant to cultural and ethnic diversity. Cities which combine these qualities are able to attract creative people and, as a result, jobs. Since Florida also assumes that jobs follow people, business will move to such places with high stocks of human (creative) capital.

The Dutch case

Tolerance as an economic force sounds very familiar to the Dutch in accounts of their economic history. The seventeenth-century Dutch 'Golden Age' is widely accepted to be related to Dutch tolerance towards (highly skilled) immigrants with various religious backgrounds (Israel, 1995). But in the present chapter we are concerned not with the position of the Netherlands among other countries, but rather with differences between regions within the Netherlands. How do tolerance features differ between cities in relation to differences in attractiveness to creative people?

In a previous paper we found significant positive correlations between the existence of a large creative class and local employment growth in the Netherlands (Marlet and Van Woerkens, 2004). Business really appears to be attracted to places with high levels of creative, highly educated people. We also found that Florida's creative class is a better measure of local stocks of human capital than education levels are. Dutch cities with high levels of the creative class perform economically better than other Dutch cities. This would seem to confirm the economic relevance of our question—to what extent do tolerance and aesthetics explain the residential patterns of the creative class in the Netherlands?

In this chapter we will try to find out which factors actually drive the Dutch creative class. We will explore all the possibilities mentioned above: tolerance and aesthetics, amenities, and job opportunities. We will do this in a cross-section of Dutch cities, using a large database of city-specific indicators developed for our yearly comparison of the country's 50 largest municipalities (Marlet and Van Woerkens, 2005). Our conclusion is that it is *not* tolerance which drives the creative class in the Netherlands. Aesthetics, however, does provide an additional explanation for the preferences shown by Dutch creative people in choosing a city of residence, complementing more traditional explanations of amenities and job opportunities.

The geography of the Dutch creative class

Richards Florida's creative class is a category of people who are not necessarily highly educated but who are engaged in creative, innovative jobs. His creative class covers about 30 percent of the American labor force. This creative class not only includes writers, designers, musicians, painters and artists, but also scientists, managers and people in computer, engineering, education, health care, legal and financial occupations (Florida, 2002).

In our previous paper we described the way we constructed a Dutch creative class. We used a narrower definition than Florida's, resulting in a 19 percent share of creative people in the total Dutch labor force. We used data on profession (EBB) on a city level from the Dutch statistical institute, CBS. The data contains the professions of a sample of inhabitants of each city. We have been more precise in selecting creative jobs. While Florida included, for example, *all* people with educational and managerial jobs in the creative class, it was in fact his own definition of creative and innovative jobs which led us to leave out several managerial, educational, administrative and governmental jobs (Marlet and Van Woerkens, 2004).

We determined and mapped out not where creative people *work* but where they *live*. This is in line with Florida's creative capital theory, claiming that where creative people live, the economy will grow faster and thus imply that, in fact, jobs follow people. The places where the creative class tends to live in the Netherlands are mapped in Figure 7.1.

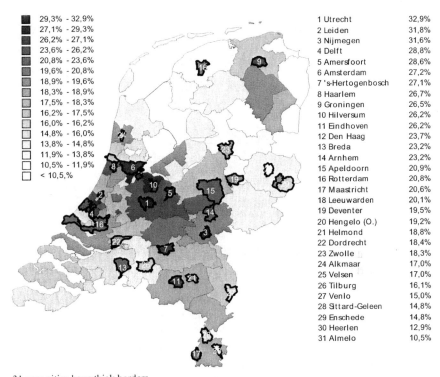

■ 29,3% - 32,9%	
■ 27,1% - 29,3%	
■ 26,2% - 27,1%	
■ 23,6% - 26,2%	
■ 20,8% - 23,6%	
■ 19,6% - 20,8%	
■ 18,9% - 19,6%	
■ 18,3% - 18,9%	
□ 17,5% - 18,3%	
□ 16,2% - 17,5%	
□ 16,0% - 16,2%	
□ 14,8% - 16,0%	
□ 13,8% - 14,8%	
□ 11,9% - 13,8%	
□ 10,5% - 11,9%	
□ < 10,5,%	

1	Utrecht	32,9%
2	Leiden	31,8%
3	Nijmegen	31,6%
4	Delft	28,8%
5	Amersfoort	28,6%
6	Amsterdam	27,2%
7	's-Hertogenbosch	27,1%
8	Haarlem	26,7%
9	Groningen	26,5%
10	Hilversum	26,2%
11	Eindhoven	26,2%
12	Den Haag	23,7%
13	Breda	23,2%
14	Arnhem	23,2%
15	Apeldoorn	20,9%
16	Rotterdam	20,8%
17	Maastricht	20,6%
18	Leeuwarden	20,1%
19	Deventer	19,5%
20	Hengelo (O.)	19,2%
21	Helmond	18,8%
22	Dordrecht	18,4%
23	Zwolle	18,3%
24	Alkmaar	17,0%
25	Velsen	17,0%
26	Tilburg	16,1%
27	Venlo	15,0%
28	Sittard-Geleen	14,8%
29	Enschede	14,8%
30	Heerlen	12,9%
31	Almelo	10,5%

31 core cities have thick borders
other cities or regions have thin lines

Figure 7.1 The geography of the Dutch creative class, 2003

Figure 7.1 suggests that creativity is concentrated in the middle and western part of the country. The ranking of the 31 core cities in the Netherlands shows that the central city of Utrecht, the fourth biggest city of the Netherlands, has the largest share of people belonging to the creative class, followed by Leiden and Nijmegen. All three cities have universities, which suggests there is a correlation between universities and stocks of creativity. But five of the other seven top 10 cities do not have universities; and university towns located on the periphery—especially Maastricht in the south and Enschede in the east—are not among the top-creative cities in the Netherlands, Enschede is even among the bottom 10. It may therefore be not universities as such that matter, but the higher concentration of universities in more agglomerated regions. The more agglomerated western part of the Netherlands (Randstad) does have relatively higher concentrations of creative class as compared to the rest of the country (see Table 7.1). The north in particular has relatively small amounts of residents belonging to the creative class.

In the regions, the creative class tends to live in cities rather than in suburbs or the countryside. In the 31 core cities of the Netherlands, 23.9 percent of the total

Table 7.1 Regional differences in share and growth of the creative class

	Share 1996 (%)	Share 2004 (%)	Increase of share (%)
The Netherlands	16.2	19.4	3.3
Core cities (K31)	20.8	23.9	3.2
Rest of the country	13.8	17.2	3.3
West ("Randstad")	19.2	22.2	3.0
North	11.7	15.1	3.4
East	14.5	17.6	3.2
South	13.8	17.6	3.8

labor force belongs to the creative class. In the rest of the country the creative class accounts for 17.2 percent of the total labor force. These findings are quite similar to the geography of creativity in the US (Florida, 2002).

This Dutch geography of creativity might confirm what Jane Jacobs has suggested—that the advantage of cities for creative, highly educated people lies in the density of diverse people and companies, which increases the possibilities of face-to-face contact, knowledge accumulation, and job opportunities (Jacobs, 1985).

However, growth figures (see Table 7.1) show that the Dutch creative class no longer tends to move to the cities, nor to the western part of the country. The increase in share of the creative class during the years 1996–2004 was roughly the same in cities and in the rest of the country. Moreover, the increase was smaller in the more agglomerated western part of the country (3.0 percent) as compared to the periphery (3.5 percent). Especially the southern parts of the

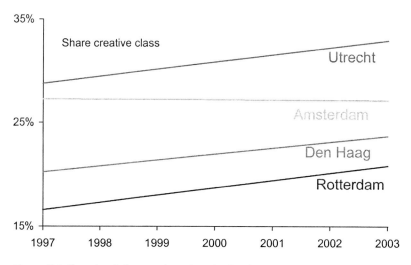

Figure 7.2 Growth of the creative class in the four largest cities of the Netherlands, 1997–2003

Netherlands saw a more than average increase in the share of people belonging to the creative class (3.8 percent).

Most of the cities with the largest increases in the share of the creative class, like Amersfoort, Nijmegen and Den Bosch, seem to lie in regions just outside the most agglomerated Randstad region. The central capital city of Amsterdam has no growth at all. Among the four large cities in the Netherlands, Rotterdam is the city whose creative class is increasing most significantly (Figure 7.2). The geography of the creative class presents a clear picture. The creative class is concentrated in the cities in the agglomerated western part of the country while seeing most of its growth outside that region.

The question is why the Dutch creative class tends to concentrate in certain cities in the western part of the country. Is it because of job opportunities, as standard economic literature suggests? Or is it because of their amenities? Or does the creative class behave differently from average people in the sense that they search primarily for aesthetically satisfying cities and a tolerant, open and diverse urban atmosphere?

A related question is why the creative class is no longer growing in the creative centers. Are congestion forces becoming more important than agglomeration forces in the Netherlands? Before we are able to answer these questions, a methodological problem needs to be tackled: How do we measure tolerance and aesthetics? And how to measure amenities and job opportunities?

Measuring tolerance, aesthetics, amenities, and jobs

Tolerance

In his *Rise of the Creative Class*, Florida suggests that local tolerance and openness can be measured by the amount of artists and gays living in the city. The importance of artists is, according to Florida's theory, not that they are artists but the fact that they are (or, to be precise, the *Bohemian Index*) is a good indicator of a city's level of openness and tolerance. Artists, gays, and the heterogeneous creative class go where a tolerant and open urban climate appears (Florida, 2005).

We have used similar indicators for tolerance. We calculated the Gay scene in Dutch cities using the subscriber postcodes of two gay magazines (*Squeeze* and *Gaykrant*) and the postcodes of members of the Dutch Gay organization, COC. The local average of these three sources as a percentage of total population is our proxy for the size of the local gay scene. Florida finds a strong correlation between the Gay Index and the share of the creative class. He regards the gay index as a "leading indication" for a place that is open and tolerant because both creative class and gays want places where they can "live as they please without raising eyebrows" (Florida, 2002).

Figure 7.3 shows the top 10 cities with largest gay scene in the Netherlands with two of the biggest cities in the western part of the country, Amsterdam and Utrecht, ranking first and third, and a smaller city in the

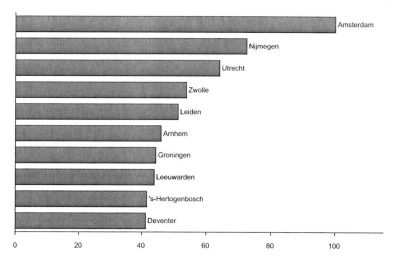

Figure 7.3 Top 10 Dutch cities with the largest gay scene

Note: Index, 100 = largest.

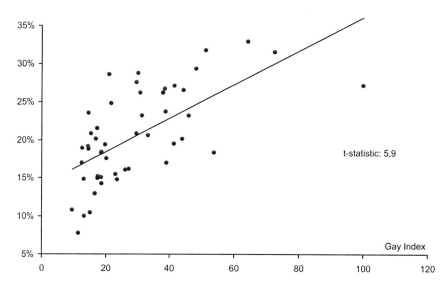

Figure 7.4 Correlation between the Gay Index and share of creative class in the 50 largest
municipalities in the Netherlands

east, Nijmegen, since the 1960s known for its large left-wing gay community, ranking second. Figure 7.4 shows a fairly strong simple correlation
between the Gay Index and share of creative class in the 50 largest municipalities in the Netherlands.

Our second indicator for tolerance is a Dutch Bohemian Index. Richard Florida's artists, measured as the so-called Bohemian Index, are in fact another proxy for tolerance and openness to diversity. According to Florida, this Bohemian Index explains the rise of the creative class in American cities because artists, like gays, tend to live in tolerant and open cities, which is exactly the urban environment where the creative class also prefers to live. He finds correlations between the Bohemian Index, on the one hand, and the share of the creative class, population growth, and local employment growth, on the other (Florida, 2002).

As a starting point for constructing our Dutch Bohemian Index we chose Florida's definition of the Bohemian Index, which includes writers, designers, musicians and composers, actors and directors, painters and sculptors, photographers and artist printmakers, dancers, artists, and performers (ibid.). However, local and regional data on the presence of artistic jobs are not available at the Dutch Bureau of Statistics (CBS). We therefore used a different source: the membership lists of various unions united in the Federation of Dutch Artists unions. Not all memberships could be included. Some membership lists were unavailable and some of the unions were considered to be less relevant for the construction of the Bohemian Index. Accordingly, a limited number of bohemians were included in our Dutch Bohemian Index: designers, visual artists, photographers, interior designers, composers, dancers, authors, painters, sculptors, and ceramic artists.

Figure 7.5 shows the top 10 cities with the largest share of bohemians in the total population. Amsterdam is, again, ranked first and Utrecht again third. The

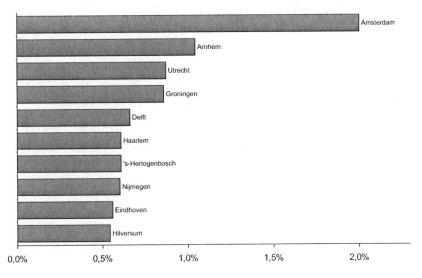

Figure 7.5 Top 10 Dutch cities with the largest artists community (as % of population)

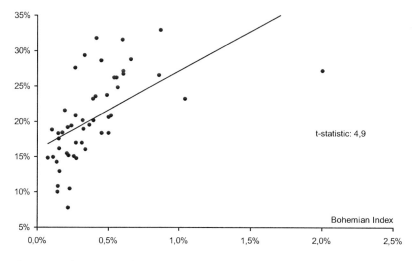

Figure 7.6 Correlation of the Bohemian Index with share of the creative class

city of Arnhem, with a well-known academy of arts and fashion (fashion designers Victor and Rolf graduated there), is ranked second on our Dutch Bohemian Index. Figure 7.6 shows the correlation of this Dutch Bohemian Index with the share of the creative class in the 50 largest Dutch cities. These findings, positive correlations between both the Dutch Bohemian Index and the Gay Index, on the one hand, and the share of the creative class, on the other, are similar to the correlations Florida finds for the US (Florida, 2005).

Florida's third and last measure for local tolerance is diversity. This diversity is measured by the so-called Melting Pot Index: the relative percentage of for-eign-born people in the city (Florida, 2002). As our own third indicator for tolerance we have used ethnic diversity. This indicator differs from Florida's Melting Pot Index because we took account of differences in ethnic background among the foreign-born people in a town. Our measure of ethnic diversity is based on the idea that the importance of diversity will increase with the chances of every urban inhabitant to coming into contact with people of a different eth-nic background.

Diversity is highest in a town where every inhabitant has a different ethnic back-ground, which is of course a theoretical case. The larger the variety of ethnic back-ground of a given town's population, the greater will be its diversity in our sense. We calculated ethnic diversity using the Hirschman-Herfindahl index, which is the sum of squared shares of the various ethnic backgrounds among total population.

Figure 7.7 ranks the top 10 cities that are ethnically most diverse, showing that the three largest cities of the Netherlands, Amsterdam, Rotterdam and The Hague, are ranked first, second and third in exactly the same order. Figure 7.8 shows the correlation between ethnic diversity and the share of the creative class in Dutch cities. In contrast to our other two diversity measures, our measure for ethnic

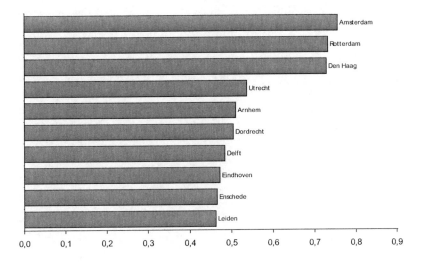

Figure 7.7 Top 10 ethnically diverse Dutch cities

Source: Hirschman-Herfindahl index.

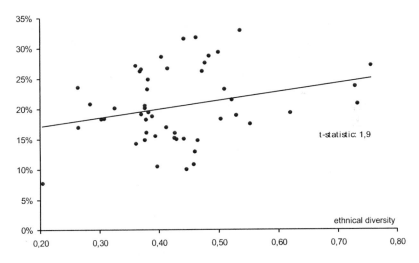

Figure 7.8 Correlation between diversity and share of the creative class in Dutch cities

diversity is not very significantly correlated to the share of the creative class. Florida, too, finds no correlation between his Melting Pot Index and the creative class in US cities (Florida, 2002).

Ethnic diversity might be an indicator not only of tolerance, but also of sorts of social problems related to immigrants. Therefore, we put several crime indicators as control variables into our models. None of these crime variables explained the share and growth of the creative class significantly; that is why they do not show up in the reduced models presented in the next section.

The indicators for tolerance introduced so far reflect tolerance and openness towards cultural and ethnic diversity. There is yet another type of tolerance and openness in cities referred to by Florida: tolerance and openness towards a diverse nightlife. The creative class, as Florida sees it, combines working hard with and intense social life: work hard and play hard (Coslor, 2001). The creative class has flexible working schedules, often working until late at night. After work, creative people want to relax in the city's venues, no matter the time of day or night. That is why, according to Florida, successful cities offer daily "around the clock" entertainment. And that again is why local governments should be tolerant of nightlife venues in town.

To account for this type of tolerance we introduced our fourth and last tolerance-indicator: *local pub closing hours*. Such an indicator, which is expected to be closely related to urban amenities as well, is not used by Florida. In the Netherlands, local government is responsible for legislation on the closing hours of pubs, clubs, and restaurants. There are huge differences between cities on this point. In some cities, pubs should be closed by 1 a.m., while other cities have no restrictions at all and many pubs are open all night during weekends. We suggest this local policy is a good indicator of local tolerance towards nightlife.

By viewing local websites or calling the town halls, we got a complete picture of the closing hours in Dutch cities. Ten out of the 50 largest municipalities in the Netherlands have no limitations on opening hours for bars and restaurants. Among them are the four biggest cities and the cities of Dordrecht, Groningen, Maastricht, and Venlo. However, there is no significant correlation between pub closing hours in cities and share of the creative class (t-value = 1.1).

Aesthetics

To indicate the aesthetic qualities of Dutch cities we used two indicators, one for urban aesthetics and one for natural beauty. Dutch environmental beauty is indicated by the proximity to nature. This is measured as a weighted sum of the natural areas surrounding the city, the weight depending on the travel time from the city to that area, being a monotonically decreasing function.

Figure 7.9 shows the ranking of Dutch cities which are the closest to nature nearby. Most of the cities ranked in this top 10 are located in the middle (Utrecht, Amersfoort, Hilversum) and eastern (Zwolle, Arnhem, Apeldoorn) parts of the country with relatively large natural sites like the Veluwe and the Utrechtse Heuvelrug. Simple correlations in Figure 7.10 suggest that these cities with most nature nearby also have a larger share of people belonging to the creative class.

The share of houses built before 1945 (pre-Second World War) as a percentage of total housing stock has been taken as an indicator of a city's historical character.

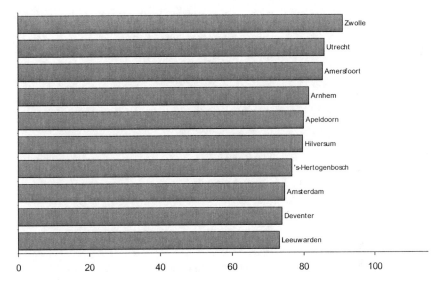

Figure 7.9 Top 10 Dutch cities with nearby scenic areas (proximity to nature)

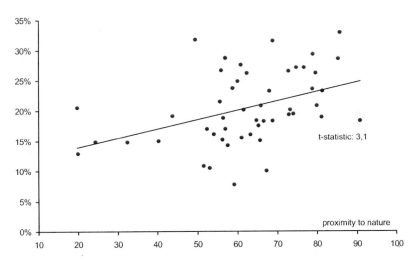

Figure 7.10 Proximity to nature correlates with share of the creative class in Dutch cities

The number of historic buildings indicates the urban aesthetics and authenticity Florida refers to. Others also emphasize the importance of historic buildings for the identity of young urban professionals (Häußermann and Siebel, 1996). Haarlem, Amsterdam, and Hilversum are ranked first, second, and third historic cities (Figure 7.11). Rotterdam is still in the top 10, but last of the four largest cities due to being

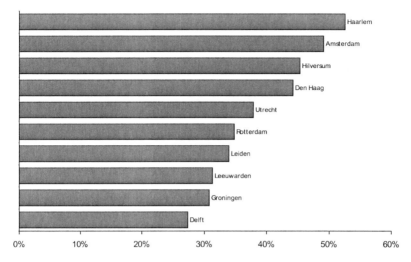

Figure 7.11 Top 10 Historical Dutch cities (pre-1945 buildings as share of total housing stock)

heavily bombed in the Second World War that destroyed large parts of the inner city. Figure 7.12 shows a positive correlation between the share of historic buildings and the share of the creative class.

In this chapter we aim to find an answer to the question of what attracts creative people in the Netherlands to a particular town: a tolerant, open and diverse

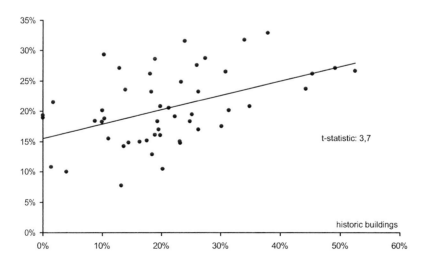

Figure 7.12 Historicity of Dutch cities correlates with share of the creative class

urban atmosphere and aesthetical beauty or the physical presence of local amenities and job opportunity? Therefore, in addition to our indicators for tolerance and aesthetics, in our models we also use indicators of local amenities and job opportunities.

Amenities

Where Florida finds tolerance and aesthetics decisive for the behavior of his creative class, American urban economics has for several decades emphasized the importance of amenities in explaining migration patterns, especially of people with high levels of education and high incomes. When incomes are rising and the location of firms no longer depends on natural resources, location-specific amenities gain importance and migration "flows to more desirable locations" (Knapp and Gravest, 2006).

In the USA, these location-specific amenities have varied from mainly climate and environmental beauty from the 1950s on (Ullman, 1954) to opera houses, sport events, pubs, and restaurants in the 1980s and 1990s (Clark, 2003). Florida does not find significant correlations between cultural amenities and share of creative class (Florida, 2005). But others, like Edward Glaeser, do find positive correlations with households' choice of location (Glaeser *et al.*, 2001).

Similar to Glaeser, we have used the amount of *live performances* per thousand inhabitants as our indicator for cultural amenities. Live performances include classical concerts, opera, dance, and theater performances, and popular music. The number of performances is determined using data from the Dutch *Uitburo* (NUB) which provides a ticket service and maintains a calendar that is used to advertise the programmed performances. In addition to our indicator for cultural amenities we used the *number of pubs* as a second indicator for urban amenities. This urban amenity is measured as the number of pubs per thousand inhabitants. The figures for the number of pubs per city are obtained from the *Bedrijfschap Horeca en Catering* (Trade Organization for the Hotel and Catering Industry).

Both theaters and pubs seem at first sight to have a problem with respect to endogeneity; in theory they not only attract people, but also are a result of the local spending of those people. But culture in the Netherlands is largely a subsidized industry, which means that national policy to a large extent decides the regional distribution of cultural supply. We have therefore assumed culture to be exogenous to our model. For pubs, the problem is more serious. Although the location of pubs and restaurants also has an important local public policy aspect and exogenous local and regional traditions play their parts as well, it is of course necessary for such venues to have local demand, and this is supposed to correlate with the presence of highly educated creative people. This problem could have been resolved by instrumenting this indicator; but since no useful instrumental variables were available we had to leave this problem unresolved.

Job opportunities

Although amenities are generally thought to have an increasing influence on living patterns of people, job opportunities still remain important. We suggest that in measuring these job opportunities, it is important to take account not only of jobs within the city, but of the proximity to jobs elsewhere as well. This was especially true in the Netherlands where none of the four biggest cities is further than 70 km from one of the others.

Therefore we included the proximity to concentrations of jobs in our models. We expect that members of the creative class prefer to live where a wide variety of jobs is available. We not only included the proximity to jobs as an agglomeration force, but also the impact of road congestion on the accessibility of jobs as a disadvantage of agglomeration (Brakman *et al.*, 2001).

Our measure for proximity is based on travel times rather than distances between locations, which are often used in other studies. Commuting times are corrected for the real effect of road congestion. Proximity is calculated as the total sum of jobs that can be reached from the city, on the assumption that there is a willingness to spend time on travel to work which is monotonically decreasing with time.[1]

Control variables

To explain the living patterns of the Dutch creative class we have used, in addition to the four categories of indicators discussed above: for tolerance, aesthetics, amenities and jobs, several control variables.

First, we included *share of owner-occupied houses* (Ministerie van VROM, n.d.). The housing supply in Dutch cities is largely determined by public policy, with large parts consisting of social housing not available for people with higher incomes. We expect this policy-driven housing supply to be important in explaining the composition of a city's population.

In our model explaining the share of creative class among local population we included the *share of students* living in town as another control variable.[2] Students during their studies do not belong to the labor force and so cannot belong to the creative class. But after completing their studies most students will be members of the creative class. Some of them will stay in the town of their studies, which implies that university towns will automatically have higher numbers of creative people in their working force.

In our growth model we have disregarded these students and replaced them by *house prices* per square meter (Marlet and Van Woerkens, 2005). We expect that high house prices will from a certain point onward prevent popular cities from growing further (Knapp and Gravest, 2006).

To compensate for possible omissions of any regional variables which might influence the share and growth of a city's creative class, we included a *spatial lag variable* in our models. The spatially lagged variable is the weighted average of the share and growth of the creative class in all (not just the cities in our sample) surrounding municipalities.[3] This spatial lag variable turned out to be insignificant in all our models. We concluded that there is no evidence for omitted regional variables in our models.

Explaining the living patterns of the Dutch creative class

In the previous sections we introduced the indicators for tolerance, aesthetics, urban amenities, job opportunities as well as the control variables which we are going to use in our models. Table 7.2 summarizes these indicators. For most of the tolerance and aesthetics indicators we found simple positive correlations with the share of the creative class in Dutch cities.

Of course, this does not mean that these factors are the real reason why these cities attract the creative class. Other factors, like job opportunities or amenities, may in fact make the difference. In this section we will therefore combine the indicators mentioned in Table 7.2 in a single model, examining the relationship between these indicators, on the one hand, and, on the other, the share and growth of the creative class. We will do this in cross-section models with a sample of the Dutch core cities.

We are taking cities, not regions, as our unit of analysis because we suggest that the creative class prefers to live in cities (see Table 7.1). We are mainly interested in the differences between cities, not between cities and suburbs. The main question is why some cities are successful in attracting or keeping members of the creative class while others are not.

We have data for only the 50 largest Dutch municipalities. The problem with this sample of 50 municipalities is, however, that there is no rationale other than the availability of these data in selecting them. That is why we prefer to

Table 7.2 Measuring tolerance, esthetics, amenities and job opportunities in Dutch cities

Category/hypothesis	Indicator
1 Tolerance	*Bohemian index*: share of artists in the city
	Gay scene: share of gays among total population
	Ethnic diversity
	Pub closing hours
2 Esthetics	Environmental beauty
	Proximity to nature
	Historic character
	Share of historic buildings
3 Urban amenities	Amount of live performances per 1,000 inhabitants
	Amount of pubs per 1,000 inhabitants
4 Job opportunities	Proximity to jobs
	Traffic congestion affecting accessibility of jobs
5 Control variables	Amount of students
	Housing prices
	Share of privately owned houses
	Crime rates

use a sample of 31 so-called core cities for our cross-section analyses. The selection of this sample of cities is based on their regional function and selected by real travel-to-work patterns (Van Oort, 2002). In using this sample of core cities we avoid the risk of comparing a core city like Amsterdam with one of its own suburbs, like Amstelveen or Haarlemmermeer, which are also in the sample of the 50 largest municipalities. We are aware of the fact that by doing so we use a rather small sample for our analyses. But then we cannot escape the fact that the country we are dealing with is small and does not have very many cities to compare.

Because of the small sample we did pay a great deal of attention to the reliability checks of our estimation results. In the tables below we only present the models that provide the best explanations, but we tried a large amount of alternative models, including and excluding indicators in different combinations (always, of course, within the boundaries of theoretically acceptable specifications). We also tried different years of observation. Finally, we actually tried the same analyses with our sample of 50 municipalities. The estimated results of these alternative models show that our main findings can remain unchanged. This gave us confidence in the robustness of our results.

With the indicators presented above and with our sample of Dutch core cities we estimated models with four categories of variables designed to explain the share and growth of the creative class in Dutch cities: tolerance, aesthetics, amenities, and job opportunities. The results of our model estimations are shown in Table 7.3 (the share of the creative class) and Table 7.4 (the growth).

In Tables 7.3 and 7.4, the results are shown of five models. Every first, second, third, and fourth column presents the results of models that comprise all indicators for aesthetics, amenities and job opportunities, adding the different tolerance indicators one by one in the four different models. Finally, we present the results of the reduced models with the best fit in column V of both tables.

The conclusions seem to be clear. As appears from our findings, the living patterns of the Dutch creative class are not explained by differences in tolerance and openness between the cities in the Netherlands. But aesthetic qualities, historical buildings in the cities and environmental beauty outside cities clearly play an important role.

Meanwhile the most important explanation is still to be found in the traditional factors: job opportunities and—less traditional—urban amenities. Our indicator "proximity to jobs" and both our urban amenities largely explain the share as well as the growth differences of the creative class between Dutch cities.

One of our two aesthetic indicators, "proximity to nature," also explains both the share and the growth of the creative class. The other one, the share of historic buildings, only explains the share of the creative class in Dutch cities, not its growth between 1994 and 2004.

That having been said, the results show that none of the tolerance indicators has a significantly positive correlation to either the share or the growth of the creative class in Dutch cities. We did find simple positive correlations between these indicators and the share of the creative class (Figures 7.6, 7.8 and 7.10), but these positive signs disappear when we enlarge our models to include indicators for aesthetic features, amenities, job opportunities, and control variables (Table 7.3).

Therefore, in contrast to Florida's findings for the United States, we may conclude that tolerance, measured in four different ways, does not explain the residential patterns of the Dutch creative class at all. The creative class does not

Table 7.3 Explaining the share of the creative class in Dutch cities, 2004

	I	*II*	*III*	*IV*	*V*
1. Tolerance					
Bohemian index	−5.5 (−0.7)				
Gay scene		5.3 (0.8)			
Ethnic diversity			−0.002 (−0.0)		
Pub closing hours				−0.0016 (−0.6)	
2. Esthetics					
Proximity to nature	0.73 (2.6)***	0.56 (1.9)*	0.65 (2.1)**	0.70 (3.1)***	0.65 (2.6)***
Share historic buildings	0.15 (3.4)***	0.13 (2.9)***	0.15 (3.3)***	0.16 (3.2)***	0.15 (3.4)***
3. Urban amenities					
Live performances per 1,000 inhabitants	10.7 (2.7)***	8.6 (2.2)**	9.9 (2.8)***	9.3 (2.6)***	9.9 (2.8)***
Pubs per 1,000 inhabitants	0.036 (1.9)*	0.031 (1.8)*	0.033 (2.0)*	0.040 (2.5)***	0.033 (2.0)*
4. Job opportunities					
Proximity to jobs	0.15 (4.5)***	0.14 (4.5)***	0.14 (4.6)***	0.14 (4.3)***	0.14 (4.6)***
Traffic congestion influencing accessibility of jobs	−0.12 (−2.1)**	−0.10 (−1.9)*	−0.11 (−2.1)**	−0.10 (−1.9)*	−0.11 (−2.1)**
5. Control variables					
Amount of students	1.22 (6.7)***	1.19 (6.8)***	1.22 (4.7)***	1.24 (6.6)***	1.22 (6.8)***
Owner-occupied houses	0.22 (6.1)***	0.22 (5.9)***	0.22 (3.0)***	0.21 (5.2)***	0.22 (6.2)***
	OLS	OLS	OLS	OLS	OLS
N	31	31	31	31	31
Moran's I	>31	>35	>29	>34	>27
R^2 adj.	0.82	0.82	0.82	0.82	0.83

Notes: Notation: coefficient (*t*-value) ***.
* Significant at a 90 level.
** Significant at a 95 level.
*** Significant at a 99 level.

tend to live or to grow in Dutch cities which have more ethnic diversity of population or with a larger gay scene. Nor do they appear to be attracted by cities whose pubs are open all night.

Conclusions about the importance of artists in a town are less clear. In our growth model, bohemians do show a significant but, unexpectedly, negative sign suggesting that the creative class tends to grow less in towns where many artists live (column I in Table 7.4). It is, however, a single city which is responsible for this negative sign: the city of Arnhem in the east of the Netherlands, which has a large community of artists but not many (other) members of the

Table 7.4 Explaining the growth of the creative class in Dutch cities, 1994–2004

	I	II	III	IV	V
1. Tolerance					
Bohemian index	−31.8				
	(−2.0)*				
Gay scene		−1.3			
		(−0.1)			
Ethnic diversity			−0.023		
			(−0.3)		
Pub closing hours				0.0034	
				(0.8)	
2. Esthetics					
Proximity to nature	1.60	1.25	1.21	1.15	1.23
	(5.0)***	(3.3)***	(3.5)***	(3.1)***	(3.8)***
Share historic	0.044	0.070	0.065	0.043	0.069
buildings	(0.4)	(0.7)	(0.7)	(0.4)	(0.7)
3. Urban amenities					
Live performances per	16.2	13.6	12.9	14.5	13.3
1,000 inhabitants	(2.5)***	(2.0)*	(1.9)*	(2.2)**	(2.1)**
Pubs per 1,000	0.055	0.061	0.061	0.048	0.061
inhabitants	(2.2)**	(2.1)**	(2.2)**	(1.4)	(2.2)**
4. Job opportunities					
Proximity to jobs	0.30	0.54	0.55	0.57	0.55
	(1.3)	(2.2)**	(2.8)***	(2.8)***	(2.8)***
5. Control variables					
House prices per	−0.070	−0.131	−0.129	−0.133	−0.133
square meter	(−1.4)	(−2.9)***	(−3.4)***	(−3.4)***	(−3.6)***
Privately owned	0.13	0.25	0.23	0.26	0.25
houses	(1.1)	(2.5)***	(2.3)**	(2.8)***	(2.8)***
	OLS	OLS	OLS	OLS	OLS
Moran's I	>58	>57	>55	>72	>57
N	31	31	31	31	31
R^2 adj.	0.39	0.31	0.31	0.32	0.34

Notes: Notation: coefficient (*t*-value) ***.
* Significant at a 90 level.
** Significant at a 95 level.
*** Significant at a 99 level.

creative class, and low levels of growth. The city of Arnhem has one thing instead: a fairly large academy of arts. Leaving Arnhem out of the sample means that the Bohemian Index does not significantly explain the growth of the creative class at all. Instead, our findings suggest that urban cultural venues, or to be precise, live performances, are the most important urban amenity attracting the creative class.

This probably provides an answer to the question whether the mere presence of artists in town constitutes a reason for the creative class to live there or, rather, their creative productions as enjoyed in museums and live performances in theaters.

Jane Jacobs recognized two major reasons why culture is important to the local economy (Jacobs, 1985). First, the cultural sector is a cauldron of creativity because it generates creative, innovative ideas benefiting other sectors in the local economy as well. Second, cultural events are a meeting place for people who exchange ideas and accordingly foster local levels of knowledge, innovation, and growth.

Which of these mechanisms is at work in the Netherlands? Is it the cultural sector itself that generates creative ideas, which in turn benefit local economies? Or is the cultural sector rather a producer of culture, which attracts highly educated, creative people, who in their turn create ideas, are highly productive, and thus stimulate economic growth? Local policy-makers in the Netherlands base their policy mainly on the first assumption. We, on the basis of our findings, both in this and in our previous paper on the creative class (Marlet and Van Woerkens, 2004), suggest the latter reason is true.

In our previous paper we found no evidence for a connection between artists and city growth, and according to the results presented in this chapter it is not artists but live performances, i.e. one of our amenity indicators, which have strong explanatory force for both the share and the growth of the creative class.

In our reduced share model the coefficient of the amount of live performances is 9.9 (column V in Table 7.3). This means that when the annual supply of theater performances in town A is one per thousand inhabitants (0.001) larger than in town B, the share of creative class in the total population is expected to be about 1 percent larger (9.9*0.001 = 0.01). For a city with 250,000 inhabitants, like Utrecht, the fourth largest city in the country, this 1 percent difference in the share of creative class means a difference of one theater with an average of 250 performances (one per thousand inhabitants) per year.

Even Florida, who introduced the Bohemian Index in his earlier work as a measure for tolerance and openness to diversity, in his later work considers bohemians as "a considerable improvement over traditional measures of amenities in that it provides a direct measure of the producers of those amenities" as well (Florida, 2005). But as we have shown, in our models for the Netherlands, it is not the presence of the producers of culture but cultural measures themselves which provide a strong explanation of the residential patterns of the Dutch creative class.

As another indicator for urban amenities beside live performances, the reduced models also show a positive correlation between the number of pubs in a town and the share and growth of its creative class (columns V in Tables 7.3 and 7.4).[4] But as we noted above, if anywhere, we face uncertainties here about the direction of the causality: the number of pubs might be the result rather than the reason for the presence of a large creative class.

That is why we are currently conducting a survey among graduates of Utrecht University, asking them where they went to live after completing their studies and why. The results of this survey, to be published soon, will give more certainty about the direction of the causal relationships found in this chapter.

This causality problem is absent from the set of highly significant aesthetic indicators: share of historic buildings and proximity to nature. These indicators are without any doubt exogenous to the model, which means we can conclude that the creative class tends to live in Dutch towns with historic character and nearby environmental beauty.

Combining these findings with those for our amenity indicators and job opportunities we get a clear picture of the type of city most popular among the Dutch creative class. These cities are most likely to be cities combining a historical inner city with many pubs and cultural venues and located in a natural environment, but still with large concentrations of jobs nearby.

Not tolerance, but aesthetic features, amenities, and job opportunities provide a strong explanation for both the share and the growth of the creative class in Dutch cities. The combination of aesthetic factors and amenities significantly explaining the living patterns of the Dutch creative class makes it possible to create an "amenity index" for the Dutch creative class. Figure 7.13 shows this index in relation to the share of people belonging to the creative class. Figure 7.13 illustrates the strong explanation we found for the regional spread of the creative class in the Netherlands.

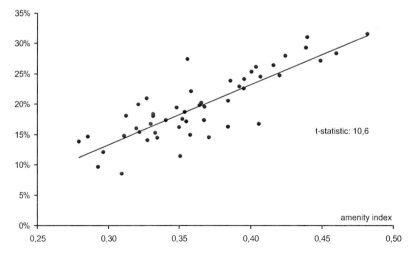

Figure 7.13 Local amenities and aesthetics explain the share of the creative class in Dutch cities

Nevertheless, in the most aesthetic and amenity-rich city of the Netherlands, Amsterdam, the creative class is no longer growing (see Figure 7.3). Our suspicion is that this has something to do with building restrictions, shortage of privately owned houses, and the comparatively high house prices resulting from this.

Although beyond the scope of this chapter, we will discuss two of our control variables here, one of them being house prices. In the reduced growth model (column V in Table 7.4), high house prices constitute a strong negative explanation for the growth of the creative class.[5] This suggests that it is indeed the lack of available and affordable houses in popular and amenity-rich cities which is causing a reverse migration from those towns. Members of the creative class who do like to live in cities like Amsterdam are no longer able to buy or rent a home there, which makes them look for alternative places. High rents are here, to put it in terms of agglomeration theory, a strong congestion force (Helpman, 1998).

We suspect that the relative stagnation of the (large) share of the creative class in Amsterdam is entirely due to extremely high rents since the end of the 1990s. The coefficient of house prices is –0.13 (column V in Table 7.4). House prices are measured in €1000 per square meter. In Amsterdam, house prices were about €2000 per square meter in 2004, which is approximately twice the prices of 1994. If Amsterdam had built more new houses and reduced price rises by 20 percent, house prices would have been €1800 per square meter, i.e. €200 (10 percent) below the present value. In this theoretical case the expected increase in the share of the creative class would have been 2.6 percent of total population (0.13*0.2 = 0.026). In that case Amsterdam would not have been in sixth position in our ranking of creative cities (see Figure 7.1), but in fourth.

An important explanatory control variable in our share models was the share of students in the population. The conclusion seemed trivial: where students live while studying, there they stay after studies. University cities would thus seem to benefit for evermore. But this is not entirely true.

For one thing, not every student in the Netherlands lives in the city where his school is located. In Holland, it is easy to travel between the major cities, which means a student can easily live in Amsterdam (the biggest city) while studying in Rotterdam (the second biggest). Work-in-progress on the location behavior of students in the Netherlands suggests that the number of students in a town greatly depends—of course—on the presence of a university. But this is not all. The availability of affordable houses and, again, amenities like culture and historic buildings explain where students tend to live.

Second, many students tend to leave their towns after completing their studies. The number of students did correlate in our models with the creative class. But other factors were also important.

This means: (1) people without a university degree may belong to the creative class; and (2) people with a university degree may after their studies belong to another town's creative class. Especially Enschede, Maastricht, Groningen, and also Rotterdam find it hard to keep their student populations after completion of studies. The reasons for students leaving these towns are primarily the nearness of jobs, but also changed living preferences. Some people prefer to live in small towns in the countryside, others in cities with more amenities.

This is confirmed by our model estimations. University towns on average have larger creative classes, university towns in agglomerated regions and with high amenity values even more so. The coefficient of the number of students explaining the share of the creative class is about 1.2 (column V in Table 7.3). But we have taken students as a percentage of the total population, and the creative class as a share of the total labor force. The labor force is approximately 60 percent of the total population, which means that the coefficient would have been around 0.7 if we took both indicators out of the total population. This means that 1,000 extra students in town will, after a while, yield an extra 700 creatives.

In a previous paper we concluded that universities do not foster growth directly, but through larger stocks of human capital (Marlet and Van Woerkens, 2004). We therefore support Richard Florida's view of the economic importance of universities, "Policy makers have overstated the degree to which universities can drive national and regional economics ... universities are far more important as the nation's primary source of knowledge creation and talent" (Florida, 2005).

Conclusion

Richard Florida states that is not (only) job opportunities or urban amenities which attract creative highly educated people to cities but, rather, tolerance and aesthetics: "Talent is not necessarily drawn to warmer climates, greater recreational amenities, or cultural amenities," but: "chief among the attractions to workers is diversity and a generalized acceptance of diversity among the local population" (ibid.).

In this chapter we have made it clear that the tolerance/creative class nexus empirically fails to materialize for the Netherlands. We have not found any significant positive correlations from our tolerance indicators—the Dutch Bohemian Index, ethnic diversity, the gay scene or pub closing hours—to the share and the growth of the creative class.

However, the aesthetic qualities of cities (historic buildings) and their location (natural environment) do provide a strong explanation for the share and the growth of the creative class in Dutch cities. Besides that, job opportunities and urban amenities are still the most important factors that influence the choice for a place of residence. These results are summarized in Table 7.5.

Our major finding was that it is not tolerance or openness to cultural or ethnic diversity that makes cities attractive to the creative class, but—beside job opportunities—aesthetic features like nature and historic buildings, and traditional amenities like culture and cafés. Or in a word: quality-of-place.

Our conclusion that tolerance is not important in the competition between Dutch cities of course depends on the empirical findings in our sample of Dutch core cities and the indicators for tolerance we chose: bohemians, gays, ethnic diversity, pub closing hours.

Table 7.5 Summary of results

	Share of the creative class	Growth of the creative class
1. Tolerance	**0**	**0**
Bohemian index	0	0
Gay scene	0	0
Ethnic diversity	0	0
Pub closing hours	0	0
2. Esthetics	+	+/0
Proximity to nature	+	+
Share historic buildings	+	0
3. Urban amenities	+	+
Live performances per 1,000 inhabitants	+	+
Pubs per 1,000 inhabitants	+	+
4. Job opportunities	+	+
Proximity to jobs	+	+
Traffic congestion influencing accessibility of jobs	–	0

This does not inevitably mean that tolerance and openness are in fact unimportant to creative, highly educated people in the Netherlands. It may mean that we have been using the wrong measures for tolerance in Dutch cities. It may also mean that Dutch cities do not differ as much as American cities do in the way of tolerance characteristics. Tolerance might well be important while not being a factor in people's choice of residence: for lack of obviously intolerant cities, people who do find tolerance important may not be either repelled or attracted by any particular city on that score.

These two reservations lead to two further lines of possible research on the supposed tolerance/growth nexus. First, measures for tolerance and openness within cities could be improved. Second, because the supposed lack of cultural differences between cities in small countries like the Netherlands, and therefore the absence of large differences in tolerance characteristics, we should enlarge our sample of research to a sample of European cities or metropolitan areas.

For if tolerance is, in spite of our findings in the Netherlands, an important living preference for creative and highly educated people, it should be possible to measure this in differences in attraction between the larger cities of various European countries like London, Paris, Milan, Berlin, Barcelona, and Amsterdam, rather than between cities within a small country like the Netherlands.

Notes

1 Proximity to jobs is calculated by the following formula:

$$\tilde{J}_i = \sum_j w(0.5 \times t_{ij}^{morning} + 0.5 \times t_{ji}^{evening}) \times J_j$$

In this formula t_{ij} is the travel time from city i to j, $w(t)$ is the share of employees that will accept t as the time needed to get to work and J_j is the number of jobs in city j.

2 Source: Informatie Beheer Groep (The *Informatie Beheer Groep* is responsible for the execution of several Acts and regulations, such as student grants and information management.)
3 The weight depending on the real travel time to those regions, and the size of the regions. See also Anselin (1988).
4 Beside live performances and pubs we also tried restaurants, museums, and crime rates as urban (dis-)amenities in our models. But these amenities did not significantly explain either share or growth of the creative class and are, for that reason, excluded from the final model specifications.
5 In one of the growth models, rents do not significantly correlate with the growth of the creative class (column I in Table 7.4), but the Bohemian Index is significant with the wrong sign here. Bohemians and rents do correlate positively (correlation coefficient = 0.3), which might mean that in the extended models the expected negative sign of house prices is absorbed by the Bohemian Index.

Bibliography

Alonso, W. (1970) *Location and Land Use: Toward a General Theory of Land Use*, Cambridge, MA: Harvard University Press.

Anselin, L. (1988) *Spatial Econometrics: Methods and Models*, Dordrecht: Kluwer.

Boarnet, M. G. (1994) "The monocentric model and employment location," *Journal of Urban Economics*, 36(1): 79–97.

Brakman, S., Garretsen, H. and Van Marrewijk, C. (2001) *An Introduction To Geographical Economics: Trade, Location and Growth*, Cambridge: Cambridge University Press. Available at: http://books.google.ca/books?hl=enandlr=andid=fMbxwuNmq7ICandoi=f ndandpg=PR9anddq=An+Introduction+to+Geographical+Economics+andots=egbB1k g61Wandsig=qSdZ6A3WbNFyCBxGRw2a6OoDcrg (accessed 16 January 2013).

Clark, T. N. (2003) "Urban amenities: Lakes, opera and juice bars: Do they drive development," *Research in Urban Policy*, 9: 103–140.

Compton, J. and Pollak, R. A. (2004) "Why are power couples increasingly concentrated in large metropolitan areas?" Washington: National Bureau of Economic Research. Available from: http://www.nber.org/papers/w10918 (accessed 16 January 2013).

Coslor, E. (2001) "Work hard, play hard: The role of nightlife in creating dynamic cities," unpublished paper, Heinz School of Public Policy and Management, Carnegie Mellon University, Pittsburgh.

Florida, R. (2002) *The Rise of the Creative Class: And How It's Transforming Work, Leisure, Community and Everyday Life*, New York: Basic Books.

Florida, R. (2004) "Response to Edward Glaeser's review of 'The Rise of the Creative Class'," available at: http://www.creativeclass.org/acrobat/ResponsetoGlaeser.pdf (accessed 29 August 2013).

Florida, R. (2005) *Cities and the Creative Class*, New York, Routledge. Available at: http://link.library.utoronto.ca/eir/EIRdetail.cfm?Resources__ID=766447andT=F (accessed 16 January 2013).

Florida, R. (2007) *The Flight of the Creative Class: The New Global Competition For Talent*, New York: HarperCollins.

Florida, R., Miller Steiger, D. and Wilson, D. (2006) *Cities and Subjective Well-being*, Gallup Organization and George Mason University.

Glaeser, E. L., Kolko, J. and Saiz, A. (2001) "Consumer city," *Journal of Economic Geography*, 1(1): 27–50.

Häußermann. H, and Siebel, W. (1996) *Soziologie des Wohnens*, Beltz Juventa, Available at: http://books.google.ca/books?hl=enandlr=andid=0iUvD9uJstACandoi=fndandpg= PA11anddq=Soziologie+des+Wohnens+andots=rt2o98KrSTandsig=Mkdynh VyY0083rcOJGuRZHZFAJQ (accessed 16 January 2013).

Helpman, E. (1998) "The size of regions," in D. Pines, E. Sadka and I. Zilcha (eds), *Topics in Public Economics: Theoretical and Applied Analysis*, Cambridge: Cambridge University Press, pp. 33–54.

Israel, J. I. (1995) *The Dutch Republic: Its Rise, Greatness and Fall, 1477–1806*, Oxford: Clarendon Press. Available at: http://www.history.ac.uk/reviews/printpdf/review/30 (accessed 16 January 2013).

Jacobs, J. (1985) *Cities and the Wealth of Nations: Principles of Economic Life*. New York: Vintage Books. Available at: http://library.wur.nl/WebQuery/clc/228968 (accessed 16 January 2013).

Knapp, T. A. and Gravest, P. E. (2006) "On the role of amenities in models of migration and regional development," *Journal of Regional Science*, 29(1): 71–87.

Marlet, G. A. and Van Woerkens, C. (2004) "Skills and creativity in a cross-section of Dutch cities," *04*, 29. Available at: http://igitur-archive.library.uu.nl/USE/2005-1129-200137/UUindex.html (accessed 16 January 2013).

Marlet, G. and Van Woerkens, C. (2005) *Atlas voor Gemeenten 2005*. Stichting Atlas voor Gemeenten. Available at: http://en.scientificcommons.org/59548357 (accessed 16 January 2013).

Putnam, R. D. (2000) *Bowling Alone: The Collapse and the Revival of American Community*, New York: Simon & Schuster.

Ullman, E. L. (1954) "Amenities as a factor in regional growth," *Geographical Review*, 44(1): 119–132.

Van Oort F. G. (2002) "Agglomeration, economic growth and innovation: Spatial analysis of growth and R&D externalities in the Netherlands," Thela thesis.

8 The creative class, related variety and economic growth in Dutch city-regions

Irina van Aalst, Oedzge Atzema,
Ron Boschma and Frank van Oort

Introduction

The 'creative class' is hypothesized to serve as the engine of the current urban economy (Florida, 2002a) in several ways: as a source of entrepreneurs establishing new firms, a location factor attracting high-tech business and by their consumption patterns and cultural preferences (i.e., purchasing power) of these individuals. Florida conceptualizes the creative class as an effective precondition for (and driving force behind) urban economic growth, whereby, 'in today's creative economy the real source of economic growth comes from the clustering and concentration of talented and productive people' (Florida, 2008: 9). The empirical literature is less extensive regarding the dynamics by which the presence of the creative class is interlinked with urban economic growth – that is, about the engine itself.

Many authors have criticized the conceptualization of the creative class on this point (Peck, 2005; Pratt, 2008; Stam *et al.*, 2008; Storper and Scott, 2009; Reese *et al.*, 2010; Perry, 2011). Storper and Scott (2009) doubt whether the spatial concentration of the creative class will explain urban economic growth. It is argued that such a theory should incorporate agglomeration economies and cumulative causation processes. According to Perry (2011: 330), the direction of causality is important in empirical testing, where it is argued that 'the amenities available at any locality should be viewed as the outcome of urban growth processes rather than independent drivers of that growth'. According to Stam *et al.* (2008: 119), 'The creative class may be enabled to grow more easily in a booming economy, rather than be the cause of economic growth.' Florida is conscious of this criticism and stated that his 'empirical models and evidence do not specify the precise nature and direction of causality' (Florida *et al.*, 2008: 643). In this chapter, we contribute to this debate by analyzing the statistical relationship between the presence of the creative class and economic growth from both sides: does the presence of the creative class affect economic growth, and does economic growth affect the presence of the creative class?

A second aim of the chapter is to test whether the geographical context influences the hypothesized relationship between the creative class and economic growth. We expect differences between countries on the basis of dissimilarities in urban structure and institutional settings. This might be the case between the extensive, highly competitive urban economic landscape in the United States and the compact, more socialized urban economic landscape in the Netherlands. However, as Andersen *et al.* (2010) have shown, important differences between European Nordic countries and Anglo-Saxon countries like the USA, Canada and Britain lead to the conclusion that 'not the "people's climate" suggested by Florida (2002a) but the opportunity of getting an attractive job and a subsequent career are vital for the location of the creative class' (2010: 1605). Explained by the relatively equal distribution of public goods and services regulated by national laws and the relatively highly subsidized cultural facilities, their study underlines the importance of an attractive urban labour market. Nevertheless, in the Nordic countries, the capital regions also score highest on Florida's indicators of a people's climate. The notion of what might be an attractive place to live and work seems to vary between places and people, even those within the creative class. Although the situation in the Netherlands is partially comparable with those of the Nordic countries, the regional differences in urbanity are much smaller in the Netherlands. As stated by Marlet and Van Woerkens (2007), the dense and well-distributed urban structure of the Netherlands and the small differences in economic growth between Dutch city-regions would appear to offer less room for Florida's theory, which especially focuses on large cities and city-regions.

In this chapter, we will investigate to what extent the hypothesis of mutual relationships between the presence of the creative class and economic growth can be applied to Dutch city-regions. The following three questions will be central to our investigation:

1 Are there significant differences in the size and composition of the creative class between city-regions in the Netherlands?
2 Does growth in employment, after controlling for other variables such as residential factors, contribute to differences in the size and composition of the creative class in Dutch city-regions?
3 To what extent does the presence of the creative class, after controlling for other variables such as the relatedness of industries, contribute to economic growth in Dutch city-regions?

We will use city-regions as spatial research units. These regions are urban employment markets, similar to American MSAs.

This chapter is organized as follows. In Section 2, we will look more closely at Florida's hypothesis considering the importance of the creative class for economic growth in city-regions. Section 3 describes the regional distribution of the creative class in the Netherlands. To obtain more insight into how this distribution can be explained, in Section 4, we relate a number of factors to the attraction of the regional creative class (using correlation analysis), such as a high level of urban facilities, employment growth and a local culture of tolerance and openness. In Section 5, we consider whether these factors are significant for growth in the Dutch case using multiple regression analysis and determine the effect of the creative class on economic growth in the urban regions of the Netherlands using regression analysis. Section 6 concludes and provides a discussion on the role of related variety in relation to urban economic growth processes and the creative class.

The creative class and the economic growth of city-regions: a Dutch perspective

Long before Florida (2002a) introduced his ideas about the rise of the creative class, there was an old adage in Europe that 'people make the city'. Nevertheless, Florida's proposal was innovative in linking this adage to the urban economy, specifically by proposing that economic growth has become increasingly dependent on the creativity of the urban population. Florida's ideas go beyond the classical benefits of urban economic specialization because the creative class crosses various economic sectors. This phenomenon is at odds with the prevailing view that innovation mainly takes place in certain sectors (ICT, biotechnology, semiconductors, etc.). The economic strength of a city, Florida argues, lies in the diversity of its creative working population. Moreover, Florida suggests that creativity has little to do with education, stating that value creation is irrespective of the education level of the creator. Florida has been challenged on this point by Glaeser (2004), who, on the basis of Florida's US data, has shown that education, not creativity, offers the better explanation for the differences in economic growth between American cities. According to Glaeser, the well-established human capital theory would be more applicable than Florida's creative capital theory in explaining urban growth differentials.

However, Florida also suggests that the significance of the creative class to the urban economy lies mainly in their lifestyles, which are made up of a mix of a Calvinist work ethic and hedonistic consumption. Historically, this image of the creative class corresponds perfectly with Dutch history. The country has a long Calvinistic tradition of serving as a sanctuary for art and spiritual life (Israel, 1995). In the seventeenth century, Dutch cities like Amsterdam were textbook examples of tolerant societies. For example, the characteristic tolerance of New York – formerly New Amsterdam – originated in Amsterdam (Shorto, 2004). According to Mak and Shorto (2009), both cities still enjoy the benefits of this seventeenth-century tolerance, even though in the present global society they are no longer alone in this regard. However, path dependence does occur. For example, Amsterdam confirmed its reputation as a tolerant city in the 1960s as the 'magical centre of the world' and continues to do so even today with its permissive attitude towards the use of soft drugs and its well-known 'coffee shops'. As Bontje and Musterd (2009) note, the creative fields (defined as multi-scalar networks of (potential) firms and workers in the creative industries; Scott, 2006) of European city-regions are strongly affected by their path dependencies. They show that policy-makers in city-regions with long traditions in trade, culture, creativity and business-to-business services, such as Munich, Barcelona and Amsterdam, are more adaptive to the demands of a creative economy than city-regions that must reinvent themselves and depart from a specialization in mass industrial production, such as Manchester, Birmingham, Leipzig and even Helsinki. These qualities attributed to Amsterdam also apply to other Dutch cities, as many Dutch cities can also be characterized as creative cities. However, does this mean that the creative class is of real importance to the economic growth of cities in the Netherlands? Florida denoted this importance with his famous '3Ts' of economic development: talent, technology and tolerance (2002b). He sees the city as a magnet for a wide variety of talent. The concentration of innovation and technology in an urban region is an indicator of the second T, technology. Tolerance is ultimately openness towards newcomers, other races and lifestyles. Cities with many immigrants and artists (referred to as bohemians), in particular, should be prime examples of tolerance. A truly creative city, according to Florida, attracts a constant stream of newcomers who bring fresh creative blood to the city (Florida, 2005).

As in other European countries, Florida's ideas have quickly become very popular among Dutch policy-makers. However, in creating the creative city, many policy-makers have become stuck in the rut of city promotion alone, which is often nothing more than the idea that creative cities will be attractive to the creative class as long as these cities are also known to be so. There is hope that awareness of the creative image of the city will attract creative people and, along with them, creative businesses. The central idea then soon becomes that the authorities must deploy all their available resources – also in terms of culture and creativity – to improve the competitive position of the city and thus strengthen its economic growth (Landry, 2000). In addition, in the Netherlands, prestigious cultural activities are increasingly used as a sign of being a creative city. Art and creativity are assigned a role in the economic competitive battle between cities and regions and are also utilized to improve the quality of life in the city (e.g., Van Aalst and Boogaarts, 2002; Miles and Paddison, 2005). With a view to this international competition, city councillors work on 'image building' and increasingly sell their cities as a product. Many cities run promotional campaigns through advertising in newspapers, posters and brochures with the aim of promoting themselves as 'the place to be' for residents, tourists and companies. In addition to this practice, cities compete with one another for major events and festivals within city limits, thus putting the city on the national and international map for a time (e.g., Van Aalst and Van Melik, 2012). However, this is not what Florida had in mind as the role of creativity in the growth of the urban economy. As indicated, he links this to the presence of a creative class. Florida states that it is through their pattern of activity that members of the creative class create a vibrant economy with high added value. The spatial scale on which the creative economy is played out is an essential point in Florida's theory. In his view, the growth effects of the creative class appear in the labour market at the urban regional level. Such city-regions, he believes, carry the creative economy. In this context, Florida states that 'places have replaced companies as the key organizing units in our economy" (Florida, 2002a: 30). In his book *Who's Your City?*, Florida argues that mega-cities are the most relevant scale on which to analyze the creative economy (Florida, 2008). According to him, the Netherlands forms part of the 'Am-Brus-Twep' region with 60 million inhabitants. Clearly, this mega-city extends beyond the national boundaries of the Netherlands.

For the Dutch case, we will investigate the mutual relations between the creative class and economic growth. We agree with Florida that these relations fit in the scale of urban labour markets, and we will use city-regions as a proper scale to do so.

Regional distribution of creative classes in the Netherlands

The size of a creative class depends on the definition taken. In his book *The Flight of the Creative Class* (2005), Florida uses both narrow and broad definitions. The broad definition covers 'scientists, engineers, artists, cultural creatives, managers, professionals, and technicians' (ibid.: 272). The narrow definition excludes technicians. The relative position of countries differs depending which definition is applied. For instance, the positions of Canada and the United States, as well as Greece, the United Kingdom and Spain, are lower in the broader definition than in the narrow definition, while Norway and the Czech and Slovak Republics score high under the broad definition because of the presence of technicians. The Netherlands scores extremely high under both definitions. The Netherlands leads worldwide under the broad definition. However, in this chapter, we investigate the mutual relation between the creative class and economic growth not at the national level but at the city-region level.

Our definitions of the creative class closely resemble those of Florida's broad and narrow definitions. Under Florida's definition, the creative class comprises two groups: the 'super-creative core' and 'creative professionals'. The first group is focused mainly on 'problem-finding', while creative professionals are mainly concerned with 'problem-solving' (Florida, 2002a: 68–69). Creative professionals are therefore seen as the creative executors of the new ideas of the creative core. Comparable to Florida (2005), we use a broad definition of creative class, the so-called *European definition*, and a narrow definition, the so-called *Dutch definition*. Both definitions are based on the 1992 Standard Profession Classification (SBC 1992) of the Bureau of Statistics of the Netherlands. This classification system covers 1211 professions. The broader European definition stems from an international comparative study in Europe (see Chapter 11 by Boschma and Fritsch in this volume). In this European definition, the common denominator in the definitions of the national statistical bureaux of the participating countries has been taken. It is unavoidable that many details will be lost under the resulting European definition. The narrow Dutch definition of the creative class is based on a bottom-up selection of skills that contribute to either 'problem-solving' or 'problem-finding'. We linked professions in Art and Design to 'problem-finding'; professions in Management, Consultancy and Government to 'problem-solving'; and professions in 'Research' to both categories, which resulted in a final number of 487 professional activities that can be allocated to the creative class in the Netherlands under the Dutch definition.

Both definitions match with regard to the growth of the creative class. Under the European definition, the Dutch creative class in 1996 amounted to 43.1 per cent of the total labour population, and in 2002, this share had risen to 47.2 per cent. According to the narrower Dutch definition in 1996, the creative class comprised 15.6 per cent of the total labour population, and in 2002, this percentage rose to 17.6 per cent. Irrespective of the definition used, the size of the creative class appears to be growing, both in absolute and relative terms.

The creative class in the Netherlands consists of relatively many 'creative professionals'. Under the European definition, approximately one-third of the Dutch active working population is 'creative professionals'. The percentage for the 'super-creative core' is much lower (12 per cent). The figures under the Dutch definition show that the share of purely 'problem finders' remains at approximately 5 per cent of the labour population. The share of 'problem solvers' increased from 9.1 per cent in 1996 to 10.2 per cent in 2002.

Looking at the regional distribution, the four largest city-regions in the Netherlands (Amsterdam, Rotterdam, The Hague, and Utrecht) accommodate the most sizeable creative class. The urban dominance of the creative class becomes clear from the fact that nine of the top 10 regions in the Netherlands with regard to the presence of the creative class are situated in the Randstad, which is the most urbanized part of the Netherlands.

In Figure 8.1, we differentiate between night-time and daytime creative class distributions. The resident creative class (night-time) is compared with the total population living in each area; the working creative class (daytime) is compared with total employment. The resident creative class lives in a broad urban region with high concentrations in the northern wing of the Randstad (Amsterdam, Utrecht, Leiden, Haarlem and Hilversum) and in the southeastern part of the country (Den Bosch, Eindhoven). The regional distribution of the working creative class reflects the polycentric urban structure of the Netherlands. An important part of the resident creative class lives in suburban regions some distance from the four major city centres, as well as in the medium-sized city-regions outside the Randstad (for instance, in Groningen in the north of the country).

Within the Dutch 'urban field', the differences in the share of the creative class between city-regions and within city-regions are small. Nevertheless, there are important qualitative differences between the city-regions. The largest share of the 'super-creative core' lives in the four biggest urban regions, while 'creative professionals' with their higher average income live in more opulent suburban regions. The urban purchasing power effect of the creative class assumed by Florida will, in their case, depend on the distance and accessibility of the central cities from their suburban homes. However, in a small country like the Netherlands, this distance can easily be covered.

Economic growth and the presence of the creative class

In this section, we will correlate the regional distribution of the creative class with variables used by Florida (see Figure 8.2). Based on Florida (2002a; 2002c), we

Home location creative class (European definition)   Home location creative class (Dutch definition)

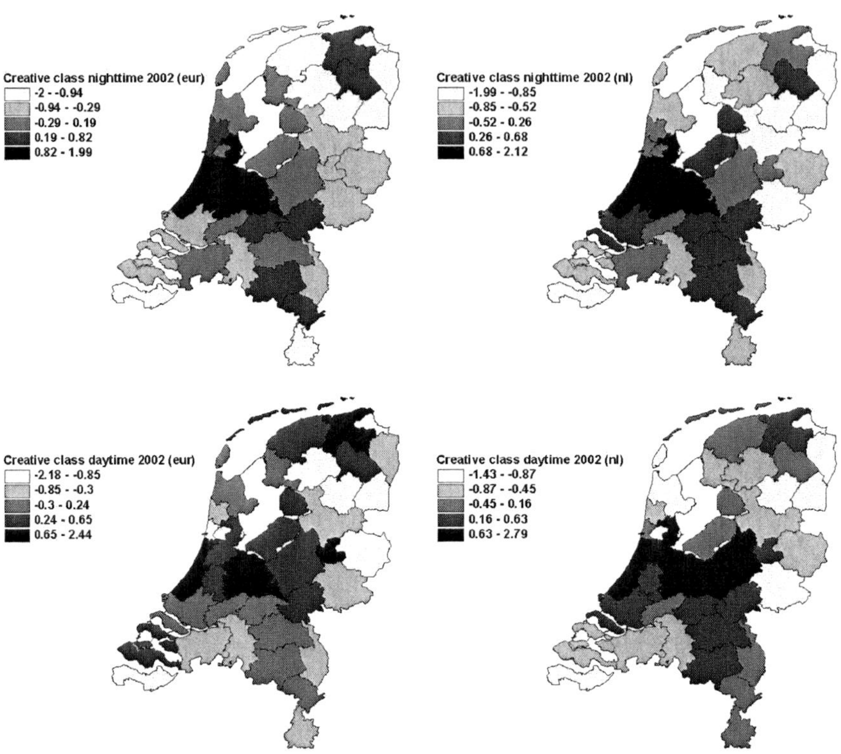

Creative class nighttime 2002 (eur)
☐ -2 - -0.94
▨ -0.94 - -0.29
▨ -0.29 - 0.19
▨ 0.19 - 0.82
■ 0.82 - 1.99

Creative class nighttime 2002 (nl)
☐ -1.99 - -0.85
▨ -0.85 - -0.52
▨ -0.52 - 0.26
▨ 0.26 - 0.68
■ 0.68 - 2.12

Creative class daytime 2002 (eur)
☐ -2.18 - -0.85
▨ -0.85 - -0.3
▨ -0.3 - 0.24
▨ 0.24 - 0.65
■ 0.65 - 2.44

Creative class daytime 2002 (nl)
☐ -1.43 - -0.87
▨ -0.87 - -0.45
▨ -0.45 - 0.16
▨ 0.16 - 0.63
■ 0.63 - 2.79

Work location creative class (European definition)   Work location creative class (Dutch definition)

Figure 8.1 Regional distribution of the creative class in the Netherlands by home and work location, 2002

Source: Statistics Netherlands (Survey of Working Population). Adapted by the authors.

have selected two independent variables that indicate the tolerance and openness of the urban environment: the 'Bohemian' index and the 'Openness' index. The 'Bohemian' index (Florida, 2002a: 260–266) shows an over- or under-representation of the number of writers, designers, musicians, actors, painters, sculptors, photographers and dancers (the so-called bohemians) per region, relative to the national average in 2002. As suggested by Florida, people in the creative arts and professions add a certain artistic air or bring a particular liberal atmosphere to an urban area. The 'Openness' index or Diversity index is the counterpart of Florida's melting pot index (ibid.: 252–253) and measures the relative percentage of the number of people in a region born abroad. Florida defines 'tolerance' as openness, inclusiveness, and diversity to all ethnicities, races, and walks of life. The openness of cities can be described as the provision of low barriers of entry and good opportunities for integration and participation with international populations (Clark, 2009). A large number of studies (including Florida, 2005) gauge 'openness' or tolerance by measuring the share of immigrants in the general population. This index is controversial because it assumes that a high proportion of immigrants in a region will always be matched by tolerance towards newcomers. However, this share will greatly depend on the housing supply in a region, particularly the share of cheap, rented public housing. A better measure, without doubt, is the attitudes towards ethnic people or the degree of workforce participation among immigrants because this indicator gives a better picture of tolerance and acceptance of newcomers in the labour market. However, there are no such data available. The same is true for the third measure for diversity Florida uses (2002a: 255–258), the so-called 'Gay' index.

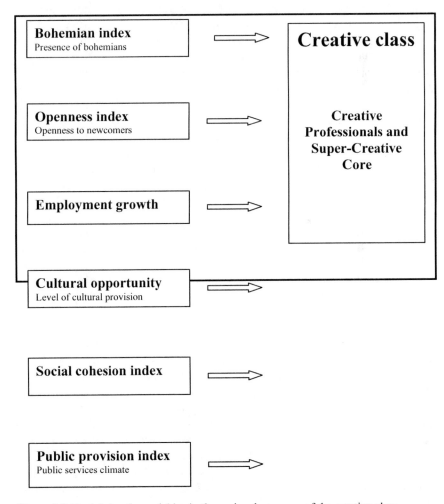

Figure 8.2 Explaining the variables in the regional presence of the creative class

The assumption is that the better a region performs economically, the more of an attractive force it will have on the creative class. To test this assumption, we use *Growth of Employment* (1996–2002) as an independent variable. Separate from this economic growth variable, we use the *'Cultural Opportunity' index*. This index captures the cultural, recreational, and leisure climates in a region. According to Florida, such opportunities play an important role in cities' ability to attract the creative class. The index is measured on the basis of the number of museums, art galleries, theatres, sports facilities, restaurants, and bars in a region per 1,000 inhabitants. The *'Social Cohesion' index* is an indicator of the social climate in an area. It may be expected that there will be a high degree of social cohesion in an area associated with a relatively large creative class. To obtain an internationally comparable measure, based on perceived inequality, we took the level of unemployment in an area (see also Clifton, 2008: 69). Unfortunately, more natural indicators, such as income equality, crime, and social capital, were unavailable due to a lack of data. In our study, unemployment was therefore taken as a proxy for a level of exclusion from mainstream economic activity and thus the possible presence of social problems in an area. Although internationally perhaps not an ideal and inclusive measure of social cohesion, PBL (2010: 108) shows that unemployment is directly (and negatively) related to livability and firm dynamics in Dutch neighbourhoods. For the Netherlands, the unemployment rates makes sense as an indicator of social cohesion. The index was measured on the basis of the percentage share of unemployed per area relative to the total working population in that area, i.e., the unemployment percentage. Finally, the *'Public Provision' index* measures the public services climate in an area. The assumption with this index is that the better the public services in a region, the more attractive it will be to the creative class as a place to live. In the public provision index, levels of employment in education and healthcare (2003; NACE codes 80 and 85) for a given locality are expressed as a proportion of the resident population. We are aware of the weakness of the indicators of this index. Following Clifton (2008), there seems to be a need to further take account of the European context, given the high levels of private employment-based provision in the USA, particularly for healthcare. It is questionable if, and to what extent high-quality social welfare provision might be a quality of place factor for the European creative class.

Correlation analyses show that only the two indices that measure the degree of openness and tolerance in an urban region (*Bohemian, Openness*) have a statistical correlation with the presence of the creative class (see Figures 8.3 and 8.4 for scatterplots of these relations). These correlations are otherwise weak, which suggests that only part of Florida's theory is applicable in the Dutch urban context. Furthermore, in the Netherlands, there is no statistical correlation on the regional level between employment growth and the presence of the creative class. In the Netherlands, it is not the case that regions with relatively high economic growth attract more people from the creative class. These results, however, are in agreement with Florida's view that, in exercising their regional preferences about where to live, people from the creative class are not primarily influenced by the vicinity of regional growth centres.

In the Dutch context, Florida's suggestion that the creative class is attracted by recreational and socio-cultural provision is not confirmed (Figures 8.3 and 8.4).

For example, the variables *Cultural Opportunity*, *Social Cohesion index* and *Public Provision index* show no correlation whatsoever with the distribution of the creative class in the Netherlands. As these results show, attracting the creative

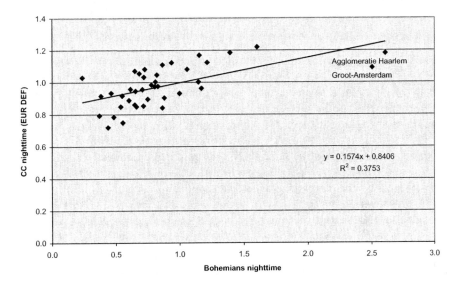

Figure 8.3 The correlation between the 'Bohemian' index and the creative class in the Netherlands at the regional level in 2002 (night-time, home location, European definition)

Source: Statistics Netherlands (Survey of Working Population), adapted by UU/RPB.

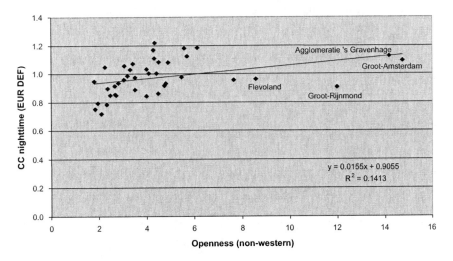

Figure 8.4 The correlation between openness and the creative class in the Netherlands at the regional level in 2002 (night-time, home location, European definition)

Source: Statistics Netherlands (Survey of Working Population), adapted by UU/RPB.

class is not so much a matter of the facilities provided in an area but rather of the cultural qualities as a whole, such as a social environment of tolerance and openness. The correlations were the same for both definitions, as all of the results for the Netherlands turned out to be extremely robust.

The presence of the creative class and economic growth

The next step is to look at what impact the presence of the creative class has on regional economic growth (Figure 8.5). For this purpose, a regional econometric model was estimated that takes into account not only control variables but also the possible effects of spatial vicinity or growth effects on nearby regions (spatial autocorrelation, see van Oort, 2004, and Frenken *et al.*, 2007).

Each of the three dependent variables measures economic growth in a specific manner. The first variable, *high-tech employment growth*, matches Florida's supposition that high-tech industry is found mainly in places with high concentrations of the creative class. The second variable, *total employment growth*, shows the general growth effect. The third variable, *growth in new business activities*, directly measures economic dynamism and innovation in the business population (Van Oort, 2004). Lee, Florida and Acs (2004) argue

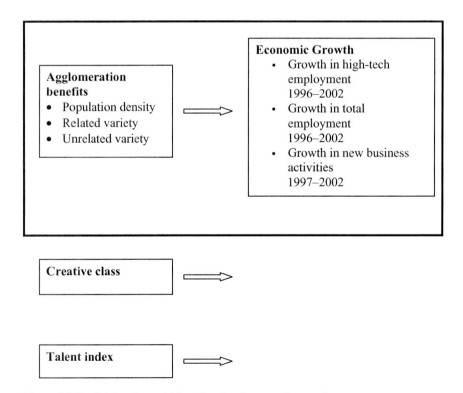

Figure 8.5 Explaining the variables of regional economic growth

that there are low barriers to entry in the diversified creative economy that generate a relatively high amount of entrepreneurial activity. They note that human capital, income change and population growth influence a region's firm formation as well. Hackler and Mayer (2008), however, find that regional growth in new business activities is better explained by opportunity structures instead of the creative milieu. By improving their skills, creative workers have better access to a variety of financial sources that facilitate their access to markets. The tangible assets of a region, such as the accessibility of financial capital, seem to be more decisive for the founding a new firm than intangible assets such as creativity (Potts, 2011).

For the independent variables, the contribution to economic growth due to the benefits of urban agglomeration was first estimated. The underlying principle is that companies in large cities benefit from a large and diverse local labour market, the proximity of suppliers and customers, and local access to knowledge spillovers (Karlsson and Picard, 2011). It was then determined whether this agglomeration effect also differs across cities. For this analysis, the regional economy's sectoral make-up was examined (Van Oort, 2004). Florida (2005) places much emphasis on this point, although like Jacobs (1961; 1969), he is purely interested in the diversity of the production structure itself. In our analysis, a distinction was made here between 'related variety' and 'unrelated variety' (Frenken *et al.*, 2007). Related variety concerns complementary sectors that have a certain affinity in terms of knowledge and competences; as a result, it may be expected that there will be a large amount of knowledge spillover, leading to growth, in cities or regions where there are many related sectors. Effective knowledge transfer, however, can be largely ruled out in urban regions with businesses in many diverse, unrelated sectors. Because a bicycle manufacturer will have little to learn from a company like Microsoft and vice versa, no significant knowledge spillovers are likely. However, a positive portfolio (hedging) effect may be expected in regions where there is much unrelated variety. This means that regions with sectors that have little to do with each other are more resilient to economic shocks or crises in specific sectors through growth in other sectors and therefore, do not experience negative impacts on the employment trend. The advantage of this independent variable is that the theoretical basis for the contribution made by 'related variety' to regional growth in employment is larger than the otherwise hardly specified term 'diversity'. Furthermore, this contribution has already been empirically demonstrated for the Netherlands' economy on the same regional level (ibid.). Measuring diversification over sectors in regional economies is sensitive to the indicator applied. In our empirical analysis of related and unrelated variety, we apply an entropy measure. The main reason to use this measure is its decomposable nature. In the context of measuring regional variety to analyze the effects on growth, decomposition is informative, as one expects entropy/variety at a high level of sector aggregation to have a portfolio effect on the regional economy, protecting it from unemployment and shocks, while one expects entropy/variety at a low level of sector aggregation to generate knowledge spillovers and employment growth. Put differently, entropy at a high level of sector aggregation measures unrelated variety, while entropy at a low level of sector aggregation measures related variety. See Frenken *et al.* (2007) for a detailed description of the entropy indicators used in our analyses.

The second category of independent variables in the model concerns the creative class itself. Florida notes the economic importance of large creative classes in cities, which, as our previous analyses have shown (Hutton, 2008), are found mainly in cities that are open and tolerant. Here, too, cities and regions differ from one another in how creative classes consequently affect growth. It is worth noting that our model does not include the economic impact of spending by the creative class. This effect will very likely be considerable, given that the creative class is generally prosperous and earns more than average (Florida, 2002a). However, as we noted above, a proportion of the wealthy creative class lives outside the large cities in suburban regions.

The third category in the model relates to the level of educational attainment of the population. Endogenous growth theory, in particular, attaches a great deal of importance to 'human capital' (Romer, 1986; Glaeser and Saiz, 2003), and as mentioned, Florida (2002a) often makes reference to this theory. The effect of education was taken into account in this study for two reasons. First, critics of Florida assert that, even at a regional level, education and the creative class generally go together and that these two variables therefore essentially measure the same thing. Therefore, we tested this. The second reason is directly related to the first. Glaeser (2004) proposes that the creative class may make a positive contribution to economic growth, but as soon as the education factor is introduced into the estimation model, education takes over this effect from the creative class. Marlet *et al.* (2007), conversely, refute this criticism on the basis of empirical research in the Netherlands. They showed that, education aside, the creative class holds explanatory power in their model. In our model, the share of the active working population with a bachelor's degree or high school diploma was included as a control variable to be able to estimate whether the creative class makes an additional or differentiated contribution to economic growth.

The main results are shown in Table 8.1. Appendix Table A1 shows the correlations of the variables used. As no correlation is particularly high, multicollinearity is not a problem in our models.

Only in one of the presented models is the creative class a factor of significance in explaining economic growth at the regional level, i.e., the positive and significant coefficient for the presence of the creative class under the home definition in the total growth in employment model. This relation is in agreement with Florida's theory. The positive employment effect of the creative class occurs predominantly in regions where the creative class lives, not where they work.

More striking in light of Florida's conceptualization and theory is the conclusion that on the regional level in the Netherlands, the creative class does not appear to have a relationship with the development of high-tech employment. However, this finding is explained by the decentralized nature of high-technology industrial locations outside of the largest cities in the country, see, for example, Raspe and Van Oort (2006). Hence, population density is negatively related to

Table 8.1 OLS regression results for different indicators of regional economic growth

	Growth in high-tech employment, 1996–2002		Growth in employment, 1996–2002		Growth in new businesses, 1997–2002	
	Home	Work	Home	Work	Home	Work
Constant	0.118	0.123	0.126	0.138	0.024	0.032
	(0.179)	(0.178)	(0.131)	(0.156)	(0.141)	(0.147)
Urbanization	−0.467**	−0.344	−0.742**	−0.662**	−0.200	−0.130
	(0.233)	(0.252)	(0.170)	(0.221)	(0.192)	(0.209)
Related variety	0.220	0.284	0.412**	0.553**	0.283*	0.374**
	(0.190)	(0.183)	(0.139)	(0.160)	(0.149)	(0.151)
Unrelated variety	−0.195	0.333	−0.085	−0.068	0.102	−0.030
	(0.216)	(0.208)	(0.158)	(0.182)	(0.170)	(0.173)
Creative class (EU definition)	−0.135	−0.414	0.861**	0.297	0.356	0.075
	(0.297)	(0.336)	(0.216)	(0.294)	(0.232)	(0.279)
Education	0.428*	0.479**	−0.244	−0.019	0.162	0.186
	(0.251)	(0.209)	(0.183)	(0.219)	(0.197)	(0.207)
R^2	0.18	0.20	0.54	0.34	0.32	0.25

Notes: N = 40 labor market (COROP) regions, standard errors reported between parentheses.
* $p < 0.10$, ** $p < 0.05$.
See, for a detailed description of the dat,a Van Oort (2004). Growth in new businesses is measured as percentage of existing businesses. Models that control for spatial autocorrelation (available upon request) show similar magnitudes and slopes of coefficients. All independent variables are measured in 1996.

Source: Statistics Netherlands (Survey of Working Population) and National Employment Register (LISA), adapted by the authors.

high-tech development. As we found that there is a statistical correlation between the degree of urbanization and the distribution of the creative class, it is not surprising that no significant correlation was found between the presence of the creative class and growth in high-tech employment. Education, however, does have a strong, positive effect on the growth of high-tech employment. For the case of the Netherlands, we have to reject Florida's argument that high-tech employment follows from the spread of the creative class.

Furthermore, it would appear that in other models (employment growth and new businesses) education does not make a genuine or an additional contribution to the economic growth of urban regions. This finding agrees with the results of Marlet *et al.* (2007) that Glaeser's criticism does not necessarily apply to the case of the Netherlands. We do not observe that education takes over or obviates the effect of the creative class on economic growth. Education only has a positive effect on the growth in employment in high-tech industries, without the creative class having any influence. This most likely has to do with the specific labour requirements of the sector and the fact that 'nerds' only form a small proportion of the entire creative class. The creative class in the Netherlands mainly comprises 'creative professionals' who more often have humanities, languages, or generalist backgrounds rather than science backgrounds.

Finally, we examined whether growth effects in one region depended on growth effects in neighbouring regions (Anselin, 1988). The statistical correlations previously found turned out to be robust for corrections because of spatial autocorrelation (results available on request). The spatial dependence on neighbouring regions is either absent or relatively small. This finding is not too surprising, as we were interested in the differences in development between urban regions that function as labour markets (Frenken *et al.*, 2007).

A form of spatial heterogeneity, which was tested separately, concerned the matter of whether regions in the most urban part of the Netherlands (the Randstad) show a different relationship between economic growth and the explanatory factors than regions outside the Randstad. This was not the case. This finding also confirms that the spatial correlations found are regionally isolated and spill over only into regions that are very close by. Furthermore, it shows that, regarding the causality between the presence of the creative class and the economic growth of city-regions within the Netherlands, there are not two separate spatial systems in operation (with the urbanized Randstad, on the one hand, and smaller and medium-sized cities outside the Randstad, on the other).

Conclusion

In this chapter, we investigated to what extent the mutual relationships between the presence of the creative class and economic growth can be applied to Dutch city-regions. We asked the following three questions: (1) what is the variation in the size and composition of the creative class between city-regions in the Netherlands?; (2) does growth in employment contribute to differences in the size and composition of the creative class in Dutch city-regions?; and (3) to what extent does the presence of the creative class contribute to economic growth in Dutch city-regions, especially in relation to the relatedness of industries (related variety)?

We found that at the level of labour market regions, there is a relationship between the presence of the creative class and economic performance in urban regions in the Netherlands, but this relation is still weak. This is not because of the size of the creative class, which is large enough, but more due to the relatively even regional distribution of the creative class. The regional differences in the Netherlands in the concentration of the places where the creative class lives and works are not large. The main regional differences are of a qualitative nature: most urban regions have an over-representation of the 'creative core', while the 'creative professionals' are more often found in more suburban areas. On the whole, the same applies to the differences between parts of the country, i.e., between the urbanized Randstad and the rest of the Netherlands.

In the Netherlands, Richard Florida's theory, which suggests that tolerance leads to a large creative class (talent), which in turn leads to the development of technology, appears to be only partly true. The first part of the theory can be confirmed. Openness (towards newcomers) and tolerance (with regard to free and creative activities) are both relevant to the spatial distribution of the creative class in the Netherlands. Urban regions, which score well in both of these factors, have a relatively large creative class within their boundaries. Dutch cities validate their reputation as tolerant environments, and this condition brings with it relatively many creative people who choose to live and work there. In this regard, Amsterdam tops the bill, which is understandable from a historical point of view.

Our results confirm Florida's suggestion about the importance of a 'people climate' over a 'business climate' with respect to the locational preferences of the creative class. Culture, in the broadest sense of the word, is important for the distribution of the creative class. A narrow definition of culture, for example, by pointing to the presence of socio-cultural provision, is less useful. Such facilities do not appear to have a demonstrable effect on the distribution of the creative class in the Netherlands. Policy-makers in the Netherlands who believe that they can bind a large creative class to the city by investing in cultural provision may find themselves disappointed.

The second aspect of Florida's theory on the geography of the creative class was not confirmed by the empirical results of our study. A relatively large creative class in a region is not accompanied by high-tech development. Nevertheless, there is a relationship between talent (i.e., high levels of education) and technology in the Netherlands, though not via the creative class. The regional differences in growth in employment in the high-tech sector depend not on the degree of urbanization, not on the production structure, and not on the creative class. Instead, these differences depend on the educational level of the working population living there.

In the Netherlands, however, the creative class is a structuring factor in the growth of employment, as an additional factor related to agglomeration economies. The positive influence of the creative class on growth is most profoundly noticed in regions with a production structure characterized by a related variety in business activities. It is only then that this phenomenon leads to the creation of new businesses. This finding clearly relates to the current discussion on the role of (sector-specific) localization and urbanization economies in the economic agglomeration debate. Urbanization economies are often interchangeably mentioned with Jane Jacobs' diversity externalities, as (sectoral) diversity tends to be larger in cities than it is outside them. Our empirical findings, in line with Frenken *et al.* (2007), show that a distinction between variety and diversity externalities and urbanization economies is necessary. A large body of empirical literature has grown around testing these types of externalities in relation to knowledge spillovers using sectoral specialization, sectoral diversity and density data from cities. This literature has evolved into a rather polarized discussion on the question of whether sectoral specialization (clusters) or sectoral diversity matter for economic growth and innovation in cities. Recent meta-analyses and overviews clearly show the limitations of this empirical approach (Beaudry and Schiffauerova, 2009); the outcomes of the many empirical analyses on agglomeration externalities appear to be highly dependent on spatial scale, sectoral detail, time frame, institutional context and the construction of indicators and variables. In principle, scientifically, this is a rather unsatisfactory basis for understanding the relation between urban growth, spillovers and innovation. It is very plausible that the prevailing urban economic modeling approaches fall short conceptually, and are unable to test this important issue satisfactorily in its present form (McCann and Van Oort, 2009). The concept of related variety, indicating that successful sectors in regions diversify over time, though mostly in relation to existing competences and specializations, is an important exponent of new conceptualizations in the agglomeration, innovation and growth discussion – and this becomes more fruitful in relation to analyzing the creative class. In particular, the presence of the creative class may be an important regional condition in the case of labour mobility as part of related variety in a region (Van Oort and Lambooy, 2013).

Finally, our empirical tests show that there is a positive relation between the creative class and new business activities and between the creative class and overall employment growth, but these relations do not apply in reverse. This finding suggests that the criticism levelled at Florida's theory – that the creative class settles in places where there is already growth – is not valid, but this issue obviously needs more thorough testing on causality. Although the large geographical differences (in size and urban structure) that exist between the United States and the Netherlands make comparison difficult, Florida's theory regarding the creative class and the urban economy turned out to be a fruitful starting point for analyzing the dynamics in Dutch urban regions.

Bibliography

Andersen, V., Hansen, H. and Raunio, M. (2010) 'Nordic city-regions in the creative class debate: Putting the creative class thesis to a test', *Industry and Innovation*, 17: 215–240.

Anselin, L. (1988) *Spatial Econometrics: Methods and Models*, Dordrecht: Kluwer.

Beaudry, C. and Schiffauerova, A. (2009) 'Who's right, Marshall or Jacobs? The localization versus urbanization debate', *Research Policy*, 38: 318–337.

Bontje, M. and Muster, D. (2009) 'Creative industries, creative class and competitiveness: Expert opinions critically appraised', *Geoforum*, 4: 849–852.

Clark, G. (2009) OPENCities Feasibility Study: Summary. *UrbAct II*, available at: http://urbact.eu (accessed 29 August 2013).

Clifton, N. (2008) 'The "creative class" in the UK: An initial analysis', *Geografiska Annaler B*, 90: 63–82.

Florida, R. (2002a) *The Rise of the Creative Class And How It's Transforming Work, Leisure, Community and Everyday Life*, New York: Basic Books.

Florida, R. (2002b) 'The economic geography of talent', *Annals of the Association of American Geographers*, 92: 743–755.

Florida, R. (2002c) 'Bohemia and economic geography', *Journal of Economic Geography*, 2: 55–71.

Florida, R. (2005) *The Flight of the Creative Class*, New York: Harper Business.

Florida, R. (2008) *Who's Your City?*, New York: Basic Books.

Florida, R., Mellander, C. and Stolarick, K. (2008) 'Inside the Black Box of regional development – human capital, the creative class and tolerance', *Journal of Economic Geography*, 8: 615–649.

Frenken, K., van Oort, F. G. and Verburg, T. (2007) 'Related variety, unrelated variety and regional economic growth', *Regional Studies*, 41: 685–697.

Glaeser, E. L. (2004) 'Review of Richard Florida's "The Rise of the Creative Class"', available at: http://www.creativeclass.com/rfcgdb/articles/GlaeserReview.pdf (accessed 29 August 2013).

Glaeser, E. L. and Saiz, A. (2003) 'The rise of the skilled city', Harvard Institute of Economic Research and NBER Discussion Paper No. 2025.

Hackler, D. and Mayer, H. (2008) 'Diversity, entrepreneurship, and the urban environment', *Journal of Urban Affairs*, 30(3): 273–307.

Hutton, T. (2008) *The New Economy of the Inner City: Restructuring, Regeneration and Dislocation in the 21st Century Metropolis*, London: Routledge.

Israel, J. (1995) *The Dutch Republic: Its Rise, Greatness and Fall, 1477–1806*, Oxford: Oxford University Press.

Jacobs, J. (1961) *The Death and Life of Great American Cities*, New York: Random House.

Jacobs, J. (1969) *The Economy of Cities*, New York: Random House.

Karlsson, C. and Picard, R. (eds) (2011) *Media Clusters: Spatial Agglomeration and Content Capabilities*, Cheltenham, UK: Edward Elgar.

Landry, C. (2000) *The Creative City: A Toolkit for Urban Innovators*, London: Earthscan.

Lee, S.Y., Florida, R. and Acs, Z. (2004) 'Creativity and entrepreneurship: A regional analysis of new firm formation', *Regional Studies*, 38(8): 879–891.

McCann, P. and van Oort, F. G. (2009) 'Theories of agglomeration and regional economic growth: A historical review', in R. Capello and P. Nijkamp (eds), *Handbook of Regional Growth and Development Theories*, Cheltenham, UK: Edward Elgar, pp. 19–32.

Mak, G. and Shorto, R. (2009) *1609 – The Forgotten History of Hudson, Amsterdam and New York*, New York: Henry Hudson Foundation,

Marlet, G. and van Woerkens, G. (2007) "The Dutch creative class and how it fosters urban employment growth', *Urban Studies*, 44: 2605–2626.

Miles, S. and Paddison, R. (2005) 'The rise and rise of culture-led urban regeneration', *Urban Studies*, 42: 833–839.

PBL (2010) *Firm Dynamics and Livability in Dutch Urban Neighborhoods*, The Hague: Netherlands Environmental Assessment Agency (PBL).

Peck, J. (2005) 'Struggling with the creative class', *International Journal of Urban and Regional Research*, 29: 740–770.

Perry, M. (2011) 'Finding space for the creative class: A review of the issues', *Urban Policy and Research*, 29: 325–341.

Potts, J. (2011) *Creative Industries and Economic Evolution*, Cheltenham, UK: Edward Elgar.

Pratt, A .C. (2008) 'Creative cities: The cultural industries and the creative class', *Geografiska Annaler B*, 90: 107–117.

Raspe, O. and van Oort, F.G. (2006) 'The knowledge economy and urban economic growth', *European Planning Studies*, 14: 1209–1234.

Reese, L., Faist, J. M. and Sands, G. (2010) 'Measuring the creative class: Do we know it when we see it?', *Journal of Urban Affairs*, 32: 345–366.

Romer, P. M. (1986) 'Increasing returns and long-run growth', *Journal of Political Economy*, 94: 1002–1037.

Scott, A. J. (2006) 'Creative cities: Conceptual issues and policy questions', *Journal of Urban Affairs*, 28: 1–17.

Shorto, R. (2004) *The Island at the Center of the World: The Epic Story of Dutch Manhattan and the Forgotten Colony that Shaped America*, New York: Vintage Books.

Stam, E., de Jong, J. P. J. and Marlet, G. (2008) 'Creative industries in the Netherlands: Structure, development, innovativeness and effects on urban growth', *Geografiska Annaler B*, 90: 199–132.

Storper, M. and Scott, A. (2009) 'Rethinking human capital, creativity and urban growth', *Journal of Economic Geography*, 9: 147–167.

Van Aalst, I. and Boogaarts, I. (2002) 'From museum to mass entertainment: The evolution of the role of museums in cities', *European Urban and Regional Studies*, 9: 195–209.

Van Aalst, I. and van Melik, R. (2012) 'City festivals and urban development: Does place matter?', *European Urban and Regional Studies*, 19: 195–206.

Van Oort, F. G. (2004*) Urban Growth and Innovation: Spatially Bounded Externalities in the Netherlands*, Aldershot, UK: Ashgate.

Van Oort, F. G. and Lambooy, J. (2013) 'Cities, knowledge and innovation', in M. Fischer and P. Nijkamp (eds), *Handbook of Regional Science*, Berlin: Springer (forthcoming).

Appendix

Table A1 Correlation matrix of variables used in regression analysis

	[1]	*[2]*	*[3]*	*[4]*	*[5]*	*[6]*	*[7]*	*[8]*	*[9]*
High-tech employment growth 1996–2002 [1]	1	0,27	0,33	–0,15	0,13	–0,14	0,08	–0,03	0,23
Employment growth 1996–2002 [2]		1	0,38	–0,17	0,42	–0,01	0,38	0,11	0,08
Growth in new businesses 1996–2002 [3]			1	0,18	0,45	–0,09	0,44	0,31	0,37
Urbanization 1996 [4]				1	0,41	–0,34	0,59	0,61	0,49
Related variety 1996 [5]					1	–0,05	0,47	0,43	0,33
Unrelated variety 1996 [6]						1	–0,49	–0,46	–0,41
Creative class EU-definition, HOME, 1996 [7]							1	0,73	0,67
Creative class EU-definition, WORK, 1996 [8]								1	0,69
Education, 1996 [9]									1

9 Location, quality of place, and outcomes

Applying the '3Ts' model to the UK

Nick Clifton

Introduction

In a knowledge economy, the ability to attract and retain highly skilled labour is perceived as crucial to the current and future prosperity of regions as well as entire nations. Florida (2000) has argued that in the knowledge economy, regions develop advantage based on their ability to quickly mobilize the best people, resources and capabilities required to turn innovations into new business ideas and commercial products. In particular, the ability to attract creative people in arts and culture fields and to be open to diverse groups of people of different ethnic, racial and lifestyle groups provides distinct advantages to regions in generating innovations, growing and attracting high-technology industries, and spurring economic growth (Gertler *et al.*, 2002). This research demonstrates that quality of place must be understood in broader terms than we have traditionally been accustomed to: while the attractiveness and condition of the natural environment and built form are certainly important, so too are the presence of a rich cultural scene and a high concentration of people working in cultural occupations (most specifically the 'bohemians'). According to the results from Florida *et al.*'s research, the underlying hypothesis is that the presence and concentration of bohemians in an area create an environment or milieu that attracts other types of talented or high human capital individuals. The presence of such human capital in turn attracts and generates innovative, technology-based industries (Florida, 2002b; Florida *et al.*, 2008).

However, given the interest Florida's writings have received from academics, policy-makers and the media alike, it is no surprise that they have been the subject of a high degree of critical examination. This critique has centred most notably around the apparent fuzziness of some of the concepts, definitions and causal logic Florida employs, the seemingly convenient appeal of his ideas to the agendas of a multitude of urban actors and policy-makers, and conversely the minimal attention paid to difficult issues such as the potential inequalities and negative externalities implied by a creative class model of regional development.[1] More fundamentally, a number of authors question the very concept of a 'new economy' that can deliver prosperity in tandem with greater levels of self-determination to an ever-expanding body of knowledge workers (Brown and Lauder, 2006).

With specific regard to the UK, culture and the creative industries have for a number of years been positioned at the centre of many urban and regional development policies, becoming a delivery vehicle for all manner of outcomes including social cohesion, sustainability, economic growth, civic pride, mental and physical well-being, social inclusion, and an ever-increasing array of other social, economic and environmental goals. The government has explicitly drawn on Florida's discourse, stating, 'Richard Florida, a professor of regional economic development, has set out a convincing argument as to why environments with strong cultural facilities and creative networks are key to economic success in modern urban societies' (DCMS, 2004: 40). Sometimes seen as a quintessentially New Labour project, this interest has, if anything, increased following the election of the Conservative-Lib Dem coalition in May 2010. Similarly, government-sponsored reviews, such as the Cox Review, have promoted the apparent importance of creativity to improving the competitiveness of UK firms (HM Treasury, 2005). As a counterbalance, some commentators have sought to temper the view that the concept of 'creativity', and its enhancement, represent either a higher form of development or more of a 'policy panacea' than previous 'prescriptions' (Clifton, 2008; Pratt, 2008). Overall, the spatial focus of creative industry policy in the UK has centred on the role of cities and city-regions, with the metropolitan arena seen as key for developing and enhancing 'creative clusters' (DCMS, 2000; 2007; 2008).

This chapter essentially then seeks to apply Florida's model systematically in the UK context,[2] using a comprehensive dataset designed to mirror that used in the North American analysis. This research took place within the context of a wider project entitled 'Technology, Talent and Tolerance in European Cities: A Comparative Analysis', involving matched datasets and research partners in Denmark, Sweden, Norway, Finland, the Netherlands and Germany. The structure of the chapter is therefore as follows: the theoretical basis of the creative class approach is outlined in more detail below, with significant reservations and criticisms from the literature introduced as appropriate. Data sources and methodologies are then described, with the consequent results presented. These are focused around the three principal research questions: (1) where is the creative class located in the UK?; (2) what is the impact of quality of place upon this dispersion?; and (3) what is the connection between the location of the creative class and inequalities in technical and economic outcomes within the UK? Finally, conclusions are drawn and implications for future research considered in the light of these questions.

The creative class: review of theoretical perspectives

A distinct advantage of city-regions is their ability to produce, attract and retain those workers who play the lead role in knowledge-intensive production and innovation – who provide the ideas, know-how, creativity and imagination so crucial to economic success. The idea that growth-based development agendas can be actively pursed at the city level is, however, not a new one, see, for example, the 'urban entrepreneurialism' documented by Leitner (1990). If we accept that the value creation in many sectors of the economy rests increasingly on non-tangible assets, the locational constraints of earlier eras – for example, the access to good natural harbours or proximity to raw materials and cheap energy sources – no longer exert the same pull they once did. Instead, what the emerging geography of creativity suggests now matters most are those attributes and characteristics of particular places that make them attractive to potentially mobile, much sought-after *talent*. A key reason for believing that a significant shift has occurred taking us into a knowledge economy is that the data suggests this to be true. Thus, the book value of intangible assets compared to raw materials has shifted from 20:80 in the 1950s to 70:30 in the 1990s (De Laurentis, 2006; Cooke *et al.*, 2007). Consequently, the distribution of talent, or human capital, is an important factor in economic geography, as this is a key intermediate variable in attracting high-technology industries and generating higher regional incomes. This makes it an important research task to explore the factors that attract talent and its effects on high-technology industry and regional incomes (Florida 2002c). The replacement of natural resources with human capital and creativity as the crucial wellspring of economic growth means that, in order to be successful, regions must develop, attract and retain talented and creative people who generate innovations, develop technology-intensive industries and power economic growth. Such talented people are not spread equally across space, but tend to concentrate within particular city-regions (Gertler *et al.*, 2002). According to the creative class thesis, economic outcomes are ultimately linked to places' ability to attract and retain mobile creative individuals. The 'quality of place' factors valued by these people are suggested to be tolerance and openness to different ethnic, racial and lifestyle groups, an authentic and attractive built environment, high levels of social cohesion, and the opportunity to take part it (or at least consume) a variety of cultural activities and related amenities. The presence of this creative class is then assumed implicitly to provide distinct advantages to regions in generating innovations, growing and attracting high-technology industries, and spurring economic growth.

As Wojan *et al.* (2007) describe, theorizing on how local environments influence economic outcomes has a long and rich history, the two dominant views of which may be traced back to Marshall (1920) – agglomerations, industry/firm-focused – and Jacobs (1961, 1969) focusing on variety and people. Traditional theories of economic growth and development tended to emphasize the role of natural resources and physical assets. Such theories were used to inform strategies typically based on various incentives to try to alter the location decision of firms. In recent years, several more related theories have emerged. The first, associated with the work of Porter (2000) and others, emphasizes the role of clusters of related and supporting industries. According to this work, clusters operate as geographically concentrated collections of interrelated firms in which demanding local customers and strong competition with other firms in the same industry drive the innovation process. A second view associated with Lucas (1988) and Glaeser (1998) focuses on the role of human capital – that is, primarily highly educated people. It argues that places with higher levels of human capital are more innovative and grow more rapidly and robustly over time. A third approach, associated with Florida (2002b; Florida *et al.*, 2008) emphasizes the role of creative capital, arguing that certain underlying conditions of places, such as their ability to attract *creative people* and be open to diversity, drive innovation and growth. Peck (2005) remarks upon how the creative class thesis has tapped into many of the same 'cultural circuits of capitalism' (Thrift, 2001) as much of the immediately preceding work on the knowledge (or new) economy. It should also be noted that there is work preceding the first accounts of the 'creative class' which makes explicit reference to quality of place and locational choice factors in the UK, including Wong (2001), which in turn may be linked back to Hall *et al.* (1987).

Such constellations of talent are – as already mentioned – most commonly found in large city-regions where the diversity of urbanization economies is most abundant. Thus, labour markets characterized by high demand for skilled personnel, cultural diversity and tolerance, low entry barriers and high levels of urban amenities, largely determine the economic geography of talent and of creativity. According to Cooke *et al.* (2007), cities on average are twice as advantaged by their knowledge intensity over towns and rural areas compared to their already existing advantages from agglomeration economies. This means that if a city scores 50 per cent above the mean in GDP per capita, it is likely to score 100 per cent above it in terms of its knowledge-based industry. Consequently there is more chance of knowledge economy employment in the city than in the country, a major contributory factor in the renewed migration of young people from rural to urban areas in many European countries, making the knowledge economy unevenly distributed and knowledge poverty a new kind of locational disadvantage (ibid.).

Thus, it is not enough to attract firms: the 'right' people also need to be attracted. A creative class approach calls for firm-attraction policies to be complemented by those aimed at attracting people, which means addressing issues of 'people climate' as well as of 'business climate' (Florida, 2002c). Indeed, the former is seen as basic to the latter, in that the presence of human capital and talent is essential for attracting and developing high-tech industries and consequently for economic growth.[3] This suggests that the attention of politicians and planners should be directed towards people, not companies, that is, away from business attraction to talent attraction and quality of place (ibid.). Critics of this viewpoint have, however, pointed to what they consider the 'easy-sell' of this message to urban policy-makers; Peck (2005: 752) in particular has dissected in some detail what he regards as the eminently 'deliverable supply-side policy prescriptions' that flow implicitly from acceptance of the creative class thesis, and which thus (either by design or otherwise[4]) find a ready market among these newly 'legitimized' urban actors.

The knowledge economy means then that the ability to attract and retain highly skilled labour is crucial in terms of both the current and future prosperity of city-regions as well as entire nations. The pioneering research around this question on American metropolitan areas indicated that talent is attracted to and retained by cities, but not just *any* cities The central finding of this work was that the social character of city-regions has a very large influence over their economic success and competitiveness (Florida and Gates, 2001; Florida, 2002a; 2002b; 2002c). In particular, Florida and his colleagues found that those places which offered a high quality of life and best accommodated diversity enjoyed the greatest success in talent attraction/retention and in the growth of their technology-intensive economic activities. Diversity as a key aspect of successful places concerns entry barriers facing newcomers: cities with great diversity are understood as places where people from different backgrounds (nationality, race, ethnicity and sexual orientation) can easily fit in (Florida 2002c). A key indicator of diversity in this research is the 'melting pot index', reflecting the proportion of a city-region's population that is foreign-born; this is the indicator we employ in the present study.

Creativity, class and the economic 'mainstream'

The idea of a creative class relates more generally to a reassessment of the idea that 'bourgeois' values of business and profit (inherently linked to a wider conservative value system) are by definition mutually exclusive to 'bohemian' values of creativity, the embracing of new ideas and valuing of diversity. Brooks (2000) actually merged the two words themselves in describing the emergence of the *bobos* – a new group of people in which bourgeois and bohemian values are blended into the creative, unconventional but also entrepreneurial (Brooks' depiction is, however, an inherently less sympathetic one than Florida's description of his creative class). This idea has some intrinsic appeal when the nature of 'cool' jobs in technology, new media and so on is considered (Heath and Potter, 2006). The use of the word *class* comes of course with a certain baggage in that it implies some kind of self-identity and consistent value system within a socio-political hierarchy. Whether the creative class really is a class in some kind of Marxist sense is something of a moot point; the broad attitudes held and approaches to life that Florida (and others) describe does suggest that at least the term is not wholly erroneous in this context, but this argument is not an entirely convincing one. These traits include personal attire and style, beliefs and values, attitudes to work – to old-style demarcations of blue collar and white collar is added the 'no-collar' workplace; viewed through the eyes of someone used to the traditional demarcations of the workplace, these are people 'who seem to be always working, and yet never working when they are supposed to' (Florida, 2002b: 5).

The points that Markusen (2006) makes regarding the fuzziness of Florida's definitions and causal logic are thus warranted in certain respects, albeit that the comment 'it is rather amusing to think of the vast bulk of artists as making common urban or economic cause with bankers, real estate developers' (Markusen, 2006: 1937) does seem something of a straw man. Artists (i.e. the bohemians) are treated as a distinct group even within Florida's creative class. Indeed, the bohemians are essentially posited as a quality of place factor in their own right; that is, one which is attractive to the wider creative class in general, which does not necessarily imply a complete commonality of values and beliefs.[5] Furthermore, the ingenious study by Wojan *et al.* (2007) did find evidence for a positive 'artistic milieu' effect upon regional growth outcomes; these authors attempt to avoid the potential bohemians-lead-to-growth, growth-leads-to-bohemians circularity by controlling for both supply and demand-side factors for artists, and in turn using the residuals from this model (i.e. unexplained variations in the presence of bohemians) to predict economic growth. The positive result does not of course necessarily mean that artists themselves are the conscious hard-nosed economic drivers of the localities in which they find themselves concentrated. Either way, a conceptual route into these issues of shared versus divergent preferences is offered by an analysis of the knowledge bases which differentiate occupations within an aggregate creative class (Asheim and Hansen, 2009). We are not able to emulate that here, but we can at least specify separate models for the creative core, creative professionals and combined creative class.

However, even when the creative class is defined in its widest sense, this still implies that around 60 per cent of the workforce is engaged in 'non-creative' activities. The role of this non-creative class was typically neglected in the earlier writings on the subject. Peck (2005) going so far as to suggest that Florida advocates a form of what he (Peck) terms 'creative trickle-down'; that is, there is an acknowledgement of the potential inequalities and negative externalities associated with high-growth locations, but very little in the way of concrete policies for how these might be addressed. There has been some attempt to deal with these concerns outside the US context (Cannon *et al.*, 2003, in the UK; Bradford, 2004, in Canada) within some of the creative cities literature, but typically these amount to little more than somewhat ad hoc social objectives bolted on to an underlying creative class orthodoxy. It should be acknowledged that in his more recent work Florida does consider at some length the ever increasing levels of economic polarization that have typically been the flip side of economic development in recent years: indeed, he now regards the creative class as a 'privileged minority', who connect with each other from across the global peaks of an increasingly 'spiky world' (Florida, 2007: 33).

Whatever the subtleties of the debate, however, the fundamental point remains that a dichotomous split between the bohemian and the bourgeois, or the businesslike and the creative, is no longer adequate in describing how a significant group of people live and work, and that this creative class is now very much part of the economic mainstream.

Research questions

Significantly, the pioneering work of Florida and his associates (Gertler *et al.*, 2002) was undertaken with reference to North America. Although Europe and North America share many common values and institutions, there are aspects of their respective societal development that show strong divergence; for example, with regard to political priorities, functioning of labour markets, economic growth processes and social outcomes (see Hall and Soskice, 2001). Indeed, there is now growing empirical evidence that the European context has implications for the trans-national application of the creative class thesis (Boschma and Frisch, 2009; Hansen and Niedomysl, 2009; Asheim, 2009; Andersen *et al.*, 2010a; Andersen *et al.*, 2010b; Martin-Brelot *et al.*, 2010). Therefore, the research reported in this chapter represents an analysis of quality of place and the dispersion of the creative class in the UK, building upon the work described above in order to understand whether similar processes concerning the relationship between creativity, human capital and high-technology industries are at work, as is claimed elsewhere. The questions we seek to address are then essentially:

1   Where is the creative class located in the UK?
2   What is the impact of quality of place upon this dispersion? Does the creative class thesis appear valid within the UK context?
3   What is the connection between the location of the creative class and inequalities in technical and economic outcomes within the UK?

To address these issues, the role of human capital, creative capital and diversity in technology-based economic development in the UK is investigated. The research uses the two measures developed by the North American studies: the Bohemian Index to reflect creative capital, and the Diversity (Mosaic) Index to reflect openness. This suggests that there will be a relationship between openness and the ability to support high-tech industries and economic development based on talented workers. New indices are developed in order to grasp the fundamental differences in certain aspects of life between North American and European societies (see the following section). As noted, this analysis has the potential to shed important new light on the role of quality of place in shaping the competitiveness of city-regions in the UK.

Data and methodology

The key variables for the analyses are the Creative Class Index, the Bohemian Index, and the Openness (Diversity) Index. These mirror variables employed in the work of Florida (2002a; 2002b; 2002c) and Gertler *et al.* (2002) on the geography of the creative class in North America. In addition, indicators for cultural and recreational amenities (the Cultural Opportunity Index) are also considered. A new measure is introduced to reflect the particular European context of this research; the Public Provision Index, capturing the supply of public sector goods such as education, health care, and social security. Specifically, the variables we construct and analyse with respect to each spatial unit are:

- *Creative Class, Creative Core and Creative Professionals*: All three variables are calculated as shares of people employed in the relevant occupational group for any given location. These variables are also used in a Location Quotient (LQ) where each case is represented relative to the national average.[6]

- *Public Provision Index (PPI)*: The number of employed in the public service sectors related to health and education per 1000 inhabitants in a region (NACE 80, 85).
- *Bohemian Index*: The share of the working population in artist-related occupations.
- *Cultural Opportunity Index (COI):* The number of people employed in culture and experience related industries by 1000 inhabitants (NACE 553, 554, 922, 923, 925, 926).
- *Openness to foreigners*: The share of the population that is born in a foreign country.
- *Employment Growth (annual average 1993–2003)*: the average growth rate of the number of employed in a 10-year period.
- *Milken Techpole Index*: The share of all employed of those who are employed in the high-tech industries (defined as per DeVol *et al.*, 2007).
- *New firms by 1000 inhabitants:* the growth in numbers of firms divided by 1000 inhabitants.

With respect to the levels of geography (i.e., spatial units employed in the analysis) employed- partner countries in the wider European research accounted for large variations in size, governance structure, patterns of population dispersion and so on, thus it was impractical to impose a single standard definition. In practice, such definitions typically have different functional meanings dependent upon the context in which they are applied; as we were seeking definitions that encapsulated something approaching functional labour markets (analogous at least in part to the municipal city-regions employed in the North American research[7]) it was decided that the most meaningful functional unit in each national context would be used, subject to this also being a level at which the necessary statistical data were available from the relevant national agencies. As Parr (2005) notes, standard UK administrative geographies do not typically relate in a systematic way to any theoretical construct of the city-region; for the UK this meaningful unit was primarily the NUTS3 definition (105 spatial units in England and Wales). Due to the sometimes complex and non-hierarchical nature of these standard geographies, this is supplemented by analysis using the Unitary/County Authority level (171 units).[8]

Results and analysis

Mapping the creative class in England and Wales

As shown in Table 9.1, the creative class in England and Wales accounts for some 37.3 per cent of the workforce, substantially greater than the 'more than 30 per cent' figure that Florida (2002b) himself quotes with regard to the USA. Problems in obtaining consistent occupational time series data mean that it is difficult to draw many conclusions with regard to how the size of the creative class may be changing over time. However, if the major group Professional

Table 9.1 Creative class as a percentage of the labour force

	England and Wales (%)	Highest locality (%)	Lowest locality (%)
Creative core	9.7	13.7	5.0
Creative professionals	25.5	44.3	17.7
Bohemians	2.1	8.8	0.8
Creative class in total	37.3	64.9	24.1

Source: Census of Population (2001).

Occupations is taken as a proxy for the creative core, then an increase is observed from below 9 per cent of the workforce in the 1991 Census to over 11 per cent in 2001, suggesting significant growth in these occupations.

The total figure for the creative class is split between the creative core (9.7 per cent of the workforce), the creative professionals (25.5 per cent) and the bohemians (2.1 per cent). As Table 9.1 shows, there is considerable variation around the England and Wales percentages. It is worth noting here that the two NUTS3 areas of Inner London West and Inner London East between them account for the highest percentages across all four creative class categories shown. Other than Inner London West (64.9 per cent), only Inner London East (at just under 52 per cent) possesses a labour force of which the creative class comprises more than half. For the bohemians, an even greater concentration is observed: after the two Inner London areas (both above 7 per cent) the highest percentage is found in Brighton and Hove at 4.4 per cent of the labour force.

At the opposite end of the spectrum, the same localities also tend to crop up across the board, albeit with some variation; Stoke on Trent possesses the lowest proportion of total creative class and also creative core, Gwent Valleys the lowest share of bohemian occupations, while the lowest share of creative professionals is found in Hull. Despite this apparent variation, the same localities are typically found within a few places of each other at both the top and bottom of the rankings. This effectively demonstrates that although there are variations in the overall make-up of the creative class in any given place, there is little correlation between this variation and the actual size of the creative class in that place.

Table 9.2 shows the top 15 and the bottom 15 NUTS3 areas in England and Wales ranked in terms of their population size. The actual populations vary from just under 1.8m down to around 69,000, with a median size of just over 360,000. The corresponding ranks in terms of creative class location quotient (LQ) are also shown. The LQ itself is a measure of spatial concentration, expressed as a proportion such that the average for England and Wales is 1. These data highlight the sometimes arbitrary nature of NUTS3 geography in the UK, with counties, towns, cities and urban metropolitan areas all being represented. Many of the smaller areas are particular accidents of geography such as islands and relatively isolated smaller towns and cities.

Table 9.2 Creative class location and population rank

Population size rank	Locality (NUTS3)	Creative class LQ rank
1	London (Inner, West)	1
2	London (Outer, West and N West)	4
3	London (Outer, East and N East)	29
4	Kent	36
5	Greater Manchester (South)	35
6	Essex	25
7	Hampshire	17
8	Greater Manchester (North)	75
9	London (Outer, South)	6
10	Lancashire	50
11	Surrey	3
12	Hertfordshire	9
13	Birmingham	54
14	London (Inner, East)	2
15	Calder, Kirlees and Wakefield	66
91	York	32
92	Swindon	47
93	Herefordshire	51
94	Southend	26
95	Telford and Wrekin	73
96	Peterborough	55
97	Thurrock	97
98	Blackpool	86
99	Blackburn and Darwen	87
100	Isle of Wight	65
101	Torbay	68
102	Powys	80
103	Gwynedd	70
104	Darlington	56
105	Anglesey	76

Source: Census of Population (2001).

One thing which Table 9.2 does highlight are the differences that exist *within* London, particularly the relatively low ranking in terms of creative class LQs of the more peripheral areas in contrast to the central areas. Although London looms large over the UK picture, there are other regional centres of high creativity (and high concentrations of bohemians). The situation tends to differ in the smaller countries, where the capital may be the only realistic locational choice for many specialized professional workers (see also Clifton *et al.*, 2012). Moreover, the status of London as a genuine global city is significant, as it is therefore competing for creativity (to use the fashionable rhetoric) on the world stage, with the different tensions that this brings. One of these may be a latent conflict between national capital versus international roles, perhaps generating competing pressures or funding priorities, for example, resources which are ostensibly earmarked for local regeneration might be spent with one eye on the potential national or international payoffs.

As the UK's 'second city', Birmingham is an interesting case; with statistics relating to the central area (population of about 1m) it ranks proportionally much lower for the creative class (54th) than it does in terms of population (13th); variations around this urban core are, however, apparent in Figure 9.1, discussed below. Despite these discrepancies and data issues, there is some evidence of an association between size of agglomeration and creative class concentration, a rank correlation between the two producing a coefficient of 0.41. In order to explore this agglomeration effect further, the association between population density and creative class concentration was investigated; somewhat surprisingly, virtually no link was found, with a correlation coefficient of only 0.1.[9] Clearly, then, it is not just size or density of population, the higher levels of which are typically found in metropolitan areas and urban centres, that is associated with the

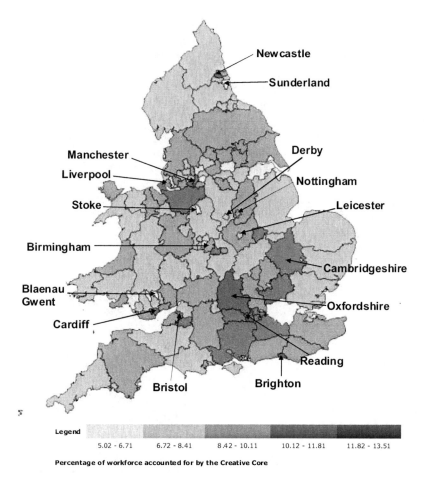

Figure 9.1 Location of the creative core in England and Wales

Source: Nomis.

location of the creative class. This could reflect different preferences within the agglomerated creative class, as suggested by some of the literature reviewed earlier. It also suggests that different spatial levels of analysis might be appropriate, in order, for example, to zoom in on micro-level neighbourhood effects not currently captured in the data. More generally, these issues highlight the importance of investigating additional quality of place factors (quantitative and if possible qualitative) in seeking to explain the distribution of the creative class; see the section on the creative class and quality of place below.

Table 9.3 provides a slightly different view of creative class distribution, in this case showing the ten highest and lowest unitary/county authorities, ranked with respect to their creative core LQs. There are in total 171 of these localities in England and Wales, and this level of geography allows a little more detail to become apparent than is the case with NUTS3. Further to this end, the 33 unitary authorities that comprise London have been combined into the single standard NUTS1 UK region; this provides a view of how London as a whole is positioned, but equally important is the fact that 18 of the top 20 creative core UAs in England and Wales are located in the capital,[10] and so collapsing these into a single figure allows detail elsewhere to emerge.

As might be expected (see e.g., Hall *et al.* 1987), localities in the west-of-London M4 corridor area (Wokingham, Reading, Oxfordshire, Windsor and Maidenhead) feature heavily in the top ten creative core LQs. In addition to London, ranked at number seven, Cambridgeshire completes the third facet of the 'Golden Triangle' of the UK's knowledge economy. What is perhaps more interesting is that in addition to those areas which might be expected to feature, a number of less obvious regional centres of creativity emerge – Cardiff in the west, Manchester in the northwest (Trafford lying just to the west of the city centre with Manchester itself ranked only four places below at 14), and Newcastle in the northeast. Finally, our rankings confirm the perception of Brighton and Hove as a creative centre with its unique bohemian image and relative proximity to London.

Table 9.3 Creative core location by unitary authority/county

Top 10 localities	LQ	Bottom 10 localities	LQ
1. Wokingham	1.46	1. Barnsley	0.63
2. Reading	1.42	2. Tameside	0.62
3. Cardiff	1.39	3. N.E. Lincolnshire	0.61
4. Oxfordshire	1.34	4. Knowsley	0.60
5. *London**	*1.33*	5. Kingston upon Hull	0.58
6. Newcastle	1.32	6. Sandwell	0.57
7. Cambridgeshire	1.31	7. Thurrock	0.56
8. Brighton and Hove	1.31	8. Blackpool	0.52
9. Windsor and Maidenhead	1.31	9. Blaenau Gwent	0.51
10. Trafford	1.27	10. Stoke on Trent	0.49

Source: Census of Population (2001).

Note: * Combined NUTS1 region.

Turning attention to the bottom ten UAs, a number of these are places suffering the protracted after-effects of the loss of heavy industry, either as distinct localities (Blaenau Gwent, Stoke on Trent, Barnsley) or the deindustrialized areas of large cities, for example, Tameside (Manchester), Knowsley (Liverpool) and Sandwell (Birmingham). These localities typically face a long-standing and often deeply embedded mixture of social, economic, and environmental problems that give a narrow economic base and a vulnerability to both to short-term employment shocks and long-term economic decline. More specifically:

- a weak local tradition of entrepreneurship and small independent enterprise;
- high unemployment, particularly among young people and older men;
- the paradox of skill shortages in certain key sectors through an inability to attract and retain the necessary human capital;
- a history of under-investment and continuing deterioration in the natural and built environment with special problems in the area of housing;
- mixed multi-ethnic populations as a result of previous waves of immigration before the advent of decline.[11]

Figure 9.1 shows how the creative core are distributed within the Unitary/ County districts of England and Wales, with London shown as a single standard NUTS1 region. A number of locations are highlighted on the map; this is not necessarily a comprehensive listing of the highest or lowest ranked places, rather, they are intended to serve as illustrative examples. The concentration creative core in the south-east of England generally and the M4 corridor area in particular is apparent; within this area the Unitary Authority of Reading is highlighted, immediately to the south-east is Wokingham, and Windsor and Maidenhead lie to the east again (not shown).

The three cities of the East Midlands (Derby, Leicester and Nottingham) serve to illustrate the way in which urban centres do not necessarily possess a consistent relationship with their surrounding hinterland in terms of where the creative core congregate – one of these cities (Leicester) has a significantly higher concentration than the corresponding county area, while in the other two cases it is approximately equal. There is a wider point to note on this in that as alluded to earlier, explanations of creative class distribution go beyond a simplistic urban vs. rural issue, though this may play some part in the process. This type of pattern is further revealed when the major cities are examined, in that localities which make up the wider city area are often very different with respect to levels of the creative core, despite quite small distances being involved. Examples of this are apparent in Birmingham, with the district of Sandwell immediately to the west placed fifth lowest (see Table 9.3) while directly to the east lies Solihull (22nd of the 138 Unitary Authorities and Counties outside London). A similar situation is observed with respect to Manchester: Tameside to the east, Trafford to the (south) west, placed in the bottom ten and top ten respectively of the creative core ranking. The north-east of England provides another example of contrasting creative class patterns existing in close proximity; this is, however, different in one key aspect in that, though adjacent to one another, Newcastle and Sunderland are two distinct cities with their own identities, not to mention rivalries. Newcastle's much higher levels of creative core may in part be assigned to its role as a regional capital and administrative centre, but in recent years it has seen extensive cultural development and has acquired something of a boho image that is more complex to explain.

Focusing on those areas of England and Wales that are less well placed in terms of creativity, as discussed above, a number of larger city areas fall into this category, along with distinct 'post-industrial' regions such as the South Wales valleys and the former coalfield areas in the north of England. It is notable that the former exist in relative proximity to Cardiff, one of the highly placed cities for creative core in England and Wales, and it is significant that of these Blaenau Gwent is one of the two valley areas that does not share a border with either Cardiff or Newport to the east (the other being Merthyr Tydfil).

The creative class and quality of place

As outlined earlier, Florida (2002a; 2002b) suggests that the creative class is highly mobile, with strong preferences for certain aspects of quality of place. In conjunction with Canadian researchers (see e.g. Gertler *et al.* 2002), he shows that in North America cities with high levels of the creative class tend to be open, tolerant and diverse places, with high levels of recreational and cultural opportunity. According to Florida, an open environment is one in which people are accepted and allowed in, on the basis of their skills rather than their similarity to the existing gatekeepers. As such, another indicator of tolerance we can employ is the proportion of bohemians in any given location. This group often stands out compared to mainstream culture, lifestyle and values, and thus in order to thrive requires high levels of tolerance. The idea therefore is that bohemians seek the opportunity to experience a diversity of impressions, and are thereby themselves indicators of a tolerant and open environment (it may be recalled from previous sections that this view has been critiqued as revealing a somewhat simplistic view of the locational choices of arts- and culture-based professionals, e.g., Markusen, 2006; Wojan *et al.*, 2007). In order to reflect the European context of our research, to these indicators have been added those of Public Provision and Unemployment (as a proxy for Social Cohesion).

We do not suggest that all aspects of a concept as nebulous as quality of place can be perfectly captured by these relatively simplistic statistics; it is possible, however, to construct some general indicators, underpinned by the creative class theory. In this section we analyse the association between these indicators and the location of the creative class in England and Wales. An analysis is conducted of the bivariate correlations between the individual quality of place indicators and the location of the creative class; we then combine these indicators into a single multiple regression model, which allows an estimation of the overall explanatory value of these variables on the distribution of the creative class.

Table 9.4 Quality of place indicators: overview

	England and Wales (%)	Highest locality (%)	Lowest locality (%)
Openness (diversity)	8.9	36.2	1.6
Bohemians	2.1	8.8	0.8
Cultural opportunity	2.9	15.2	1.3
Public provision	9.0	17.6	5.4
Unemployment	5.1	10.5	2.1

Source: Census of Population (2001); Annual Business Inquiry, Employee Analysis (2002).

Table 9.4 shows summary values of the quality of place indicators for England and Wales. The distribution of the bohemians has been discussed above and so will not be commented upon here. Levels of diversity, defined as the percentage of residents that are foreign-born, shows quite considerable variation; the three highest values are accounted for by London NUTS3 areas (of which there are five) with Inner London East being the highest. The highest placed non-London locality is Leicester, a city with a long tradition of immigration from the Indian subcontinent. This result does highlight concerns over this particular indicator, and these are subsequently discussed. Conversely, the Gwent Valleys is the least diverse locality in England and Wales by this measure, closely followed by the other Valleys area (Central).

Cultural opportunity also sees wide variations; Inner London West is a significant outlier, unsurprisingly, given the concentration of high profile museums and galleries therein. Perhaps more surprising is that the next highest placed locality is Blackpool (4.1 per cent of employment). Again this highlights how certain quality of place indicators can be influenced by underlying factors which are not necessarily consistent – the Blackpool figure is almost certainly largely derived from a high concentration of bars and amusements rather than the 'high' culture found in central London. Once again, the lowest value of the indicator (1.3 per cent) is accounted for by the Gwent Valleys region.

Finally, with regard to the Public Provision index (PPI), it is quite hard to discern any pattern within the results, with two of the top three being cities of the East Midlands (Nottingham and Leicester respectively), separated only by Inner London west. Again, different forces are likely to be at work here.

As shown in Table 9.5, the indicators for both diversity and the bohemians are positively correlated with the localization of the creative class and both of its subgroups. This means that the creative class in England and Wales tends to live in places that also have high levels of bohemians and diversity. Both relationships are quite strong, particularly so between the creative class and the location of the bohemians. The Openness index is a fairly simplistic measure of tolerance to diversity and as such might not be sufficient. A more focused measure on levels of actual integration, or the labour market participation of highly educated foreign-born workers might capture the real openness of a community better. Such measures are, however, restricted by data problems. Nonetheless, from the above we can tentatively conclude that the creative class and tolerance (measured as

Table 9.5 Quality of place: bivariate correlations

	Correlation with creative class	Correlation with creative core	Correlation with creative professionals
Openness (diversity)	0.52**	0.44**	0.50**
Bohemians	0.72**	0.58**	0.71**
Cultural opportunity.	0.52**	0.29**	0.56**
Public provision	0.02	0.21*	−0.07
Unemployment	−0.31**	−0.21*	−0.33**

Source: Census of Population (2001); Annual Business Inquiry, Employee Analysis (2002).

Notes: * significant at the 95% level; ** significant at the 99% level.

ethnic diversity, and the presence of bohemians) do correlate in the same way that is found in the North American analyses.

Figures 9.2 and 9.3 show graphical representations of the relationship between the Creative Class and respectively the bohemians and openness. Figure 9.2 demonstrates a strong and positive relationship as predicted, with the four NUTS3 areas of London, along with Brighton and Hove as significant outliers (i.e., they have higher concentrations of bohemians for their observed levels of creative core employment than is typical). This makes intrinsic sense given the locations in question. Figure 9.3 illustrates the point made earlier that despite a significant trend line, localities can possess identical levels of openness (as we measure it), but very different levels of the creative core. Different local and regional trajectories (and thus potentially different relationships) are likely to underpin this observation.

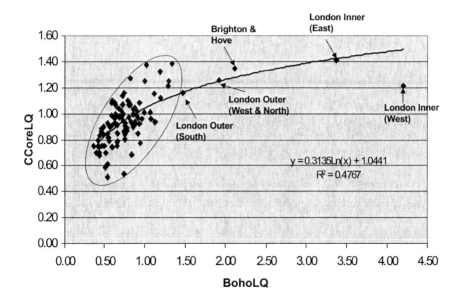

Figure 9.2 Creative core and bohemians (Boho LQ)

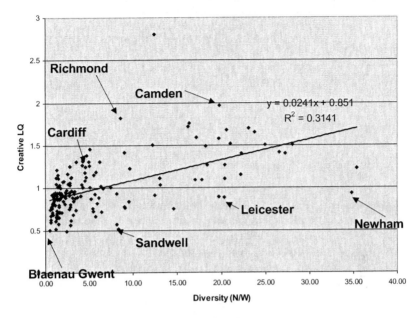

Figure 9.3 Creative core and openness (diversity)

With regard to cultural opportunity, a positive and statistically significant relationship exists between the presence of the creative class in a location, and that location's cultural and recreational offering. This finding is again compatible with those of the North American research. This relationship is quite strong for the creative class as a whole and for the creative professionals, but somewhat puzzlingly weaker for the creative core.

The concepts of public provision and social cohesion are actually quite abstract, and are therefore somewhat difficult to operationalize in practice. The relative provision of public goods and services in healthcare and education is measured here by levels of employment in these sectors. Conversely, unemployment (i.e., exclusion from the labour market) is one of the main manifestations of social exclusion. For public provision, a significant and positive (but weak) association is observed for the creative core only. For unemployment, the relationship is consistently negative, although moderate and weak with respect to the creative core, meaning that municipalities with high levels of unemployment tend to have a low concentration of the creative class.

Overall, it would appear that the creative class in England and Wales shows a similar pattern of distribution with respect to quality of place, as is observed in North American cities. High concentrations are typically found in places which are tolerant, diverse, bohemian, socially cohesive and which offer higher levels of cultural opportunity, but the overall pattern is quite complex.

In order to test a unified creative class model, the multiple regression method is used. The advantage of using this method is that all indicators are tested in one

Table 9.6 Results of the Combined Model: summary

	Total creative class	Creative core	Creative professionals
Openness (diversity)	+	n/s	+
Bohemians	+	+	+
Cultural opportunity.	n/s	−	+
Public provision	n/s	+	−
Unemployment	−	−	−
Adjusted R²	0.664	0.484	0.698

Note: Where a significant result at the 5 per cent level of confidence is observed this is represented by the + symbol, − when the result is significant but in the opposite direction to that predicted. A statistically insignificant result is denoted by n/s.

model, and therefore it is possible to control for any multicollinearity between the independent variables. A total of six models were produced; for each of the creative class and the two subgroups (the creative core and the creative professionals) two models were calculated for each dependent variable, including either all foreign-born citizens or non-Western foreign-born citizens as the Openness variable. These results are summarized in Table 9.6: this reveals some variation across the regressions: the model for the creative core has the lowest explanatory power (.484), while that of the creative professionals has the highest (.698). There was also some variation across the quality of place variables, for example, Cultural Opportunity was negatively associated with the creative core (the opposite direction than predicted), and not significant within the Total Creative Class model. The Public Provision index was also not significant for the Total model, but positively associated with the creative core (the direction predicted).

The model shown in full in Table 9.7 – creative professionals as the dependent variable with all foreign-born citizens as a dependent variable – had the greatest explanatory power of those constructed. In total, this model explains around 70 per cent of the distribution of the Creative Professionals. All of the independent variables are significant at the 99 per cent level, with the exception of Openness (95 per cent).

The location of the bohemians, Openness and the Cultural Opportunity index is positively correlated with the localization of the Creative Professionals. This means that, consistent with the theory of the creative class, wherever these quality of place indicators are high, levels of creative professionals will also tend to be higher. Moreover, from the standardized coefficients shown in Table 9.7 we can infer that of these variables, it is the presence of the bohemians that has the greatest influence. With regard to the other two independent variables, as expected, unemployment is negatively associated with the location of the creative professionals; the nature of causality behind this relationship is open to debate. On the one hand, it may represent (as intended) an association with higher levels of social cohesion, while on the other it could be related to labour market in that creativity is a growing area of employment and as such would be expected to coincide with lower unemployment. Finally, the public provision index is negatively linked to

Table 9.7 Results of the Combined Model: detail

Indicators	Unstandardized coefficients		Standardized coefficients	t	Sig.	Collinearity statistics	
	B	Std. Error	Beta			Tolerance	VIF
(Constant)	27.882	1.097		25.406	0.000		
Openness	0.143	0.060	0.218	2.360	0.020	0.345	2.897
Bohemians	3.235	0.906	0.414	3.572	0.001	0.221	4.530
Public Provision	−0.423	0.126	−0.223	−3.356	0.001	0.670	1.492
Cultural Opportunity	0.877	0.265	0.302	3.313	0.001	0.356	2.807
Unemployment	−0.903	0.145	−0.385	−6.231	0.000	0.776	1.289

Dependent variable: creative professionals

Model summary

Model	R	R square	Adjusted R square	Std. error of the estimate
1	0.844(a)	0.713	0.698	2.19272

the distribution of the creative professionals, which is the opposite of what might be expected. This could be due to the nature of public sector employment in the UK, which tends to be proportionally higher in less prosperous areas, reflecting a lack of private sector jobs in combination with a conscious policy of employment redistribution (see Clifton *et al.*, 2012, for more on this). On the one hand, Tables 9.6 and 9.7 would appear to be *prima facie* evidence of systematic variation between sections of the creative class; however, we need to be wary of data or other specification issues; this is a clear area for further research and one in which qualitative (casual) evidence will need to play a role.

The creative class and indicators of prosperity, growth and technology

Having examined where the creative class is located in England and Wales, and how this distribution is associated with various indicators of quality of place, attention is now turned to the relationship between the creative class and basic indicators of prosperity. Constraints of space prevent our reporting a full analysis of the geographical variations within each of these indicators here; thus Table 9.8 shows overall bivariate correlations between the three creative class groupings and the five indicators of prosperity, growth and technology.[12]

The association between the two general indicators of prosperity (i.e. population growth and employment growth) and the localization of the creative class is statistically significant and positive. The relationship between creative class location and population growth is quite strong for both the creative class as a whole and the creative professionals, but weak for the creative core. For employment

Table 9.8 Indicators of prosperity: bivariate correlations

	Correlation with creative class	Correlation with creative core	Correlation with creative professionals
Population change	0.51**	0.29**	0.56**
Employment change	0.27**	0.23**	0.25**
Milken Techpole Index	0.64**	0.49**	0.63**
Employment change (Hi tech)	0.04	0.01	0.05
New firm formation	0.76**	0.46**	0.82**

Source: ONS, various datasets
Notes: * significant at the 95% level; ** significant at the 99% level.

growth, the relationship is, however, quite weak for both the creative class and its two sub-groups. Overall, therefore, a high concentration of the creative class tends to be found in places that have growing populations and rising employment. This may be interpreted as evidence in support of the 'jobs follow people' aspect of the Florida thesis; that is, that the creative class creates prosperity by its very presence. Bivariate correlations can, however, only indicate association (i.e., covariance) and do not themselves imply any causal relationships between the variables involved. Put simply, it may be that the creative class also follows prosperity, rather than creating it. As noted above, conclusions regarding causality will need to be informed by more qualitative data.

With regard to employment in the Tech-pole sectors, the relationship between the creative class and share of 'high-tech' employees is positive and significant; this relationship is somewhat stronger for the creative class in general and the creative professionals in particular than it is for the creative core. This means that a high concentration of resident creative class tends to be associated with the presence of relatively high levels of employment in technology-based businesses. This preponderance for the creative class to be collocated with high-technology activities is consistent with what is observed in the North American research (Florida, 2002a; 2002b; 2002c; Gertler *et al.*, 2002). There is, however, no evidence to suggest that the presence of the creative class (in any of its guises) is associated with any *growth* in employment in these activities, these correlations not being significantly different from zero. This is, on the face of it, a major difference between the UK and the US/Canada creative class results, and one that requires further investigation, given the central tolerance and diversity begets creativity begets technology-based employment growth theme of the creative class model.

Finally, the correlation between the presence of the creative class (in all its forms) and the rate at which new firms are created is positive and significant. The relationship is strong with respect to the creative class as a whole, and for the creative professionals but less so for the creative core. This means that localities in which the creative class in England and Wales is concentrated typically exhibit higher levels of new firm formation; this is consistent with the Florida thesis but again open to interpretation with regard to causality.

Conclusion and issues for further research

Our first research question was concerned with mapping the size and distribution of the creative class in England and Wales. In its widest definition it currently accounts for just over 37 per cent of all employment, yet the dispersion is somewhat uneven. High concentrations are typically an urban and metropolitan phenomenon, but not exclusively so, a number of inner city areas having some of the lowest rankings observed, in common with a number of localities and regions afflicted by the long employment decline within traditional industries. It should be noted that the level of geography employed does have an impact here, and striking the balance between highlighting distinct localities and functional labour markets, on the one hand, and being able to observe interesting variations and idiosyncrasies, on the other, is not always easy. Particularly within the larger cities, the findings of Markusen (2006) and Wojan *et al.* (2007) suggest the need to investigate the subtleties of bohemian and creative class distribution at the sub-metropolitan (or even neighbourhood) level.

Attention was focused upon how variations in quality of place are related to the location of the creative class. This analysis of this second research question showed statistically significant relationships between the localization of the creative class and these indicators. Tested individually, all the indicators were significantly correlated in the directions hypothesized with the exception of the Public Provision index, which was partially so.[13] The strength and significance level of these correlations showed some variation by creative class type (i.e. creative class as a whole, creative core and creative professionals). The combined quality of place regression model produced high levels of explanatory power with independent variables largely significant in the direction suggested by Florida's theory; there are, however, some variations depending upon which creative class subgroup is employed as the dependent variable.

Do these variations reflect 'real' differences in, for example, preferences for quality of place? Alternatively, are they more likely to derive from data/model specification issues, or from such factors as urban hierarchy or national political system (see Clifton *et al.*, 2012)? Perhaps one way forward for future research here might be to control for population density (and/or human capital) in the regression models as a way to isolate agglomeration effects unrelated to the creative class *per se*. The observed differences between the creative class groupings underline the potential value in seeking to unpack the sometimes amorphous set of occupations included; the knowledge base approach taken by Asheim and Hansen (2009) with respect to creative workers in Sweden may represent a fruitful method of doing just this for the UK. Essentially this would require the re-coding of the creative class dataset into (in their methodology) the users and creators of symbolic, analytical, and synthetic knowledge. Another way to achieve greater understanding could be to explore life-stage affects of location choice, for example, as per the Markusen and Johnson (2006) study of artists in Minneapolis. More generally, it may also be insightful to bring together research on the hard and soft infrastructures of a given place. For example, what types of spaces, natural or built environments might aid (or hinder) milieu effects? At present, these are essentially assumed to happen inside a spatial black box.

Indicators of prosperity, technology and growth are all significant and positively associated with the presence of the creative class, and again variations in the significance and strength of relationships were observed by creative class subgroups. The notable exception to this pattern was technology-based employment growth, which showed no association with the location of the creative class. This suggests the representation of both technology entrepreneurs and bohemians in the same places in North America, while in the UK, by contrast, bohemians are concentrated in the London area and in a few other creative centres (Brighton, for example); technology entrepreneurship is less common but may also be found in (for example) smaller university cities.

Overall, we generally conclude that the creative class in England and Wales displays similar properties to those ascribed to it in the USA (Florida, 2002a; 2002b; 2002c) and Canada (Gertler *et al.*, 2002), albeit with certain caveats as noted. It should also be noted here that though our quantitative results provide evidence of consistency with the creative class theory through numerous correlations and associations, it is much more difficult to draw inferences relating to actual causality. This will be an issue that more qualitative research can address, with interviews and case studies designed to uncover the motivations and thought processes behind locational choices (i.e. designed to probe the *causations* that underpin the observed *correlations*). A good example of this is the association of creative class and openness: does this correlation between the creative class and diversity arise merely from a more or less coincidental location in certain metropolitan and urban areas with little or no interaction, is it primarily a kind of consumption relationship in which the creative class are able to access, for example, exotic ethnic shops and a wide variety of interesting restaurants, or is it a reflection of the creative class's genuine preference to live and work in an open, tolerant and diverse community, as Florida describes? Each of these outcomes would potentially be consistent with the findings we present here.

On the issue of diversity, Figure 9.2 suggests a number of places that have arrived at similar levels (as we are able to measure it) but almost certainly for very different reasons, and with different outcomes likely. Clearly the whole issue of diversity and tolerance needs further exploration; one possibility is using the census data to examine variations within the overall foreign-born or non-Western figures; at present, it is not possible to distinguish between places that have equal-sized foreign-born communities originating from one or one hundred different parts of the world. Intuition alone would suggest that such places are likely to be very different. In addition, on the wider point of measuring tolerance, one of the key insights of Florida and Gates (2001) is the linking of gay and hi-tech indices, something not possible in the UK using secondary data. Brighton is the classic example from the UK of a locality whose position in the tolerance rankings would be significantly affected if this alternative measure were used. To widen this point out, Florida himself has suggested that since his original studies of the creative class, the USA is now starting to lose its dominance in what he refers to as 'the new global competition for talent' (Florida, 2004); if this is indeed the case, what might be the potential impact on both policy and potential economic outcomes for Europe in general, and the UK more specifically? Perhaps the most pressing research priority though is the fate of the non-creative class, which, after all, comprises more than 60 per cent of the labour force. Will they be limited to those meagre trickle-down benefits of creativity, or can everyone become more creative?; and who will be responsible for making this happen, given the essential hegemony of 'neo-liberal' (Sager, 2011) urban planning policies? The urban leaders driving forward the creative class agenda? Or national governments? Or will it be left to the creative class themselves to 'grow up' and take responsibility as Richard Florida himself proposes? Analogously, there are similar questions to be resolved regarding non-creative places. Peck (2005) warns against the creation of 'cargo cults', vainly attempting to flag down footloose creativity much in the same way that cities and regions used to enter into zero-sum games chasing old-style inward investment. Perhaps it would be an interesting exercise for further research to revisit the sites of creativity attraction programmes, to systematically evaluate their impacts, successful or otherwise.

Although the link between the creative class, culture, competitiveness, and growth can, and will, continue to be debated, as Huggins and Clifton (2011) argue, the crux of the matter from a UK competitiveness perspective is to ensure fair access to economic opportunity across the nation as a whole. In the current economic (and policy) climate, it is increasingly difficult to see how this will happen; though many lagging places do possess a tradition of loyalty to the locality and a strong spirit of community, together with well-established traditions of partnership and association, they essentially lack the endogenous capacity to reconnect themselves with the growth poles of the UK economy. In the parlance of Putnam (2000), they possess *bonding* social capital but are lacking in the *bridging* social capital required for development. This situation will inevitably be exacerbated by the coming cuts in central government departmental budgets over the next four years; the most pertinent being Local Government down by 27 per cent, Communities by 51 per cent, and Culture, Media and Sport 24 per cent (all in excess of the average 19 per cent reduction in revenue spending across all UK Government departments). Moreover, at a time when place matters as much if not more than it ever did, the disbanding of the regional development agencies (RDAs) in 2010 in England and their replacement by Local Enterprise Partnerships and 'Core City' arrangements (ODPM, 2012) adds another level of uncertainty to the picture. Culture and creativity cannot in themselves create employment. Regeneration also requires the mobilization of more tangible resources to encourage the process.

Acknowledgements

Research was funded by the UK Economic and Social Research Council as a project entitled 'Technology, Talent and Tolerance in European Cities: A Comparative Analysis' (Grant No. RES-000-230467). The usual disclaimer applies.

Notes

1 Most notably (but not necessarily restricted to) gentrification, and so on.
2 For data reasons the analysis presented here excludes Northern Ireland and Scotland, thus it represents approximately 90 per cent of the total UK population.
3 As Saxenian (2005) notes, this is not necessarily a zero-sum game of static talent attraction – high levels of *circulation* are also important for a region's development.
4 Peck (2005) also notes the use of disarming terminology that invites positive association, and asks who indeed would seek to be rigid, narrow-minded and conservative when they could be flexible, open and creative?
5 Indeed, as Markusen herself notes, visual artists, for example, may well have significantly different locational preferences to, say, performing artists.
6 For a detailed explanation of the indicators employed here, see Andersen *et al.* (2010a), and Clifton (2008).
7 Not in terms of absolute size – the USA and Canadian regions typically being much larger – but rather having a similar role within the national context in question.
8 There has of course been considerable debate around what constitutes an appropriate functional unit –Travel To Work Areas being the most obvious example – but, as noted, the key driver here was the availability of the necessary data.
9 This figure rises slightly to 0.28 for the bohemians only.
10 This statistic should not obscure the fact that massive variation exists within London, with some very low Creative Core LQs found therein (for example, Barking and Dagenham, at 0.51, the third lowest in England and Wales).
11 Although beyond the scope of the discussion presented here, studies such as that of Bobo and Licari (1989) which investigates the association between tolerance and levels of education suggest that causality is a complex issue here. More generally, we should be wary of 'blaming the victim' when reviewing non-diverse, non-creative places.
12 For a more comprehensive discussion of the outcomes of creative class location around the broader concept of 'competitiveness' see Huggins and Clifton (2011).
13 This suggests the need to revisit this indicator in future research; for example, maybe the constituent components of health and education actually exert conflicting influences due to demographic effects.

Bibliography

Andersen, K., Buggee, M., Hansen, H., Isaksen, A., and Raunio, M. (2010b) 'One size fits all? Applying the creative class thesis onto a Nordic context', *European Planning Studies*, 18: 1591–1609.
Andersen, K., Hansen, H., Isaksen, A. and Raunio, M (2010a) 'Nordic city regions in the creative class debate: Putting the creative class thesis to a test', *Industry and Innovation*, 17: 215–240.
Asheim, B. (2009) 'Guest Editorial: Introduction to the creative class in European city regions', *Economic Geography*, 85: 355–362.

Asheim, B. and Hansen, H. (2009) 'Knowledge bases, talents and contexts: On the useful-ness of the creative class approach in Sweden', *Economic Geography*, 85(4): 425–442.

Bobo, L. and Licari, F. (1989) 'Education and political tolerance: Testing the effects of cognitive sophistication and target group affect', *Public Opinion Quarterly*, 53: 285–308.

Boschma, R. and Frisch, M. (2009) 'Creative class and regional growth: Empirical evidence from seven European countries', *Economic Geography*, 85: 391–423.

Bradford, N. (2004) 'Creative cities: Structured policy dialogue report', Background paper F45, Family Network, Canadian Policy Research Networks, Ottawa, ON.

Brooks, D. (2000) *Bobos in Paradise: The New Upper Class and How They Got There*, New York: Simon & Schuster.

Brown, P. and Lauder, H. (2006) 'Globalisation, knowledge, and the myth of the magnet economy', *Globalisation, Societies and Education*, 4: 25–57.

Cannon, T., Nathan, M. and Westwood, A. (2003) *Welcome to the Ideopolis*, London: The Work Foundation.

Clifton, N. (2008) 'The "creative class" in the UK: An initial analysis', *Geografiska Annaler, Series B*, 90: 63–82.

Clifton, N., Cooke, P. and Hansen, H. (2012) 'Towards a reconciliation of the "context-less" with the "space-less"? The creative class across varieties of capitalism: New evidence from Sweden and the UK', *Regional Studies*, iFirst: 1–15.

Cooke, P., De Laurentis, C., Todtling, F. and Trippl, M. (2007) *Regional Knowledge Economies: Markets, Clusters and Innovation*, Cheltenham, UK: Edward Elgar.

DCMS (Department for Culture, Media and Sport) (2000) *Creative Industries: The Regional Dimension*, London: TSO.

DCMS (Department for Culture, Media and Sport) (2003) 'Manchester is favourite with "new bohemians"', available at: http://www.demos.co.uk/media/pressreleases/bohobritain.

DCMS (Department for Culture, Media and Sport) (2004) *Culture at the Heart of Regen-eration*, London: TSO.

DCMS (Department for Culture, Media and Sport) (2007) *The Creative Economy Programme: A Summary of Projects Commissioned in 2006/7*, London: TSO.

DCMS (Department for Culture, Media and Sport) (2008) *Creative Britain: New Talents for the New Economy*, London: TSO.

De Laurentis, C. (2006) 'Digital knowledge exploitation: ICT, memory institutions and innovation from cultural assets', *Journal of Technology Transfer*, 31: 77–89.

DeVol, R., Bedroussian, A. and Kim, S. (2007) *Best Performing Cities 2007: Where America's Jobs Are Created and Sustained*, Santa Monica, CA: Milken Institute.

Florida, R. (2000) *Competing in the Age of Talent: Quality of Place and the New Economy*, Pittsburgh, PA: R.K. Mellon Foundation.

Florida, R. (2002a) 'Bohemia and economic geography', *Journal of Economic Geography*, 2: 55–71.

Florida, R. (2002b) *The Rise of the Creative Class*, New York: Basic Books.

Florida, R. (2002c) 'The economic geography of talent', *Annals of the Association of American Geographers*, 92: 743–755.

Florida, R. (2004) *The Flight of the Creative Class: The New Global Competition for Talent*, New York: HarperCollins.

Florida, R. (2008) *Who's Your City?*, New York: Basic Books.

Florida, R. and Gates, G. (2001) *Technology and Tolerance: The Importance of Diversity to High-Technology Growth*, Survey Series 1, Center on Urban and Metropolitan Policy, Washington, DC: The Brookings Institution.

Florida, R., Mellander, C., and Stolarick, K. (2008) 'Inside the Black Box of regional development – human capital, the creative class and tolerance', *Journal of Economic Geography*, 8: 615–649.

Gertler, M. S., Florida, R., Gates, G. and Vinodrai, T. (2002) *Competing on Creativity: Placing Ontario's Cities in North American Context*, report prepared for the Ontario Ministry of Enterprise, Opportunity and Innovation and the Institute for Competitiveness and Prosperity. Munk Centre for International Studies, University of Toronto, Toronto, ON.

Glaeser, E. L. (1998) 'Are cities dying?', *Journal of Economic Perspectives*, 12: 139–160.

Hall, P., Breheny, M., McQuaid, R. and Hart, D. (1987) *Western Sunrise: The Genesis and Growth of Britain's Major High Tech Corridor*, London: Allen & Unwin.

Hall, P. and Soskice, D. (2001) 'An introduction to varieties of capitalism', in P. Hall and D. Soskice (eds), *Varieties of Capitalism: The Institutional Foundations of Comparative Advantage*, Oxford: Oxford University Press, pp. 1–68.

Hansen, H. K. and Niedomysl, T. (2009) 'Migrations of the creative class: Evidence from Sweden', *Journal of Economic Geography*, 9: 191–206.

Heath, J. and Potter A. (2006) *The Rebel Sell: How the Counter Culture Became the Consumer Culture*, Chichester: Capstone.

HM Treasury (2005) *The Cox Review of Creativity in Business: Building on the UK's Strengths*, London: TSO.

Huggins, R. and Clifton, N. (2011) 'Competitiveness, creativity, and place-based development', *Environment and Planning A*, 43: 1341–1362.

Jacobs, J. (1961) *The Death and Life of Great American Cities*, New York: Random House.

Jacobs, J. (1969) *The Economy of Cities*, New York: Random House.

Leitner, H. (1990) 'Cities in pursuit of economic growth: The local state as entrepreneur', *Political Geography Quarterly*, 9: 146–170.

Lucas, R. E. (1988) 'On the mechanics of economic development', *Journal of Monetary Economics*, 22: 3–42.

Markusen, A. (2006) 'Urban development and the politics of a creative class: Evidence from a study of artists', *Environment and Planning A*, 38: 1921–1940.

Markusen, A. and Johnson, A. (2006) *Artists' Centers: Evolution and Impact on Careers, Neighborhoods and Economies*, Minneapolis, MN: Hubert H. Humphrey Institute of Public Affairs, University of Minnesota.

Marshall, A. (1920) *Industry and Trade*, London: Macmillan.

Martin-Brelot, H., Grossetti, M., Eckert, D., Gritsai, O. and Kovacs, Z. (2010) 'The spatial mobility of the creative class: A European perspective', *International Journal of Urban and Regional Research*, 34: 854–870.

ODPM (Office of the Deputy Prime Minister) (2012) *Unlocking Growth in Cities*, London: TSO.

Parr, J. B. (2005) 'Perspectives on the city-region', *Regional Studies*, 39: 555–566.

Peck, J. (2005) 'Struggling with the creative class', *International Journal of Urban and Regional Research*, 29: 740–770.

Porter, M. E. (2000) 'Location, clusters, and company strategy', in G. L. Clark, M. P. Feldman and M. S. Gertler (eds), *The Oxford Handbook of Economic Geography*, Oxford: Oxford University Press, pp. 253–274.

Pratt, A. C. (2008) 'Creative cities: The cultural industries and the creative class', *Geografiska Annaler Series B*, 90: 107–117.

Putnam, R. (2000): *Bowling Alone: The Collapse and Revival of American Community*, New York: Simon & Schuster.

Sager, T. (2011) 'Neo-liberal urban planning policies: A literature survey, 1990–2010', *Progress in Planning*, 76: 147–199.

Saxenian, A. (2005) 'From brain drain to brain circulation: Transnational communities and regional upgrading in India and China', *Studies in Comparative International Development*, 40: 35–61.

Thrift, N. J. (2001) '"It's the romance, not the finance, that makes the business worth pursuing": Disclosing a new market', *Economy and Society*, 30: 412–432.

Wojan, T. R., Lambert, D. M. and McGranahan, D. A. (2007) 'Emoting with their feet: Bohemian attraction to creative milieu', *Journal of Economic Geography*, 7: 711–736.

Wong, C. (2001) 'The relationship between quality of life, local economic development: An empirical study of local authority areas in England', *Cities*, 18: 25–32.

10 The geography of creative people in Germany revisited[1]

Michael Fritsch and Michael Stuetzer

Introduction

Creativity as a source of growth has gained increasing attention in recent years. Creativity is the ability to create new knowledge or to transform existing knowledge. In his book *The Rise of the Creative Class* (2004),[2] Richard Florida has shown that the part of the labour force in the USA which is active in creative occupations is distributed unequally across space. According to Florida's analysis, people in creative occupations are concentrated in a few key large city-regions, which he regards as hubs of technical and social innovation. Accordingly, these creative cities can be regarded as hothouses for future growth and development. Florida goes one step further in arguing that the creative people have pronounced locational preferences and that they represent a main source for attracting innovative activity from outside the region. His recommendation for regional policy-makers is, therefore, to create a suitable environment for creative people in order to account for the key importance of this part of the regional population.

This chapter analyzes the geography of people with creative occupations in Germany. We build on our previous work (see Fritsch and Stuetzer, 2009) by analyzing more recent data. Several questions drive this updated work: where do these people live and work? What is it that characterizes regions with a high share of creative inhabitants? Following an introduction of some basic hypotheses (section 2), the indicators for a creative population are introduced (section 3). Section 4 gives an overview of the regional distribution of the creative people. Results of multivariate analyses of the share of the population in creative occupations are presented in section 5, while section 6 concludes.

Review of the theory and empirical evidence

Creativity is often defined as the ability to recombine existing knowledge in new ways, thereby generating new ideas or products (Sternberg and Lubart, 1996; Runco, 2004; Hennessey and Amabile, 2009). Creativity is not restricted to outstanding scientists and artists such as Edison, Einstein, Goethe, Shakespeare, and Leonardo da Vinci. On the contrary, it is an ability inherent in all people who find ways to express their creativity in many different fields (Hartley and Cunningham, 2002). Since Richard Florida's (2004) seminal work, this creation has been attributed to members of the 'creative class'. Florida's main hypothesis is that creative class is an important driver for regional development as it generates innovations and fosters entrepreneurship. However, Florida's theory is not limited to the potential effects of creative people, as it also addresses the factors driving their location choice. In that sense, Florida offers a holistic theory of regional development, emphasizing the sociocultural underpinnings of regional well-being. In the following, we present theoretical arguments and empirical evidence regarding these two main streams of thought. In the third section we will also review some of the critiques that have been brought forward.

Location choice of creative people

Florida (2003, 40; 2004) identifies 'three interrelated types of creativity: (1) *technological creativity* or innovation, (2) *economic creativity* or entrepreneurship, and (3) *artistic or cultural creativity*'. He argues that these three types of human creativity influence and reinforce each other. According to Florida, a main factor in explaining creativity-driven growth is the locational choice of creative people. He suggests that creative people do not solely base their decision to live in a certain location because of job opportunities available there. According to him, factors such as the variety of the cultural supply, tolerance and openness towards new ideas, towards people of different ethnic background, of different sexual orientation or different styles of living are just as important as the regional labour market to creative individuals. Florida (2004) assumes that creative people prefer a diversity of small-scale cultural activities with a vibrant night-life and an innovative music scene over traditional cultural events such as museums, operas, ballets or professional sports teams.

According to Florida (ibid.), these factors are important for two reasons. First, it is easier for people to integrate in such an environment without having to abandon their own identity. Second, tolerance and openness may lead to variety and diversity. This gives creative people the opportunity to gain new experiences that can be a stimulus and inspiration for the creative process (ibid.; Andersen and Lorenzen, 2005). Florida (2004) applies a number of indicators for openness, tolerance and cultural variety, such as the share of the foreign-born population (the Melting Pot Index), the share of people in artistic occupations (the Bohemian Index) or the share of homosexual people (the Gay Index). For the USA and some European countries, a couple of studies provide some evidence for this hypothesis. Boschma and Fritsch (2009) find that in many European countries, bohemians tend to live in regions characterized by a high share of immigrants and cultural activities. Asheim and Hansen (2009) also report positive correlations between the presence of artists and the regional share of creative people in Sweden. The attractive force of bohemians and cultural amenities becomes evident when looking at other variables than population shares. Analyzing a large-scale database of US citizens, Florida, Mellander and Stolarick (2011) found that the existence of cultural opportunities is an important determinant of higher community satisfaction. The presence of bohemians is also related to higher housing prices – even when controlling for economic factors (Florida and Mellander, 2010). Some other studies have found that the gay and lesbian population, indicating an open and tolerant climate, is correlated with the presence of the creative class (e.g., Wojan *et al.*, 2007; Florida *et al.*, 2008).

A further important element of Florida's approach is the hypothesis that creative people show no pronounced tendency to locate in regions where they can expect to have good employment opportunities (the idea that 'people follow jobs') but rather that companies locate in regions where they can find the creative people they need ('jobs follow people'). Therefore, the concentration of creative people in a few locations can be regarded as the reason for the clustering of economic activity. This is particularly true for activities with a high demand for high qualified labour such as research and development, design and marketing and high-tech industries (Arora *et al.*, 2000). There is mixed evidence for this specific hypothesis. While Boschma and Fritsch (2009) find a significantly positive relationship between regional employment change and the share of people in creative occupations in the European countries analyzed, employment growth is not related to changes of the share of the creative population in US regions (McGranahan and Wojan, 2007).

Economic impact of creative people

Florida's main hypothesis regarding the economic impact of creative people is that members of the creative class generate new knowledge that can be commercialized by start-ups but also of course in incumbent firms. The main reason why openness, tolerance, and variety may provide a good breeding ground for new knowledge is that the combination of people with different backgrounds can stimulate the combination of their knowledge (Desrochers, 2001; Boschma and Fritsch, 2009). This newly combined knowledge may then constitute an important source of innovation and the formation of new firms which are important drivers of economic development (Schumpeter, [1911] 1934; Feldman, 2000; Fritsch, 2013).[3] Florida's argument is congruent to Jane Jacobs' (1970; 1985) ideas about the important role of cities as well as the basic hypotheses of the new economic growth theory (see Lucas, 1988; Romer, 1986; 1993).

A number of studies have investigated the links between the creative class and several economic performance indicators. In two early studies, Florida and Gates (2001) and Lee, Florida and Gates (2002) demonstrate that there is a positive empirical relationship between ethnic diversity and innovation in US metropolitan areas. When looking at patents as a dependent variable, studies find a positive relationship between the density of creative workers and patenting activity in US regions (Knudsen *et al.*, 2008) and in German regions (Boschma and Fritsch, 2009). This suggests the importance of the creative class in generating knowledge. As well as innovation, entrepreneurship is another mechanism of how the creative class might impact the economy. Quite a number of studies suggest that the creative class as a whole, or subgroups thereof such as bohemians, can be an important source of start-ups (see Bieri, 2010; Boschma and Fritsch, 2009; Fritsch and Rusakova, 2012; Lee *et al.*, 2004) or the expansion of existing firms (Stolarick *et al.*, 2011). Another group of studies have investigated the link between the creative class and more general indicators of economic performance. Although these studies are not completely convincing in terms of methodology and econometric strategy, there is some evidence that the creative class is related to productivity, income and employment (Florida, *et al.*, 2008; Boschma and Fritsch, 2009; McGranahan and Wojan, 2007).

Critique of Florida's creative class theory

Florida's ideas have provoked considerable controversy. One strand of criticism is directed towards the definitions of creative people used as the foundation for empirical analysis on the basis of occupations. Many of the occupations that Florida regards as creative require a relatively high level of qualification, resulting in critics stating that he measures the impact of qualification, not creativity on economic development (Glaeser, 2005; Markusen, 2006). This kind of critique is correct to the extent that there tends to be a highly positive correlation between the share of people in creative occupations and the share of people with a higher level of education. However, for the contribution to economic development, the way how qualification is applied may be of importance. A taxi driver with a PhD may be highly qualified, but is he more creative than other people? Even if he was a rather creative taxi driver, can he, in his position, have a significant influence on the creation and the application of new ideas? A review of the empirical studies indeed shows that in most cases creative class indicators outperform indicators of education when analyzing regional growth (McGranahan and Wojan, 2007; Florida *et al.*, 2008; Boschma and Fritsch, 2009).

An additional point of criticism is directed towards the impact of people in artistic occupations – the bohemians – on economic development (Malizia and Feser, in Lang and Danielsen, 2005; Markusen, 2006). These critics doubt that there is a causal relationship between a high share of bohemians in a region and economic development. Correlations and regressions relating the share of people in creative occupation today to the current wealth level or to economic growth are not really convincing in this respect because there is a 'chicken or the egg problem' with regards to the underlying causality: Does the presence of creative people cause growth or do growth and wealth induce spending on cultural amenities? In the latter case, a high share of people in cultural occupation would not be a cause but more a symptom of economic prosperity. Falck, Fritsch and Heblich (2011) tried to overcome this problem by using the presence of an opera house built in the Baroque era before the year 1800 as an indicator for cultural activity. They argue that, in the case of Germany, proximity to a Baroque opera house still has a significantly positive impact on the regional distribution of high-skilled employees as well as on regional growth today.

Who are the creative people?

Florida's creative class (2004: 8) consists of people who

> engage in complex problem solving that involves a great deal of independent judgment and requires high levels of education of human capital … Those … in the Creative Class are primarily paid to create and have considerable more autonomy and flexibility than the other … classes to do so.

According to Florida, the core of the creative class includes 'people in science and engineering, architecture and design, education, arts, music and entertainment, whose economic function is to create new ideas, new technology and/or new creative content' (ibid.). Surrounding this creative core is 'a broader group of creative professionals in business and finance, law, health care and related fields'. An important sub-group of the creative core is the bohemians, which includes the artistically creative people such as 'authors, designers, musicians, composers, actors, directors, painters, sculptors, artists, printmakers, photographers, dancers, artists, and performers' (ibid.: 333).

For this empirical analysis, the different categories of creative people are identified by their occupation. The main data source used for this is the German Social Insurance Statistics (see Fritsch and Brixy, 2004, for a brief description). All persons contained in the data set can be assigned to the place of their employment. This information was classified according to the International Standard Classification of Occupations (ISCO) in the 1988 version (see for the ISCO classification, Elias, 1997). We use an updated list of creative occupations that takes into account the criticism regarding construct validity (McGranahan and Wojan, 2007). Table A1 in the Appendix shows the definitions of the different types of creative occupations according to the ISCO classification.

One shortcoming of the German Social Insurance Statistics is that entrepreneurs, freelancers and civil servants are not included. This is particularly relevant for the bohemians, because many of these occupations are characterized by a relatively high share of freelancers. It is estimated that about half of the active artists in Germany are working as freelancers and are not recorded in the Social Insurance Statistics (Haak, 2005). Information about the freelance artists is drawn from the *Künstlersozialkasse*, a special insurance created for those artists who are not in regular employment and, therefore, not subject to obligatory social insurance payments.[4] According to this data source, the freelance artists are assigned to their place of residence. Information on a regional basis about entrepreneurs or civil servants that indicates the creativity of their activity is not available. Therefore, this category of people is not covered in the empirical analysis.

Where do the creative people live and work?

According to the Social Insurance Statistics, in 2007, the share of employees in Germany engaging in creative occupations was 14.3 per cent (Table 10.1). The

Table 10.1 Population share of people with creative occupations and location coefficients in different types of regions 2007 (share of population/location coefficient) (%)

	Germany	Agglomerations			Moderately congested regions		Rural areas
		Overall	Core cities	Rest	Overall	Core cities	
Creative class	14.4/1.00	17.1/1.19	22.2/1.54	12.3/0.86	12.6/0.87	23.0/1.60	11.2/0.78
Creative core	2.2/1.00	2.9/1.31	3.9/1.77	1.9/0.89	1.7/0.80	3.9/1.79	1.4/0.62
Creative professionals	11.8/1.00	13.7/1.16	17.5/1.48	10.0/0.85	10.6/0.89	18.5/1.57	9.7/0.82
Employed bohemians	0.19/1.00	0.25/1.36	0.38/2.05	0.13/0.72	0.14/0.74	0.36/1.91	0.11/0.61
Freelance artists	0.20/1.00	0.29/1.48	0.47/2.37	0.13/0.66	0.12/0.62	0.24/1.21	0.10/0.51
Writers	0.05/1.00	0.08/1.60	0.13/2.65	0.03/0.63	0.03/0.50	0.05/1.02	0.02/0.42
Performing arts	0.02/1.00	0.04/1.59	0.06/2.71	0.01/0.55	0.01/0.51	0.02/1.10	0.01/0.44
Music	0.05/1.00	0.07/1.31	0.10/1.88	0.04/0.79	0.04/0.78	0.07/1.39	0.03/0.64
Fine arts	0.07/1.00	0.11/1.48	0.17/2.40	0.04/0.63	0.04/0.62	0.09/1.25	0.04/0.51

creative professionals made up the largest part of the three sub-groups, accounting for 11.8 per cent of the population. The creative core occupations were the second largest group with a share of 2.2 per cent. The share of employed bohemians made only 0.19 per cent of the population. The share of the freelance artists was about 0.20 per cent. The largest group among the freelance artists were in the fine arts (0.07 per cent) followed by musicians (0.05 per cent), writers (0.05 per cent), and performing artists (0.02 per cent).

In the period 1993–2007, the share of creative occupations of all employees in Germany, as recorded in the Social Insurance Statistics, increased from 37.1 per cent to 42.3 per cent. Most notably the share of creative core occupations increased from 5.1 to 6.5 per cent. Unfortunately, the information for the freelance artists does not allow meaningful longitudinal comparisons due to increasing coverage of the basic population over time (Haak, 2005).

More than half of the creative people in all categories live or work in the agglomerations,[5] while the share of creative people located in rural regions is less than 20 per cent. Since the population is rather unevenly distributed among the different spatial categories, information on the share of creative people in different types of regions makes only limited sense. In order to judge to what extent a concentration of creative people is found in certain regions, their share is related to the share of the population. This is done by calculating a location coefficient according to:

$$\text{Location coefficient} = \frac{\dfrac{\text{Number of creatives}_{\text{region}}}{\text{Population}_{\text{region}}}}{\dfrac{\text{Number of creatives}_{\text{Germany}}}{\text{Population}_{\text{Germany}}}}$$

This location coefficient indicates to what extent the share of creative people in a region is above or below the national share. The more the location coefficient exceeds unity, the more above the national average the share of creative people is. A value below unity indicates a share of people in creative occupations below the national average.

According to the location coefficients, the shares of the different types of creative people are above average mainly in cities (Table 10.1). In rural areas and in the moderately congested regions, the value of the location coefficient is almost always below 1, thus, indicating a relatively low share of creative people in this type of region. The maps with the population share of freelance artists and employed bohemians make the differences between the two categories rather obvious (Figure 10.1). The highest share of freelance artists is found in Munich, Cologne, Berlin, Freiburg, Hamburg, Düsseldorf and Frankfurt (Main). There are also remarkably high shares of freelance artists in regions which are regarded as having a high quality of living such as the area around Freiburg and the region south of Munich which borders the Alps. Compared to the freelance artists, the employed bohemians are more evenly distributed in space. The share of employed

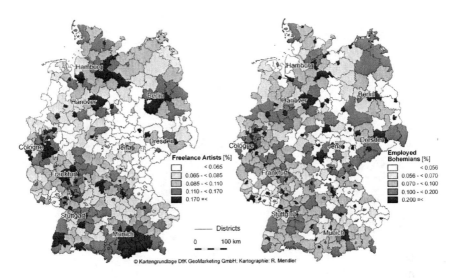

Figure 10.1 Population share of freelance artists and employed bohemians in German districts, 2007

bohemians is relatively high in the cities, and low in remote rural areas. The main reason why the locations of the freelance artists are more scattered throughout the cities may be that they are assigned to their place of residence while the employed bohemians are assigned to the location of their workplaces, which are concentrated in the cities.

The share of employees in the creative core is also relatively high in the cities (Figure 10.2). However, the cities with the highest share of creative core employees are medium-sized cities such as Erlangen, Darmstadt, Heidelberg, Ulm, Wolfsburg, Regensburg and Jena; many of these have a large manufacturing sector and the headquarters of a large firm. The only two larger cities with high shares of creative core employment are Munich and Stuttgart. The population share of the creative class as a whole ranges from a high of 47.1 per cent in the City of Erlangen, to a low of 4.27 per cent in Südwestpfalz. Relatively high shares are found in the cities of Düsseldorf, Frankfurt (Main), Munich and Stuttgart.

In the discussion about the long-lasting economic weakness of the East German economy, it has sometimes been argued that the share of creative people in the East is relatively low because the creative part of the population migrated outward during the GDR regime and thereafter. The share of the creative class is, indeed, 1.7 per cent lower in the East as compared to the West (Table 10.2). This result can particularly be attributed to the relatively low share of creative professionals in East Germany. However, the share of the creative core in East Germany is only slightly below the Western level,

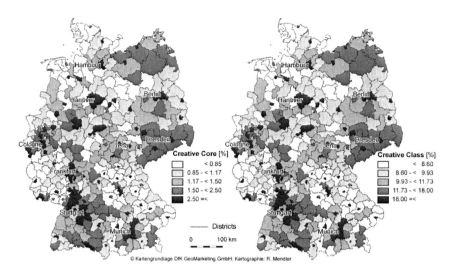

Figure 10.2 Population share of creative core and creative class in German districts, 2007

and the share of employed bohemians and freelance artists is higher in the East than in the West. These results are largely due to a high concentration of people with creative occupations, particularly the employed bohemians and freelance artists, in Berlin. If Berlin is excluded, the location coefficients for people in creative occupations in East Germany are clearly below the West German level.

Table 10.2 Population share of people in creative occupations and location coefficients in East and West Germany, 2007 (%)

	West	*East (including Berlin)*	*East (Berlin excluded)*	*Berlin*
Creative class	14.7/1.02	13.0/0.90	12.2/0.85	15.9/1.11
Creative core	2.2/1.01	2.1/0.95	1.9/0.89	2.5/1.16
Creative professionals	12.1/1.03	10.5/0.89	10.0/0.85	12.3/1.04
Employed bohemians	0.18/0.98	0.20/1.07	0.16/0.88	0.34/1.81
Freelance artists	0.18/0.93	0.25/1.27	0.11/0.55	0.80/4.06
Writers	0.05/0.92	0.07/1.30	0.02/0.48	0.23/4.62
Performing arts	0.02/0.84	0.04/1.62	0.01/0.54	0.14/5.83
Musicians	0.05//0.95	0.06/1.19	0.04/0.69	0.16/3.12
Fine arts	0.07/0.96	0.08/1.17	0.04/0.51	0.26/3.75
Employees with social insurance	34.0/1.01	29.9/0.94	31.4/0.94	32.0/0.96

What determines the regional share of creative population?

In order to explain the regional share of creative population, three hypotheses are tested:

- First, a high quality of life in a region attracts creative people. We use two indicators for the regional quality of life. One indicator is the abundance and the variety of the cultural supply in a region as measured by the share of employed bohemians and freelance artists (Artist-Bohemian Index). A second indicator is the share of the employees in public health care and education (Public Provision Index).
- Second, creative people value a regional environment that is characterized by openness and tolerance. The measure for openness and tolerance is the share of people with foreign citizenship who are dependently employed in a region (Openness Index). This indicator corresponds to Florida's (2004) Melting Pot Index.
- Third, job opportunities on the regional labour market are relatively unimportant for the locational choice of the creative people. Regional opportunities of employment are measured by the average employment growth rate in the preceding three and seven years.

Population density is included in the regressions as a catch-all variable to control for all kinds of regional characteristics such as land prices, size of the labour market and availability of public infrastructure. In order to account for the special situation in East Germany, a dummy variable for a location in the East (including Berlin; 1 = East, 0 = West) is entered into the regressions. Since the share of population with foreign citizenship is generally lower in the East, an interaction of the dummy for a location in East Germany with the Openness Index is also included. In order to facilitate a comparison of the different independent variables, the tables show the standardized regression coefficients (beta coefficients). The higher the absolute value of a beta coefficient, the stronger the impact of the respective variable on the share of creative people is. All independent variables are lagged by one year. Table 10.3 shows descriptive statistics for the variables included in the regressions.

The regressions for the share of the creative class and the creative core (Tables 10.4 and 10.5) clearly indicate a positive impact on the share of employed bohemians and the freelance artists. A slightly larger positive effect can also be found for the Openness Index. Population density is only statistically significant for the share of the creative class, not for the creative core. The level of public services, as measured by the Public Provision Index, does not seem to have an effect on the presence of people in creative occupations. The dummy for location in East Germany has a significantly positive value, indicating a relatively high share of creative employment in the East. The negative sign for the interaction of location in East Germany and the Openness Index show that the positive effect of the population with foreign citizenship is considerably weaker in the East. The effect

Table 10.3 Descriptive statistics for the distribution of the variables used in the regressions in the share of creative occupations (Table 10.4–Table 10.7)

Variable	Mean	Standard deviation	Minimum	Maximum
Index creative class (without bohemians)	12.89	6.46	4.19	46.67
Index creative core	1.85	1.62	0.30	16.68
Index employed bohemians	0.15	0.17	0.02	1.83
Index freelance artists	0.13	0.11	0.03	0.82
Artist-Bohemian Index	0.28	0.25	0.06	2.10
Public Provision Index	7.74	2.34	1.76	17.45
Openness index	7.23	4.55	0.70	25.20
Population density	515.52	669.7	20.63	4,162.73
Employment growth rate previous three years	0.02	0.03	−0.05	0.15
Employment growth rate previous seven years	−0.07	0.06	−0.27	0.10
Employment growth rate 2007–2008	0.02	0.01	−0.03	0.07

of employment growth on the share of creative people in a region turns out to be relatively weak as compared to the results for the other variables. The higher beta coefficient for the seven-year employment growth rate indicates that the effect of

Table 10.4 Determinants of the regional share of creative class, 2007 (without bohemians)[a]

	Share of creative class (ln)			
	(I)	*(II)*	*(III)*	*(IV)*
Artist-Bohemian Index (ln)	0.508** (12.70)	0.482** (11.66)	0.469** (11.28)	0.465** (11.24)
Public Provision Index (ln)	0.024 (0.65)	0.005 (0.12)	0.012 (0.32)	0.012 (0.33)
Openness Index (ln)	0.595** (9.84)	0.519** (7.59)	0.516** (7.60)	0.482** (7.00)
Population density	–	0.108* (2.39)	0.119** (2.62)	0.139** (3.01)
Location in East Germany (Dummy)	0.249** (3.71)	0.227** (3.37)	0.222** (3.31)	0.253** (3.75)
Openness Index * location in East Germany (interaction)	−0.181** (2.62)	−0.159* (2.30)	−0.169* (2.44)	−0.151* (2.19)
Employment growth rate previous three years	–	–	0.064* (2.14)	–
Employment growth rate previous seven years	–	–	–	0.094** (2.79)
R^2adj.	0.647	0.651	0.654	0.657

Notes: [a] Beta coefficients of robust least square regressions; *t*-values in parentheses; ** statistically significant at the 1 per cent level, * statistically significant at the 5 per cent level; number of observations: 410.

Table 10.5 Determinants of the regional share of creative core, 2007[a]

	Share of creative core population (ln)			
	(I)	(II)	(III)	(IV)
Artist-Bohemian Index (ln)	0.431** (11.26)	0.427** (10.75)	0.416** (10.39)	0.404** (10.25)
Public Provision Index (ln)	0.061 (1.74)	0.059 (1.63)	0.065 (1.81)	0.070* (1.99)
Openness index (ln)	0.744** (12.87)	0.734** (11.18)	0.733** (11.20)	0.683** (10.43)
Population density	–	0.014 (0.31)	0.023 (0.53)	–
Location in East Germany (Dummy)	0.359** (5.59)	0.356** (5.49)	0.351** (5.44)	0.393** (6.13)
Openness Index * location in East Germany (interaction)	−0.343** (5.19)	−0.340** (5.10)	−0.348** (5.24)	−0.328** (5.02)
Employment growth rate previous three years	–	–	0.059* (2.00)	–
Employment growth rate previous seven years	–	–	–	0.135** (4.22)
R²adj.	0.677	0.677	0.679	0.690

Notes: [a] Beta coefficients of robust least square regressions; *t*-values in parentheses; ** statistically significant at the 1 per cent level, * statistically significant at the 5 per cent level; number of observations: 410.

Table 10.6 Determinants of the regional share of employed bohemians, 2007

	Share of employed bohemians (ln)			
	(I)	(II)	(III)	(IV)
Public Provision Index (ln)	0.300** (6.79)	0.222** (5.01)	0.229** (5.20)	0.226** (5.09)
Openness Index (ln)	0.617** (8.80)	0.359** (4.39)	0.349** (4.30)	0.325** (3.89)
Population density	–	0.300** (5.61)	0.311** (5.84)	0.321** (5.89)
Location in East Germany (Dummy)	0.512** (6.30)	0.416** (5.18)	0.400** (5.02)	0.432** (5.37)
Openness Index * location in East Germany (interaction)	0.130 (1.50)	0.177* (2.10)	0.157 (1.88)	0.180* (2.15)
Employment growth rate previous three years	–	–	0.100 (2.78)	–
Employment growth rate previous seven years	–	–	–	0.076 (1.86)
R²adj.	0.436	0.475	0.484	0.478

Notes: [a] Beta coefficients of robust least square regressions; *t*-values in parentheses; ** statistically significant at the 1 per cent level, * statistically significant at the 5 per cent level; number of observations: 410.

employment opportunities is particularly relevant in the long run. It can be concluded from these results that creative people do not completely ignore their employment opportunities on the local labour market and that they *do* tend to follow jobs, but that the effect is relatively small as compared to other characteristics of a region.

The analyses for the share of employed bohemians (Table 10.6) show a rather strong positive effect for the Public Provision Index and the Openness Index. The positive effect of population density is probably due to a concentration of cultural establishments such as theatres, opera houses, etc. in larger cities. The significantly positive coefficient for the East Germany dummy may also be an effect of relatively high numbers of cultural establishments in the East. As in the regressions for the creative class and the creative core, the interaction between the East dummy and the Openness Index shows a significantly negative effect. No significant effect can be found for employment growth.

In the regressions for the share of freelance artists (Table 10.7), the effect of the Public Provision Index is much weaker than for the employed bohemians. The dummy variable for location in East Germany is only significant or insignificant at the 10 per cent level and the interaction between the East dummy and the Openness Index has a not so significant positive sign. While the employment growth rate over the three years is not statistically significant, we find a significantly positive effect for the seven years employment growth rate, indicating a particular dependence on regional prosperity.

Table 10.7 Determinants of the regional share of freelance artists, 2007[a]

	Share of freelance artists (ln)			
	(I)	(II)	(III)	(IV)
Public Provision Index (ln)	0.286**	0.232**	0.237**	0.238**
	(6.05)	(4.74)	(4.85)	(4.90)
Openness Index (ln)	0.432**	0.247**	0.240**	0.188*
	(5.72)	(2.75)	(2.67)	(2.05)
Population density	–	0.215**	0.223**	0.253**
		(3.66)	(3.79)	(4.24)
Location in East Germany (Dummy)	0.240*	0.171	0.160	0.199*
	(2.74)	(1.94)	(1.81)	(2.27)
Openness Index * location in East Germany (interaction)	0.180	0.213*	0.200*	0.220*
	(1.93)	(2.31)	(2.16)	(2.40)
Employment growth rate previous three years	–	–	0.072	–
			(1.80)	
Employment growth rate previous seven years	–	–	–	0.135**
				(3.00)
R^2adj.	0.351	0.364	0.368	0.376

Notes: [a] Beta coefficients of robust least square regressions; *t*-values in parentheses; ** statistically significant at the 1 per cent level, * statistically significant at the 5 per cent level; number of observations: 410.

Conclusion and discussion

The aim of this chapter was to investigate the geography of the creative class in Germany. Our first main finding is that the creative class is not equally distributed in space. Quite in contrast, the majority of the creatives live and work in agglomerated areas and cities. This clustering is particularly prevalent for members of the creative core, bohemians and freelance artists. With respect to the determinants of this observed unequal distribution, we find that the creative class is located in regions with high quality of life (operationalized by the Artist-Bohemian Index and the share of employment in education and public health care). Another important predictor for the regional share of the creative class is an open and tolerant environment (measured by the share of people with foreign citizenship). In contrast, job opportunities (though a statistically significant predictor) seem to be of less importance for the locational choice of the creative class. Taken together, this supports Richard Florida's basic hypotheses that the creative are attracted by a friendly 'people climate'. Hence, regions lacking features such as small-scale cultural amenities or a culture open towards newcomers and new ideas are in danger of experiencing a continued drain of creative people.

A critical issue that is of crucial importance for the empirical study of the creative class is the identification of creative people. Creativity of people can hardly be assessed directly and is not a characteristic that is reported in official statistics. Therefore, Florida's approach of measuring the immeasurable by identifying the creative class by occupation cannot be regarded as more than a rather rough approximation. The creative class, according to this definition, is a rather heterogeneous crowd. It includes people of different ages and stages of their career; scientists, engineers, highly paid managers as well as poor artists without a regular income. These people may have rather different preferences as well as degrees of freedom in making locational choices. The basic idea that creativity and knowledge constitute key drivers of regional development and that policy should account for people, who embody these important resources, has great appeal. Yet, we need to know considerably more about these types of people and their role in the local social system in order to be able to draw substantiated policy conclusions.

Notes

1 This chapter is a revised and updated version of Fritsch and Stuetzer (2009).
2 The first edition of the book appeared in 2002. We refer to the revised paperback edition from 2004.
3 The main reason for a person to set up a new firm is that knowledge and ideas may hardly be tradable on the market. Therefore, setting up one's own firm may be the only way for someone to realize her or his ideas (Audretsch, 1995; Wennekers und Thurik, 1999; Klepper und Sleeper, 2005).
4 We are indebted to Harro Bruns of the *Künstlersozialkasse* for providing these data.
5 The definition of the spatial categories is from the *Bundesamt für Bauwesen und Raumordnung* (BBR) (2003).

Bibliography

Andersen, K. V. and Lorenzen, M. (2005) 'The geography of the Danish creative class: A mapping and analysis', Copenhagen: Copenhagen Business School. Available at: http://www.kreativeklasse.dk/index.php?id=75 (accessed 29 August 2013).

Arora, A., Florida, R., Gates, G. J. and Kamlet, M. (2000) 'Human capital, quality of place, and location', Pittsburgh: H.J. Heinz III School of Public Policy.

Asheim, B. and Hansen, H. K. (2009) 'Knowledge bases, talents, and contexts: On the usefulness of the creative class approach in Sweden', *Economic Geography*, 85: 425–442.

Audretsch, D. B. (1995) *Innovation and Industry Evolution*, Cambridge, MA: MIT Press.

Bieri, D. S. (2010) 'Booming bohemia? Evidence from the US high-technology industry', *Industry and Innovation*, 17: 23–48.

Boschma, R. A. and Fritsch, M. (2009) 'Creative class and regional growth: Empirical evidence from seven European countries', *Economic Geography*, 85: 391–423.

Desrochers, P. (2001) 'Local diversity, human creativity and technological innovation', *Growth and Change*, 32: 326–354.

Elias, P. (1997) 'Occupational Classification (ISCO 88): Concepts, methods, reliability, validity and cross-national comparability', Labour Market and Social Policy Occasional Papers No. 20, Paris: OECD.

Falck, O., Fritsch, M. and Heblich, S. (2011) 'The phantom of the opera: Cultural amenities, human capital, and regional development', *Labour Economics*, 18: 755–766.

Feldman, M. (2000) 'Location and innovation: The new economic geography of innovation, spillovers, and agglomeration', in G. Clark, M. Gertler and M. P. Feldman (eds), *The Oxford Handbook of Economic Geography*, Oxford: Oxford University Press, pp. 373–394.

Florida, R. (2003) 'Entrepreneurship, creativity and regional economic growth', in D. M. Hart (ed.), *The Emergence of Entrepreneurship Policy: Governance, Start-Ups, and Growth in the US Knowledge Economy*, Cambridge: Cambridge University Press.

Florida, R. (2004) *The Rise of the Creative Class*, revised paperback edition, New York: Basic Books.

Florida, R. and Gates, G. (2001) *Technology and Tolerance: The Importance of Diversity on High Technology Growth*, Washington, DC: Brookings Institution.

Florida, R. and Mellander, C. (2010) 'There goes the metro: How and why bohemians, artists and gays affect regional housing values', *Journal of Economic Geography*, 10: 167–188.

Florida, R., Mellander, C. and Stolarick, K. (2008) 'Inside the Black Box of regional development: Human capital, the creative class and tolerance', *Journal of Economic Geography*, 8: 615–649.

Florida, R., Mellander, C. and Stolarick, K. (2011) 'Beautiful places: The role of perceived aesthetic beauty in community satisfaction', *Regional Studies*, 45: 33–48.

Fritsch, M. (2013) 'New business formation and regional development: A survey and assessment of the evidence', *Foundations and Trends in Entrepreneurship*, 9 (forthcoming).

Fritsch, M. and Brixy, U. (2004) 'The establishment file of the German social insurance statistics', *Schmollers Jahrbuch/Journal of Applied Social Science Studies*, 124: 183–190.

Fritsch, M. and Stuetzer, M. (2009) 'The geography of creative people in Germany', *International Journal of Foresight and Innovation Policy*, 5: 7–23.

Fritsch, M. and Rusakova, A. (2012) 'Entrepreneurship and cultural creativity,' in R. Sternberg and G. Krauss (eds), *Handbook of Research on Entrepreneurship and Creativity*, Cheltenham, UK: Elgar.

Glaeser, E. L. (2005) 'Review of Richard Florida's "The rise of the creative class"', *Regional Science and Urban Economics*, 35: 593–596.

Haak, C. (2005) 'Künstler zwischen selbstständiger und abhängiger Erwerbsarbeit', *Schmollers Jahrbuch /Journal of Applied Social Science Studies*, 125: 573–595.

Hartley, J. and Cunningham, S. (2002) 'Creative industries: From blue poles to fat pipes', in M. Gillies, M. Carroll and J. Dash (eds), *The National Humanities and Social Sciences Summit: Position Papers*, Canberra: DEST.

Hennessey, B. A. and Amabile, T. M. (2009) 'Creativity', *Annual Review of Psychology*, 61: 2.1–2.30.

Jacobs, J. (1970) *The Economy of Cities*, New York: Vintage Books.

Jacobs, J. (1985) *Cities and the Wealth of Nations*, New York: Vintage Books.

Klepper, S. and Sleeper, S. D. (2005) 'Entry by spinoffs', *Management Science*, 51: 1291–1306.

Knudsen, B., Florida, R. L., Stolarick, K. and Gates, G. (2008) 'Density and creativity in US regions', *Annals of the Association of American Geographers*, 9: 461–478.

Lang, R. and Danielsen, K. (2005) 'Review roundtable: Cities and the creative class', *Journal of the American Planning Association*, 71: 203–220.

Lee, S. Y., Florida, R. L. and Gates, G. (2002) 'Innovation, human capital, and creativity', Working Paper, Pittsburgh: Carnegie Mellon University.

Lee, S. Y., Florida, R. L. and Acs, Z. (2004) 'Creativity and entrepreneurship: A regional analysis of new firm formation', *Regional Studies*, 38: 879–891.

Lucas, R. E. (1988) 'On the mechanics of economic development', *Journal of Monetary Economics*, 22: 3–42.

McGranahan, D. A. and Wojan, T. R. (2007) 'Recasting the creative class to examine growth processes in rural and urban communities', *Regional Studies*, 41: 197–216.

Markusen, A. (2006) 'Urban development and the politics of a creative class: Evidence from the study of artists', *Environment and Planning A*, 38: 1921–1940.

Romer, P. (1986) 'Increasing returns and long-run growth', *Journal of Political Economy*, 84: 1002–1037.

Romer, P. (1993) 'Economic growth', in D. R. Henderson (ed.), *The Fortune Encyclopedia of Economics*, New York: Time Warner Books.

Runco, M. A. (2004) 'Creativity', *Annual Review of Psychology*, 55: 657–687.

Schumpeter, J. ([1911] 1934) *Theorie der wirtschaftligen Entwicklung*. English translation 1934: *The Theory of Economic Development*, Cambridge, MA: Harvard University Press.

Sternberg, R. J. and Lubart, T. I. (1999) 'The concept of creativity: Prospects and paradigms', in R. J. Sternberg (ed.), *Handbook of Creativity*, Cambridge: Cambridge University Press, pp. 3–15.

Stolarick, K., Lobo, J. and Strumsky, D. (2011) 'Are creative metropolitan areas also entrepreneurial?', *Regional Science, Policy & Practice*, 3: 271–287.

Wennekers, S. and Thurik, R. (1999) 'Linking entrepreneurship and economic growth', *Small Business Economics*, 13: 27–55.

Wojan, T. R., Lambert, D. M. and McGranahan, D. A. (2007) 'Emoting with their feet: Bohemian attraction to creative milieu', *Journal of Economic Geography*, 7: 711–736.

Appendix

Table A1 The creative occupations

Groups of creative people	Occupations (ISCO-Code)
Creative core	Computing services department managers (1,236), Research and development department managers (1,237), Physicists, chemists and related professionals (211); Mathematicians, statisticians and related professionals (212); Computing professionals (213); Architects, engineers and related professionals (214); Life science professionals (221); College, university and higher education teaching professionals (231); Secondary education teaching professionals (232); Primary and pre-primary education teaching professionals (233); Special education teaching professionals (234); Other teaching professionals (235); Archivists, librarians and related information professionals (243); Social sciences and related professionals (244); Primary education teaching associate professionals (331); Pre-primary education teaching associate professionals (3,320); Special education teaching associate professionals (3,330); Other teaching associate professionals (3,340); Statistical, mathematical and related associate professionals (3,434); Jewelry and precious-metal workers (7,313); Glass, ceramics and related decorative painters (7,324); Tailors, dressmakers and hatters (7,433)
Creative professionals	Legislators, senior officials and managers (1; except 1,236 and 1,237); Medical doctors and other health professionals (222); Business professionals (241); Legal professionals (242); Public service administrative professionals (247); Physical and engineering science associate professionals (31); Broadcasting and telecommunications equipment operators (3,132); Life science and health associate professionals (32); Finance and sales associate professionals (341)
	Business services agents and trade brokers (342); Legal and related business associate professionals (3,432); Athletes, sportspersons and related associate professionals (3,475); Musical instrument makers and tuners (7,312); Handicraft workers in wood and related materials (7,331); Handicraft workers in textile, leather and related materials (7,332)
Employed bohemians	Writers and creative or performing artists (245)
	Photographers and image and sound recording equipment operators (3,131)
	Artistic, entertainment and sports associate professionals (347); Fashion and other models (521)
Freelance artists	Writers, performing arts, fine arts, music

11 The location of the creative class in seven European countries

Ron Boschma and Michael Fritsch

Introduction

A debate has recently emerged about the role of creative people on economic growth (Lang and Danielsen, 2005). In his book, *The Rise of the Creative Class*, Richard Florida (2004) argued that creative people are a key driver of urban and regional development. According to his empirical analysis for the USA, the creative class is not evenly distributed among cities and regions, and rather, is especially attracted to places, which are characterized by an urban climate of tolerance that is open to new ideas and newcomers. Florida states that it is this type of 'people climate', rather than 'business climate' (such as low taxes or good infrastructure *per se*) that is crucial for regional growth. He argues that creative people induce and attract new economic activities, such as start-ups and high-tech firms.

However, there are hardly any empirical studies available that provide information on creative people in countries other than the USA, or that make a systematic comparison between regions in different countries. This chapter aims to fill in this gap. We present results of a large research project on the creative class and regional development in seven European countries: Denmark, Finland, Germany, Netherlands, Norway, Sweden, and the United Kingdom (see Boschma and Fritsch, 2009, for details). In this research project, data on creative employment and development at the regional level have been collected by using similar definitions, thus, trying to make the information comparable between the countries.

We deal with two research questions. First, how concentrated is the distribution of the creative class among European regions? Second, what are the determinants of the share of creative population in a region? In the following section, we briefly set out the main ideas of Richard Florida's work that will be tested with the European data set. Section 3 provides details on this data set, and section 4 summarizes the spatial distribution of the creative class in the seven European countries. In section 5, we will explain this European pattern by means of a regression analysis. The final section (section 6) draws conclusions.

The creative class, urban climate and regional growth

A basic idea of Florida's (2004) work on the role of the creative class for economic development is that geography matters. He asserts that the creative class is especially attracted to places that are characterized, among other things, by a tolerant urban climate that is open to new ideas and to newcomers. According to Florida, creative people tend to be attracted to tolerant and open regional societies that are home to a diversified group of people with different cultural and ethnic backgrounds. The main reason for this preference is that diversity serves as a source of inspiration in the innovation process (Andersen and Lorenzen, 2005). In addition, the creative class attaches great value to urban facilities and cultural services such as cinemas, bars, museums, art galleries, restaurants and trendy shops. In other words, Florida places emphasis on the socio-cultural underpinnings of regional development. It is an urban culture characterized by tolerance, diversity and open-mindedness that constitutes an important asset for economic development because it attracts creative class people (Peck, 2005). These are not places with high levels of social capital that consist of homogeneous communities with strong ties between their members, as according to Florida (2004), these environments tend to suppress creativity and new ideas.

According to Florida, this type of 'people climate' provides an environment that is conducive to regional growth. This stands in contrast to conventional beliefs that refer to quality of places in terms of 'business climate' characteristics, such as low taxes or good infrastructure. The essence of Florida's proposition is that instead, places with a good 'people climate' retain and attract creative people who, in turn, induce new economic activities, such as start-ups and high-tech firms. Therefore, the creative class is not attracted to places with high growth *per se*. On the contrary, regional growth is expected to be more of an outcome of the presence of creative people, or in the terminology of Florida, jobs will follow people instead of people following jobs.

With its focus on creative people, Florida argues that it is what people actually do is what enhances regional growth, rather than their sector affiliations or educational attainment (Markusen and Schrock, 2006; Markusen *et al.*, 2008). This abandonment of an industry perspective implies that urban and regional growth is primarily based on creative occupations that are not industry-specific. Though creative and cultural industries have attracted a lot of attention in this respect (Power and Scott, 2004), the creative class is found not only in those industries (Stam *et al.*, 2008). This take also makes Florida's approach different from the literature on agglomeration externalities (such as Glaeser *et al.*, 1992) that merely focuses on the question whether regional specialization or regional diversity enhance innovation and regional growth. Instead of concentrating on regional externalities between firms and industries, Florida focuses on creative individuals who generate spillovers and innovation in a region (Stolarick and Florida, 2006).

Florida's ideas about the role of the creative class for economic development have also induced considerable controversy. A major part of the debate concerns the question whether creative people are really different from educated and skilled persons. According to Glaeser (2004), creative capital equals human capital, as most, if not all, members of the creative class are skilled and highly educated individuals. Therefore, Glaeser claims that it is no use to include creative capital in a growth model that already accounts for the effect of human capital. Running regressions using Florida's data, Glaeser's analysis shows that human capital removes the positive effect of the creative class on urban growth in the USA in the 1990s. In fact, the creative class variables become negative and statistically insignificant in his regressions when adding human capital.

Another related issue that remains almost untouched in Florida's thesis is the importance of knowledge spillovers for regional growth. All that matters is the presence of the creative class; cities grow more when they attract a disproportionate share of creative people, not because cities cause the creative class to be more productive and more innovative. Other critiques of Florida's work mainly concern empirical issues (see e.g., Hansen and Niedomysl, 2009), which will be dealt with in subsequent sections.

The measurement of the creative class

In his empirical analyses, Florida (2002a; 2002b; 2003; 2004) based his definition of the creative class on professions, not industries. According to Florida, the creative class is a category of people who are engaged in creative, innovative jobs that can be found in every industry. Creative people are defined as workers who are engaged in identifying problems, figuring out new solutions and combining pieces of knowledge in new and innovative ways. While the general idea behind the creative class may sound plausible and appealing, its definition and measurement are still problematic. A main weakness of this kind of definition is that assigning certain professions to the creative class tends to be biased towards the highly educated, largely excluding creative people in occupations that require low or no level of education (Markusen and Schrock, 2006; Markusen *et al.*, 2008).

In our empirical approach, we have used Florida's definition of the creative class for a purely pragmatic reason. One of the objectives of the European project was to conduct a comparative analysis of European regions similar to the study for the USA. Using comparable definitions (based on professions) allows us to investigate the similarities and differences between the US and the European case. Three steps have been taken to define and measure the creative class:

As a starting point, we adopted the definitions of creative occupations as given by Florida (2004). We followed his idea of distinguishing between the creative core, creative professionals and bohemians. Creative core members are those individuals who invent. They basically are comprised of occupations in Research and Development and higher education. Creative professionals include educators, managers and health care professionals. Bohemians are engaged in cultural and artistic occupations. Bohemians fulfil two roles: they are part of the creative class, and they reflect an urban culture of tolerance; thus they act as a key factor in attracting the two other categories of creative people. According to Florida, the creative core and the bohemians are mainly engaged in 'problem finding' activities, i.e., creating new ideas, knowledge, technology, designs and content. By contrast, creative professionals are active in 'problem solving' activities. We largely followed Florida's work in assigning the professions to these three main categories.

In order to secure international comparisons, we used the International Standard Classification of Occupations (ISCO 88) to select professions that belong to the creative class. This classification scheme has been developed by the International Labour Office (ILO) and is based on the types of skills that are necessary to conduct a profession. The selected 3-digit ISCO categories are presented in Table 11.1.

Each country team applied these classifications to their national data sources. Due to data availability and different ways of measurement, it is unavoidable that country-specific effects may occur in the data, which result in limited comparability between countries. In our analyses, we will account for this problem by including country dummies in our estimation models.

Table 11.1 The creative occupations (ISCO)

Groups of creative people	*Occupations (ISCO-Code)*
Creative core	Physicists, chemists and related professionals (211); Mathematicians, statisticians and related professionals (212); Computing professionals (213); Architects, engineers and related professionals (214); Life science professionals (221); Health professionals (except nursing) (222); College, university and higher education teaching professionals (231); Secondary education teaching professionals (232); Primary and pre-primary education teaching professionals (233); Special education teaching professionals (234); Other teaching professionals (235); Archivists, librarians and related information professionals (243); Social sciences and related professionals (244); Public service administrative professionals (247)
Creative professionals	Legislators, senior officials and managers (1); Nursing and midwifery professionals (223); Business professionals (241); Legal professionals (242); Physical and engineering science associate professionals (31); Life science and health associate professionals (32); Finance and sales associate professionals (341); Business services agents and trade brokers (342); Administrative associate professionals (343); Police inspectors and detectives (345); Social work associate professionals (346)
Bohemians	Writers and creative or performing artists (245); Photographers and image and sound recording equipment operators (3131); Artistic, entertainment and sports associate professionals (347); Fashion and other models (521)

Because of the special character of bohemian occupations, we depart from Florida's approach (2004) of including bohemians in the creative core and instead create a separate category specifically for them. Accordingly, we use two different definitions of the creative class: Creative Class A is the sum of the Creative Core and the Creative Professionals; Creative Class B contains the Creative Core, the Creative Professionals, and the bohemians.

After identifying the professional categories of the creative class, we calculated their numbers in each country and region, making use of national employment data that are provided by profession and by region in or around the year 2002.[1] Our results show that the creative class (including the bohemians) consists of about 26,065,907 persons in 2002, which comprises about 37.7 per cent of the total workforce in the seven European countries, and about 15 per cent of their total population. The total workforce was calculated for each country as the total number of workers who work at least half the regular full-time employment hours per week. The Creative Professionals form the largest category (18,179,184 persons), followed by the Creative Core (6,782,995 persons). The number of bohemians is comparatively small, amounting to 1,103,728 employees.

The spatial distribution of the creative class in Europe

For most of the countries, the data are available at the level of NUTS III–regions, which more or less correspond to city regions or labour market areas.[2] At this rather detailed spatial scale, the place of residence and place of work are expected to coincide. The data set we use comprises information for 471 regions.

In the regions of the seven European countries as a whole (Table 11.2), the descriptive statistics of the share of the creative class are in line with Florida's statement that the creative class is highly unevenly distributed across geographic space. For example, the lowest share of the creative class records a share of almost 3 per cent, while the maximum value amounts to 33 per cent.

Table 11.2 Descriptive statistics for variables

Variable	Mean	Median	Minimum	Maximum	Standard deviation
Creative core (ln)	1.074	1.252	−1.529	2.163	0.659
Creative professionals (ln)	2.137	2.149	0.953	3.024	0.407
Creative class A (ln)	2.446	2.500	1.045	3.377	0.443
Bohemians (ln)	−1.112	−1.032	−5.048	1.409	0.907
Openness index (ln)	1.674	1.674	−0.724	4.018	0.770
Public provision index (ln)	2.144	2.248	1.155	3.000	0.414
Cultural opportunity index (ln)	0.276	0.256	−1.061	2.637	0.561
Employment growth 1993–2002	1.076	0.875	−2.780	8.232	1.531

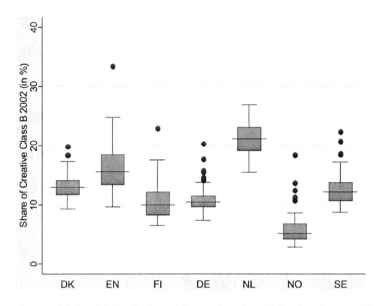

Figure 11.1 Spatial distribution of the creative class (defined as Creative Class B) in each of the European countries in 2002*

Note: * DK: Denmark, EN: England/Wales, FI: Finland, DE: Germany, NL: The Netherlands, NO: Norway, SE: Sweden.

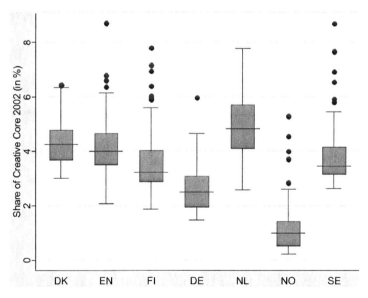

Figure 11.2 Spatial distribution of the share of creative core occupations in the population in the European countries in 2002*

Note: * DK: Denmark, EN: England/Wales, FI: Finland, DE: Germany, NL: The Netherlands, NO: Norway, SE: Sweden.

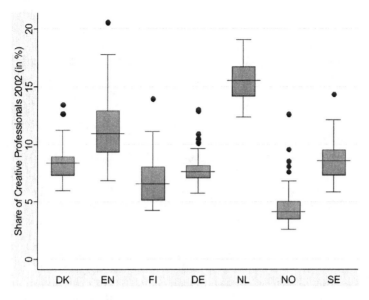

Figure 11.3 Spatial distribution of the share of creative professional occupations in the population in the European countries in 2002*

Note: * DK: Denmark, EN: England/Wales, FI: Finland, DE: Germany, NL: The Netherlands, NO: Norway, SE: Sweden.

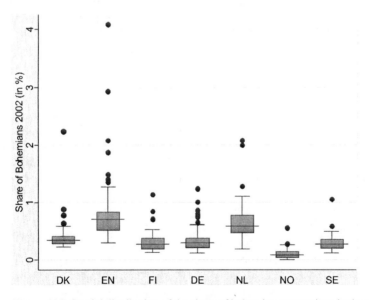

Figure 11.4 Spatial distribution of the share of bohemian occupations in the population in the European countries in 2002*

Note: * DK: Denmark, EN: England/Wales, FI: Finland, DE: Germany, NL: The Netherlands, NO: Norway, SE: Sweden.

Figures 11.1 to 11.4 show the spread of creative occupations for the entire creative class (i.e., including the bohemians, what we call Creative Class B) and the subcategories within each of the seven European countries. The line in the middle of the shaded box indicates the median value. The shaded box comprises the values of the second and the third quartile (i.e., between the 25th and 75th percentile of the distribution). The lines extending from the boxes (whiskers) show the adjacent values. The adjacent values are calculated by utilizing the interquartile range (IQR), which is the difference between the first and third quartile values. The upper adjacent value is the highest data value that is less than or equal to the third quartile plus 1.5 * IQR; the lower adjacent value is the smallest data value that is greater than or equal to the first quartile minus 1.5 * IQR. Values exceeding the upper and lower adjacent values are displayed as markers. Differences in the level of the shares between countries may be caused by different definitions and procedures of data collection and thus should be interpreted with caution. Nevertheless, the figures suggest that, broadly speaking, the Netherlands is well supplied with all categories of the creative class, whereas Norway is less so.[3]

Each of the Figures 11.1–11.4 displays outlier regions with relatively high shares of creative population. All of these outlier regions are the main cities of the respective country. In Germany, the Munich region has the highest values in all categories of creative occupation, followed by Frankfurt, Hamburg, Stuttgart, and Berlin. In Denmark, the outliers are Arhus and Copenhagen. In Finland, it is Helsinki. In the Netherlands, the leading regions are part of the northern wing of the Randstad area, with high scores for Amsterdam, Haarlem, and Utrecht. In Norway, by far the highest share of creative occupations is found in Oslo, followed by Kongsberg, and Trondheim. The leading Swedish region is Stockholm, with Uppsala, Linköping, and Gothenburg next in line. Unsurprisingly, in the UK, the London region is the clear winner as to highest share.

How to explain the spatial distribution of the creative class in Europe?

In order to analyze the reasons for the uneven spatial distribution of the creative class across Europe, we conducted multiple regressions that allow the assessment of the relative importance of the different factors.[4] The dependent variable in these regressions is the share of employees with creative occupations in the total number of regional employment in the year 2002. We split the creative class into three categories – the creative core, the creative professionals and the bohemians – because different explanations may apply for these different types of creative occupations. Hence, we ran various regressions explaining the European spatial pattern for each of these categories separately.

Three types of influences on the share of creative occupations were tested. The first type of influences is *regional culture*, which is closely associated with particular cultural qualities of regions such as tolerance and openness. Following Florida, we used two indicators to account for this effect.[5] The first indicator is the share of bohemian occupations in the total workforce in each region that, according to Florida (2004), should have a positive effect on the presence of other creative occupations. The idea is that a high proportion of bohemians indicates a kind of local culture, lifestyle and set of values that are different from the mainstream. Being artistically creative, bohemians add a meaning of liveliness to a particular place ('the place to be') and tolerance (openness to different lifestyles and values), which makes a region attractive for the other two categories of the creative class. The second measure is the share of foreign-born people, which is expected to have a positive effect on the presence of creative occupations.[6] Following Florida, this *openness index* is used as a proxy for the degree of open-mindedness, tolerance, cultural diversity and openness to newcomers.

The second type of explanatory factors can be labelled *regional facilities*. First, the *public provision index* has been measured by the share of the labour force working in public health care and public education (NACE codes 80 and 85). Second, the so-called *cultural opportunity index* is given by the share of the workforce, which is active in cultural and recreational activities.[7] Following Florida, we expect that both kinds of facilities are highly appreciated by the creative class. For analytical reasons, we have excluded those professions from the creative class that could be associated with these two indicators, in order to empirically disentangle the dependent from the independent variables.

The third type of explanation concerns a pure economic indicator. It is measured as the *annual employment growth rate* in the preceding ten years (1993–2002); this indicates job opportunities in a region. To control for country-specific differences (e.g., with regard to the measurement of creative occupations), we included country dummies.[8] Table 11.3 provides descriptive statistics for the variables included in the analysis.

Table 11.3 shows the results of the regression analyses with the shares of creative population as a dependent variable. We present the standardized regression coefficients (beta coefficients) here, which allow the direct comparison of the relative importance of the different variables (Greene, 2003). The analyses show that the share of bohemians in a region has a considerable positive impact on the share of the creative core and creative professional employment. We have, however, to be cautious in interpreting this result, because the share of bohemians shows a high correlation (0.66) with the other indices of the creative class. Moreover, there is also a high correlation between the share of bohemians and the cultural opportunity index (0.63). Due to the fact that the presence of bohemians could be a result of rich employment opportunities in cultural industries as indicated by the cultural opportunity index, we also ran a model where the share of bohemians is omitted in model II. It was found that there is, indeed, a considerable higher coefficient for the cultural opportunity index if the share of bohemians is omitted (model II). However, comparing the results of the different models indicates that the impact of the share of bohemians is considerably stronger than that of cultural opportunity.[9]

The results of the regression analyses tend to confirm our expectations. First, there is a close relationship between the presence of bohemians and the other creative class categories at the regional level in Europe. Even when the cultural

Table 11.3 Regressions to explain the share of the creative population

	Creative core (ln)		Creative professionals (ln)		Creative class A (ln)		Bohemians (ln)
	I	II	I	II	I	II	I
Share of bohemians (ln)	0.5378**	–	0.4118**	–	0.4613**	–	–
	(7.95)		(6.51)		(7.70)		
Openness index (ln)	0.0817	0.1815**	0.0889*	0.1675**	0.0938**	0.1812**	0.2102**
	(1.89)	(4.09)	(2.57)	(4.38)	(2.88)	(4.95)	(5.75)
Public provision index (ln)	0.2226**	0.2075**	–0.1117*	–0.1195*	0.0096	–0.0005	–0.0143
	(3.85)	(3.02)	(2.50)	(2.17)	(0.23)	(0.01)	(0.27)
Cultural opportunity index (ln)	0.0078	0.2742**	0.0828	0.2862**	0.0647	0.2926**	0.4944**
	(0.15)	(4.86)	(1.86)	(6.97)	(1.52)	(6.77)	(10.19)
Employment growth 1993–2002	0.0931**	0.1681**	0.2170**	0.2731**	0.1929**	0.2560**	0.1377**
	(2.90)	(4.67)	(5.97)	(6.45)	(6.21)	(6.74)	(3.49)
Population density (ln)	0.0050	0.0984	0.0613	0.1294**	0.0375	0.1447*	0.1369**
	(0.10)	(1.61)	(1.41)	(2.58)	(0.91)	(2.29)	(2.81)
R^2adj	0.845	0.795	0.896	0.867	0.905	0.864	0.825
F-value	129.86**	103.93**	213.49**	198.26**	226.08**	195.78**	117.32**
Number of observations	443	444	443	444	443	444	443

Notes: Beta coefficients, robust estimates (t-values in parentheses); country dummies included; * statistically significant at the 5 per cent-level; ** statistically significant at the 1 per cent-level.

opportunity index is included, the beta coefficients for the share of bohemians show the highest values in the model. The openness index has the expected positive impact on the presence of the creative class, but the effect is relatively small. This leads us to conclude that a regional climate of culture and openness tends to attract members of the creative class. By contrast, the public provision index (the level of supply in health care and education) only has a significantly positive effect on the regional share of the creative core employment. For creative professionals, it is significantly negative, while for the creative class (A) as a whole, it is insignificant. Thus, in general, the provision of public facilities has a slight, if any, impact on the presence of the creative class.

According to the beta coefficients, the annual employment growth in the preceding years in a region has the second largest impact on the regional share of creative occupations. The effect is relatively low for the creative core and for the bohemians, but quite pronounced for the creative professionals and the overall creative class (A). Finally, population density seems to only have a positive impact on bohemians, but it shows no effect on the other indicators of the creative class. This result suggests that the creative class is not attracted to highly urbanized regions *per se*, but to regions with a particular regional climate.

Conclusion

The results of our empirical analysis for regions in seven European countries tend to confirm a number of the hypotheses on the creative class as suggested by Florida (2004). We find that the creative class is highly unevenly distributed across Europe. A regional climate of tolerance and openness has a positive effect on the regional share of the creative class. The creative class is not attracted to highly urbanized regions *per se*, while the provision of public facilities in healthcare and education only has a minor, if any, impact on the presence of the creative class.

We consider our analysis as a first step towards a better understanding of the relationship between regional climate, creative class and regional growth in Europe. No doubt better indicators to measure creativity are a prerequisite for accomplishing such a task (Rantisi and Leslie, 2006; Markusen *et al.*, 2008). We need to define more precisely, for instance, which workers are really creative, in order to link them more directly to the other variables in the analysis.[10] We should also try to have a better understanding of the relationship between creativity and education, as well as the role of knowledge spillovers. Another key question concerns the relationship between a climate of tolerance, and the presence of the creative class. And we need better indicators to measure a tolerant climate or culture of openness.

Another issue to be taken up by future research is whether a high share of creative class people in a firm and the recruitment of new employees from the creative class actually enhance the performance of firms. Boschma *et al.* (2009) found empirical evidence that plants perform better when they employ individuals with related skills and when they hire new employees who bring in new knowledge related to the knowledge base of the plant. This idea could be extended to creative individuals.

An important question that we have not dealt with here is the relationship between the creative class and regional growth.[11] Does the presence of creative people *per se* contribute to regional growth, or do they mainly generate (localized) knowledge spillovers that have an additional effect on regional growth? What is the relationship between the presence of creative people in a region and high levels of education? In empirical analyses, education and creative capital need to be disentangled in order to be able to identify their effects. We need to be able to better specify through which mechanisms regional conditions (e.g., a regional climate of tolerance) affect human capital, creativity and growth, and in what ways public policy could make a positive contribution.

Notes

1 The creative class data for Denmark are from 1999, for Finland from 2000, for England/ Wales from 2001, and for Norway from 2004. The workforce data are for 2002.
2 NUTS (*Nomenclature des Unités Territoriales Statistiques*) is a hierarchical regional classification system used for the member states of the European Community. The data for the Netherlands are for 40 regions, the data for the UK comprise 106 regions. The 47 Swedish regions are defined as labour market regions (A-Regioner) based on travel to work patterns. In Switzerland, 25 city-regions as defined by the statistical offices were included. In Finland, there are 25 regions. The 77 Norwegian regions are so-called city-regions. These concern NUTS4 for most of the regions and combinations of several NUTS4 for the larger cities. In Denmark, the information is available for the 35 city-regions. Because the NUTS III regions for Germany are not always functional units, the analysis for this country is at the level of 93 planning regions, which are functional regions in the sense of travel-to-work areas and comprise at least one city and its surroundings. For a more detailed description of the German data, see Fritsch and Stuetzer (2009).
3 The low figures for the creative class in Norway are due to several reasons. First, the Norwegian figures do not include employees in the public health sector, which has relatively many creative class workers. Second, the Norwegian regions are comparatively small, and the most peripheral regions do not contain a city or town, which particularly lowers the share of creative class members in these small, peripheral regions of the country.
4 Many have criticized Florida's analyses that would rest on suggestive correlations rather than causality (e.g., Peck, 2005; Markusen and Schrock, 2006).
5 Another indicator of tolerant and open urban climate that has been applied by Florida in his analysis for the United States is the so-called Gay Index which measures 'the over- or under-representation of coupled gay people in a region relative to the United States as a whole' (Florida, 2004: 333). This type of index could not be calculated for the European countries because of a lack of data at the NUTS 3 level.
6 A better indicator would have been the rate of labour market participation of immigrants because, among other things, it reflects how open the region is to absorb and integrate people of different descent and cultures into the regional labour market. However, such an indicator was not available in the European countries at the regional level.
7 We have assigned these types of activities to the NACE codes 553 (restaurants), 554 (bars), 921 (activities in the field of film and video), 922 (radio and television), 923 (entertainment), 925 (libraries, public archives, museums and other cultural activities) and 926 (sports).

8 The results for these country dummies are not reported here due to space limitations. To account for the differences that still exist between East and West Germany (Fritsch, 2004), we included separate dummies for the two parts of the country.
9 The coefficients for the share of bohemians are slightly higher if the cultural opportunity index is omitted. This does, however, not lead to any substantial changes in the results.
10 Boschma and Fritsch (2009) and Lee, Florida and Acs (2004) find evidence for a positive effect of creative people on the regional level of new business formation. Boschma and Fritsch (2009) also provide empirical evidence for a positive relationship between creative class and the number of patents that are generated in the respective region.
11 For an attempt of such an analysis for Germany and the Netherlands, see Boschma and Fritsch (2009). Falck, Fritsch and Heblich (2011) discuss the causal link between cultural amenities and regional development presenting empirical evidence for the case of Germany.

Bibliography

Andersen, K. V. and Lorenzen, M. (2005) 'The geography of the Danish creative class: A mapping and analysis', Copenhagen: Copenhagen Business School. http://www.kreativeklasse.dk/index.php?id=75 (accessed 29 August 2013).

Boschma, R. and Fritsch, M. (2009) 'Creative class and regional growth: Empirical evidence from seven European countries', *Economic Geography*, 85: 391–423.

Boschma, R., Eriksson, R. and Lindgren, U. (2009) 'How does labour mobility affect the performance of plants? The importance of relatedness and geographical proximity', *Journal of Economic Geography*, 9: 169–190.

Falck, O., Fritsch, M. and Heblich, S. (2011) 'The phantom of the opera: Cultural amenities, human capital, and regional economic growth', *Labour Economics*, 18: 755–766.

Florida, R. (2002a) 'The economic geography of talent', *Annals of the Association of American Geographers*, 92:743–755.

Florida, R. (2002b) 'Bohemia and economic geography', *Journal of Economic Geography*, 2: 55–71.

Florida, R. (2003) 'Entrepreneurship, creativity and regional economic growth', in D. M. Hart (ed.), *The Emergence of Entrepreneurship Policy: Governance, Start-Ups, and Growth in the US Knowledge Economy*, Cambridge: Cambridge University Press.

Florida, R. (2004) *The Rise of the Creative Class*, revised paperback edition, New York: Basic Books.

Fritsch, M. (2004) 'Entrepreneurship, entry and performance of new businesses compared in two growth regimes: East and West Germany', *Journal of Evolutionary Economics*, 14: 525–542.

Fritsch, M. and Stuetzer, M. (2009) 'The geography of creative people in Germany', *International Journal of Foresight and Innovation Policy*, 5: 7–23.

Glaeser, E. L. (2004). Book review of Richard Florida's "The rise of the creative class", Available at: http://post.economics.harvard.edu/faculty/glaeser/papers/Review_Florida.pdf (accessed 29 August 2013).

Glaeser, E., Kallal, H., Schinkmann, J. and Shleifer, A. (1992) 'Growth in cities', *Journal of Political Economy*, 100: 1126–1152.

Greene, W. H. (2003) *Econometric Analysis*, 4th edn, New York: Prentice Hall.

Hansen, H. K. and Niedomysl, T. (2009) 'Migration of the creative class: Evidence from Sweden', *Journal of Economic Geography*, 9: 191–206.

Lang, R. and Danielsen, K. (2005) 'Review roundtable: Cities and the creative class', *Journal of the American Planning Association*, 71: 203–220.

Lee, S. Y., Florida, R. and Acs, Z. (2004) 'Creativity and entrepreneurship: A regional analysis of new firm formation', *Regional Studies*, 38: 879–891.

Markusen, A. and Schrock, G. (2006) 'The artistic dividend: Urban specialization and economic development implications', *Urban Studies*, 43: 1661–1686.

Markusen, A., Wassall, G., DeNatale, D. and Cohen, R. (2008) 'Defining the creative economy: Industry and occupational approaches', *Economic Development Quarterly*, 22: 24–45.

Peck, J. (2005) 'Struggling with the creative class', *International Journal of Urban and Regional Research*, 29: 740–770.

Power, D. and Scott, A. (2004) *Cultural Industries and the Production of Culture*, London: Routledge.

Rantisi, N. M. and Leslie, D. (2006) 'Guest editorial: Placing the creative economy – Scale, politics, and the material', *Environment and Planning A*, 38: 1789–1797.

Stam, E., de Jong, J., and Marlet, G. (2008) 'Creative industries in the Netherlands: Structure, development, innovativeness and effects on urban growth', *Geografiska Annaler Series B, Human Geography*, 90: 119–132.

Stolarick, K. and Florida, R. (2006) 'Creativity, connections and innovations: A study of linkages in the Montreal region', *Environment and Planning A*, 38: 1799–1817.

Part III

Australia and Asia

12 The creative class 'down under'

Exploring the creative class theory in Australia

Kevin Stolarick

Introduction

Arguably, the creative class theory has made a bigger splash 'down under' in Australian cities than in most other countries. The works of Landry (2000) and Florida (2002), on the creative city and the creative class respectively, have had monumental impacts on policy-makers and economic development strategists in Australia. Inherent in this literature is the magnitude with which this theory has been adopted, which in turn has sparked considerable debate among policy-makers and commentators (see Montgomery, 2005; Atkinson and Easthope, 2008, 2009). In addition to exploring the rise of the creative class theory in Australia, the role of neoliberal policies will also be examined in this context. It is important to recognize that these theories have been applied to both urban and rural settings.

Throughout all of this scholarship, the focus has been on research, critiques and suggestions around implementation of creative economy-based programs and policies. However, little work has been done to actually investigate whether or not these ideas are valid in an Australian context. What has clearly – if contestedly – been shown in the context of the USA, Europe, and Canada may not actually apply in Australia. Key questions need to be addressed: First, where is the creative class in Australia? Second, are the creative city ideas that are being pursued and criticized so vigorously in academic and policy circles likely to result in economic benefits for Australian regions and metros?

Using data from the Australian Bureau of Statistics (2001; 2005; 2006a; 2006b; 2006c), primarily from the Australian Census, this chapter examines the applicability of the creative class thesis in an Australian context. Using data on Local Government Areas (LGAs), information on a variety of measures for technology, talent, and tolerance (the 3Ts) is presented. Basic correlations among these measures exhibit the generally expected relationships with each other and with increasing prosperity, measured as income growth, but not with total population growth.

This chapter will begin by reviewing some of the work that has been done on creativity as an economic development tool in the Australian context. This will be followed by a discussion of the available data and data sources for Australia, an explanation of Richard Florida's (2002) '3Ts' or economic development: talent, tolerance, and technology, and an analysis of the 3Ts in the Australian context. Following the results of this analysis, the chapter will conclude with a discussion of implications and future work.

The creative class comes to Australia

As evidenced by Freestone *et al.*'s (2006) book, *Talking About Sydney*, the city has experienced rapid economic, cultural and social change in recent decades. Creative cities theory has been at the heart of debates around the nature of this change in Sydney and the country at large. While there are opportunities for Sydney to increase its standing as a global city, challenges remain with respect to managing population growth, affordability and new economic opportunities. Fortunately, there is a great deal of government outreach and scholarship on the topic, such as Throsby's (2008) paper in collaboration with the Australian Census Bureau, which examines the role of creativity in terms of creative work and workers, the creative class and participation and recreation.

Atkinson and Easthope (2008) examine the creative cities concept in Australia, which has grown, due to implementation of economic development strategies that focus on 'soft' attributes of prosperity that including creativity and livability. Using a case study of student attraction and retention strategies, they argue that a city's livability is a key element capitalized on in order to attract students and further the region's creative economy (ibid.). Building on their earlier work, Atkinson and Easthope (2009) examine how creative city strategies of economic growth, outlined by Florida and Landry, have impacted a broad spectrum of Australian urban environments, mainly focusing on arts projects, gentrification, affordable housing, issues surrounding public space and relative rates of social investment. In particular, Atkinson and Easthope argue that when policy-makers endeavour to strengthen the creative economy, they often fail to consider the needs of those who are excluded from participating in the economy and the possible negative impacts such policies can have on certain neighbourhoods, such as a loss of sense of place or increased social fragmentation. Interestingly, as Atkinson and Easthope (2009) note, of all Australia's major cities, only Brisbane has a formal creative city strategy. Cities such as Adelaide and Sydney, conversely, have less explicit creative city strategies. Despite the lack of a formal strategy, however, they argue that policy-makers apply the creative city tagline in an ad-hoc manner to justify a host of urban development initiatives.

It is frequently argued that creative city strategies are a central part of urban neoliberal agendas, which often force urban regions to compete with one another for economic dominance. Some authors have even gone so far as to argue that cities should 'beware (of) the creative class' because of the assumption that the policies catering to the creative class have negatively impacted on urban regions (Montgomery, 2005). The extent to which creative city policies are attributed to, and associated with, neoliberalization, is particularly prevalent in the literature focusing on Australia, where some have cited the relationship between intra-urban competition to attract the creative class (see Gibson and Klocker, 2005). For example, according to Gibson and Klocker (2005), the creativity index, which measures spatial patterns of creativity, is argued to be a key factor for economic success and a requirement in those cities lacking it, in order to be regional leaders in the changing economy. They conclude that: 'We need creativity in policy-making much more than overt policy prescriptions about creativity' (ibid.: 101).

Building upon this argument, scholars have also raised concerns that creative city policies cause economic and social marginalization. Barnes *et al.* (2006) utilize a case study of Wentworth Street in Wollongong, New South Wales, to evaluate the methods through which place-making and creative cities strategies are being applied on the ground. The authors observed that during a specific revitalization initiative designed to transform a depressed street into an 'urban village', marginalization did in fact occur. Similarly, in recognition of the argued political failures and market-based policies, Smyth, Redell and Jones (2005) explore the ways in which social policies focused on reforming spatial inequalities have emerged.

However, it is important to recognize that creative cities strategies do not exclusively affect urban dwellers, particularly in Australia. Collis, Felton and Graham (2010) argue that while the majority of creative city policies target inner city environments, the majority of Australians live in the outer suburbs, and as such, are possibly being both underserved and under-utilized by these policy initiatives. *Creative Suburbia* reveals that the outer suburbs have tremendous creative potential that will only increase as more creative people move into suburban environments (ibid.). As such, there is a significant opportunity to develop creative industries' and enterprises' links between suburban and inner city locations, which has the potential of spurring income and employment growth. Using a case study of Launceston, Tasmania, Verdich (2010) examines how creative class attraction and retention strategies have affected a small, suburban regional centre. In the context of shifting policy and planning attraction strategies away from infrastructure development and towards amenities and entertainment, it is argued that the works of Florida (2002; 2009) have been vital to these policy changes. In Launceston the characteristics typically associated with small towns, such as outdoor amenities, strong community and easy access to the natural environment were deemed to be more attractive to incoming residents than the diversity of lifestyle factors typically associated with the creative class (ibid.). However, Verdich found that once residents had settled in Launceston, cultural amenities were appreciated, even if they were not the driving factor in their resettlement.

Examining creative class theories in rural Australia, Tonts and Greive (2002) performed a case study of Bridgetown, West Australia, and found that the city's creative class-driven economic development strategies led to the commodification of the rural landscape. They argue that unmanaged growth strategies and 'the growing level of political contestation in Bridgetown is a reflection of the "creative-destructive" tendencies of capitalism and their impact on rural space' (ibid.: 68). The implementation of a new planning strategies and more nuanced creative-based economic development strategies, in the authors' opinion, is required to protect rapidly changing rural communities and mitigate social and economic marginalization. In the context of tropical Darwin, Northwest Territory, Australia, Luckman, Gibson and Lea (2009) examine the role of creative industries in remote locations in an attempt to evaluate the transferability of creative cities policies beyond urban environments. Gibson and Lea argue that because the existing history and attributes of a particular location are integral to successful economic development policies, creative cities policies can only be transferred in part to remote regions (ibid.). Furthermore, they advocate for more nuanced interpretations and implementation of these policies in order to ensure that the needs of the existing population are met and that other vital issues, such as social justice and environmental protection, are not overlooked in the discussion and application of creative cities strategies.

Moving to Western Australia, Bennett (2010) examines the migration patterns of creative artists who typically forgo operating in smaller towns and regional centres in favour of major cities that provide the greatest financial opportunities. In particular, Bennett argues that the domination by Australia's central cities of the country's knowledge-based economies has caused out-migration of creative and talented individuals, including artists, from smaller cities (ibid.). Moreover, Masters, Russell and Brooks (2011) examined the demand for the creative arts in three suburban Victoria locations to provide key insights of creative cities outside traditional urban cores. Demographic characteristics, such as older respondents, women and festival attendees, were found to have the highest local demand for the arts, while respondents in these three suburban communities had overall high levels for demands of the arts.

This chapter will proceed by first presenting information about the available data and the local government areas (LGAs) analyzed. Information will first be presented on the 3Ts of technology, talent, and tolerance for the Australian municipalities. This will be followed by summary rankings using the 'creativity index' which combines the 3Ts and simple, high-level correlational analysis comparing the 3Ts to measures of regional growth and prosperity. A brief overall discussion concludes this chapter.

Empirical analysis of the 3Ts in Australia

All data is from the Australian Bureau of Statistics (ABS). The primary data is from the National Regional Profiles from the 2006 Census. Data is summarized by Local Government Area (LGA).[1] LGAs effectively use political boundaries and are defined as cities, towns, and other local government entities. While LGAs are not the most ideal definition (Mitchell and Stimson, 2010; Stimson *et al.*, 2011) for identifying metropolitan areas, which are the traditional focus of creative class and creative economy research (Florida, 2002), they are the only urbanized area definition that is consistently available on a national basis for all of Australia's states and territories in the Census of Australia for 2006 and earlier years. As the focus for this analysis, only the 57 LGAs with a population above 100,000 will be considered.

Table 12.1 shows the ten most populous Australia LGAs. Brisbane is the largest city by far. Gold Coast comes in second, and is just south of Brisbane in Queensland in eastern Australia. Blacktown, Sutherland Shire, Wollongong, Lake Macquarie, and Fairfield are located in the Greater Sydney area. Canberra and Casey are part of the Australian Capital Territory, which has independent territorial status. Geelong and Melbourne are in Victoria in the southwest of the country, and Stirling is close to Perth in Western Australia.

As with any study, this has its limitations. Not least of which is the problem of the actual unit of analysis. For the Census years considered, the only units available are the local government areas (LGAs) – effectively municipal political boundaries that are not always the best spatial units to use when approximating the bounds of metropolitan regions. It is the more inclusive, more functionally defined, labour market and commuting-based areas that normally are used to research the creative economy around the world. Although changes were made to the 2011 Australian Census to create a more functionally defined region, while this study was being conducted, these had yet to be implemented and thus we were unable to incorporate them in the analysis. It remains to be seen whether these changes will be made available on a limited basis for historical research. However, since positive results were found using this more limited regional definition, it is expected that future research capable of using the newly amended metropolitan regional definitions will find stronger results.

Table 12.1 Ten largest Australian Local Government Areas

Rank	LGA	Population 2006
1	Brisbane	956,132
2	Gold Coast	472,280
3	Blacktown	271,711
4	Casey	214,962
5	Sutherland Shire	205,449
6	Greater Geelong	197,477
7	Wollongong	184,209
8	Lake Macquarie	183,142
9	Fairfield	179,892
10	Stirling	176,867

Variables in the analysis

In order to create the 3T indices and to test them against Australian regional economic development, we employ a number of variables (summary statistics are included in the Appendix).

Economic and demographic variables

- *Population*: We employ three different population variables: total population, population density per square kilometre and population growth.
- *Wages*: This variable is earned income, and we employ both average wage and wage growth in the analysis.
- *Income*: This variable includes wages, but also other received incomes. Again, we employ both average income (measured in Australian Dollars), as well as income growth.

All economic and demographic variables are for the year 2006 with the exception of the growth variables which are for the years 2001–2006. Average population growth for all of Australia (1.31 per cent) was essentially the same as the average growth for the 57 largest LGAs (1.35 per cent). While average wages and income are slightly higher in the LGAs than for the country overall, this is likely due to higher growth in LGAs than the country as a whole. While the average density of Australia is 2.7 people per sq km, that number is less informative. Across the 57 largest LGAs average density is 1,191 people per sq km. The highest density is in Sydney with 6,158 people per sq km, and the least densely populated LGA is in the Shire of Yarra Ranges in Victoria in the far outskirts of Melbourne with only 58.7 people per sq km.

3T variables

Technology

In order to create the Technology Index, we employ a combination of high-technology employment by location quotient (LQ) and internet access for the year 2006. The high-tech location quotient is calculated as the share of regional high-tech employment divided by the overall national average high-tech employment. With limited data available, high-tech employment is limited to employment in the following industries: transportation, communication, finance and insurance. Internet access is calculated as the share of households in the region with internet access (broadband, dial-up or other). While we realize that a significant share of the population has internet access today, this measure is relevant because it indicates which regions have been early adopters of technology.

As with most countries, high-tech industries and employment are more prevalent and concentrated in larger metropolitan regions. Over half (51 per cent) of the country's total high-tech employment is located in the largest 57 Australian LGAs. In these LGAs, high-tech employment comprises 2.4 per cent of all jobs compared to fewer than 2.0 per cent of all jobs for the whole country. Not surprisingly, as a result, the average high-tech location quotient across these regions is well above 1.0 at 1.19, but while concentrated in larger regions, the highest LQ is only 1.63, which says that no region has an extremely high concentration. This is also likely due to the lack of detailed regional industry employment information.

While 40 per cent of the country has broadband access, interestingly, living in a large city does not increase the number of homes with internet by very much (it increases to 44.2 per cent) which indicates that price or other factors, rather than availability, may be limiting internet access. The larger metropolitan areas are also home to more innovative companies. While the Survey of Innovation (Australian Bureau of Statistics, 2005) reports that 54 per cent of all companies in Australia implemented a product, process, or management process improvement in the previous year, nearly 60 per cent of companies in the largest LGAs did so. Innovative companies are spread fairly evenly across all of the largest cities.

Talent

The Talent Index combines Human Capital and Creative Class Share for the year 2006. The Creative Class Share is the share of total workforce in the creative class using Florida's (2002) occupational typology. This includes the following occupations: computer and math, architecture and engineering, science, education, arts, media, design, finance, managers, law, health, and high-end sales. Human Capital is measured through the share of the population 15 years and older that has obtained a bachelor's degree or above.

For the entire country, 34.1 per cent of the workforce has a creative occupation, compared with 36.5 per cent in service-based jobs and 29.4 per cent in the working class. While the creative number is similar to what is seen in other developed countries, the service class number is lower and the working class is higher. These numbers are fairly consistent with what is reported for the largest cities (33.9 per cent creative, 37.3 per cent service, 28.8 per cent working). However, for many of the LGAs included in this study, the creative workforce is significantly higher than the national average. Across Australia, only 11.6 per cent have obtained a bachelor's degree. Interestingly, unlike the typical situation in other developed countries, educational attainment does not change very much (if at all) in the larger metropolitan areas.

Tolerance

The Tolerance Index is a combination of three different variables (all for the year 2006): (1) the share of the population that is foreign-born; (2) the estimated share of families in the region with same sex couples[2] (the Gay Index); and (3) a location quotient for bohemian occupations (the Bohemian Index).

As expected, Australia's larger cities are more diverse places. The bohemian, foreign-born, and gay/lesbian populations of the largest cities are higher than for the country overall. Compared to 24 per cent of the entire population, 29 per cent of the population in cities are foreign-born. As is expected, some regions, particularly near major metropolitan centres, have significantly higher proportions of foreign-born residents. For example, in Fairfield, New South Wales, west of Sydney, over 55 per cent of the population is foreign-born and 71 per cent speak a language other than English at home. While the bohemian index shows that in some places the concentration of those in bohemian occupations is nearly double the national average, the average of the location quotient across the largest cities is below 1.0 (0.94) which indicates that Australia's bohemians are spread across the country and not just living in cities. The gay and lesbian population, while based on an estimate, shows a fairly even spread across the country, but is at its highest concentration in Sydney (3.32).

Mapping the Australian 3Ts

Technology

In order to find out more about the distribution of the 3Ts across Australian regions, we start by ranking and mapping its indicators of broadband internet connectivity and high-tech firm location quotient (Table 12.2). In Ku-ring-gai, 83.4 per cent of the population has access to broadband internet, followed closely by Baulkham Hills (82.7 per cent), Hornsby (79.3 per cent), Joondalup (77.7 per cent) and Boroondara (76.1 per cent). The remaining cities have over 70 per cent of the population with access to broadband internet ranging from Pine Rivers in sixth place (75.1 per cent) to Sutherland Shire (71.6 per cent).

Moving beyond internet access, we examined the clustering of high-technology firms in Australia's LGAs using location quotients. All of the top ten cities have

Table 12.2 Technology variables rankings

Rank	LGA	Broadband (%)	Rank	LGA	High-tech firm LQ
1	Ku-ring-gai	83.4	1	Blacktown	1.63
2	Baulkham Hills	82.7	2	Campbelltown	1.60
3	Hornsby	79.3	3	Wyndham	1.55
4	Joondalup	77.7	4	Penrith	1.48
5	Boroondara	76.1	5	Bankstown	1.45
6	Pine Rivers	75.1	6	Pine Rivers	1.43
7	Warringah	73.4	7	Moreland	1.42
8	Manningham	73.4	8	Casey	1.40
9	Sydney	72.4	9	Brimbank	1.38
10	Sutherland Shire	71.6	10	Knox	1.38

scores above 1.0, which indicates an above average clustering of high-tech firms. Blacktown ranks first on this index, with a score of 1.63, followed by Campbelltown (1.60), Wyndham (1.55) and Penrith (1.48). Bankstown ranked fifth (1.45), followed closely by Pine Rivers (1.43), Moreland (1.42) and Casey (1.40). Brimbank and Knox each score (1.38) to round out the Index.

Combining these indicators (internet access and high-tech firm LQ) forms the Technology Index (Table 12.3). Using this combined index, the city of Pine Rivers, a suburb of Brisbane, leads all other LGAs with a score of 0.912. It is followed by Hornsby, a suburb of Sydney, and Wyndham and Kimberly, two

Table 12.3 The Technology Index top 9

Rank	LGA	Technology Index score
1	Pine Rivers	0.912
3	Hornsby	0.842
3	Wyndham	0.842
4	Knox	0.825
5	Joondalup	0.772
8	Ku-ring-gai	0.763
8	Casey	0.763
8	Monash	0.763
8	Blacktown	0.763

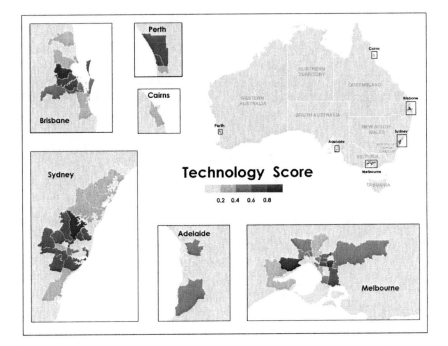

Figure 12.1 Map of the Technology Index

suburbs of Melbourne, who both scored (0.842). Knox, a suburb of Melbourne, ranks fourth with a score of 0.825, followed by Joondalup, a suburb of Perth, with a score of 0.772. Two of Sydney's suburban cities, Ku-ring-gai and Blacktown, round out the top ten in the Tech Index, tying with two cities in the Australian Capital Territory, Casey and Monash, with a score of 0.763. Figure 12.1 visualizes the Technology Index: Brisbane (1st), Melbourne (2nd), Sydney (3rd), Perth (4th).

Talent

Next, we move on to the ranking and mapping of the second of the 3Ts – Talent, which combines the occupational-based creative class with the educational-based human capital. Table 12.4 presents the top ten LGAs for the creative class and for human capital. Ku-ring-gai has the largest creative class share in Australia, with 60.9 per cent of the workforce in the creative class, followed closely by Boroondara with 58.4 per cent. Hornsby (50.9 per cent), Glen Eira (49.6 per cent) and Whitehorse (47 per cent) all have approximately half of their workforce employed in creative industries, closely followed by Manningham, Baulkham Hills and Sydney, with approximately 46 per cent of their labour force in the creative class, which in turn are followed by Randwick (45.3) and Warringah (43.8 per cent).

However, being a member of the creative class is not dependent on holding a bachelor's degree or higher, as many creative occupations do not require academic credentials. When examining the educated population within Australia's LGAs, Ku-ring-gai also ranks first, with 27.3 per cent of the population holding a bachelor's degree or above, followed closely by Boroondara (26.9 per cent) and Sydney (22.2 per cent). Approximately one-fifth of the remaining cities of Glen Eira (21.4 per cent), Hornsby (20.6), Randwick (19.5 per cent) and Whitehorse (18.7 per cent) have a bachelor's degree, while Manningham, Baulkham Hills and Montash are tied with approximately 17.9 per cent each.

Table 12.4 Talent variables rankings

Rank	LGA	Creative class share (%)	Rank	LGA	Bachelor's degree (%)
1	Ku-ring-gai	60.9	1	Ku-ring-gai	27.3
2	Boroondara	58.4	2	Boroondara	26.9
3	Hornsby	50.9	3	Sydney	22.2
4	Glen Eira	49.6	4	Glen Eira	21.4
5	Whitehorse	47.0	5	Hornsby	20.6
6	Manningham	46.9	6	Randwick	19.5
7	Baulkham Hills	46.9	7	Whitehorse	18.7
8	Sydney	46.3	8	Manningham	17.9
9	Randwick	45.3	9	Baulkham Hills	17.9
10	Warringah	43.8	10	Monash	17.8

Combining the two together gives us the Talent Index for Australian regions. Table 12.5 ranks the top ten LGAs. Three of the top five cities are in the Greater Sydney Metropolitan Area, with Ku-ring-gai, placed first with a ranking of 1.0 on the Index, followed by two Melbourne suburbs, Boroondara (0.982) and Glen Eira (0.947) and rounded out by Hornsby (0.947), and Sydney itself with a score of 0.921 rounds out the top five. Whitehorse, a suburb of Melbourne, ranks sixth with 0.912, followed closely by Manningham, outside of Adelaide, scoring (0.890), the Sydney suburbs of Randwick scoring 0.886 and Baulkham Hills scoring 0.882, while Monash, outside of Brisbane, rounds out the top ten with a score of 0.833. Figure 12.2 illustrates the distribution of the Talent Index across Australian

Table 12.5 The Talent Index top 10

Rank	LGA	Talent Index score
1	Ku-ring-gai	1.000
2	Boroondara	0.982
4	Glen Eira	0.947
4	Hornsby	0.947
5	Sydney	0.921
6	Whitehorse	0.912
7	Manningham	0.890
8	Randwick	0.886
9	Baulkham Hills	0.882
10	Monash	0.833

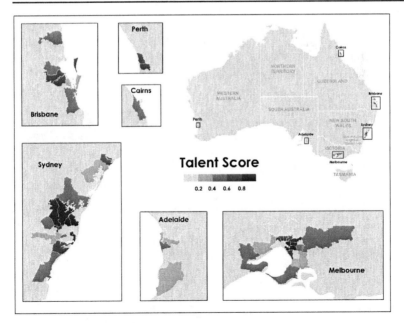

Figure 12.2 Map of the Talent Index

LGAs and shows the concentration of cities on the Talent Index in Perth, New South Wales, Victoria and Queensland: Sydney (1st), Melbourne (2nd), Adelaide (3rd), Brisbane (4th).

Tolerance

Moving to the Tolerance Index, we examine three different variables: the Gay Index, the Bohemian Index, and the Foreign-Born share of the population. Table 12.6 ranks the top ten LGAs for each of these variables. The first factor we examine is the Gay Index. Here the dominance of Australia's larger cities becomes apparent, with Sydney ranking first on the Index with a score of 3.32. Following Sydney are Moreland (1.65), Darebin (1.53) and Randwick in fourth with a score of 1.50. The remaining cities score below 1.50, with Parramatta (1.25), Brisbane (1.23), Stirling (1.19), Wyndham and Wanneroo (1.18 respectively) and Cairns with 1.16.

Looking at the Bohemian Index, which simply measures the concentration of an area's population that is in a bohemian occupation, Randwick (2.00) edges out Sydney (1.69) for first place, which in turn is followed closely by Warringah (1.47), Glen Eira (1.42), Darebin (1.27) and Moreland (1.24). The Gold Coast (1.20) and Moonee Valley (1.20) are tied for seventh place on the index, followed by Wyong (1.18) and Boroondara (1.18), which are tied for eighth.

The third component of this index is the share of the population that is foreign-born, which signifies an area with low barriers to entry into economic and social networks as well as high levels of openness. Greater Dandenong ranks first, with 55.9 per cent of the population being foreign-born, followed by Fairfield (55.2 per cent) and Canterbury (51.2 per cent). Brimbank and Sydney each have approximately 46 per cent of the population that is foreign-born, followed by Parramatta (43.7 per cent), Monash (42.1 per cent) and Liverpool (41.2 per cent). Randwick (39.3 per cent) and Bankstown (38.6 per cent) round out the top ten.

Table 12.6 Tolerance variables rankings

Rank	LGA	Gay Index	Rank	LGA	Bohemian Index	Rank	LGA	Foreign-born (%)
1	Sydney	3.32	1	Randwick	2.00	1	Greater Dandenong	55.9
2	Moreland	1.65	2	Sydney	1.69	2	Fairfield	55.2
3	Darebin	1.53	3	Warringah	1.47	3	Canterbury	51.2
4	Randwick	1.50	4	Glen Eira	1.42	4	Brimbank	46.7
5	Parramatta	1.25	5	Darebin	1.27	5	Sydney	46.0
6	Brisbane	1.23	6	Moreland	1.24	6	Parramatta	43.7
7	Stirling	1.19	7	Gold Coast	1.20	7	Monash	42.1
8	Wyndham	1.18	7	Moonee Valley	1.20	8	Liverpool	41.2
9	Wanneroo	1.18	8	Wyong	1.18	9	Randwick	39.3
10	Cairns	1.16	8	Boroondara	1.18	10	Bankstown	38.6

We bring these indicators (Gay Index, Bohemian Index, and share of the population that is foreign-born) together to form the Tolerance Index (Table 12.7), where Sydney tops all LGAs with a score of 0.971. Randwick, a suburb of Sydney, comes second with a score of (0.936), and is followed by two suburbs of Melbourne, Moreland and Darebin, each with 0.880 respectively. Another suburb of Melbourne, Glen Eira is fifth on the Tolerance Index (0.804), followed by Warringah (0.760), outside of Sydney, Moonee Valley (0.743), a suburb of Melbourne, and a suburb of Perth, Stirling, with a score of (0.708). Parramatta (0.684), a western suburb of Sydney, and the sixth most populous city in the country, Gold Coast (0.681), round out the top ten. Figure 12.3 displays the Tolerance Score: Sydney (1st), Melbourne (2nd), Perth (3rd), Brisbane (4th).

Table 12.7 The Tolerance Index top 10

Rank	LGA	Tolerance Index score
1	Sydney	0.971
2	Randwick	0.936
4	Moreland	0.880
4	Darebin	0.880
5	Glen Eira	0.804
6	Warringah	0.760
7	Moonee Valley	0.743
8	Stirling	0.708
9	Parramatta	0.684
10	Gold Coast	0.681

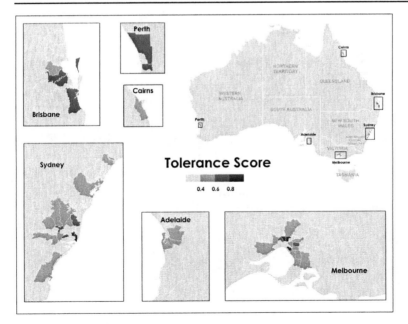

Figure 12.3 The Tolerance Index

Bringing it all together: the Creativity Index for Australia

Finally, we combine the Talent, Tolerance, and Technology Indices to form the overall Creativity Index (Table 12.8). Randwick, a suburb of Sydney, leads all other LGAs with a score of (0.886), despite the metro's low score on the Technology Index. Two additional LGAs in New South Wales, Sydney (0.848) and Hornsby (0.816), follow in second and third place respectively. Monash, in the Australian Capital Territory (0.813), and Ku-ring-gai, a northern suburb of Sydney (0.810), are followed by another suburb of Sydney, Warringah, and two suburbs of Melbourne, Whitehorse and Glen Eira, all with scores of (0.801). The top ten are rounded out by Paramatta, a Sydney suburb, with a score of (0.766) and Brisbane, the third most populous city in the country, with a score of (0.757). The Creativity Index for the Australian regions is visualized in Figure 12.4.

Table 12.8 The Australian Creativity Index top 10

Rank	LGA	Score
1	Randwick (C)	0.886
2	Sydney (C)	0.848
3	Hornsby (A)	0.816
4	Monash (C)	0.813
5	Ku-ring-gai (A)	0.810
7	Whitehorse (C)	0.801
7	Warringah (A)	0.801
7	Glen Eira (C)	0.801
9	Parramatta (C)	0.766
10	Brisbane (C)	0.757

Note: (C) (A).

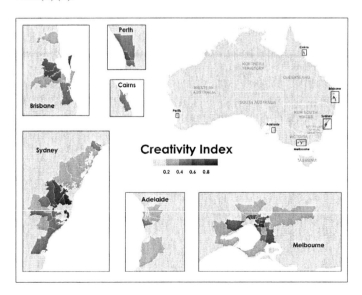

Figure 12.4 The Creativity Index

Technology, talent and tolerance and regional economic development in Australia

Next, we will examine to what extent the variables included in the 3Ts, as well as the 3T indices, relate to the main economic and demographic variables across Australian regions. We employ basic bivariate correlation analysis, in order to examine whether technology, talent and tolerance relate significantly to other key development indicators in Australia. Table 12.9 illustrates the result from this analysis. Table 12.9 shows the correlations among the 3T index measures, their component parts and measures of regional growth and prosperity. Overall, the results suggest that the relationships for Australia's municipalities (as measured using the LGA definition) are similar to creative economy findings in other countries. None of the measures have a significant relationship with population, so the city size is not a driving factor in the Australian creative economy. This may be a result of the non-metropolitan region definition provided by the LGAs. (The results for wages and income effectively parallel each other and will be discussed together.)

The results for technology in Australia are different than what is usually seen. While wages/income are positively related to broadband internet availability, that is most likely an income effect of internet providers making the service available in places with more money. The high-tech location quotient (and other measures of technology not shown here) do not indicate any significant relationships, including population, density, growth, and wages/income. It appears as if the technology focus in Australia (for the 2006 period) is more on mining, agriculture, and other more remotely located industries so there is no urbanization or agglomeration impact from technology.

Talent, measured either as creative class or human capital, is positively associated with population density and wages/income. It does not show any significant relationships with growth measures. Tolerance measures also have significant and positive relationships with population density and wages/income. But, foreign-born population and the Gay Index have a negative relationship with wage/income growth. The positive relationship between the Gay Index and population growth helps to explain some of this. The growing regions of Australia have a fairly strong correlation with service class workers which are lower wage jobs. Places that are growing have larger gay/lesbian populations but are also growing in lower wage jobs.

The Creativity Index pulls all of the 3Ts together. It shows that the combination of technology, talent, and tolerance across Australia's regions is more prevalent in more densely populated regions and is also strongly associated with higher wage and income levels. As discussed above, growth in Australia is generally more associated with lower incomes so the Creativity Index does not have a positive or significant relationship with population, wage, or income growth.

Conclusion

The aim of this chapter was to identify a set of measures from what the ABS (Australian Bureau of Statistics) makes available to be able to take a first look

Table 12.9 Correlation analysis for the 3Ts and regional economic and demographic development

	Population	Population density	Population growth	Wages	Wage growth	Income	Income Growth
Technology Index	0.071	0.037	0.127	0.393***	0.067	0.348***	−0.044
High-tech location quotient	−0.054	−0.005	0.012	−0.029	0.057	−0.092	−0.149
Broadband	0.109	0.021	0.139	0.673***	0.075	0.671***	0.102
Talent Index	0.075	0.504***	−0.225*	0.733***	−0.021	0.738***	0.020
Creative class	0.018	0.445***	−0.238	0.844***	0.000	0.859***	0.047
Human capital	0.060	0.573***	−0.186	0.843***	−0.051	0.850***	−0.015
Tolerance Index	0.111	0.673***	0.148	0.249*	0.026	0.234*	0.018
Foreign-born	−0.050	0.572***	−0.067	0.103	−0.142	0.067	−0.267**
Gay Index	0.058	0.645***	0.365***	−0.022	−0.429***	−0.047	−0.384***
Bohemian Index	0.066	0.397***	−0.015	0.465***	−0.001	0.475***	0.073
Creativity Index	0.122	0.546***	0.017	0.653***	0.065	0.629***	0.023

Note: * Indicates significance at the 10 per cent level, ** at the 5 per cent level, and *** at the 1 per cent level.

at how creative economy ideas work in Australian regions. Using data from the Australian Census, regional economic and demographic variables, as well as variables for technology, talent, and tolerance were identified and created. We also combined our technology, talent and tolerance measures to form an Overall Creativity Index. While this is only a first look and purely descriptive, the results show that there is a relationship between the 3Ts and levels of economic performance, but not necessarily growth. This study found results consistent with and supportive of previous investigations into the creative economy. That being said, significant work still remains to be carried out to fully understand the creative cities theory in the Australian context. The measures created and identified here would allow this more in-depth work to be undertaken and the results obtained indicate that completing this additional research would be a worthwhile endeavour.

Acknowledgements

Special thanks to Taylor Brydges and Garrett Morgan for research and editorial assistance and to Zara Matheson for her always excellent map-making ability.

Notes

1 According to the Australian government: 'Local Government Areas (6 LGAs) are an ABS approximation of officially gazetted LGAs as defined by each State and Territory (S/T) local government departments', see http://www.abs.gov.au/ausstats/abs@.nsf/mf/1270.0.55.003 (accessed 29 August 2013).
2 Detailed regional data was not reported by ABS for this, but estimates at the national level were provided. The national numbers were combined with regional data on family structure and age to estimate the number of same sex couples across the region.

Bibliography

Atkinson, R. and Easthope, H. (2008) 'The creative class in utero? The Australian city, the creative economy and the role of higher education', *Built Environment*, 34: 307–318.
Atkinson, R. and Easthope, H. (2009) 'The consequences of the creative class: The pursuit of creativity strategies in Australia's cities', *International Journal of Urban and Regional Research*, 33(1): 64–79.
Australian Bureau of Statistics (2001) '2001 Census of Population and Housing: Socio-Economic Indexes for Areas (SEIFA), Australia', available at: http://www.abs.gov.au/ausstats/abs@.nsf/allprimarymainfeatures/C53F24374E92E8D3CA2573F0000DA0BE?opendocument (accessed 1 November 2012).
Australian Bureau of Statistics (2005) '2005 Innovation Survey', available at: http://www.abs.gov.au/AUSSTATS/abs@.nsf/Lookup/8158.0Main+Features12005?OpenDocument (accessed 1 November 2012).
Australian Bureau of Statistics (2006a) '2006 Census of Population and Housing, Socio-Economic Indexes for Areas (SEIFA), Australia', available at: http://www.abs.gov.au/ausstats/abs@.nsf/mf/2033.0.55.001/ (accessed 1 November 2012).

Australian Bureau of Statistics (2006b) 'National Regional Profile 2006', available at: http://www.ausstats.abs.gov.au/ausstats/nrpmaps.nsf/NEW+GmapPages/ national+regional+profile (accessed 1 November 2012).

Australian Bureau of Statistics (2006c) 'Manufacturing Industry, Australia, 2006–07', available at: http://www.abs.gov.au/AUSSTATS/abs@.nsf/Lookup/8221.0Main+Features12006-07?OpenDocument (accessed 1 November 2012).

Barnes, K., Waitt, G., Gill, N. and Gibson, C. (2006) 'Community and nostalgia in urban revitalization: A critique of urban village and creative class strategies as remedies for social "problems"', *Australian Geographer*, 37: 335–354.

Bennett, D. (2010) 'Creative migration: A Western Australian case study of creative artists', *Australian Geographer*, 41(1): 117–128.

Collis, C., Felton, E. and Graham, P. (2010) 'Beyond the inner city: Real and imagined places in creative place policy and practice', *The Information Society*, 26(2): 104–112. doi:10.1080/01972240903562738.

Florida, R. (2002) *The Rise of the Creative Class*, New York: Basic Books.

Florida, R. (2009) *Who's Your City?: How the Creative Economy is Making Where to Live the Most Important Decision of Your Life*, New York: Random House.

Freestone, R., Randolph, B. and Butler-Bowdon, C. (2006) *Talking about Sydney: Population, Community and Culture in Contemporary Sydney*, Sydney: UNSW Press.

Gibson, C. and Klocker, N. (2004) 'Academic publishing as "creative" industry, and recent discourses of "creative economies": Some critical reflections', *Area*, 36: 423–434.

Gibson, C., and Klocker, N. (2005) 'The "cultural turn" in Australian regional economic development discourse: Neoliberalising creativity?', *Geographical Research*, 43(1): 93–102.

Landry, C. (2000) *The Creative City: A Toolkit for Urban Innovators*, London: Earthscan.

Luckman, S., Gibson, C. and Lea, T. (2009) 'Mosquitoes in the mix: How transferable is creative city thinking?', *Singapore Journal of Tropical Geography*, 30: 70–85.

Masters, T., Russell, R. and Brooks, R. (2011) 'The demand for creative arts in regional Victoria, Australia', *Applied Economics*, 43: 619–629.

Mitchell, Q. and Stimson, R. (2010) 'Creating a new geography of functional economic regions to analyze aspects of labour market performance in Australia', Working Paper 10-09. Centre of Full Employment and Equity: University of New Castle, Australia.

Montgomery, J. (2005) 'Beware "the creative class": Creativity and wealth creation revisited', *Local Economy*, 20: 337–343.

Smyth, P., Reddel, T. and Jones, A. (2005) *Community and Local Governance in Australia*, Sydney: UNSW Press.

Stimson, R. J., Mitchell, W., Rohde, D. and Shyy, P. (2011) 'Using functional economic regions to model endogenous regional performance in Australia: Implications for addressing the spatial autocorrelation problem', *Regional Science Policy & Practice*, 3(3): 131–144.

Throsby, D. (2008) *Creative Australia: The Arts and Culture in Australian Work and Leisure*, available at: http://apo.org.au/?q=node/3770 (accessed 29 August 2013).

Tonts, M. and Greive, S. (2002) 'Commodification and creative destruction in the Australian rural landscape: The case of Bridgetown, Western Australia', *Australian Geographical Studies*, 40: 58–70.

Verdich, M. (2010) 'Creative migration? The attraction and retention of the "creative class" in Launceston, Tasmania', *Australian Geographer*, 41: 129–140.

Appendix

Table A1 Descriptive statistics

Variable	N	Mean	Std dev	Minimum	Maximum	Australia
Economic and demographic						
Population	57	166,398	118,935	100,532	956,132	20,701,488
Population density	57	1,191	1,207	59	6,158	2.7
Population growth	57	0.01	0.02	0.00	0.07	0.01
Wages	57	40,614	6,132	33,492	70,305	40,585
Wage growth	57	0.04	0.01	0.02	0.05	0.04
Income	57	42,497	7,042	35,159	78,102	42,634
Income growth	57	0.04	0.01	0.01	0.06	0.04
Technology Index						
High-tech location quotient	57	1.19	0.19	0.83	1.63	1.00
Broadband	57	0.44	0.09	0.27	0.69	0.40
Talent Index						
Creative class	57	0.34	0.10	0.20	0.61	0.34
Human capital	57	0.12	0.05	0.05	0.27	0.12
Tolerance Index						
Foreign-born	57	0.29	0.11	0.10	0.56	0.24
Gay Index	57	1.03	0.37	0.50	3.32	1.00
Bohemian Index	57	0.94	0.29	0.45	2.00	1.00

13 Regional development and the creative class in Japan

Hans Westlund and Federica Calidoni

Introduction

What is the 'secret' to successful regional economic development? Is it the traditional prescription of access to the factors of production in just the right amounts? What is the role of capital, land and labour, and how does this recipe change across geography? Ever since Weber's (1904/05) study on the work ethics of Protestantism and its spatial impact on capitalism's development in Europe, understanding the factors of regional growth have been at the heart of the discipline.

There are many theories of economic development; each trying to pinpoint the key ingredients of economic growth. Adam Smith (1776) introduced the concept of specialization and the division of work in the rationalization of industrial production. Writing a hundred years later, Marshall (1880) built upon these ideas by arguing that the specific knowledge inherent in the environment of specialized industrial districts led productivity gains in these regions. The works of Schumpeter ([1911] 1934) and Knight (1921) argued for the importance of entrepreneurship and risk-taking as integral factors of economic development. Scholars more recently, such as Westlund and Bolton (2003), have built on their work, focusing on the spatial dimensions of this work.

More recently, the work of economists such as Porter (e.g. 1990) and Krugman (e.g. 1991) has led to the development of theories of regional specialization or clustering, which has had a considerable policy impact. Novel combinations of these ideas have combined many of these concepts to develop theories such as 'learning regions' (Florida, 1995; Asheim, 1996), 'localized learning' (Maskell and Malmberg, 1995) and human capital (Schultz, 1961; Becker, 1964) as sources for regional development.

Building throughout history has been the importance of intangible factors on regional economic growth. Learning, entrepreneurship and risk-taking are all emerging through themes such as values, culture, norms, networks and tacit knowledge, as vital to economic development. This chapter will utilize two concepts that have emerged out of – and come to define – this influential school of thought: Richard Florida's *creative class* and Robert Putnam's *social capital*.

Using a case study of Japan, this chapter will test the theories of Florida and Putnam. This chapter is structured as follows. Section two will introduce the hypotheses of Florida and Putnam respectively, while section three provides an overview of the existing research on these issues. Section four describes the methods and the data used before presenting our empirical results in section five. We conclude with final remarks in section six.

Values, preferences and economic transformation

It may be that creativity, entrepreneurship and innovation, to some extent, all depend on the degree of diversity in a society. To Schumpeter, the entrepreneur not only spurred new growth in the form of more efficient firms, but can also be responsible for the orchestration of bankruptcies, unemployment and other problems if the old businesses could not survive. An entrepreneur therefore can threaten his competitors, but also the economic stability of their local community; causing tensions and unease. This dual role of the entrepreneur helps to explain why entrepreneurship often meets resistance:

> In the breast of one who wishes to do something new, the forces of habit rise up and bear witness against the embryonic project ... the reaction of the social environment against one who wishes to do something new ... any deviating conduct by a member of a social group is condemned.
>
> (Schumpeter, [1911] 1934: 86)

Therefore, it is not surprising that the dominant values of society can prevent entrepreneurship in history. Different values of individuals and groups, and their organized expressions, are housed in the civil society. Old and new ideas and interests are opposite each other, but most often certain values dominate. In general, it is reasonable to assume some interaction between the economic and the dominant values of society. In this way it is possible to explain why the values of civil society have resisted innovations, but after their success, have supported the new situation. This slowed the pace of change in periods of transformation, but during periods of stable growth in industrial society, contributed to higher growth.

This means that the relation between society's diversity and values, and economic growth over time might be described as an inverted U-curve. A stable, conservative agrarian society, typified by pre-industrial communities, produced little in the way of creativity and economic growth rates. However, the increasing diversity spurred by industrialization and urbanization increased opportunities for social interactions, diversity and creativity in the population; all spurring economic growth. With diversity came social tensions that reduced social cohesion and tolerance, and, among other things, resulted in class and ethnic conflicts that have negative effects on growth.

Society after World War II paved the way for new institutions to the market economies, allowing forms of stability that supported growth. Innovations on the cusp of mass production in the nineteenth century, like the car, now became the engines of growth. This led to a period of growth, but not necessarily innovation.

However, when the crisis of the 1970s hit, it was regions with rigid industrial economies that saw much of their workforce and technologies wiped away, due to the lack of entrepreneurial spirit and drive to innovate that was required to overcome the economic challenges of the day (Westlund, 2006).

Economic growth after the 1970s in OECD countries took on a new shape and identity. This growth was concentrated in mid-sized university cities and metropolitan regions with diverse economies. The usual explanation is that growth in knowledge-intensive industries occurred in regions with a diverse labour pool of highly skilled workers. In turn, the large labour markets of metropolitan regions worked to attract people to these regions, spurring growth. As has been argued, there are many explanations for regional economic growth, of which the civil society of the region is central. From variation in the dominant values of a society to diversity of values in a community, the markers of tolerance and creativity range from society to society. A city with a dominant industry and a metropolis with a wide range of occupations differ in these respects.

Florida's creative class

According to Florida's (2002) theory of economic development, the creative class is the engine of economic growth. The locational decision of this class is argued to be fundamental to the economic growth of regions. There are several factors that Florida argues can attract the creative class to a region, including: a diverse labour market and horizontal mobility, myriad lifestyle options and amenities, openness to difference and low barriers to entry, and authenticity. It becomes evident therefore that the identity of a region speaks to the creative class, and influences their lifestyle and professional considerations when deciding where to live, work and play.

To further his argument, Florida argues there are 3Ts of economic growth: talent, technology and tolerance. All three are not a sufficient condition in themselves, as all three are needed in a region. Introducing variables such as the Bohemian Index, and the Melting Pot Index, Florida shows the existence of relationships between the growth of high-tech industries, creativity and modern lifestyles. Florida suggests a cause and effect: 'talent or creative capital is attracted to places that score high on our basic indicators of diversity' (Florida, 2003: 10), which can be interpreted to mean that tolerance is an attracting force for talent. Other research, such as that of Florida, Mellander and Stolarick (2007), has isolated the special role of tolerance in the cause-and-effect chain of regional development.

Putnam's social capital and Florida's criticism

Florida formulated his hypothesis on the 3Ts and the creative class in explicit opposition to another hypothesis concerning the impact of civil society on regional development, namely, Putnam's (2000) social capital hypothesis. According to Putnam, rather than a diverse community with loose connections being vital to support regional development, it is argued that a community with strong social networks with uniform standards and values spurs growth. Central to this is the notion of trust between actors, which, it is argued, can reduce the cost of transaction and improve business conditions. It is these networks of mutual trust that attract people to the region, thus positively affecting regional development.

It therefore becomes clear there are clear methodological and ontological variations between Florida's and Putnam's theoretical approaches, methods and conclusions. The aim of this chapter, rather than consider all the elements of these theories, is to focus on the common elements of these theories and examine their impact on regional economic development.

In discussing norms, values and social networks, Florida presents a strong criticism of Putnam's view that social capital is a factor contributing to current regional development. He argues, 'Where strong ties among people were once important, weak ties are now more effective. Those social structures that historically embraced closeness may now appear restricting and invasive' (Florida, 2002: 6). To highlight the differences between his measures of diversity and tolerance and Putnam's measures of social capital, while Putnam uses the term 'social capital', Florida refers to 'creative capital' instead.

Both Florida and Putnam are dealing with the physical spaces, in which norms, values and networks are distributed, in their individual examination of 'social capital' and 'creative capital' respectively. However, while Putnam describes social capital in a homogeneous civil society with common bonds and networks, Florida centres his work on a diverse community with differing norms and a myriad of networks. Westlund (2006) has suggested that Putnam mainly is referring to the relatively stable civil society in well-established, industrial communities. Florida, on the other hand, is examining patterns of economic growth in the knowledge economy's innovating and expanding regions. In line with this, in terms of economic renewal, it can be argued that Florida's perspective seems connected to path-breaking innovations of the Schumpetarian type, while Putnam's approach can be connected to incremental innovations of the Kirznerian type.

Research overview

Research connected to Florida's and Putnam's hypotheses

Diversity – in all its forms – has long been argued to be vital to innovation-led growth, and this dates back to the work of Schumpeter. There are many types of diversity, from economic (see Glaeser *et al.*, 1992; Feldman and Audretsch, 1999; Anderson *et al.*, 2005) to cultural (Jacobs, 1961). Both Lazear (2000) and Fujita and Weber (2003) have provided influential arguments for the impact of diversity on economic growth. The work of Ottaviano and Peri (2006), examining regional productivity in the United States, found that ethnic and cultural diversity are vital ingredients. Audretsch *et al.*'s (2009) study in Germany found that cultural diversity had a positive impact on technology-oriented start-ups, while examining regional R&D. Niebuhr (2006) also argues that cultural diversity affects regional innovation activity, as the differences in knowledge and capabilities of workers spur the creation of new ideas.

With respect to the contentious work of Florida, many quantitative analyses have been undertaken to challenge and unearth these findings. Perhaps the most influential critique of Florida's is that of Glaeser (2005) which, by using Florida's own data, called into question the statistical relationships between Florida's Gay Index and the Bohemian Index, when combined in multiple regressions analyses with a measure of human capital. It was found that human capital was the most influential factor in understanding population growth in 242 US metropolitan regions in 1990–2000.

Lee, Florida and Acs (2004) studied factors behind entrepreneurship in the USA, finding strong correlations between creativity/bohemians and entrepreneurship. Interestingly, measures of diversity in the form of location quotients of the gay population and the foreign-born, were in most cases non-significant. With respect to unearthing the statistical significance of talent, Hansen and Niedomysl (2009) used human capital as a proxy for the creative class in Sweden, and failed to find evidence that the presence of a 'people climate' is influential in the locational decisions of the creative class. Also probing the creative class hypothesis are Comunian *et al.* (2010), who investigated the prospects of 'bohemian' graduates in the British labour market, where the economic reality of low salaries and poor career prospects confront the portrayal of bohemians as being the engines of economic growth.

However, there is also quantitative support for this theory. In a study of the determinants of innovation in the USA by Knudsen, Florida, Gates and Stolarick (2007), there were no statistically significant results for the bohemian and gay measures, but the measure of 'creative capital' was highly significant in explaining innovation. Mellander and Florida (2006) carried out 'path analyses' of Sweden's labour market areas in which tolerance was shown to have a significant covariation with size of university, service diversity and human capital. Florida, Mellander and Stolarick's (2007) study of US Metropolitan areas found significant covariations between tolerance and university faculty per capita, consumer services, human capital, the creative class and its 'super-creative' core.

Switching gears now to social capital theory, this section will examine the relevant literature in this field, which has taken off in the past 15 years. However, as shown in a meta-study by Westlund and Adam (2010), the impacts of social capital on regional and national growth are not at all unambiguous. A substantial number of studies found no impact of social capital on regional/national growth.

Another empirical observation that opposes Putnam's hypothesis is that economic growth was high in the United States during the 1990s, despite the reduction of capital of civil society that Putnam (2000) showed evidence of. It is observed that in the United States, there is a seemingly inverse relationship between the principal component of Putnam's social capital – trust – and regional development.

Trust is higher in declining rural areas, while it is low in the expanding metropolitan areas (Putnam, 2001).

This section has demonstrated that to date, there is a limited and conflicting body of literature, which has sought to empirically test the relationship between civil society/social capital and regional development, suggested by Florida and Putnam respectively. Throughout this review, the contested nature of this field has been demonstrated, highlighting the tension in the field. While the theses of both Putnam and Florida have gained international prominence, neither has been given adequate attention in the context of Japan: the world's third largest economy.

The civil society of Japan[1]

For most of recent history, 'culture' has been the factor attributed to the unprecedented growth in the Japanese economy. Group culture is identified as a key factor by Zhang (1998) as providing the ability of the Japanese population to adapt to societal changes. While requiring strict observance of its members and group cooperation, under the right circumstances, an individual can contribute to the changing and recombination of groups, even if the particular group does not remain. In addition to this factor, Zhang also identifies Confucianism as a vital ingredient in Japan's economic success. It is argued that the Japanese interpretations of Confucianism have contributed to a strong group culture and loyalty, which provided the foundation of economic nationalism in the region. In the context of Western challenge in the nineteenth century, this group culture allowed the Japanese economy to focus on the national goal of rapid industrialization and 'catching up with the West'. As such, it is argued that the traditional group culture supported the Japanese industrialization strategy, allowing it to thrive.

Although often overlooked, a key feature of Japan's culture and civil society are local community and residential networks. These networks are dominated by 'invisible' women, who while men are at work, have had an extremely influential role in shaping the trajectory of civil society's social capital. While this may be reflective of limited interactions between civil society and the economy, it can also be argued this environment has provided favourable conditions for the men to concentrate on their job, thus spurring economic growth. However, the impact of Japanese civil society on economic growth has been relatively understudied, when compared to its European and American counterparts in particular.

The state, however, has been a more thoroughly examined, and influential, factor in the development of civil society and the economy in Japan (Schwartz, 2003). Government at all levels has had a key impact on the economic development of the region. Non-governmental organizations have also played a key role in the civil society of the country, working hand in hand with the government. Since post-World War II, at both the central and local levels, government has influenced the mandate of these organizations, not to mention the fact that the majority of non-governmental organizations have received a large portion of their incomes from the public sector and service fees. The Kobe earthquake served as a turning point in Japan, spurring growth of non-profit, grassroots organizations focused at the local level and engaged in issues dealing with the environment, at the community and the international level. But, as Schwartz (2003) argues, the strict regulatory environment these organizations operate in contributes to impede the growth of civil society in this sphere.

Thus, the connections between civil society and economic development in Japan seem unclear and contradictory. The relative small size of civil society suggests that it cannot have contributed much to economic growth, but the homogeneous group culture and its importance for economic development are well in line with Putnam's hypothesis.

Considering Florida's hypothesis, it has often been argued that Japan is lacking some of the essential features of the knowledge society, primarily creativity and individualism, as both strongly connected to entrepreneurship. Japan's long-term strategy of being a follower and an improver of foreign innovations has – in combination with traditional 'hierarchical groupism' and risk aversion – come to a dead end when there is no one to follow. The crucial question is how much the relations, norms and institutions of the industrial economy can contribute to the knowledge economy's growth.

Being a society considerably more culturally and ethnically homogeneous than its American and European counterparts, Florida's hypothesis would suggest severe problems for the high-tech industries in Japan. Even if the two decades of economic stagnation after 1990 mainly can be explained by other factors (the finance bubble, the bank system and a political wish to avoid changes), Florida's hypothesis might perhaps serve as an additional explanation.

Data and methods

When it comes to examining the impact of civil society on economic growth, are quantitative methods the most effective tools? As has been demonstrated, the literature on economic development and civil society has sought to quantify civil society such as measuring and ranking indicators of diversity, such as bohemians and gays. But there are several limitations to these methods. The mere presence of these organizations does not provide any indication as to the activities of these organizations and their contribution to civil society. The data itself does not let us know about the values, norms and attitudes held by these organizations and their members. As such, this research seeks to build on – and enhance – the previous work done in this field, by including explanatory variables such as values and attitudes to truly examine the impact of civil society on regional development.

The data used in this study to examine social values are collected from the Japanese General Social Surveys' International Comparative Survey on Values and Behavioral Patterns 2003. This is a data set consisting of 3663 valid responses, from which three indexes have been developed for 46 of Japan's 47 prefectures.[2] Appendix 1 provides details of how the indexes were constructed. It should be pointed out that the limited number of responses per prefecture means that the indexes contains a certain degree of uncertainty. Appendix 2 is a map of Japan's prefectures.

This analysis will test the assumptions of both Florida and Putnam, to examine the ways in which *tolerance, diversity* and *talent* of Florida, and *trust* and *homogeneity* of Putnam, are factors behind regional development. Two additional variables have been added to this analysis: first, the number of non-profit organizations (NPOs) per capita,[3] as a proxy to measure civil society, and second, an additional measure of diversity in the form of the share of foreigners of the total population. Diversity and homogeneity are considered as each other's opposites and measured by the *Homogeneity/Diversity Index*. Quantitative aspects of the civil society are measured by the number of civil organizations and the diversity of the population, measured by the share of foreigners.[4] The impact of the values of civil society on regional development is measured by indexes of tolerance and diversity (Florida) and trust and homogeneity (Putnam).

Building on this analysis, the *Aggregate Accessibility Index* was created using data on inter-regional accessibility; the National Integrated Transport Analysis System (NITAS) developed by the Japanese Ministry of Land, Infrastructure and Transport (MLIT), for 2002, giving the population potential for each prefecture:

$$A_j = \sum_{i=1}^{n} \frac{P_i}{D_{i,j}}$$

In this model, P is the population of each prefecture and D is the average distance between prefecture i and prefecture j. The Aggregate Accessibility Index is used as an approximate measure to examine variables which typically show spatial covariation. This includes, but is not limited to, access to spatially determined markets for input (including labour) and output (including market segments for highly specialized products), access to university and industry R&D and facilities, access to venture capital and traditional forms of financial capital. Finally, the last variable added to this analysis is human capital, defined as the share of the population who has completed university education.

We then introduce four alternative variables for our dependent variable of regional development: *population growth*, 2000–2005, the share of the total workforce of the *high-tech sector*, 2003/2004 and a part of that sector, the *high-tech services*, 2004, and *net growth of enterprises* as a percentage of stock, 2001–2004.[5] As an additional check, we have added an alternative dependent variable through testing *value added growth*.

Briefly, a note about data sources: the definition of high-tech sector used is that of the Milken Institute (DeVol, 1999: 34) which forms the basis of Florida's work as well.[6] The *Japan Statistical Yearbook*, edited by Statistical Research and Training Institute (MIC), was the source for data on population and the share of foreigners. Employment data is from the Japanese Ministry of Economy, Trade and Industry (METI) for the year 2003. Data on employment in service sectors

Table 13.1 Descriptive statistics

	N	Minimum	Maximum	Mean	Std Deviation
Employment HT services 2004	46	0.02	0.06	0.03	0.01
Population growth 2000–2004	46	−0.02	0.04	0.00	0.01
Employment high-tech 2003–2004	46	0.03	0.17	0.06	0.03
Growth enterprises 2001–2004	46	−0.07	−0.04	−0.06	0.01
Accessibility	46	3.86	7.48	5.36	0.92
Trust Index	46	0.30	0.78	0.48	0.09
Tolerance Index	46	0.34	0.73	0.53	0.09
Homogeneity Index	46	0.07	0.15	0.12	0.02
NPOs per 10,000 inhabitants	46	0.10	3.90	0.45	0.61
Human capital	46	0.00	0.14	0.02	0.03

defined as high-tech were available only for 2004, and the sum of these two variables combined formed the total employment in high-tech 2003/2004. As no detailed data for the service sectors are available at the regional level for earlier years, estimations of the growth of the total high-tech industry was not possible. On the whole, the limited availability of Japanese regional data has prevented the construction of time series and the calculation of employment changes in high-tech industries. Table 13.1 shows the descriptive statistics for the variables used in the regression analysis.

Results and discussion

The first test of the covariations between the dependent and the explanatory variables is shown in Table 13.2. All explanatory variables except NPOs per capita show positive correlations with population growth, but there is a clear difference between the variables measuring qualitative values of the civil society and the three quantitative variables, the latter showing considerably higher correlations. Concerning employment in the total high-tech sector (industry and services), the civil society variables seem completely insignificant, while they have stronger, positive covariations when only the high-tech services are taken into account. None of the explanatory variables seem to have an impact on the growth of enterprises.[7]

It should also be noted that there are strong positive correlations between human capital, accessibility and foreigners, and to a lesser extent between the group Trust-Tolerance and the Homogeneity/Diversity Index. The highly significant *share of foreigners* is, as said above, connected to diversity in Florida's hypothesis, but the variable's very strong correlation with accessibility is probably an indication of a general global pattern, namely, that the largest city-regions with the highest national accessibility have higher international interactions and exchanges. Thus, the share of foreigners is mainly an expression of the prefectures' size, something which probably is positively connected to creativity. But in this relation the share of foreigners seems to be a dependent variable, and accordingly,

Table 13.2 Correlation matrix of all variables (N = 46 prefectures)

	Population growth 2000–04	Employment high-tech 2003/2004	Employment HT services 2004	Growth enterprises 2001–04	Trust index	Tolerance index	Homogeneity index	Foreigners	Human capital	NPOs per capita	Accessibility
Population growth 2000–04	1										
Employment high-tech 2003/2004	0.51	1									
Employment HT services 2004	0.46	0.33	1								
Growth enterprises 2001–04	0.37	0.18	-0.03	1							
Trust Index	0.13	0.01	0.25	-0.12	1						
Tolerance Index	0.17	0.06	0.25	0.16	0.26	1					
Homogeneity Index	0.11	-0.03	0.03	-0.04	0.33	-0.08	1				
Foreigners	0.64	0.56	0.31	-0.15	0.02	0.11	-0.08	1			
Human capital	0.60	0.36	0.70	-0.06	0.17	0.26	0.00	0.55	1		
NPOs per capita	0.00	-0.12	0.05	-0.12	-0.11	-0.01	-0.08	0.22	0.21	1	
Accessibility	0.70	0.53	0.45	-0.01	0.07	0.27	-0.02	0.75	0.81	0.06	1

accessibility is the basic independent variable. For this reason, we omit the variable *share of foreigners* from the further analysis.

As discussed above, the relationship between society's diversity and values and its economic performance probably describes an inverted U-curve over time. However, as we are studying a very short time period (due to the lack of available data), of a country that also is considered a very homogeneous one, we expect the relationship to be linear. Thus, the second step in the analysis is ordinary least square regressions. The following estimations were made:

$$Pop_{i,t-1,t} = \alpha + \beta_1 tr_{i,t-1} + \beta_2 tol_{i,t-1} + \beta_3 ho_{i,t-1} + \beta_4 acc_{i,t-1} + \beta_5 hk_{i,t-1} + \beta_6 ngo_{i,t-1} + \mu_t$$
$$L_{i,t} = \alpha + \beta_1 tr_{i,t-1} + \beta_2 tol_{i,t-1} + \beta_3 ho_{i,t-1} + \beta_4 acc_{i,t-1} + \beta_5 hk_{i,t-1} + \beta_6 ngo_{i,t-1} + \mu_t$$
$$Lht_{i,t-1,t} = \alpha + \beta_1 tr_{i,t-1} + \beta_2 tol_{i,t-1} + \beta_3 ho_{i,t-1} + \beta_4 acc_{i,t-1} + \beta_5 hk_{i,t-1} + \beta_6 ngo_{i,t-1} + \mu_t$$
$$Est_{i,t} = \alpha + \beta_1 tr_{i,t-1} + \beta_2 tol_{i,t-1} + \beta_3 ho_{i,t-1} + \beta_4 acc_{i,t-1} + \beta_5 hk_{i,t-1} + \beta_6 ngo_{i,t-1} + \mu_t$$

where $Pop_{i,t-1,t}$ is the rate of growth of population by prefecture i between $t-1$ (2000) and t (2004); $L_{i,t}$ is the share of employment in high tech over total employment in each prefecture i at time t; $Lht_{i,t}$ is the share of employment in high-tech service sectors over total employment in each prefecture i at time t; and $Est_{i,t-1,t}$ is the rate of growth of establishments by prefecture i between $t-1$ (2000) and t (2004), while $tr_{i,t-1}$, $tol_{i,t-1}$ and $ho_{i,t-1}$ are the level of Trust, Tolerance and Homogeneity in 2000 respectively, as explained in Appendix 1; and $acc_{i,t-1}$, $hk_{i,t-1}$ and $ngo_{i,t-1}$ are the quantitative measures of Accessibility, Human capital and NPOs respectively.

The results of the regression analyses are shown in Table 13.3. Three results stand out as obvious: (1) the civil society variables do not have any significant influence on any of the regional development variables, measured at the prefecture level; (2) accessibility and human capital show a high correlation with population growth and employment in the high-tech sector and high-tech services; and (3) none of the variables have any covariation with entrepreneurship.

As mentioned above, the Japanese General Social Surveys' International Comparative Survey on Values and Behavioural Patterns contains a small number of observations per prefecture, which means that the indexes measuring various aspects of civil society to a certain extent might be a snapshot of what a larger number of observations might give.[8] In order to reduce the possible errors from the limited number of observations, regressions were also run for the 23 prefectures (i.e. half the prefectures) with the largest populations. However, the results do not deviate in any significant way from those of the previous tables; each of the quantitative variables stays positively significant if single, and the civil society variables stay insignificant.

The same regressions have been run inserting the growth rate of value added per capita between 2000 and 2004 as a fifth, alternative dependent variable. The results do not differ consistently from the previous ones. Moreover, the growth rate of value added per capita minus percentage population growth was tested as a combined dependent variable, against all other variables. As shown in Table 13.4, the results are not significant for any of the variables.

Table 13.3 OLS regressions, by prefecture (N = 46)

Population growth 2000–2004

	(1)	(2)	(3)	(4)
Trust	0.005 *(0.28)*	0.008 *(0.31)*	-0.003 *(-0.15)*	0.008 *(0.42)*
Tolerance	0.025 *(1.06)*	0.005 *(0.25)*	0.005 *(0.25)*	-0.002 *(-0.14)*
Homogeneity	0.080 *(0.89)*	0.081 *(0.67)*	0.090 *(0.91)*	0.079 *(0.91)*
NPOs	-1.243 *(-0.36)*	0.448 *(0.10)*		
Human capital	0.046 *(0.44)*		0.299*** *(4.57)*	
Accessibility	0.009** *(3.13)*			0.010*** *(6.14)*
Constant	-0.057** *(-2.55)*	-0.024 *(-1.15)*	-0.015 *(-0.96)*	-0.065*** *(-4.21)*
R-squared	0.51	0.48	0.37	0.50

Employment High-tech 2003/2004

	(1)	(2)	(3)	(4)
Trust	0.005 *(0.09)*	-0.000 *(-0.21)*	-0.012 *(-0.21)*	0.004 *(0.08)*
Tolerance	-0.031 *(-0.62)*	0.020 *(0.35)*	-0.010 *(-0.19)*	-0.031 *(-0.63)*
Homogeneity	-0.071 *(-0.29)*	-0.064 *(-0.22)*	-0.041 *(-0.15)*	-0.056 *(-0.23)*
NPOs	-8.869 *(-0.95)*	-8.129 *(-0.78)*		
Human capital	-0.153 *(-0.53)*		0.443** *(2.48)*	
Accessibility	0.023** *(2.79)*			0.019*** *(4.03)*
Constant	-0.021 *(-0.34)*	0.074 *(1.49)*	0.070 *(1.64)*	-0.018 *(-0.42)*
R-squared	0.32	0.19	0.13	0.29

Employment High-tech services 2004

	(1)	(2)	(3)	(4)
Trust	0.008 *(0.64)*	0.023 *(1.34)*	0.014 *(1.09)*	0.022 *(1.43)*
Tolerance	0.007 *(0.56)*	0.019 *(1.23)*	0.004 *(0.33)*	0.008 *(0.56)*
Homogeneity	-0.005 *(-0.08)*	-0.012 *(-0.14)*	-0.006 *(0.10)*	-0.014 *(-0.18)*
NPOs	-2.612 *(-1.16)*	1.457 *(0.49)*		
Human capital	0.354*** *(5.11)*		0.233*** *(5.78)*	
Accessibility	-0.004* *(-2.02)*			0.04** *(2.96)*
Constant	0.040** *(2.66)*	0.006 *(0.39)*	0.015 *(1.52)*	-0.009 *(-0.66)*
R-squared	0.56	0.11	0.51	0.26

Growth of enterprises 2001–2004

	(1)	(2)	(3)	(4)
Trust	-0.012 *(-1.06)*	-0.013 *(-1.18)*	-0.011 *(-1.02)*	-0.012 *(-1.09)*
Tolerance	0.014 *(1.33)*	0.014 *(1.32)*	0.015 *(1.41)*	0.014 *(1.34)*
Homogeneity	0.010 *(0.18)*	0.010 *(0.19)*	0.011 *(0.21)*	0.012 *(0.22)*
NPOs	-1.563 *(-0.76)*	-1.789 *(-0.93)*		
Human capital	-0.020 *(-0.30)*		-0.022 *(-0.61)*	
Accessibility	0.000 *(0.08)*			-0.000 *(-0.34)*
Constant	-0.057*** *(-4.18)*	-0.055*** *(-6.00)*	-0.059*** *(-6.96)*	-0.057*** *(-6.06)*
R-squared	0.08	0.07	0.06	0.06

Note: *t*-statistic in italics. * = 0.10; ** = 0.05; *** = 0.01.

Ramsey test shows that there is no evidence of omitted variables to include in the model. Breusch-Pagan/Cook-Weisberg test for heteroskedasticity shows small chi-square values, indicating that heteroskedasticity is not a problem.

Table 13.4 OLS regressions (N = 46) for value added growth per capita minus percentage population growth (2000–2004) as dependent variable

Variable	Value added growth minus population growth (2000–2004)
Trust	0.235
	1.43
Tolerance	0.091
	0.581
Homogeneity	−0.021
	−0.134
NPOs	−0.211
	−1.39
Human capital	0.646
	1.26
HT services	−0.235
	−0.997
Employment HT	−0.280
	−1.72
Growth of establishments	−0.153
	−0.98
Accessibility	−0.674
	−1.563
Constant	−0.307
	−0.301
R-squared	0.28

This leaves us with the conclusion that, in the way the hypotheses have been operationalized in this chapter, the results do not give any significant support for either Putnam's or Florida's hypotheses, when the share of foreigners is considered as a variable dependent on accessibility.

Thus, the basic hypothesis on the impact of civil society on regional development in Japan did not find any support on the level studied. What can be the reason for that? The following explanations are possible:

1   *The hypotheses might be of relevance only in a longer time perspective.* The time span of this analysis is limited to a relatively short period around the year 2000, the main reason being the availability of data. However, it is likely that the impact of sluggish, intangible factors of the type we here have tried to analyze is discernible only in the long run. The lack of data constitutes a problem when performing such long-term analyses.

2   *Civil society might have an influence on regional economic development in the USA (and maybe in Europe) but not in Japan.* Japan might be too homogeneous a country to permit regional differences of civil society to have any impact on regional development. Due to historical reasons, civil society in Japan is a younger, less developed feature of society – and might therefore be less connected to the regions' economic performance – compared with its

European and American counterparts. Instead of the social networks of civil society, it might be the social networks of business life (see Westlund and Nilsson, 2005) that, together with other factors, influence regional economic development in Japan.

3   *Other aspects of civil society than those measured in this study have an impact on regional development in Japan.* Trust, tolerance and diversity are without doubt important expressions of civil society's norms and values. However, it is possible that it is not differences in values and norms that influence regional development in Japan, but the diversity of leisure activities and opportunities for social interaction, which are aspects of Florida's hypothesis not being tested in this study – or it might be the strength and or/size of social networks (independent of the general trust people express) to mention an element of Putnam's hypothesis not being investigated here.

4   *Civil society might be of some importance in regional development but other factors are more important.* The assumption that a civil society with certain qualities has a positive impact on the regional economy and high-tech industries is built on some results of studies of Italy (Putnam, 1993) and the USA (Florida, 2002; 2003). However, as shown in this study, it is highly probable that the high-tech industry's regional growth pattern in Japan is affected by a number of other factors, such as accessibility, existing industries, labour market size, regional R&D capacity, etc., to such an extent that makes the civil society insignificant.

5   *Civil society might affect other aspects of regional development than those tested in this chapter.* In this study we tested four (five) measures of regional development, of which two (total high-tech sector and high-tech services) are explicitly connected to Florida's hypothesis. However, it is possible that civil society might have an impact on other aspects of regional development, i.e., other economic and social factors. This remains to be investigated.

6   *The measures of trust, tolerance and diversity used in this study might deviate too much from the ideal measures to be able to exert any real influence on regional development.* Transforming theory to empirical facts is always a problem. It is seldom possible to find or construct the ideal measure of a factor. This study is no exception. Although we think that our constructed indexes are fairly good empirical approximations of the theoretical concepts, based on the only existing compiled data in this field, it cannot be denied that they diverge too much from the ideal to show any explanatory power.

7   *Finally, the spatial unit used in the analysis (46 Prefectures) might be too limited to reflect differences in civil society.* Even if regional variations within Japanese civil society do exist, it is not clear where the important regional borders are. It is possible that a number of adjacent prefectures have similar regional characteristics. If this is the case, the analysis should be performed on larger spatial units.

It is not possible to investigate the validity of most of these possible explanations with the limited availability of regional data for Japan. However, the spatial level of the analysis can be changed. This was done by calculating weighted average values of each prefecture and its adjacent prefectures for each variable and testing them in models with a selection of variables. However, this did not provide any results that in a considerable way were different from the previous results as regards civil society variables. None of them turned significant in any of the regressions.

Conclusion

This chapter has begun to examine the economic impact of cultural factors on the economic development of Japan. Basing this work on the theories of Florida (2002) and Putnam (2000), on the role of civil society in particular, has been the focus of this study, to examine the ways in which the social milieu of a region can contribute to the vital ingredients of economic growth: creativity, diversity, innovation and entrepreneurship. However, as this analysis has demonstrated, due to the lack of data available, these hypotheses have yet to be fully tested. In conclusion, this research has provided several possible alternative avenues of research for future study.

Acknowledgements

The authors are grateful for scientific support and assistance from Kiyoshi Kobayashi and Masamitsu Onishi of Kyoto University, Makoto Tsukai of the Ritsumeikan University in Kyoto, and Kyoko Nakazato of the Swedish Office for Science and Technology in Tokyo. We are also grateful for comments from Charlotta Mellander, Mikael Nordenmark, Håkan Gadd, Taka Ueda, Kakuya Matsushima, Roger Stough, Fumi Kitagawa, Franco Malerba and anonymous referees. All possible flaws and misinterpretations are the sole responsibility of the authors.

Notes

1 This subsection is mainly based on Westlund (2006).
2 Due to its special conditions and remote location, the prefecture of Okinawa was not included in the analysis.
3 Data on NPOs was collected from the Japanese Research Institute of Economy, Trade and Industry, the 2004 Investigation of NPO Corporate Bodies.
4 Other measures of civil society at the prefecture level have been difficult to come across. It has not yet been possible to find data on membership of the majority of NPOs, NGOs or similar organizations. Nor has it been possible to find data to construct a regional 'Gay Index'.
5 The available data was for the whole stock of enterprises, primary sector enterprises included.
6 The Milken Institute's American definition was based on the US Standard Industrial Classification (SIC). This was transformed into the OECD's International Standard Industrial Classification (ISIC) which in its turn was transformed into the Japanese Standard Industrial Classification (JSIC).

7 This is probably a reflection of the insignificance of new enterprises on the regional development in Japan. In all international comparisons of entrepreneurship, Japan scores lowest (see Reynolds *et al.*, 2002). A supplementary explanation to the non-existent connections between the explanatory variables and growth of enterprises might be that it was not possible to exclude primary sector enterprises from the calculation. However, even if growth of enterprises is poorly connected to regional development in Japan, due to the lack of alternative measures, we continue to use the variable as a measure of entrepreneurship.
8 The number of replies and the reply rate for each prefecture are presented in Appendix 3.

Bibliography

Anderson, R., Quigley, J. and Wilhelmsson, M. (2005) 'Agglomeration and the spatial distribution of creativity', *Papers in Regional Science*, 83: 445–465.

Asheim, B. (1996) 'Industrial districts as "learning regions": A condition for prosperity', *European Planning Studies*, 4: 379–400.

Audretsch, D., Dohse, D. and Niebuhr, A. (2009) 'Cultural diversity and entrepreneurship: A regional analysis for Germany', *Annals of Regional Science*, 45: 55–85.

Becker, G. (1964) *Human Capital*, Chicago: University of Chicago Press.

Comunian, R., Faggian, A. and Li, Q. (2010) 'Unrewarded careers in the creative class: The strange case of bohemian graduates', *Papers in Regional Science*, 809: 389–410.

DeVol, R. (1999) *America's High-Tech Economy: Growth, Development, and Risks for Metropolitan Areas*, Santa Monica, CA: Milken Institute.

Feldman, M. and Audretsch, D. (1999) 'Innovation in cities: Science-based diversity, specialization and localized competition', *European Economic Review*, 43: 409–429.

Florida, R. (1995) 'Toward the learning region', *Futures: The Journal of Forecasting and Planning*, 27: 527–536.

Florida, R. (2001) *Technology and Tolerance: The Importance of Diversity to High-Technology Growth*, Washington, DC: The Brookings Institution, Survey Series.

Florida, R. (2002) *The Rise of the Creative Class: And How It's Transforming Work, Leisure, Community and Everyday Life*, New York: Basic Books.

Florida, R. (2003) 'Cities and the creative class', *City & Community*, 2: 3–19.

Florida, R. (2005) *The Flight of the Creative Class: The New Global Competition for Talent*, New York: HarperCollins.

Florida, R., Mellander, C. and Stolarick, K. (2007) 'Inside the Black Box of regional development: Human capital, the creative class and tolerance', CESIS Electronic Working Paper No. 88. Available at: http://www.infra.kth.se/cesis/documents/WP88.pdf (accessed 29 August 2013).

Fujita, M. and Weber, S. (2003) 'Strategic immigration policies and welfare in heterogeneous countries', Working Paper No. 569, Institute of Economic Research, Kyoto University.

Glaeser, E. (2005) 'Review of Richard Florida's "The rise of the creative class"', *Regional Science and Urban Economics*, 35: 593–596.

Glaeser, E., Kallal, H., Scheinkman, J. and Schleifer, A. (1992) 'Growth in cities', *Journal of Political Economy*, 100: 1126–1152.

Hansen, H. and Niedomysl, T. (2009) 'Migration of the creative class: Evidence from Sweden', *Journal of Economic Geography*, 9: 191–206.

Jacobs, J. (1961) *The Death and Life of Great American Cities*, New York: Random House.

Japanese General Social Surveys (2006) Available at: http://jgss.daishodai.ac.jp/english/eframe/englishtop.html (accessed 29 August 2013).

Knight, F. (1921) *Risk, Uncertainty and Profit*, Boston: Houghton Mifflin.

Knudsen, B., Florida, R., Gates, G. and Stolarick, K. (2007) 'Urban density, creativity and innovation', Working Paper. Available at http://www.creativeclass.com/rfcgdb/articles/Urban_Density_Creativity_and_Innovation.pdf (accessed 29 August 2013).

Krugman, P. (1991) 'Increasing returns and economic geography', *Journal of Political Economy*, 99: 483–499.

Lazear, E. (2000) 'Diversity and immigration', in G. J. Borjas (ed.), *Issues in the Economics of Immigration*, Chicago: University of Chicago Press, pp. 117–142.

Lee, S., Florida, R. and Acs, Z. (2004) 'Creativity and entrepreneurship: A regional analysis of new firm formation', *Regional Studies*, 38: 879–891.

Marshall, A. (1880) *Principles of Economics: An Introductory Volume*. London: Macmillan.

Maskell, P. and Malmberg, A. (1995) 'Localized learning and industrial competitiveness', BRIE Working Paper No. 80. Available at: http://brie.berkeley.edu/publications/WP%2080.pdf (accessed 29 August 2013).

Mellander, C. and Florida, R. (2006) 'The creative class or human capital? Explaining regional development in Sweden', Working Paper Series in Economics and Institutions of Innovation No. 79. Royal Institute of Technology, CESIS, Centre of Excellence for Science and Innovation Studies.

Niebuhr, A. (2006) 'Migration and innovation: Does cultural diversity matter for regional R&D activity?', paper presented at the 46th Congress of the European Regional Science Association Volos, Greece, August 30–September 3.

Ottaviano, G. I. P. and Peri, G. (2006) 'The economic value of cultural diversity: Evidence from US cities', *Journal of Economic Geography*, 6: 9–44.

Porter, M. (1990) *The Competitive Advantage of Nations*, Basingstoke: Macmillan.

Putnam, R. (1993) *Making Democracy Work: Civic Traditions in Modern Italy*, Princeton, NJ: Princeton University Press.

Putnam, R. (2000) *Bowling Alone: The Collapse and Revival of American Community*, New York: Simon & Schuster.

Putnam, R. (2001) 'Social capital community benchmark survey: Community result matrix', available at: http://www.ksg.harvard.edu/saguaro/communitysurvey/results_matrix.html (accessed 29 August 2013).

Research Institute of Economy, Trade and Industry (2004) 'Investigation of NPO corporate bodies', available at: http://www.rieti.go.jp/en/index.html (accessed 29 August 2013).

Reynolds, P., Bygrave, W., Autio, E., Cox, L. and Hay, M. (2002) *Global Entrepreneurship Monitor Executive Report*, London: Babson College, Ewing Marion Kauffman Foundation, London Business School.

Schultz, T. (1961) 'Investment in human capital', *The American Economic Review*, I: 1–17.

Schumpeter, J. ([1911] 1934) *Theorie der wirtschaftligen Entwicklung*. English translation 1934: *The Theory of Economic Development*, Cambridge, MA: Harvard University Press.

Schwartz, F. (2003) 'Introduction: Recognizing civil society in Japan', in F. J. Schwartz and S. J. Pharr (eds), *The State of Civil Society in Japan*, Cambridge: Cambridge University Press.

Smith, A. (1776) *An Inquiry into the Nature and Causes of the Wealth of Nations*, London: Printed for W. Strahan and T. Cadell.

Weber, M. (1904/05) *Die protestantische Ethik und der 'Geist' des Kapitalismus*, Archiv für Sozialwissenschaft und Sozialpolitik 20: 1–54 and 21: 1–110. English translation: *The Protestant Ethic and the Spirit of Capitalism*, trans. Talcott Parsons, 1931/2001, London: Routledge Classics.

Westlund, H. (2006) *Social Capital in the Knowledge Economy: Theory and Empirics*, New York: Springer.

Westlund, H. and Bolton, R. (2003) 'Local social capital and entrepreneurship', *Small Business Economics*, 21: 77–113.

Westlund, H. and Nilsson, E. (2005) 'Measuring enterprises' investments in social capital: A pilot study', *Regional Studies*, 39: 1079–1094.

Westlund, H. and Adam, F. (2010) 'Social capital and economic performance: A meta-analysis of 65 studies', *European Planning Studies*, 18: 893–919.

Zhang, W. (1998) *Japan Versus China in the Industrial Race*, London: Macmillan.

Appendix 1

1. **Tolerance Index**, consisting of the regional unweighted averages of the individuals' replies (1 = tolerant, 0 = intolerant) based on the questions:

✓ **Divorce**: when a marriage is troubled and unhappy, is it generally better if the couple gets divorced? (yes = 1 no = 0)

✓ **Foreign**: are you for or against an increase in the number of foreigners in your community? (yes = 1 no = 0)

✓ **Contfor**: have you had any contact with foreigners in Japan? (yes = 1 no = 0)

✓ **Fjob1**: if a husband has sufficient income, is it better for his wife not to have a job? (yes = 0 no = 1)

✓ **Fjob2**: can a working mother establish just as warm and secure a relationship with her children as a mother who does not work? (yes = 1 no = 0)

✓ **Fjob3**: a husband's job is to earn money; a wife's job is to look after the home and family. Do you agree? (yes = 0 no = 1)

✓ **Fjob4**: is having a job the best way for a woman to be an independent person? (yes = 1 no = 0)

✓ **Kill**: when a person has a fatal disease, do you think doctors should be allowed by law to end the patient's life by some painless means if the patient and his/her family request it? (yes = 1 no = 0)

✓ **Homo**: do you think that sexual relations between two adults of the same sex are wrong? (yes = 0 no = 1)

2. **Trust Index**, consisting of the regional averages unweighted of dummy variables (1 = trust in people, 0 = no trust) based on the questions:

✓ **Trust1**: generally speaking, would you say that most people can be trusted? (yes = 1 no = 0)

✓ **Evil**: do you think human nature is good or evil? (good = 1 evil = 0)

The Japanese General Social Surveys' International Comparative Survey on Values and Behavioral Patterns contains data at micro level. 3663

(Continued)

(Continued)

yes–no answers to each of the questions above were transformed to dummy variables (0 and 1) and an average for each question and each prefecture was calculated and then aggregated to indexes.

Homogeneity/Diversity Index. The Homogeneity Index is based on the above 11 questions. The index is based on the assumption that a prefecture with a wholly homogeneous opinion in one question would either have the average reply 0 or 1. A prefecture with maximum heterogeneity (diversity) would have the same amount of 0 and 1 replies respectively and thus have the average reply 0.5. Hence we estimate the deviation of the real average for each question from 0.5 and summarize them for the 11 questions for each prefecture. In this way a *Homogeneity index* is obtained. Positive co-variations with the dependent variables might be interpreted as support for Putnam's hypothesis, while negative covariations might be interpreted as support for Florida's hypothesis.

Appendix 2 The Japanese prefectures

Japan is divided into the following 47 prefectures:

1 Hokkaido, 2 Aomori, 3 Iwate, 4 Akita, 5 Miyagi, 6 Yamagata, 7 Fukushima, 8 Ibaraki, 9 Tochigi, 10 Gunma, 11 Chiba, 12 Saitama, 13 Tokyo, 14 Kanagawa, 15 Niigata, 16 Toyama, 17 Ishikawa, 18 Nagano, 19 Gifu, 20 Fukui, 21 Yamanashi, 22 Shizuoka, 23 Aichi, 24 Shiga, 25 Kyoto, 26 Hyogo, 27 Mie, 28 Nara, 29 Osaka, 30 Wakayama, 31 Tottori, 32 Shimane, 33 Okayama, 34 Hiroshima, 35 Yamaguchi, 36 Kagawa, 37 Tokushima, 38 Ehime, 39 Kochi, 40 Fukuoka, 41 Saga, 42 Nagasaki, 43 Oita, 44 Kumamoto, 45 Miyazaki, 46 Kagoshima, 47 Okinawa.

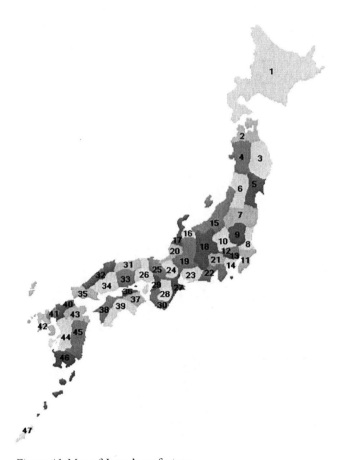

Figure A1 Map of Japan's prefectures

Appendix 3

Table A1 Number of replies and reply rates for the Japanese Value Survey per prefecture

	Prefecture	Total answers	% answers		Prefecture	Total answers	% answers		Prefecture	Total answers	% answers
1	Hokkaido	161	82.6	16	Toyama	44	86.4	31	Tottori	19	89.5
2	Aomori	45	84.4	17	Ishikawa	45	82.2	32	Shimane	33	78.8
3	Iwate	52	82.7	18	Fukui	32	84.4	33	Okayama	53	83.0
4	Miyagi	82	81.7	19	Yamanashi	44	77.3	34	Hiroshima	100	89.0
5	Akita	49	87.8	20	Nagano	76	85.5	35	Yamaguchi	57	89.5
6	Yamagata	48	79.2	21	Gifu	62	96.8	36	Tokushima	23	87.0
7	Fukushima	67	83.6	22	Shizouka	93	84.9	37	Kagawa	53	88.7
8	Ibaraki	86	86.0	23	Aichi	181	80.7	38	Ehime	38	84.2
9	Tochigi	71	83.1	24	Mie	61	80.3	39	Kochi	40	80.0
10	Gunma	63	85.7	25	Shiga	48	87.5	40	Fukuoka	154	83.8
11	Saitama	148	85.8	26	Kyoto	71	77.5	41	Saga	40	75.0
12	Chiba	153	75.8	27	Osaka	202	84.2	42	Nagasaki	52	86.5
13	Tokyo	272	78.7	28	Hyogo	134	85.1	43	Kumamoto	49	77.6
14	Kanagawa	200	77.5	29	Nara	47	80.9	44	Oita	53	77.4
15	Niigata	87	86.2	30	Wakayama	34	70.6	45	Miyazaki	45	77.8
								46	Kagoshima	54	88.9

14 China's development disconnect*

Richard Florida, Charlotta Mellander
and Haifeng Qian

Introduction

Over the past three decades, China's massive economic growth, rapid urbanization and expansion of its cities have put it on the world scene. China's economy
has grown at an average rate of above 9 percent per year. Some 46.6 percent of
China's population lived in urban areas in 2009, compared with only 17.9 percent in 1978 (Xinhuanet, 2010). China has 118 cities with more than a million
people (ibid.).

Conventional wisdom and a large body of the academic literature (e.g., Cai *et al.*,
2002; Chow and Li, 2002; Wang and Yao, 2003) have identified physical capital
accumulation as the major source of China's economic growth. China has been
posed as a manufacturing miracle—the world's factory, producing manufactured
goods especially for the developed world. Despite its rapid growth, China ranks
27th on the Davos Global Competitiveness Index (Schwab, 2010) and 89th on the
UN Human Development Index (UNDP, 2010).

But another perspective has emerged. OECD (2008) has noted that China is
increasing its innovative capabilities. According to its report, *Reviews of Innovation Policy: China*, the country's R&D spending exhibited an annual growth
rate of 19 percent, and R&D intensity (R&D/GDP) doubled in the decade of
1995–2005. Since 2000, China has had the second largest number of researchers in the world, however, the productivity of those researchers in publications
and patents is low compared with advanced countries. Enrollment at Chinese
universities has significantly expanded and the quality of those universities has
improved. A growing number of American, European and Asian multinational
companies have opened laboratories and R&D facilities there. According to its
Ministry of Science and Technology, China devoted 461.6 billion Yuan to R&D
in 2008, ranking fourth in the world. China's economic development has been
oriented toward higher human capital and knowledge-based industries. Meanwhile a top national policy priority has been to build an innovative country.

* This chapter was previously published as: Florida, R., Mellander, C., and Qian, H. (2012)
"China's Development Disconnect," *Environment and Planning A*, 44(3): 628–648.
Reprinted with permission of the publisher, Pion Ltd, London, www.pion.co.uk and www.
envplan.com.

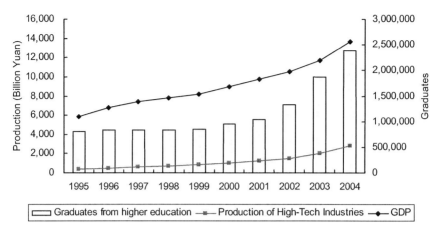

Figure 14.1 Graduates from higher education, production of high-tech industries and GDP
of China, 1995–2004

Source: *China Statistical Yearbook* (2005) and *China Statistical Yearbook on High Technology Industry* (2005).

Figure 14.1 illustrates the growth of human capital and high-tech industries for the period of 1995–2004. Scholars have also started to examine innovative activity in China (e.g., Sun, 2002; Zhou *et al.*, 2011).

This leads to an important and understudied question. We know that cities are key organizing units for knowledge, human capital, creativity and innovation (Florida, 2002c; Glaeser *et al.*, 1992; Jacobs; 1961; 1969). To what degree have China's rapidly growing cities and regions come to reflect the underlying human capital, technology and creativity required for innovation-led economic growth? Do China's cities and regions reflect the underlying characteristics associated with the high human capital, creative class, and innovative cities, characteristic of knowledge-based economic development in more advanced economies?

To answer the question, our research looks at the role of three key clusters of factors in economic development. The first of these is technology, long identified as shaping knowledge-based economic development by scholars such as Schumpeter (1942), Solow (1956), and Markusen (2004), as key to economic development. The second is the effect of human capital or talent identified in the work of Barro (1991, 1997), Lucas (1988), Jacobs (1969), Glaeser *et al.* (1992) among others. While there is a general consensus as to the important role played by human capital in regional development, debate has emerged on two key issues. The first involves the efficacy of educational versus occupational measures of talent. In this study we use both. This brings us to the third, somewhat more contentious factor. Recent research has argued that there are other place-based factors that shape the distribution of both technology and human capital. Florida *et al.* (2008) in particular argue that these are better conceived less as stocks and more as flows. We examine several factors that have been shown to affect the distribution of technology and human capital in studies of advanced economies: universities (Anselin *et al.*, 1997; Cheshire and Magrini, 2000; Florida *et al.*, 2006), consumer amenities (Roback, 1982; Glaeser *et al.*, 2001), and openness, diversity, and tolerance (Florida *et al.*, 2008; Mellander and Florida, 2011; Page, 2007). We now turn to broader discussion of the theory and constructs that lie behind the effects of these three factors on regional development and which, in turn, motivate our empirical research.

Theories and concepts

Our understanding of the transformation from traditional industrial to knowledge-based economies is based largely on the experience of the advanced nations. A key feature of this study is that it tries to examine this transformation as it is currently occurring in China, a county that is actively developing policies to pursue this transformation. Three key factors have been found to shape such economic transformation as noted above.

The first is technology. Initially identified by Marx (Marx *et al.*, 1848) and Schumpeter (1942), Solow (1956) famously isolated the role of technology in the form of the error term, which is associated with productivity gains that cannot be explained by changes related to labor or capital. In other words, he treated technology as an exogenous factor. Romer (1986; 1987; 1990) allowed technology to be explained endogenously. Investment in R&D is thereby seen as a purposeful activity, one that generates technology and productivity improvements.

The second is human capital. Initially identified by Adam Smith (1776) as the fourth factor of production, empirical studies by Barro (1991; 1997) document the role of human capital in national economic development. Following Jacobs (1961; 1969), Lucas (1988) noted that human capital externalities found in cities are the primary mechanism of economic development. Lucas (1988) let the human capital factor be embodied in individuals and investments in human capital that generate productivity gains and growth. He also stressed the role of cities as interactive places for human capital, places where knowledge is exchanged and created. By reducing the transaction cost of knowledge generation, cities become engines for economic growth.

The role of cities has also been identified by Jacobs (1961; 1969) who argued that a diversity of firms and individuals is associated with economic growth. She also illustrated the role of cities' scale and diversity in the generation of new ideas. Andersson (1985a; 1985b) explored the subject of creativity in cities and metropolitan regions historically, stressing the importance of knowledge, culture, and communications in stimulating regional growth.

On the empirical side, Barro's large-scale empirical tests of the human capital influence on national economic performance (1991; 1997) have been followed by several influential studies, including Rauch (1993), Simon and Nardinelli (1996), Simon (1998), and others. Further studies have shown that talent (human capital or the creative class) can serve as an attractor for the technology industry (Florida, 2002b; Florida *et al.*, 2008; Mellander and Florida, 2011).

The third cluster of factors revolves around those that affect the distribution of technology and of human capital across regions. Economists have typically conceptualized these factors as stocks, but Florida *et al.* (2008) contend they are more appropriately conceived as flows. A number of key factors have been shown to affect the distribution of human capital and technology. The role of amenities was introduced in a neoclassical framework by Roback (1982). The traditional attractor for households in general is higher living standards through higher wages or lower living costs. In the Roback context, migration patterns not explained by those two factors could be explained by regional differences in amenity levels. Later, Glaeser *et al.* (2001) suggested that several factors help increase the competitiveness of the city: a variety of consumer services and goods; aesthetical and physical settings; good public services; and speed to make the city accessible. Florida (2002a; 2002b; 2002c) stressed the importance of lifestyle, culture, nightlife and entertainment as talent attractors. Shapiro (2006) illustrated the importance of quality of life over and above the employment growth effect of college graduates.

A second approach has focused on the role of diversity and openness. Jacobs (1961) stressed the importance of a diversity of individuals. Quigley (1998) argued that we have a "taste for variety" and that firm-based diversity is associated with economic growth. The importance of diversity, as expressed in higher levels of tolerance and openness, has been demonstrated by Inglehart and Norris (2003) and Inglehart and Welzel (2005) in the World Value Surveys. They examine the relationship between cultural attitudes and economic development. According to Inglehart, one of the best proxies for tolerance is openness toward gay and lesbian individuals. Studies by Florida and Gates (2001) found a positive relationship between gay concentrations and economic development in the US. Openness and tolerance may also be expressed in relation to immigrants. Florida (2002c) demonstrated a relationship between the proportion of immigrants in a population and regional economic performance. Ottaviano and Peri (2005) showed how diversity, in the form of immigrants, increases regional productivity. Qian and Stough (2011) demonstrated a positive association between cultural diversity and regional innovation. Page (2007) found that diversity leads to better decision-making, and that diversity within groups provides new perspectives. Florida (2002a) has also argued that openness and tolerance lead to a lowering of regional barriers to entry.

A third factor with a strong influence on the distribution of human capital is the location of universities which serve as talent producers. The value of such production depends on the mobility of graduates. If graduates are highly mobile and are insufficiently attracted to the region, universities may become talent exporters. This kind of migration is something several US regions have experienced and has been highlighted by Florida *et al.* (2006). When talent is less mobile or is restricted from migrating through various institutions, the role of universities may be of greater importance. In the case of China, the local universities are likely to be the key source of regional talent.

It is important to note that there has been a considerable debate over the role of tolerance, openness, and diversity. Clark (2003) suggests that the Gay Index and regional development relationship only holds for larger regions. Glaeser (2004) shows that the traditional, education-based human capital measure outperforms the Gay Index when examining the change in population between 1990 and 2000. However, Florida *et al.* (2008) suggest that the OLS frameworks and models are insufficient and do not capture the interactions among the system of factors that affect regional development. Florida (2002c) suggests that all three factors or "Ts" must act together as complementaries and not substitutes in order to achieve higher levels of development.

There has also been a considerable debate over the work by Florida (2002c). Markusen (2006) questions the creative class concept, arguing jobs included in the category have little to do with an underlying creative process but are based on the education level. She also questions the causality of talent attracting jobs, which she believes should work the other way around. On the first point, McGranahan and Wojan (2007) use detailed data on skills to reconstruct the creative class definition. They find the definition to be robust with the exception of a small number of health and education occupations. They further find a substantial correlation between Florida's original and their revised definition and that the basic conclusions hold as well. Research by Florida *et al.* (2008) directly tests the effects of human capital and the creative class on wages and income and finds that while human capital has a significant effect on income, the creative class has a more powerful effect on wages. Independent research by Gabe (2009) and McGranahan and Wojan (2007) also finds that the creative class has a significant effect on wages, controlling for other factors. Krätke (2010) suggests that the use of 3Ts is far too simplified and would not take, for example, the sectorial mix into account, which may affect regional success and innovative potential. Pratt (2008) argues that it is more appropriate to approach creativity through an industrial lens than an occupational one. This is perhaps a step backward. Research by King *et al.* (2010) on Canada, the USA and Sweden, shows the interaction of industrial and occupational approaches, focusing on the differences and similarities between the educational-based human capital and the creative class, and the role of the occupational differences within industries. Their conclusion is that occupational structures differ between regions and nations, holding industries constant.

There is also debate over whether or not the creative class approach applies outside the US context (e.g., Lorenzen and Vaarst Andersen, 2009). Boyle (2006) suggests that Florida's ideas very well may apply to the Celtic Tigers, in order to explain migration to Dublin, but that the situation needs more nuances to be fully understood. A similar finding is presented by Houston *et al.* (2008) in an examination of the Scottish regions. Krätke (2010) uses the 3T theories to explain GDP growth in Germany, and finds that industry structures alone will explain as much as industry structures in combination with the creative class. Boschma and Fritsch (2009), on the other hand, find that the creative class outperforms the educational-based human capital measure in order to explain employment growth and new firm formation in Germany. They found that tolerance and openness have strong explanatory power to explain the distribution of the creative class, and that city size alone will not explain as much. Additional comparative studies show that the creative class measure outperforms conventional human capital measures in accounting for regional wages in Sweden (Mellander and Florida, 2011) and the Netherlands (Marlet and Van Woerken, 2004).

A number of recent studies have examined the role of these factors, individually or in combination, in Chinese regional development. Zhang and Fan (2006) constructed a descriptive indicator system to explain the regional disparity of human capital in China. The system involved four categories of indicators: (1) economic performance; (2) education, science and education investments; (3) health system and medical care investments; and (4) communication investments. Jiang *et al.* (2005) mentioned the possible influences of urbanization, universities, amenities, wage levels, and government policies on China's regional talent densities. Their statistical analysis reported significant and positive effects of universities and urbanization on talent distribution. Li and Florida (2006) examined the effects of non-market factors on talent production using city-level data and concluded that there was a positive impact of openness on the number of local universities. Qian (2010) analyzed the impacts of both market factors (wage and employment) and non-market factors (universities, amenities and openness) on China's regional talent stock. He reported that the presence of universities had a strong influence on talent distribution and also highlighted the effects of openness on talent, innovation and regional economic performance.

We now turn to our data, variables and methods.

Model, variables, data, and methods

Model

A schematic picture of our general model of talent, technology, and regional development is provided in Figure 14.2. The model allows us to accomplish several useful analyses. First, it enables us to test conventional human capital measurements against occupational or creative class definitions. Second, it allows us to isolate the independent effects of talent and technology. The model also enables identification of regional cultural and institutional factors—namely, the presence of universities, level of amenities, and tolerance—as they affect the geographic distribution of talent in the first place. The arrows identify the hypothesized structure of relationships among the key variables.

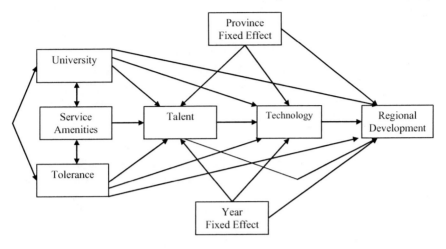

Figure 14.2 Path model of the regional development system

Variables and data

We now describe the variables and data used in the empirical model. Our analysis covers all provincial-level regions in mainland China except Tibet (which is generally considered as an outlier) for the years 2001–2005, resulting in 150 (30×5) observations. Descriptive statistics for all measures and variables are provided in Table 14.1.

Table 14.1 Descriptive statistics

	Obs.	Mean	Standard Deviation	Minimum	Maximum
Regional institutional and cultural factors:					
University	150	1.701	1.315	0.40	7.80
Tolerance	150	0.108	0.070	0.025	0.400
Service amenities	150	1.007	0.148	0.742	1.500
Talent:					
Human capital	150	7.087	4.310	2.21	26.28
Creative class	150	3.490	1.631	1.96	11.75
Technology:					
High technology	150	0.0262	0.026	0.001	0.128
Patents	150	11.033	15.528	1.299	97.434
Regional development:					
GDP per capita	150	12,140	8,754	2,893	48,490

Note: the data in this paper, except specifically noted, are from *China Statistical Yearbook* (2002–2006) edited by National Bureau of Statistics of China.

Dependent variable: regional development

Gross domestic product (GDP) is the most widely used indicator for economic performance. In China, while GDP is the single most important indicator for the promotion of local officials, GDP statistics are available at all the jurisdictional levels above counties. Accordingly, we use 2001–2005 GDP per capita (all in 2001 constant value) as the measure of regional economic performance.

While some researchers use population or job growth as measures of development, those measures fail to control for the quality of development and productivity. Not all jobs are created equal; some pay better than others. Regions increasingly specialize in different kinds of economic activity, and therefore different kinds of jobs (Markusen, 2004; Markusen and Barbour, 2007). By regional development, we mean the overall level of development and living standards underlain by productivity. While GDP per capita is not a perfect measure of overall living standards, it remains a reasonable proxy for regional development.

Independent variables

Talent

Talent can be understood as human capital or as the creative class. Earlier studies (Florida *et al.*, 2008; Mellander and Florida, 2011) have shown that the traditional human capital measure based on educational levels and the creative class measure based on occupational tasks perform differently. As a result, we employ two different talent measures. We measure human capital as those graduating with a college or higher-level degree, standardized by the local population 15 years old or older. We measure the creative class as the proportion of certified professional and technical workers (*zhuanye jishu renyuan*) within the local population 15 years old or older. Since specific occupational data are not available in China, an exact replication of the measurement methodology employed by Florida (2002c) is not possible. However, China's *zhuanye jishu renyuan* mirrors Florida's creative class to a large extent. *Zhuanye jishu renyuan* includes scientists and engineers, university professors, teachers, agricultural and sanitation specialists, aviators and navigators, economic and statistical specialists, accountants, translators, librarians, journalists, publishers, lawyers, artists, broadcasts, athletes, etc. Both the human capital and the creative class measures are based on 2001–2005 data. Data for *Zhuanye jishu renyuan* are available from the *China Labor Statistics Yearbook* (NBS, 2002–2006).

Technology

Since technological innovation is most likely to occur in high-tech industries, we have defined high technology as the proportion of value added in high technology industries to GDP. In China, the high-tech industries are officially defined as electronic and telecommunications, computers and office equipment, pharmaceuticals, medical equipment and meters, and aircraft and spacecraft. The high-tech value-added data (2001–2005) are available from the *China Statistical Yearbook on High Technology Industry* (NBS, 2005–2007).

However, the high-tech industries are not necessarily high-tech based. In China, less than 5 percent of the value added in the high-tech industries is used for R&D expenditures, much lower than in most developed countries. To better evaluate regional technology and innovation, we have used officially approved patents per 10,000 population (2001–2005) as a supplementary measure. In China, three types of patents are granted: inventions; utility models; and designs. Innovation can be measured either from the input side, such as R&D expenditures, or from the output side, in the form of patents. The output side is more reliable in the sense that high input does not necessarily lead to high output.

Universities

Universities are where most talent is produced. Regions with more universities and university students possess potential advantages in talent attraction, providing they can retain graduates. University students are often reluctant to seek a job in other places after graduation due to their well-established local network and the costs of adapting to a new environment. In China, institutional barriers (in the form of the inhabitant registration, or the "Hukou" system) further prevent the flow of university students. As a result, the university is hypothesized to play an exclusively important role in China's talent distribution. This is measured by the number of university students per 1,000 local population (2001–2005).

Amenities

The term "amenities" in this chapter refers to service amenities, as measured by the 2001–2005 location quotient of urban employment in the tertiary sector including: wholesale and retail trade, catering services; finance and insurance services; real estate trade; social services; health care, sporting and social welfare; and education, culture and arts, radio, film and television.

Tolerance, diversity, openness

Most research uses the Diversity Index or Gay Index to measure tolerance/diversity/openness (Florida, 2002a; 2002b; 2002c; Florida *et al.*, 2008; Mellander and Florida, 2011). Not surprisingly, statistical data on gays are not available in China. As an alternative, we have adopted the "Hukou Index" as a proxy for openness. In the case of China, it is a compelling measure, perhaps better than the Gay Index. The rules of Hukou (or the inhabitant registration system) are used by the central government to control internal migration. The system determines which city or county a person belongs to and whether she or he has rural or urban status. Those with a locally registered Hukou are always permanent residents and receive local economic, social and political benefits, such as social welfare, education, and voting rights. Those who live in a jurisdictional area without a local Hukou, in contrast, are always "marginal" workers or visitors. If a large proportion of an area's population is without a locally registered Hukou, this indicates that a large proportion of the population is from outside the region. The Hukou Index of openness is defined as the proportion of the population without a locally registered Hukou (2001–2005). Accordingly, the higher the Hukou Index, the more open the region.

Methods

We have used path analysis and structural equations to examine the relationships between variables in the model. Structural equation models (SEM) may be thought of as an extension of regression analysis and factor analysis, expressing the interrelationship between variables through a set of linear relationships, based upon their variances and covariances. In other words, structural equation modeling replaces a (usually large) set of observable variables with a small set of unobservable factor constructs, thus minimizing the problem of multicollinearity (further technical description in Jöreskog, 1973). The parameters of the equations are simultaneously estimated by the maximum likelihood method. For the analysis we employ a panel data set for 30 regions over a five-year time period. We assume this is a pooled data set, controlling for time and province fixed effects.

It is important to stress that the graphic picture of the structural model (Figure 14.2) expresses direct and indirect correlations, not actual causalities. Rather, the estimated parameters (path coefficients) provide information on the relations between the variables. Moreover, the relative importance of the parameters is expressed by the standardized path coefficients, which allow for interpretation of the direct as well as the indirect effects. We do not assume any causality among the university, tolerance and service amenities factors but rather treat them as correlations.

From the relationships depicted in the model (Figure 14.2) we estimate three equations simultaneously:

$$Talent = \beta_{11}\,University + \beta_{12}\,ServiceAmenities + \beta_{13}\,Tolerance +$$
$$\beta_{14}\,Year + \beta_{15}\,Province + e_1 \tag{14.1}$$
$$Technology = \beta_{21}\,University + \beta_{22}\,Tolerance + \beta_{23}\,Talent + \beta_{24}\,Year +$$
$$\beta_{25}\,Province + e_2 \tag{14.2}$$
$$RegionalDevelopment = \beta_{31}\,University + \beta_{32}\,Tolerance + \beta_{33}\,Talent +$$
$$\beta_{34}\,Technology + \beta_{35}\,Year + \beta_{36}\,Province + e_3 \tag{14.3}$$

Findings

Table 14.2 presents a correlation matrix for the major variables. While bivariate relations tell us little about how these relations hold in a multivariate context, we still

Table 14.2 Correlation matrix

	University	Service amenities	Tolerance	Human capital	Creative class	High-tech	Patents	GDP per capita
University	1							
Service amenities	0.055	1						
Tolerance	0.424***	−0.149	1					
Human capital	0.739***	0.044	0.604***	1				
Creative class	0.566***	0.028	0.626***	0.829***	1			
High-tech	0.484***	0.009	0.489***	0.309***	0.246***	1		
Patents	0.690***	−0.116	0.731***	0.650***	0.585***	0.688***	1	
GDP per capita	0.795***	−0.124	0.762***	0.757***	0.693***	0.566***	0.912***	1
Year[a]	0.594***	0.040	0.019	0.237***	−0.024	0.058	0.131	0.312***
Province[a]	−0.486***	−0.049	−0.472***	−0.402***	−0.394***	−0.407***	−0.504***	−0.578***

Notes: We use the natural logarithm term for all variables in our statistical analysis except for the fixed effect variables.
*** Significant at the 0.01 level (2-tailed).
[a] Fixed effects.

include them in order to check for possible collinearity problems in our structural equation modeling. According to Table 14.2, the presence of universities has a strong and significant correlation with talent, both in terms of human capital and of the creative class. It also presents a significant relationship with technology and patents. Relatively speaking, the university shows a stronger association with patents than with high-tech industries. This is not surprising, considering that university professors and students form one of the key groups that apply for patents and given the low level of R&D activity in China's high-tech industries. Lastly, the university is significantly associated with regional economic performance in terms of GDP per capita. There are no significant correlations between service amenities and any of the other variables. As with the presence of universities, tolerance is significantly associated with talent, technology and regional economic performance.

A further exploration of the data shows that the 30 provincial-level regions form two clusters when excluding Xinjiang as an outlier.[1] One cluster includes Beijing, Shanghai, and Tianjin, showing high levels of talent, technology, and economic performance. Those regions share several distinguishing features. First, they are all municipalities directly under the central government, with the highest political status among provincial-level regions. Second, they benefit from preferential (economic and social) central government policies. Third, they all have a high level of urbanization (with more than 70 percent of the population living in the cities). These commonalities shed light on the spiky distribution of talent in China.

Most other regions gather as another cluster, showing little connection between talent and economic performance or between talent and technology. This implies that China as a whole is not a talent-driven knowledge economy. Regional innovation and economic performance, where they exist, are likely to rely on something other than human capital or the creative class. Even so, the few talent-intensive regions (Beijing, Shanghai and Tianjin) that make up the first cluster have better technology and economic performance than the others.

Compared with studies by Florida *et al.* (2008) and Mellander and Florida (2011), we can see that the economic geography of talent in China is even more concentrated than in the West. In other words, talent distribution is spikier in China. This may be a result of the contrast between the more market-based economies of the West and a Chinese system in which the government and related non-market factors appear to be at least as important as market factors. The enormous political, economic, and social resources brought to bear by the central government render Beijing, Shanghai, and Tianjin unbeatable in attracting talent and high-tech industries and in fostering economic growth. These hard-to-measure government factors have not been incorporated into our model.

Results from path analysis and structural equations models

Model 1: Human capital, high technology and GDP per capita

We now turn to the results of the SEM models and path analysis. Figure 14.3 and Table 14.3 show the statistical results when talent is measured by human capital. It can be seen that the university holds a significant association with human capital after keeping tolerance and service amenities constant. Tolerance is also significantly associated with human capital. But this relationship, according to the path coefficients, is not as strong as that between the university and human capital. In addition, there is no significant association between service amenities and human capital.

The results are different from those observed in the West. Amenities, which appear to be a significant contributor to human capital distribution in the US and Sweden (Florida *et al.*, 2008; Mellander and Florida, 2011), are not important in China. This reflects the difference between developing and developed economies. At this earlier stage of development, Chinese talent, while experiencing higher living standards than other Chinese people, does not use quality of life as a key factor in location choice.

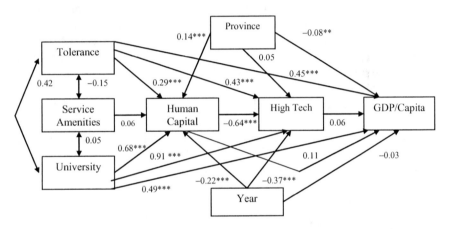

Figure 14.3 Path analysis for human capital, high technology and GDP per capita

Table 14.3 Regression results for human capital, high technology and GDP per capita

GDP per capita	Human capital		
	Talent	High tech	GDP/capita
Variables	Eq 1	Eq 2	Eq 3
Tolerance	0.294***	0.788***	0.470***
Service amenities	0.222		
University	0.583***	1.417***	0.432***
Talent		−1.170***	0.111
High technology			0.036
Year	−0.084***	−0.259***	−0.003
Province	0.009***	0.005	−0.005**
Observations	150	150	150
R^2	0.788	0.524	0.855

Note: *** Significant at the 0.01 level. ** Significant at the 0.05 level.

The presence of universities plays the leading role in forming regional human capital stock. This is in line with findings by Qian (2010). According to his study, the university is the single most important factor affecting talent distribution in China, outweighing market and other non-market factors. This is also in accordance with findings in the Western context by Berry and Glaeser (2005), Florida (2006) and Mellander and Florida (2011). Even so, it is reasonable to say that the university is more important in China than in the West. Florida *et al.* (2006) point out that US cities with a good university system do not necessarily retain talent, partially due to labor market mobility. In China, by contrast, the government controls the local population through the Hukou system. Most employers in big cities, especially in star cities like Beijing and Shanghai, have quotas of local Hukous they can issue. The local university graduates, due to their networks and other advantages in accessing job information, are better able to find and compete for opportunities, and subsequently become locally registered. This process is much more difficult for graduates from outside the local area. Therefore talent in China is much less mobile than in the US. This reinforces the power of local universities in influencing the local talent stock. It also locks in place jurisdictional advantage and prevents efficient allocation of talent or resources.

Even in China, where mobility is restricted, tolerance or openness plays a significant role in the distribution of talent. This is consistent with the research on developed countries (Florida *et al.*, 2008; Mellander and Florida, 2011) and further proves the indispensable role of tolerance in attracting talent.

Similarly, the university and tolerance are significantly associated with both high technology and GDP per capita. High-tech firms like to locate themselves near universities which provide technologies, scientists and engineers. It is also possible that open and diversified regions can better attract high-tech industries than relatively closed and homogeneous regions.

Interestingly enough, there are some counter-intuitive relationships between human capital, high technology and GDP per capita, once the university and tolerance factors are controlled for. Human capital exhibits a significant but negative relationship with high technology. While this partly can be a multicollinearity effect, the equilibrium between talent supply and demand is distorted and the market forces "disappear." Moreover, compared with the correlation matrix, the significant and positive associations between human capital or high technology and GDP per capita no long exist. This is not in line with the empirical results from analysis on developed economies. Why does this happen for China?

One possible explanation is that the restriction of population mobility decreases the role of talent in high-tech industries and economic performance. Because of the Hukou system, talent cannot freely migrate to those places with high-tech industries. Talent demand by high-tech industries and the supply by talent itself thus cannot reach market equilibriums.

Another possible explanation lies in the characteristics of China's high-tech industries. Those so-called high-tech industries are primarily based on manufacturing, processing and assembling, rather than on innovation and services. Compared with developed countries, innovative activity in the Chinese high-tech industries is very limited. According to *China Statistical Yearbook on High Technology Industry* (NBS, 2005), R&D expenditures in 2004 accounted for 4.6 percent of the total value added of the Chinese high-tech industries, much lower than 27 percent in the US in 2002 and 18.2 percent in Korea in 2003. This percentage for knowledge economies is generally above 20 percent. With limited innovative opportunities, the link between human capital and high-tech industries is weakened. A negative sign in our results suggests that high-tech firms would rather locate themselves in places with less talent. This is reasonable in that the total costs of production (including, for instance, land use costs) in those places are likely to be low. Consistent with our results, Wang *et al.* (2010) find no significant relationship between spatial agglomeration of ICT manufacturing and productivity in China.

A third possible explanation is the role of government. Although implementing economic policies of liberalization and decentralization, Chinese governments, both central and local, still exert tremendous influence on economic and social activity. For instance, Beijing is home to the nation's best education institutions and health systems, which serve as talent magnets, and benefits considerably from housing the central government. National Economic and Technology Development Zones (NETDZ) in China are the most attractive places for high-tech firms, largely because of preferential policies approved by the central government. Tianjin and Beijing have two of the largest and best such zones in China. Shanghai is home to four such zones and the only city with more than two. In addition, Shanghai, as the economic center of China, receives economic development support from the central government in all possible forms. The government, to sum up, might affect talent, technology and economic growth in ways that diminish their intrinsic relationships.

Statistically, the negative relation between talent and technology may be partly a result of the very close correlation between the university and talent. To see whether talent, the university and tolerance include the same information, we ran an OLS separately, letting high technology be explained by these three variables, including a VIF test for multicollinearity. The VIF values are distributed between 1.6 and 2.8, indicating that they to some extent include the same information. But with values less than 5 we concluded that they did not include identical information. Instead, to further explore the relation between talent and innovation, we substituted patents for high technology in the original model.

According to the results shown in Figure 14.4 and Table 14.4, the relationship between talent and patents is still negative and significant. Consistent with our explanation for the high technology case, patents in China are not necessarily innovation-based. As mentioned before, patents consist of three types: inventions, utility models, and designs. Inventions, which are the most likely to be innovation-based, accounted for only 12 percent of the total number of patents in 2004. In contrast, the less innovation-based utility models and designs represented 46 percent and 42 percent respectively. However, patents have a stronger explanatory value in relation to GDP per capita.

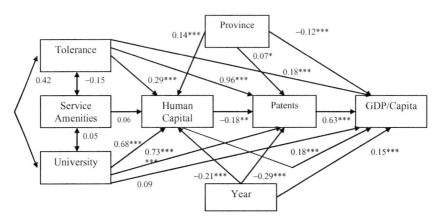

Figure 14.4 Path analysis for human capital, patents and GDP per capita

Table 14.4 Regression results for human capital, patents and GDP per capita

GDP per capita	Human capital		
	Talent	Patents	GDP/capita
Variables	Eq 1	Eq 2	Eq 3
Tolerance	0.294***	0.965***	0.192***
Service amenities	0.222		
University	0.583***	1.272***	0.079
Talent		−0.363**	0.184***
Patents			0.318***
Year	−0.084***	−0.229***	0.061***
Province	0.009***	0.009*	−0.008***
Observations	150	150	150
R^2	0.788	0.815	0.928

Note: *** Significant at the 0.01 level. ** Significant at the 0.05 level.

To make sure this is not driven by outliers, we re-ran this path/SEM, excluding the very obvious outliers, Beijing and Shanghai. The negative and significant relation between human capital and high technology still holds (see Figure 14.5 and Table 14.5).

The role of high technology in relation to GDP per capita does not change with the exclusion of outliers. Again, it is not significant. The association between tolerance and talent remains approximately at the same level. Tolerance also remains important for high technology and GDP per capita. The university still plays a significant role in relation to high technology as well as in relation to GDP per capita. As a summary, the key relations still hold after excluding outliers: the university and tolerance are still significantly associated with human capital, high technology and GDP per capita; and the relationships between human capital, high technology and GDP per capita are again counter-intuitive.

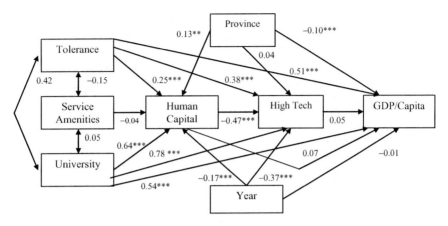

Figure 14.5 Path analysis for human capital, high technology and GDP per capita, excluding outliers

Table 14.5 Regression results for human capital, high technology and GDP per capita, excluding outliers

GDP per capita	Human capital		
	Talent	High tech	GDP/capita
Variables	Eq 1	Eq 2	Eq 3
Tolerance	0.210***	0.816***	0.507***
Service amenities	−0.114		
University	0.442***	1.416***	0.448***
Talent		−1.217***	0.007
High technology			0.021
Year	−0.046***	−0.262***	−0.005
Province	0.006**	0.005	−0.006***
Observations	140	140	140
R^2	0.596	0.518	0.803

Note: *** Significant at the 0.01 level. ** Significant at the 0.05 level.

We also re-ran these regressions, substituting patents for high technology and excluding the outliers. In this case, the relationship between talent and patents remains negative and significant.

Model 2: Creative class, high technology and GDP per capita

Earlier research (Florida *et al.*, 2008; Mellander and Florida, 2011) has shown that talent when viewed in the form of the creative occupations may reveal a different role in this economic context. Therefore, we substituted the creative class for human capital and re-ran the same regressions as for Model 1 above. The results are presented in Figure 14.6 and Table 14.6.

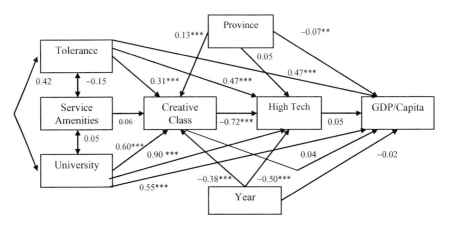

Figure 14.6 Path analysis for creative class, high technology and GDP per capita

Table 14.6 Results for creative class, high technology and GDP per capita

GDP per capita	Creative class		
	Talent	High tech	GDP/capita
Variables	Eq 1	Eq 2	Eq 3
Tolerance	0.246***	0.861***	0.493***
Service amenities	0.172		
University	0.391***	1.403***	0.483***
Talent		−1.704***	0.052
High technology			0.028
Year	−0.113***	−0.353***	−0.008
Province	0.006***	0.006	−0.005**
Observations	150	150	150
R^2	0.776	0.553	0.854

Note: *** Significant at the 0.01 level. ** Significant at the 0.05 level.

The effects of the university, service amenities and tolerance on the creative class here follow a similar pattern to human capital. The university again is the dominant factor in the distribution of the creative class. The university and tolerance are still significantly associated with both high technology and GDP per capita. As with human capital, the creative class variables are negatively and significantly associated with high technology.

As in the human capital case, we substituted patents for high technology to get closer to innovation. The significant and negative relation between the creative class and innovation is still negative and significant (as shown in Figure 14.7 and Table 14.7). This is in line with what occurred when patents were substituted for high technology in the human capital model.

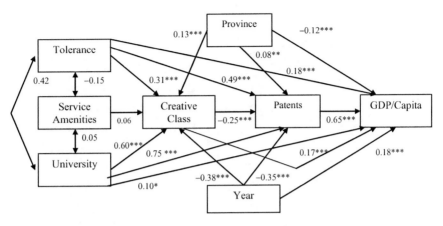

Figure 14.7 Path analysis for creative class, patents and GDP per capita

Table 14.7 Regression results for creative class, patents and GDP per capita

GDP per capita	Creative class		
	Talent	Patents	GDP/capita
Variables	Eq 1	Eq 2	Eq 3
Tolerance	0.246***	1.020***	0.185***
Service Amenities	0.172		
University	0.391***	1.323***	0.092*
Talent		−0.670***	0.223***
Patents			0.325***
Year	−0.113***	−0.274***	0.072***
Province	0.006***	0.010**	−0.008***
Observations	150	150	150
R²	0.776	0.823	0.927

Note: *** Significant at the 0.01 level. ** Significant at the 0.05 level. * Significant at the 0.1 level.

To rule out that the results are driven by a few outliers, we correct for this, and re-run the same regressions without the most extreme outliers, Beijing and Shanghai, as we did in the human capital case. Without the outliers the connection between the creative class and high technology remains negative and significant and so do the roles of the university and tolerance (see Figure 14.8 and Table 14.8). The relationship between high technology and GDP per capita remains insignificant.

We also re-ran the regressions with the outliers excluded and patents substituted for high technology. Here again the relation between the creative class and patents remains similar.

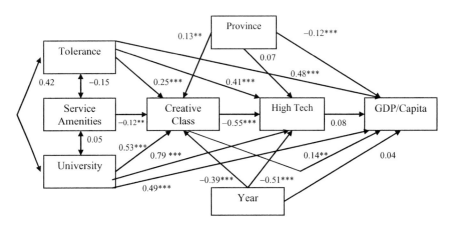

Figure 14.8 Path analysis for creative class, high technology and GDP per capita, excluding outliers

Table 14.8 Regression results for creative class, high technology and GDP per capita, excluding outliers

GDP per capita	Creative class		
	Talent	High tech	GDP/capita
Variables	Eq 1	Eq 2	Eq 3
Tolerance	0.156***	0.909***	0.474***
Service amenities	−0.252**		
University	0.272***	1.439***	0.403***
Talent		−1.953***	0.229**
High technology			0.036
Year	−0.078***	−0.368***	0.014
Province	0.005**	0.008	−0.006***
Observations	140	140	140
R^2	0.625	0.559	0.807

Note: *** Significant at the 0.01 level (2-tailed). ** Significant at the 0.05 level (2-tailed).

Discussion

Our research has examined the effect of three key factors technology, talent and tolerance on Chinese regional economic development. We used path analysis and structural equation approaches and established a three-stage model. In the first stage, we explored the institutional and cultural factors affecting the distribution of talent. Second, we examined the impact of talent distribution on regional technology. Third, we investigated the effects of the university, tolerance, talent and technology on regional economic performance. Our path/SEM model allowed us to test for the direct, indirect, separate and joint effects of those factors on regional economic performance, while minimizing the problem of multicollinearity.

To achieve solid conclusions, we used two different measures for talent (human capital versus the creative class) and two variables for technology (high-tech value added versus patents), and we examined the effects of outliers. No matter how we changed the model, the different path/SEM analyses produced four general findings. First, we found the distribution of talent in China to be very concentrated—more so than in the US or other advanced economies. Second, we found universities to be the key factor in shaping the economic geography of both talent and innovation in China. Universities not only supply educated talent to the region, but also produce new knowledge and technology through their professors, scientists and even students. However, university graduates do not necessarily stay put. A region's ability to retain and attract talent plays an even more important role in determining its talent stock. In China, mobility restrictions imposed by the inhabitant registration system make talent migration more difficult than in the West. Thus the region in China has an easier time retaining local university graduates. This indicates that the university is even more important for talent concentration in the Chinese context.

Third, we found a reasonably strong association between our variables for tolerance/openness/diversity and both talent (measured as human capital or the creative class) and our technology measures. This pattern is similar to that for the advanced nations. Although not as powerful as the effects of the university variables, tolerance is an additional significant factor in the distribution of talent across China's regions. Tolerance is likely to increase educational and occupational skill in a region by lowering the barriers to entry for talented people across gender, race, and sexual orientation. A tolerant and open social climate also nurtures new knowledge and entrepreneurial activity which in turn underpin innovation-based economic growth. To build a knowledge-based creative economy, China will have to recognize the role of such social factors, and further socially "emancipate the mind (*jiefangsixiang*)."

Fourth, we found a weak relationship between talent (measured as human capital or the creative class) on either innovation or regional economic performance. This is in many ways our most interesting, if counter-intuitive finding. It suggests that the Chinese system has not yet made the transition from an industrial to more knowledge-based model. And, it stands in some contrast to its stated efforts to invest in R&D and talent to promote domestic innovation. To gain competitiveness, high-tech firms generally invest tremendous resources in R&D and require plenty of talent to perform innovative activity. In China, however, R&D expenditures in high-tech industries are very low compared with the advanced nations. Also, most patents granted in China tend to be of the less innovation-based utility model and design varieties. Without mature platforms for innovative activity, the Chinese talent pool, though growing rapidly, makes a limited contribution to technological and economic development. Furthermore, even if high-tech firms have a high demand for talent, they may not be able to recruit what they need, since the spatial supply and demand of talent have been distorted by the government. China's inhabitant registration system prevents talent from migrating to locations where its utility can be maximized. The government also intervenes into the talent market by bestowing upon a few regions, such as Beijing and Shanghai, enormous social, economic, and political resources. This has hyper-concentrated human capital and the creative class in these places. These regions are obviously talent-intensive, but not necessarily knowledge-based.

It is nonetheless intriguing that tolerance matters to the distribution of human capital and of technology in China, even at the same time as human capital and technology are not associated with regional economic performance. We find this perplexing. Openness and universities are shaping the distribution and concentration of talent and technology. Talent and technology are more concentrated than in the US or advanced economies. Yet human capital and technology do not run out to be important factors in regional growth. Maybe even though China is not yet a knowledge economy, the highly concentrated and uneven distribution of human capital sets it up to pave the road ahead for this transformation later on.

Despite its efforts to build an innovation-based economy, China remains a developing country with a different industrial and urban structure, and the country has long restricted internal migration. Generally speaking, our empirical results suggest that China is likely to have quite a way to go before it makes the shift from the industrial stage to the knowledge/human capital/creative stage of economic development.

Our research has tried to empirically frame some of the key issues affecting regional development as China seeks to move from an industrial to a knowledge-based economy. We hope that our findings and approach encourage additional studies of the connection or disconnect between talent/human capital, innovation and economic performance in China. The relationship between amenities and talent, which is insignificant in our results and thus inconsistent with the literature, also deserves further explorations with improved measures for amenities.

Note

1 The scatter-plot graphs supporting the discussion here are not included due to space constraints. They are available from the authors upon request.

Bibliography

Andersson, Å. (1985a) "Creativity and regional development," *Papers of the Regional Science Association*, 56: 5–20.

Andersson, Å. (1985b) *Creativity: The Future of Metropolitan Regions*, Prisma: Stockholm.

Anselin, L., Varga, A. and Acs, Z. (1997) "Local geographic spillovers between university research and high technology innovations," *Journal of Urban Economics*, 42: 422–448.

Barbour, E. and Markusen, A. (2007) "Regional occupational and industrial structure: Does one imply the other?," *International Regional Science Review*, 30: 72–90.

Barro, R. J. (1991) "Economic growth in a cross section of countries," *The Quarterly Journal of Economics*, 106: 407–443.

Barro, R. J. (1997) *Determinants of Economic Growth: A Cross-Country Empirical Study*, Cambridge, MA: The MIT Press.

Berry, C. R. and Glaeser, E. L. (2005) "The divergence of human capital levels across cities," *Papers in Regional Science*, 84: 407–444.

Boschma, R. A. and Fritsch, M. (2009) "Creative class and regional growth: Empirical evidence from seven European countries," *Economic Geography*, 85: 391–423.

Boyle, M. (2006) "Culture in the rise of tiger economies: Scottish expatriates in Dublin and the 'creative class' thesis," *International Journal of Urban and Regional Research*, 30: 403–426.

Cai, F., Wang, D. and Du, Y. (2002) "Regional disparity and economic growth in China: The impact of labor market distortions," *China Economic Review*, 13: 197–212.

Cheshire, P. and Magrini, S. (2000) "Endogenous processes in European regional growth: Convergence and policy," *Growth and Change*, 31: 455–479.

Chow, G. C. and Li, K. (2002) "China's economic growth: 1952–2010," *Economic Development and Cultural Change*, 51: 247–256.

Clark, T. N. (2003). 'Urban amenities: Lakes, opera and juice bars – Do they drive development?," *Research in Urban Policy*, 9: 103–140.

Florida, R. (2002a) *The Rise of the Creative Class: And How It's Transforming Work, Leisure, Community, and Everyday Life*, New York: Basic Books.

Florida, R. (2002b) "Bohemia and economic geography," *Journal of Economic Geography*, 2: 55–71.

Florida, R. (2002c) "The economic geography of talent," *Annals of the Association of American Geographers*, 92: 743–755.

Florida, R. and Gates, G. (2001) *Technology and Tolerance: The Importance of Diversity to High-Technology Growth*, Washington, DC: Urban Institute.

Florida, R. and Gates, G. (2003) "Technology and tolerance: The importance of diversity to high-technology growth," in T.N. Clark (ed.), *The City as an Entertainment Machine*: *Research in Urban Policy*, vol. 9, Oxford: Elsevier, pp. 199–220.

Florida, R., Gates, G., Knudsen, B. and Stolarick, K. (2006) "The university and the creative economy," available at: http://www.creativeclass.org/rfcgdb/articles/University %20For %20City %20and %20Community %204.pdf.

Florida, R., Mellander, C. and Stolarick, K. (2008) "Inside the Black Box of regional development: Human capital, the creative class and tolerance," *Journal of Economic Geography*, 8: 615–649.

Gabe, T. M. (2009) "Knowledge and earnings," *Journal of Regional Science*, 49: 439–457.

Glaeser E L. (2004) "Book review of Richard Florida's 'The rise of the creative class'," *Regional Science and Urban Economics*, 35: 593–596.

Glaeser, E. L., Kallal, H. D., Scheinkman, J. A. and Shleifer, A. (1992) "Growth in cities," *Journal of Political Economy*, 100: 1126–52.

Glaeser, E. L., Kolko, J. and Saiz, A. (2001) "Consumer city," *Journal of Economic Geography*, 1: 27–50.

Houston, D., Findlay, A., Harrison, R. and Mason, C. (2008) "Will attracting the 'creative class' boost economic growth in old industrial regions? A case study of Scotland," *Geografiska Annaler: Series B, Human Geography*, 90: 133–149.

Inglehart, R. and Norris, P. (2003) *Rising Tide: Gender Equality and Cultural Change Around the World*, Cambridge: Cambridge University Press.

Inglehart, R. and Welzel, C. (2005) *Modernization, Cultural Change, and Democracy: The Human Development Sequence*, Cambridge: Cambridge University Press.

Jacobs, J. (1961) *The Death and Life of Great American Cities*, New York: Random House.

Jacobs, J. (1969) *The Economy of Cities*, New York: Random House.

Jiang, H., Xu, X. and Li, T. (2005) "An analysis of the spatial disparities of talent in China, 1990–2002," *Economic Geography*, 25: 702–706 (In Chinese).

Jöreskog, K. G. (1973) "Analysis of covariance structures," in P. R. Krishnaiah (ed.), *Multivariate analysis*, Vol. III, New York: Academic Press.

King, K., Mellander, C. and Stolarick, K. (2010) "What you do, not who you work for: A comparison of the occupational industry structures of the United States, Canada and Sweden," *Working Paper Series in Economics and Institutions of Innovation No. 221*, Royal Institute of Technology, CESIS – Centre of Excellence for Science and Innovation Studies.

Krätke, S. (2010) "'Creative cities' and the rise of the dealer class: A critique of Richard Florida's approach to urban theory," *International Journal of Urban and Regional Research*, 34: 835–853.

Li, T. and Florida, R. (2006) "Talent, technological innovation, and economic growth in China," available at http://www.creativeclass.org/ rfcgdb/ articles/ China %20report.pdf.

Lorenzen, M. and Vaarst Andersen, K. (2009) "Centrality and creativity: Does Richard Florida's creative class offer new insights into urban hierarchy?," *Economic Geography* 85: 363–390.

Lucas, R. E. (1988) "On the mechanics of economic development," *Journal of Monetary Economics*, 22: 3–42.

McGranahan, D. and Wojan, T. (2007) "Recasting the creative class to examine growth processes in rural and urban counties," *Regional Studies*, 41: 197–216.

Markusen, A. (2004) "Targeting occupations in regional and community economic development," *Journal of the American Planning Association*, 70: 253–268.

Markusen, A. (2006) "Urban development and the politics of a creative class: Evidence from a study of artists," *Environment and Planning A*, 38: 1921–1940.

Markusen, A. and Barbour, E. (2007) "Regional occupational and industrial structure: Does one imply the other?," *International Regional Science Review*, 30: 72–90.

Marlet, G. and Van Woerkens, C. (2004) *Skills and Creativity in a Cross-section of Dutch Cities*, available at: http://www.uu.nl/uupublish/content/04-29.pdf (accessed 29 August 2013).

Marx, K., Engels, F. and Hobsbawm, E. J. (1848) *The Communist Manifesto: A Modern Edition*, London: Verso reprint: 1998.

Mellander, C. and Florida, R. (2011) "Creativity, talent, and regional wages in Sweden," *Annals of Regional Science*, 46: 637–660.

NBS, National Bureau of Statistics of China, Beijing

various years *China Statistical Yearbook*.

various years *China Statistical Yearbook on High Technology Industry*.

various years *China Labor Statistics Yearbook*.

OECD (2008) *OECD Reviews of Innovation Policy: China*. Available at http://www.oecd.org/ sti/innovationinsciencetechnologyandindustry/oecdreviewsofinnovationpolicychina.htm (accessed 29 August 2013).

Ottaviano, G. I. P. and Peri, G. (2005) "Cities and cultures," *Journal of Urban Economics*, 58: 304–337.

Page, S. E. (2007) *The Difference: How The Power of Diversity Creates Better Groups, Firms, Schools, and Societies* (New Edition), Princeton, NJ: Princeton University Press.

Pratt, A. C. (2008) "Creative cities: The cultural industries and the creative class," *Geografiska Annaler: Series B, Human Geography*, 90: 107–117.

Qian, H. (2010) "Talent, creativity and regional economic performance: The case of China," *Annals of Regional Science*, 45: 133–156.

Qian, H. and Stough, R. (2011) "The effect of social diversity on regional innovation: Measures and empirical evidence," *International Journal of Foresight and Innovation Policy*, 7: 142–157.

Quigley, J. M. (1998) "Urban diversity and economic growth," *The Journal of Economic Perspectives*, 12: 127–138.

Rauch, J. E. (1993) "Productivity gains from geographic concentration of human capital: Evidence from the cities," *Journal of Urban Economics*, 34: 380–400.

Roback, J. (1982) "Wages, rents, and the quality of life," *Journal of Political Economy*, 90: 1257–1278.

Romer, P. M. (1986) "Increasing returns and long-run growth," *Journal of Political Economy*, 94: 1002–1037.

Romer, P. M. (1987) "Crazy explanations for the productivity slowdown," in *Macroeconomics Annual*, Washington, DC: National Bureau of Economic Research, Inc.

Romer, P. M. (1990) "Endogenous technological change," *Journal of Political Economy*, 98: S71–S102.

Schumpeter, J. A. (1942) *Capitalism, Socialism and Democracy*, New York: Harper & Brothers.

Schwab, K. (2010) *The Global Competitiveness Report: 2010–2011*, World Economic Forum, available at http://www.weforum.org/documents/GCR10/index.html.

Shapiro, J. M. (2006) "Smart cities: Quality of life, productivity, and the growth effects of human capital," *Review of Economics and Statistics*, 88: 324–335.

Simon, C. J. (1998) "Human capital and metropolitan employment growth," *Journal of Urban Economics*, 43: 223–243.

Simon, C. J. and Nardinelli, C. (1996) "The talk of the town: Human capital, information, and the growth of English cities, 1861 to 1961," *Explorations in Economic History*, 33: 384–413.

Smith, A. (1776) *The Wealth of Nations*, New York: Random House.

Solow, R. M. (1956) "A contribution to the theory of economic growth," *The Quarterly Journal of Economics*, 70: 65–94.

Sun, Y. (2002) "Sources of innovation in China's manufacturing sector: Imported or developed in-house?," *Environment and Planning A*, 34: 1059–1072.

UNDP (2010) "The real wealth of nations: Pathways to human development," *Human Development Report*, available at http://hdr.undp.org/en/reports/global/hdr2010/ (accessed 29 August 2013).

Wang, C. C., Lin, G. C. S. and Li, G. (2010) "Industrial clustering and technological innovation in China: New evidence from the ICT industry in Shenzhen," *Environment and Planning A*, 42: 1987– 2010.

Wang, Y., and Yao, Y. (2003) "Sources of China's economic growth, 1952–1999: Incorporating human capital accumulation," *China Economic Review*, 14: 32–52.

Xinhuanet (2010) "The second transformation of Chinese cities," Xinhuanet, available at http://news.xinhuanet.com/mrdx/2010-10/08/c_13547523.htm (In Chinese) (accessed 29 August 2013).

Zhang, W. and Fan, W. (2006) "Factor analysis on the formation regional differences in human capital," *Journal of Xi'an University of Post and Telecommunications*, 11: 3–42 (in Chinese).

Zhou, Y., Sun, Y., Wei, Y. H. D. and Lin, G. C. S. (2011) "De-centering 'spatial fix': Patterns of territorialization and regional technological dynamism of ICT hubs in China," *Journal of Economic Geography*, 11: 119–150.

15 The creative class around the world

Richard Florida and Charlotta Mellander

The chapters in this book have examined the creative class in 12 countries. So what have we learned from this cross-national, cross-regional analysis? While the studies are different in structure and orientation, they share several core similarities and explore three key questions:

- The uneven geography and concentration of the creative class within nations, and in some studies, across them.
- The factors that influence and shape the geography of the creative class.
- The effects of the creative class on regional economic performance.

Taken as a whole, the studies in this book reinforce the validity of the occupational-based analytic approach. The creative class was found to be associated with regional economic growth and development not just in the United States but across the advanced nations of Canada, Australia, the United Kingdom, Germany, the Netherlands, Denmark, and Sweden.

The chapters, and related research, also show that the occupation-based creative class differs from the more conventional human capital approach to measuring skill. As noted in Chapter 1, a study of the United States (2012) by Stolarick and Currid-Halkett found that nearly three-quarters of adults with college degrees were members of the creative class. But almost four in ten members of the Creative Class—16.6 million workers—do not have college degrees. In Denmark and Canada, the figure is 50 percent, and in Sweden it is nearly 60 (57 percent) (see Mellander *et al.*, 2011).

Chapter 2 deepens these insights, finding that while creative class and educational attainment (share of adults with college degrees) are correlated in the United States, each plays a different—but complementary—role in regional economic development. The creative class operates primarily on wages and thus exerts its chief effects on regional productivity. The share of adults with college degrees is more closely associated with higher incomes, which include not just wages but all forms of income from capital, transfers, rents and the like. Chapter 3, which looked at Canada, found regional income to be closely associated with the creative class, as well as educational levels.

The research in this book makes another important contribution by identifying for the first time the specific creative class occupations that are associated with regional economic growth and development. Human capital measures typically specify one overall educational level, for example the share of adults with college or university degrees, and in most cases data is not available by type of degree. The creative class measure is much more heterogeneous, being made up of hundreds of specific occupations, which can be analyzed separately or clustered together. As it turns out, three occupational clusters—science and technology, business and management, and arts, culture, entertainment and media—have the biggest effects on economic growth. While much has been made in academic as well as policy circles on the role in urban economic development of so-called "eds and meds—education and healthcare—the research in these pages finds that they have virtually no effect on regional economic development.

A particularly notable finding of this analysis concerns the role of artistic and cultural occupations that have been the subject of considerable debate in the literature, with many arguing that arts and culture do not contribute to but simply reflect regional development and wealth. Research in these pages suggests that artistic and cultural occupations do in fact contribute to the process of wealth generation and regional development. This offers considerable support for one of the key precepts of creative class theory, which argues that regional development is underpinned by not just technology and entrepreneurship, but by the intersection of myriads kinds of creativity—artistic creativity, technological creativity (innovation) and economic creativity (entrepreneurship) in particular places.

But that is not to say that national differences in size, scale, and institutions do not matter. There are a couple of key aspects of creative class theory where national differences matter a great deal. The first involves the geographic concentration of the creative class across regions. Overall, the chapters in this book substantiate the uneven geography of the creative class and its tendency to concentrate in large cities or those with knowledge-based institutions like universities. However, as Chapter 5 on Denmark notes, smaller nations have only one or two larger cities and their smaller cities typically have close connections to them. The creative class can and does flourish in smaller cities in such places, particularly when these cities have strong clusters of knowledge-based institutions or universities, amenities or close connections to larger cities.

One of the most interesting findings to emerge from the country studies that make up this book revolves around the role of openness and tolerance. Studies of small countries, for example Sweden in Chapter 4 or the Netherlands in Chapters 7 and 8, and Japan in Chapter 13, find little or no effect of tolerance and openness. But studies of large countries, like the United States (Chapter 2), Canada (Chapter 3), the United Kingdom (Chapter 9), and Germany (Chapter 10), or which consider relatively large numbers of European countries as in Chapter 11, find that that tolerance and openness play a significant role in both the geography of the creative class and in regional economic development. Tolerance and openness are also found to play a role in the location of the creative class in smaller countries like Denmark (Chapter 5) and Australia (Chapter 12). And, surprisingly tolerance and openness (as well as universities) were found to be associated with the creative class in China, as Chapter 14 shows.

The indications are that this is an area where national differences appear to matter very much, as do size and scale. The effects of openness are likely to be muted in small countries with relatively homogeneous populations, and much more pronounced in larger countries that have a greater diversity of cities and populations.

The creative class has truly gone global, as the research in these chapters shows. In sharp contrast to the older industrial model, where growth was powered by natural resources and physical labor, and took place around large factories, growth in the knowledge and creative age is powered by concentrations of creative people organized in and around creative cities. While jobs and economic opportunity continue to matter, factors like quality of place, amenities, and openness and tolerance play a growing role, especially in large countries or multiple countries in large regions of the world. There is no chicken-and-egg after all, just a long-term, iterative and cumulative process of creativity and skill-accumulation occurring in and around places to power economic growth.

While the studies in this book provide important insights into how human creativity and skill come together in places to impel growth, there is much additional research that needs to be done. First and foremost, we need to expand and extend the creative class approach outside of the advanced industrial nations. Only one study in this book, Chapter 14 on China, examines the role of the creative class in the economic growth process of an emerging economy. While China has clearly evolved into an industrial powerhouse, the findings from Chapter 14 suggest that its growth pattern, at least at this stage in its development, is quite a bit different from the knowledge and creativity-driven patterns found across the advanced nations. While the creative class is concentrated in China's largest cities, neither it nor technology seems to affect regional growth. The reason may be that China remains at too early a stage of development, with a relatively small creative class share of just over 7 percent of its workforce, compared to a third to more than 40 percent in the advanced nations. For all of the media hype that surrounds China as an emerging center for innovation and technology, it has yet to develop a pattern of creative and innovation powered growth.

Brazil and India—two countries that are typically grouped in with Russia and China to make up the BRIC nations—appear to be more exemplary of creative-led growth. Brazil, where the creative class makes up nearly one in five workers, has long been noted for its innovations in design and fashion as well as cutting-edge music scene. India is home to the largest film industry in the world and substantial clusters of innovation in music, fashion, and food as well as a highly regard technology complex in and around Bangalore. Studies of these two nations as well as of Latin America, Asia and the Middle East and Africa are needed to test the role and applicability of the creative class theory to emerging and developing economies.

More research is also needed to document the institutional and public policy arrangements that best support and extend creativity to more workers across the board, in effect "creatifying" more occupations and kinds of work. The advanced nations—and the world writ large—are currently engaged in yet another sweeping economic transformation, from an industrial to a creative economy. The result of this, as numerous economists have pointed out, is the decline of once high-wage blue-collar factory jobs and the bifurcation of the labor market into two tiers: the high-skilled, high wage knowledge and creative jobs we have examined in this volume, and an even larger group of low-wage/low skilled service jobs.

Two areas of research are of considerable importance to this. The first is to document the extent, nature, and make-up of the service class and more particularly the jobs and occupations of the service class that are amenable to upgrading and higher wages. A growing body of research identifies three underlying skill types that underpin creative, service and working class jobs. Creative jobs have high levels of cognitive and social engagement skills, while service work is based on more routine-oriented physical skills. But this research finds that adding cognitive and social engagement skills to service work leads to higher wages. More research is needed to document the kinds of service work that are amenable to upgrading, the path to upgrading that work, and the effects of upgraded, better paying, higher skill service work in regional and national economic development.

An additional key area of future research involves identifying the institutional settings and public policies that can support and extend creativity to a greater group of occupations, classes, and workers. There was a considerable lag between the rise of industrial capitalism in the eighteenth and nineteenth centuries and the development of new social compacts in the middle of the last century to raise working-class wages and create a broader middle class in North America and especially in Northern Europe. Perhaps the process can be accelerated when it comes to service jobs.

Further research is also needed on what the contours of a new social compact for the creative economy would look like. To what extent would it be similar or different from the old social compact of the previous industrial age? What would its key institutional supports be? Given the variation in the concentration of the creative economy across cities and regions, is it a unified national social compact, as was the older social compact, or would its contours vary across cities and regions? A new compact would need to go beyond just material support in the form of higher wages, better housing, and old age benefits, to engage the whole of the workforce in meaningful, purposeful and creative work. What kinds of public policies and/or adjustments in current social welfare and economic policy arrangements are required to accomplish this?

As is characteristic of great periods of economic transformation, ours is a time of great disruption and adjustment. The light at the end of the proverbial tunnel is that for the first time in human history, the logic of economic development requires a greater level of human development. We hope that our individual and collective efforts to chart the dawn of this new age—warts and all—will deepen not just our understanding of it, but us help set an intellectual basis for more effective urban, regional, national and international policy on this vitally important process.

Bibliography

Mellander, C., Stolarick, K. and King, K. (2011) *What You Do, Not Who You Work For: A Comparison with the United States, Canada and Sweden.* Martin Prosperity Institute Working Paper Series, available at http://martinprosperity.org/papers/Mellander%20Stolarick%20King%20(2011)%20What%20you%20do%20not%20who%20you%20work%20for.pdf.

Stolarick, K. and Currid-Halkett, E. (2012) 'Creativity and the crisis: The impact of creative workers on regional unemployment', *Cities*, doi:10.1016/j.cities.2012.05.017.

Index